Fruit of the Motherland

Fruit of the Motherland

Gender in an Egalitarian Society

•

Maria Lepowsky

Columbia University Press · New York

Columbia University Press
New York   Chichester, West Sussex

Library of Congress Cataloging-in-Publication Data

Lepowsky, Maria Alexandra.
    Fruit of the motherland: gender in an egalitarian society
/Maria Lepowsky.
        p.   cm
    Includes bibliographical references and index.
    ISBN 0-231-08120-0
    ISBN 0-231-08121-9 (pbk.)
    1. Tagula (Papua New Guinea people)—Kinship. 2. Tagula
(Papua New Guinea)—Rites and ceremonies. 3. Tagula (Papua
New Guinea people)—Social conditions. 4. Matrilineal kinship—
Papua New Guinea—Tagula Island. 5. Gender identity—Papua
New Guinea—Tagula Island. 6. Equality—Social aspects—Papua
New Guinea—Tagula Island. 7. Sex roles—Papua New Guinea—
Tagula Island. 8. Tagula Island (Papua New Guinea)—Social life
and customs.   I. Title.
DU740.42.L47   1993
305.3'09953—dc20   93-8314
                                                CIP

∞
Casebound editions of Columbia University Press books
are printed on permanent and durable acid-free paper.

Printed in the United States of America
c 10 9 8 7 6 5 4 3 2 1

Contents

Preface   *vii*

Maps   *xix*

One Island Encounters   1

Two   Fruit of the Motherland   31

Three Island Lives   81

Four   Ancestors and Other Spirits   125

Five   Sorcerers and Witches   167

Six   The Living, the Dead, and Relations of Value   206

Seven   Fruit of the Dead   241

Eight   Gender and Power   281

Notes   *307*

Glossary   *331*

Bibliography   *345*

Index   *365*

Preface

Male dominance has often been described as universal in human societies. Female subordination, this would imply, either results directly from human biology or is inherent in human cultures, and perhaps unchangeable. But what would women's and men's lives be like in an egalitarian society, one with no ideology of male superiority and no male coercive power or formal authority over women? What idioms of sociality would prevail, and how would people relate to one another under conditions of gender equality?

In this book I describe the case of Vanatinai, a small, remote island southeast of New Guinea. It is a sexually egalitarian society that challenges the concept of the universality of male dominance and contests the assumption that the subjugation of women is inevitable. Vanatinai has its own distinctive language and culture, not previously studied by anthropologists. This book is about women and men as gendered beings and the ideologies that shape their perceptions, personal qualities, and actions in a gender egalitarian but distinctively Melanesian society.

The great island of New Guinea and the smaller islands off its shores are home to over seven hundred different ethnolinguistic groups. They, and other Melanesian cultures, have frequently been described by anthropologists as egalitarian. Almost all lack chiefs, nobles, or systems of ascribed rank typical of the Polynesian cultures to the east. But that egalitarian tendency describes only relations among men and not those between men and women. Melanesian societies are generally unstratified, but most of them are based, like almost all societies, on a hierarchy of gender in which men have greater power. In addition, there are often avenues to power and prestige that may be taken by men of ambition and ability but not by women, resulting in further differences among men, with some having more authority, wealth, and knowledge than the rest.

Descriptions of powerful ideologies of male dominance and female pollution found among many of the cultural groups in the interior of New Guinea have become anthropological classics. Nevertheless, New Guinea has been known for the great diversity of gender role patterns in its many distinctive cultures since the pioneering, and still controversial, work of Margaret Mead in 1935.

In striking contrast to many Melanesian cultures and to most cultures worldwide, on Vanatinai there are no ideologies of male superiority and female inferiority. There is considerable overlap between the roles and activities of women and men, and the actions of both sexes are considered equally valuable. Men have no formal authority or powers of coercion over women except for the physical violence that both sexes abhor and that is rare in the extreme. It is not a place where women and men live in perfect harmony and where the privileges and burdens of both sexes are exactly equal, but it comes close. The rules of social life stress respect for the will and personal autonomy of each adult. There are no chiefs, and there is nobody with the formal authority to tell another adult what to do. The emphasis on autonomy is counterbalanced by a high value placed upon choosing to give to others, which is likened to parental nurturing.

The overlap of male and female roles on Vanatinai extends to the most important arena for the acquisition of personal prestige and influence over others, ceremonial exchange and an elaborate series of mortuary rituals. Both women and men give and receive ceremonial valuables, foodstuffs, goods made by women such as clay cooking pots, sleeping mats, and coconut-leaf skirts, and goods made by men such as carved hardwood bowls and lime spatulas. They exchange with partners of both sexes, and men and women may compete across gender lines to obtain the same valuable. Women travel on foot and by sailing canoe to far-flung hamlets and distant islands whose inhabitants speak other languages and have different customs. Women and men alike host the mortuary feasts held intermittently for years after each death, giving and receiving enormous quantities of customary wealth.

Vanatinai women's participation in economically and ritually essential and prestigious activities leads to their influence over others. They have equal access to material resources, and they form the core of a matrilineal kinship system. A postmarital residence pattern that alternates between the hamlet of the wife and that of the husband gives each spouse equivalent security and support. Women also have access to the culture's most significant form of authority and influence, the role of *gia*, which literally means "giver" or "big man/big woman."

The typically Melanesian institution of the big man has been the subject of anthropological debate for over a generation. Big men gain power through their assertive personalities and their ability to mobilize labor and publicly give away on ritual occasions valuables and food that they have accumulated with the aid of their supporters. This personal form of authority, achieved through competition with others, has been regarded as the hallmark of "egalitarian" Melanesian societies, which lack classes and chiefs. That these are big men, and that women in most of these societies are disenfranchised from access to the predominant form of power over others, has usually been taken for granted by anthropologists. The big women of Vanatinai offer a fresh perspective on forms of authority and constructions of personal power and influence in egalitarian societies.

On Vanatinai the same qualities of strength, wisdom, and generosity are valued in both sexes. Both sexes have access to supernatural power, through communication with ancestors and other spirits, said to underlie all human prosperity, good fortune, and health. And both sexes use techniques, gained from their elders, that harness the powers of spirits to destroy or injure others through sorcery or witchcraft. The prominent position of women in daily and ritual life is reflected in key myths about the origins of the physical world and of social relations. Gender ideology and mythology associate both women and men with crucial forms of customary knowledge and practice. Female beings first possessed the knowledge of how to cook with fire and how to exchange ceremonial valuables. Women, the islanders say, give life while men kill, and life-giving is morally superior.

I went to Sudest Island, the European name Vanatinai has been given on maps and nautical charts, because I had admittedly romantic visions of being on a South Sea island as little affected as possible by Western cultures where people lived according to "tradition." I wanted to do a holistic, old-fashioned ethnographic study, not one on a narrowly focused topic, like those most frequently published during the years that I was a graduate student. And I wanted to do it in a place that had never previously been studied by an anthropologist. I had grandiose ideas, long a staple of ethnographers, of having "my own people" to study, but I could justify them with good, scientific reasons: putting another culture on the anthropological map, value for comparative studies, efficient use of my ethnographic labor by not reworking a place that had already seen lots of anthropologists. This last was a particularly urgent problem, because several months of searching the University of California at Berkeley libraries convinced me that practically every inhabited coral islet in the Pacific had seen one if not many anthropologists. I was clearly not the only eager researcher to be lured by the South Sea island mystique.

Finally, I wanted to do research in a place where "the status of women" was high. I wanted to study a people I could really admire. I do not find ideologies of male superiority admirable, and, as a woman, I preferred not to do research in a place where such ideologies were prevalent. I had already lived with sexual inequalities in the United States. I did not want to spend my time in the Pacific trying to cajole my way into the men's cult house in order to see interesting rituals or hear esoteric ancestral lore. The more I thought about the hypothetical possibility of living in a sexually egalitarian society, the more compelling it began to be as a research problem, one that by its nature necessitated a holistic perspective on social life and custom. Did sexual equality exist? How would it come about? How was social organization engendered? Would privileges and restrictions, power and influence be parallel at each stage of the life cycle for males and females? What kinds of personal qualities would be expected, and socialized, in each sex? This was in 1974, when a feminist resurgence was starting to make an impact in anthropology but when studies of sex roles (the word gender had not yet come into vogue) or women were still unusual. In 1972 I had taken a seminar on the anthropology of sex roles, convened by May Diaz—the first ever offered at Berkeley. From across San Francisco Bay, at Stanford University, we heard reports of the course on women in cross-cultural perspective that Michelle Rosaldo, Jane Collier, and others had recently organized, which later resulted in the publication of the influential volume *Woman, Culture, and Society* (Rosaldo and Lamphere 1974).

I concentrated my search for a field site on matrilineal areas of the Pacific, figuring that a horticultural society where descent was traced through women would accord at least some cultural weight to them. This was also a way of addressing the riddle of how to find a culture with a high status of women if such a culture had never been studied. Months later I returned to an anthropological beginning. I found my research site on the map on page 30 in Malinowski's (1922) *Argonauts of the Western Pacific*, arguably the single most important work in shaping modern anthropology. About three hundred miles southeast of the Trobriand Islands, site of Malinowski's pioneering research in 1915–18, there were two islands in the lower right-hand corner of the map, Sudest and Misima, that had not been studied, as far as I knew. They were large by Pacific standards, not just dots of coral, with distinctive cultures and languages. As I describe later in this book, the whole culture area, the Massim, which is largely matrilineal, had been repeatedly described by anthropologists, for seventy years, as having a "high status of women," but nobody had yet, I thought, documented this. (Annette Weiner's influential restudy of the Trobriand Islands of 1976, focusing on women's ceremonial exchange, was published two years later.)

Fired with enthusiasm, I wrote a research proposal for a holistic study of sex roles and culture, hypothesizing—because I was applying to the National Science Foundation—that if Sudest or Misima really did have "a high status of women," it would be reflected in equal treatment in each stage of the life cycle and that women would be prominent in the interisland ceremonial exchanges and the mortuary rituals that were characteristic of the Massim culture area. Apparently, feminist winds of intellectual change had reached the anthropology panel of the National Science Foundation, because they funded my research, although a variety of circumstances delayed my departure for Papua New Guinea until 1977.

In many ways I found what I hoped to on Sudest Island, or, as those who live there call it, Vanatinai, which literally means "motherland." This includes, most importantly, a people for whom I have the greatest respect and admiration. The island culture is sexually egalitarian overall in its principles and in the daily and ritual lives of its people, but I cannot describe it as one in which there is perfect equality between the sexes.

I have tried not to write a "Western feminist allegory" (Clifford 1986) or to idealize the people of Vanatinai for rhetorical or political effect. Still, the example of Vanatinai is a countermodel to Western gender relations, one that, by its difference, is both an implicit and, finally, an explicit critique of Western ideologies of domination (cf. Marcus and Fischer 1986). But this book, I think, will fail to satisfy either of two conflicting feminist agendas that I have encountered previously when describing my research to others. The first is the wish to find corroboration of universal male dominance and the universal oppression of women, and the second is the desire to learn that, somewhere in the world, there is a place where sexual equality is real and absolute. Vanatinai is much more in the direction of the latter, though; it is a society in which there is no ideology of male superiority, and one in which women have the same kinds of personal autonomy and control of the means of production as men.

I no longer believe it possible to describe "the [single and invariant] status of women" in any society. I have tried to document multiple social positions and gender ideologies as articulated in words and actions in varying contexts, looking for congruences and contradictions and for individual variations. I have, as I initially proposed, focused on exchange and mortuary ritual—finding that women were indeed prominent in these prestigious and influential arenas—on the life cycle, and on indigenous notions of personal power.

I came to realize, beginning with my first days on the island, that "tradition," or custom, *mumuga*, as Vanatinai people say, is not something static, unified, and unchanging, but flexible, continually modified, and reinterpreted. I encountered rituals that were said to date from the "time of the ancestors," a rich and detailed body of myths, customs, and beliefs in sharp contrast to my own about such things as sorcery and witchcraft, and women in coconut-leaf skirts. I also found professed Christians who petition ancestor spirits, rituals that involved axe blades of polished greenstone but have changed dramatically within living memory, myths about a spirit who departed for the land of Europeans with gold and machinery, elderly men and women who spoke an English-based Papuan Pidgin the younger generation could not understand, and men in well-worn Bruce Lee T-Shirts. Vanatinai is a "traditional" culture, but not because it exists in (as nearly as you can find these days) some kind of pristine, primeval isolation. Its people, most of them, are militant and self-conscious cultural conservatives, who have been eclectically adapting certain ideas, customs, and technologies from Europeans over the last century and a half, from other islanders for millennia, and actively resisting others. Accordingly, I have focused on historical transformations that have shaped island lives, particularly constructions of gender.

I use a variety of approaches in this book to the problem of how to communicate my perceptions, experiences, and constructions to multiple others, an audience that includes both educated Vanatinai people and educated people from my own country. I make no claim of presenting an objective reality. I try to locate myself as a positioned subject, in Renato Rosaldo's (1989) phrase, in this text, not only to establish my ethnographic authority (cf. Clifford 1983), which I see as a worthy objective in anthropological writing, but as a way of indicating my experiences with Vanatinai people and their customs and how I have represented them.

I have interwoven the distancing rhetoric of abstraction, generalization, and interpretation with narrative and anecdote and with dense ethnography, following an old-fashioned, Malinowskian tradition. I have tried to evoke island scenes and describe islanders' thoughts and actions as I perceived or experienced them to allow readers to reach their own partially independent understandings, inevitably refracted through my subjective constructions. I present descriptions of the value of girl babies, land tenure patterns, excerpts from Captain Owen Stanley's diary from the summer of 1849 in which he relates that the women have "a certain amount of Command," warfare customs, the multiple roles of women in mortuary rituals, sorcery practices, and the myth of Bambagho, the female snake who produced the first ceremonial valuables and taught the first magic of exchange to a wise old woman.

I use the arrival trope, a convention both of ethnographic writing and other accounts of travel, because I have found it to be an effective narrative device, both in making sense of my own experiences and in communicating them to others, verbally and in writing. Mary Louise Pratt (1986) has perceptively noted that classic opening narratives of anthropological accounts from the Pacific Islands use the same devices as accounts of Pacific "discoverers." These include "the classic Polynesian arrival scene" where the European is first welcomed on the beach to a utopian world and led to the chief, and the metaphor of the castaway, at first reluctant to be, literally, stranded with the islanders but eventually absorbed into their world.

My own arrival in the islands had remarkable, and slightly unnerving, resonances with some of these earlier accounts. An island is not a bounded cultural universe, but still, the moment when you wade ashore and step onto the beach, both you and the islanders recognize that you have crossed a boundary into someplace unique and apart, a place that is theirs and where you are the visitor, *bwabwali*. The arrival narrative has a particular aptness for evoking to others what it is like to go and live on a remote island. I had the eerie, and unexpected, experience of feeling that I was living out some description of early contact written in the last century, but that was mixed with the jarring and distinctly postmodern effect of seeing such things as men wearing T-Shirts with the words "Boston Giants" (made in Singapore?) or a picture of Muhammed Ali. But it was First Contact—between me and them—and my description is First Contact for the reader. It shows the radical otherness I perceived and the otherness with which some islanders saw me at first—me with my corpselike white skin and long hair (uncut, like someone in mourning) and the island women in long "grass" skirts, bodies bare to the waist and blackened with charcoal for a mortuary ritual—and how, from my perspective, we negotiated our relationships and gradually came to know each other.

I have changed many personal names and some place names in this account of Vanatinai life in order to protect the privacy of individuals and their families.

Chapter 1 contains the narrative of my first encounters with Louisiade Archipelago peoples and of the mutual perceptions that generated my field research experiences and shaped my understandings of Vanatinai custom and thought. In chapter 2 I present a theoretical overview of gender equality and inequality, outlining different arguments and hypotheses about male dominance and female autonomy, setting the stage for using the ethnographic example of Vanatinai to see if it fits various models of dominance or equality and associated gender roles and ideologies. I introduce aspects of the social life and history of Vanatinai and their relation to changing gender relations, religious philosophy and worldview, and exchange and ritual practice. Chapter 3 focuses on the life cycles of islanders of both sexes, comparing the ideologies and expectations, privileges and proscriptions attached to being male or female at different life stages. Chapter 4 examines religion, cosmology, and supernatural bases of power and efficacy, relating them to gender ideologies and symbolism as reflected in myth, magic, and ritual. Chapter 5 looks at gender and the destructive powers of sorcery and witchcraft. Chapters 6 and 7 focus on ceremonial exchange and mortuary ritual, key arenas for the performance and validation of personal and gender identity. Finally, in chapter 8 I discuss gender roles, ideologies, and power in this egalitarian society, their cultural and historical contexts, their significance for the cross-cultural analysis of gender relations, and their implications for the possibilities of changing relations between women and men elsewhere in the world.

The research on which this book is based was carried out in Papua New Guinea for sixteen months in 1977–79, two months in 1981, and three months in 1987. I am grateful for the following sources of financial support: the National Science Foundation, the Chancellor's Patent Fund and Department of Anthropology of the University of California at Berkeley, the Papua New Guinea Institute of Applied Social and Economic Research, the Wenner-Gren Foundation for Anthropological Research, the National Institute of Child Health and Human Development of the National Institutes of Health, and the Graduate School of the University of Wisconsin, Madison. The maps were prepared with the assistance of the Cartography Laboratory, University of Wisconsin, Madison.

Short sections of this book were previously published in earlier versions as parts of "Big Men, Big Women, and Cultural Autonomy," *Ethnology* (1990), 29(1):35–50; "Gender in an Egalitarian Society: A

Case Study from the Coral Sea," in Peggy Sanday and Ruth Goodenough, eds., *Beyond the Second Sex: New Directions in the Anthropology of Gender*, Philadelphia: University of Pennsylvania Press, 1990, pp. 171–223; "Sudest Island and the Louisiade Archipelago in Massim Exchange," in Jerry Leach and Edmund Leach, eds., *The Kula: New Perspectives on Massim Exchange*, Cambridge: Cambridge University Press, 1983, pp. 467–501; and "Death and Exchange: Mortuary Ritual on Vanatinai (Sudest Island)," in Frederick Damon and Roy Wagner, eds., *Death Rituals and Life in the Societies of the Kula Ring*, De Kalb: Northern Illinois University Press, 1989, pp. 199–229. The table and figures 1 and 2 previously appeared as well, in slightly different form, in my chapter in *Death Rituals and Life in the Societies of the Kula Ring*. I thank the publishers for the permission to use this material here.

Since 1977 I have been helped in diverse ways by many sympathethic and knowledgeable people. In Port Moresby these include Mary-Jane Mountain, Barry Shaw, the Honorable Rabbie Namaliu, Margaret Nakikus, Charles Lepani, Sue Andrews, Gary Simpson, Mac Marshall, Leslie Marshall, Michael and Elahe Walter, Jacob Simet, Wari Iamo, the students, faculty, and staff of the Department of Anthropology and the Department of Community Medicine of the University of Papua New Guinea, and the staff at the Institute of Applied Social and Economic Research. In Alotau I am grateful for the assistance of Jack Bagita, Lepani Watson, Virgil Matalale, John Rorossi, Murray and Cathy Abel, Dr. Colin Lewis, Dr. Festus Pawa, Ron Baloiloi, and the staff of the Milne Bay Provincial Government Office and the Milne Bay Provincial Health Department. I thank Weli Edoni at Samarai. At Misima I would like to thank the Honorable Jacob Lemeki and to give special thanks to Rachel and Teddy Imatana and family. Three district officers, Jon Bartlett, Victor Arme, and Kevin Kadadaya, and their staffs provided assistance. I also thank Albie and Ruth Munt, David Hanton, Benoni Kadulu, Meri Latu, John Fifita, and the captains and crews of MV *Lilivaso*, MV *Misima*, and MV *Laba*.

At Tagula Station, Sudest Island, I gratefully acknowledge the assistance of Officers in Charge Matthew Pabarikia and his wife, Josephine, Nou Labui and his wife, Philomena, and Mr. and Mrs. Francis Yuwa. I also thank John Maika, Boas Tubaria, and the staff at

Tagula Station. Special thanks go to Mathew and Timaima Paulisbo at Badia and to Theodore and Veronica Kopu. At Nimowa I thank Father Joseph Ensing, Father Kevin Young, Mother Antoninus, Sister Margaret, Sister Maria Cornelia, Sister Juliana, and Sister Marlene for their kindness and hospitality. At Jinjo, Rossel Island, my thanks go to Father Kevin English, Sister Brenda, Sister Mary, and Sister Caritas, and, at Pambwa, to Mr. and Mrs. Gabriel Kieke.

I am deeply grateful to many people on Vanatinai and nearby islands for their hospitality, interest, friendship, and assistance. In the Jelewaga area, I would particularly like to thank Kaile, Pode, Mulia, Salome, Dante, Denden, Malabwaga, Koita, Sebo, Sete, Josephine, Lote and family, Friday, Eimi, Beda, Kai, Kay, Gole, Sikoya, Bwaka, Ebenel, Saina, Sididi, Zilo, Barbara, Koya and family, Abel and family, Kelela, Nanosi, Kowak, Bwanaiwe, Sapili, Potete and family, Ludi, Yadama, Sale, Piron, Jita, Bwawa, Dobo, Boi and family, Kemp and Villo Harre, Tagilan, Dosin, Ulawa, and the people of Eyuba, with special thanks to Missis Joan Ulawa, Koita Dosin, Kasiman Dosin, and Tielly Tagilan. My thanks go also to Tabiau and family, Irene and Joseph, Theresa, Maria and Frank, Kandewe, Peter Edoni and Denise, Sisi, Geraldine, John Walia, Gus, Magani, Padi, Kadau, Stanley Siai, Dabua, Didimali and family, Latage and family, Patrick, Joseph, Bogau, Tom, Antonita, Barbara, Bwaileta, Martin Siyabibi, and Nilla. I give special thanks to Rorosi Tomiebe and family, Vitalis Rorosi, Noelene, and everyone at Grass Island Village.

My greatest debt and my deepest thanks go to Martin Peter, Nora Moses, Thomas Robutu, and Jimmy, Daisy, and Hina Martin, who accepted me into their home and family and tried to teach me about life on Vanatinai.

Ago laghie moli ghea ghemi giagia na!

I thank the people who have offered useful comments and criticisms of various incarnations of this book and its ideas. They include Margaret Mackenzie, Elizabeth Colson, Margaret Clark, Sheldon Margen, William Shack, Burton Benedict, David Baker, Wari Iamo, Sharon Hutchinson, Robert Brightman, Kirin Narayan, Fitz Poole, and several anonymous reviewers. I thank my parents, Robert and Florence Lepowsky, for their comments, for teaching me to value equality and to respect the will of others—values I found so prominent on Vanatinai—and for their continual encouragement and moral support.

I dedicate this book to the people of Vanatinai and their neighbors, with deepest admiration and respect. I hope they will forgive my mistakes and misunderstandings and realize that I have tried to do what I was instructed, "to write it down properly."

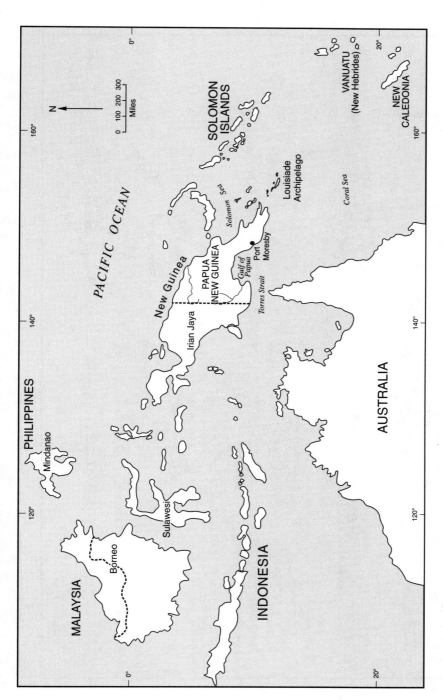

Southwest Pacific

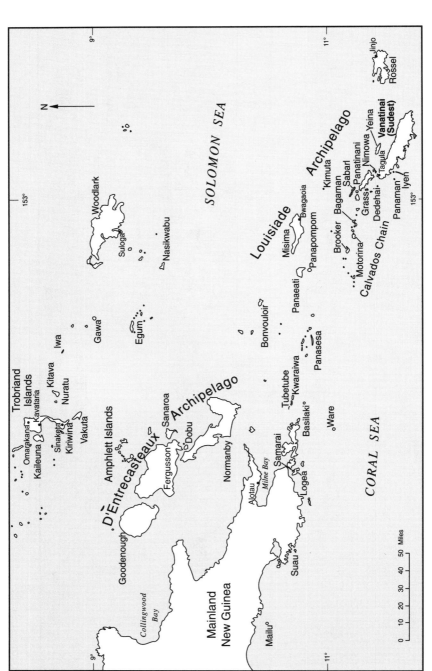

Islands of Southeastern New Guinea — The Massim

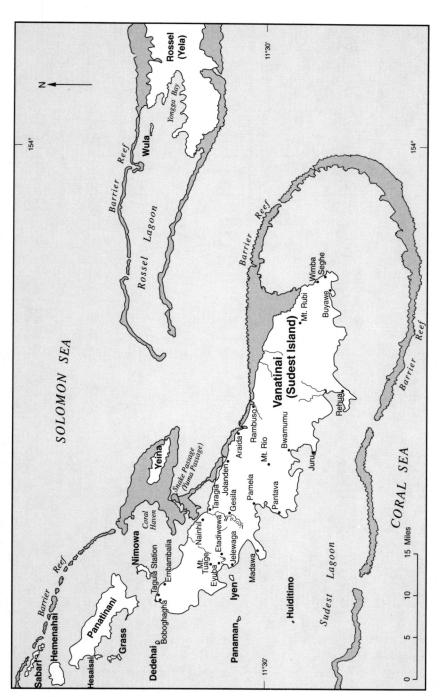

Vanatinai (Sudest Island)

Fruit of the Motherland

Chapter One

Island Encounters

The small government-owned boat pulled slowly away from the dilapidated wharf, the sudden roar of a marine diesel engine shattering the morning stillness. We skirted the shoreline fringed with mangroves and swung around Western Point, with its nearby village strung along a fine sandy beach, toward the south coast of Sudest Island. A chain of smaller islands was visible across the lagoon to the northwest, beginning only a few miles away and vanishing into the hazy distance. I was finally on my way to the village where I would live during my research. I stood at the rail as we chugged along the coast, skirting coral patches and bouncing over oncoming swells. An offshore wind brought occasional gusts of moist air laden with intoxicating smells from the rain forest slopes, mixing the sweetness of unknown flowers with rotting vegetation. But the rugged mountains—vivid green and uninterrupted by signs of human settlement for almost twenty miles—seemed ominous and threatening, and I wondered whether or not I had made the right decision in choosing to make the island my home for a year or more.

I had flown from Port Moresby, the national capital of Papua New Guinea, to Alotau, at the tip of the mainland. Transportation to the more remote islands lying to the east and southeast was generally dependent upon hitching a ride on a government, trading, or mission boat that might happen to be heading in your general direction. Sometimes it was necessary to wait for weeks. Although there were airstrips on most of the larger islands, including, since 1969, Sudest, and there were two flights a week from the mainland to the Trobriand Islands, there were no scheduled flights to Sudest during the time I first came to the region. The private airline had canceled its twice-monthly, nine-seater plane since there were not enough passengers to make it worthwhile, and the government had not yet instituted its charter flights every other week (which often did not arrive, anyway).

I had been lucky enough to catch a ride to Misima Island, ninety miles north of Sudest, on a government boat chartered by a local official. I then had to look for another boat at Misima to take me the rest of the way. While I was waiting on the wharf at Alotau, I met a young man from Dobu Island who was on his way to Port Moresby to begin his studies at the University of Papua New Guinea. He had met anthropologist Reo Fortune on a return visit to Dobu in 1969 and been impressed with Fortune's fluency in the Dobu language. When he heard that I planned to go to Sudest to conduct an anthropological study, he looked worried. I should be very careful, he warned. The people of Sudest were dangerous sorcerers who knew all the poisonous plants. Some Sudest men were presently in jail for sorcery at Giligili, the prison only a few miles along the bay from where we were. I learned from him for the first time that sorcery was a crime in independent Papua New Guinea, just as it had been in the colonial days before 1975. I told him that Reo Fortune had written a book, famous to anthropologists, called *Sorcerers of Dobu*. He laughed in surprise and said that the people of Dobu were afraid of the sorcerers of Sudest.

We left the tropical fjord of Milne Bay in late afternoon, docking overnight at Samarai, the former capital of British New Guinea. It is a tranquil port on an island so small that, as four generations of visitors have written, you can walk around it in half an hour. The voyage to Misima took two days. We put in at Panasesa, an uninhabited atoll island, and had lunch in the tall coconut groves of an abandoned plantation. My companions pointed out the embers and fragments of crabshell on the beach, which marked the recent presence of visitors, most likely fisherman from Panaeati Island, fifty miles to the east across open sea, who would have sailed to Panasesa in their outrigger canoes.

We anchored offshore until one in the morning and then rolled east with the ocean swells in starlight to cross into Panaeati Lagoon during high tide in the early morning. The captain cautiously traversed the passage through the reef and brought us into the haven of the lagoon, where half a dozen magnificently carved single-outrigger sailing canoes glided with surprising speed across the still, almost transparent water. I stayed in one of the village houses, which stand on stilts on the beach and have walls of sago palm bark lashed to a wood frame and a roof of sago palm leaves. The people of Panaeati, the most prolific builders and traders of sailing canoes in the region, were kind and hospitable, and I slept for the first time on a finely woven pandanus-leaf mat.

Misima, which we reached the following afternoon, was a single forest-covered mountain range plunging precipitously into the deep sea, with no sheltering lagoon except at the east end. Garden areas clung to the steep slopes at seemingly impossible angles, and the houses were strung out along the shore.

Although Sudest is the largest island in the Louisiade Archipelago at fifty miles long by eight to fifteen miles wide, it was home in 1978 to only 2,075 people. Misima, one-quarter its size, supported a population of nearly 8,000. Misima is the normal point of entry into the Louisiade region. District headquarters are located there, and its nearby airstrip was visited twice weekly by nine-seater commercial planes. Though there was no scheduled shipping, several privately owned cargo boats and government vessels occasionally made the run into Samarai or Alotau on official business or to sell Louisiade copra and pick up trade goods. Misima had been the center of mission activity for the archipelago since 1891 and the regional headquarters for colonial and now national government since early in this century. Misimans are enthusiastic churchgoers and adherents of the United Church Mission, formerly the Australasian Methodist Missionary Society. They still hold the series of feasts, or *hagali*, which custom requires after someone dies, but the time spent in preparing for and holding the feasts has been effectively curtailed by local government and mission edicts.

The offical with whom I had been traveling tried to persuade me to remain on Misima and go to his home village to conduct my research. He said that if I did so I would give Misima a big name and bring tourists to the island. "Dr. Malinowski came and wrote a book about Kiriwina, and now Kiriwina is famous, and the tourists go there. And Kiriwina is nothing! It is overpopulated—they have no land!" It is true that Kiriwina, about the size of Sudest but with a population then of 11,000, was seriously overcrowded.

I had realized even before coming to Papua New Guinea that I would very likely have to choose between doing fieldwork on Misima, where I would be closer to transportation, supplies, medical aid, and mail, and the much more remote and probably more culturally conservative islands to the southeast. Now, during the time I spent on Misima waiting for a boat, looking at old government patrol reports, and visiting the villages on the east end, I began to question people about living conditions on Sudest Island. The answers I received from both Misimans and expatriates were almost uniformly discouraging, at least in their intent. I was told that I would be unable to purchase any store-bought foods or supplies and that I would have no access to medical aid in case of an emergency. There was a dangerous, mile-wide fringing reef obstructing navigation, the island was full of swamps, and the swamps were full of crocodiles, so I would be unable to walk around. The people spoke no English, they were unfriendly, and they would not come and sit with me like Misimans or talk to me except to demand tobacco. They were well known for not paying their head taxes. A government official characterized the Sudest people as obsessed by sorcery, commenting that they did not seem to find much time to spend on either gardening or fishing, since no sooner had they dealt with one case of sorcery accusations than they were faced with another. I was also told they spent most of their time attending and hosting feasts. Finally, I heard that most of them were pagans. Naturally, I was both worried by descriptions of the physical and social difficulties with which I would be faced but tremendously intrigued by the stereotypes of these "sorcerers of Sudest."

But one Misima woman, who became my friend, told me that if I really wanted to study "custom" I should go to Sudest and not stay on Misima. She said that her generation had been forced to attend mission boarding schools and forbidden to go to feasts. Consequently, she said, nowadays the grandparents' generation was having to teach the young people of Misima about their customs at Culture Day once a week in the government primary schools, since the middle-aged people did not know their own customs properly. I learned that mission activity on Sudest had only begun in 1947, that no white missionaries had ever lived there, and that there were in fact no whites living on the island at all. Still, despite my attraction, I was intimidated by everyone else's warning.

By a stroke of good luck a small local trading vessel had been chartered by representatives of the Milne Bay Provincial Government for a political education mission. It was leaving immediately on a three-week tour of all the major coastal settlements on Sudest and Rossel Islands plus most of the inhabited islands in the Calvados Chain. The trip was planned so that local politicians could explain to the villagers about the formation of the new provincial government—part of a nationwide policy of governmental decentralization—and inform them of their role in it, which was to elect representatives to the new provincial assembly. I received permission to go along, and thus had a most unusual opportunity to survey the region, including even the rarely visited south coasts of Sudest and Rossel Islands. I could meet the local people and then decide where I would live and conduct my research for the next year or more.

The boat was simultaneously picking up copra (smoked, dried coconut meat) and selling tobacco, rice, canned fish, fish hooks, steel knives, and other goods to the islanders. The piercingly sweet, rancid smell of copra, the mainstay of South Sea island commerce, clung to the hold, the cargo, and soon to the bodies and clothing of all of us passengers. I was taken aback when I noticed a torn, yellowing certificate under plastic on the cabin wall that read, "Territory of Papua. License to Trade with Natives."

Martin Peter was the first Sudest person I ever met. A slender, intelligent man of about thirty, he was returning to his home at Jelewaga Village on the south coast of Sudest Island from the Louisiade Local Government Council meeting. Misimans described him to me as the leader of the Sudest councillors. Martin had already heard about me, and after we talked for a while he invited me to live with him and his wife and young children at Jelewaga either for the duration of my stay or until a separate house could be built for me if I wished. I thanked him gratefully for his most generous and surprising offer and told him that I would give him my decision by the time we reached Jelewaga. Martin got off the boat at the small government station on the northwest tip of Sudest Island to walk the seventeen miles to his home through the rain forest. Meanwhile, we continued along the northern coast of Sudest and then headed across the treacherous passage to circumnavigate Rossel Island before returning to the Sudest south coast.

By the time I saw my first Sudest village, Embambalia, I had decided that it would be worth the extra hardship and isolation to live and conduct research on Sudest Island. As we walked ashore along a path through the mangroves I could see clay pots full of pork boiling over stone tripods set on the bare ground. We had arrived at the end of a mortuary feast. While almost all of the women on Misima wore garments of store-bought cloth, most of the Sudest women were barebreasted and wearing knee-length skirts made of thin strips of young coconut leaves or, in other words, what is usually referred to inaccurately as a grass skirt. A few women wore coarser, ankle-length coconut-leaf skirts, and their bodies were blackened from head to toe with burnt coconut husks. The Misimans told me these women were in mourning and that Misimans had previously followed the same customs but nowadays wore black cloth dresses instead until the final memorial feast.

Even coming from the tranquility of Misima, visiting Sudest was almost like visiting another world. While the Misimans had seemed calmly curious and friendly but unsurprised upon encountering me, the Sudest people were clearly stunned to find a white woman on their island. Some small children shrieked in terror upon catching sight of me and fled in the opposite direction, to the amusement of my Misiman companions, who explained that they were terrified of my strange white skin and long hair, as they had never have seen a white person before. Some of the women had never seen a white woman before either. A couple of old women crossed their arms over their breasts, put their heads down, and, to my dismay, ran for the forest as well. But most of the adults and older children clustered around me, talking and laughing loudly in obvious excitement and, to my surprise, eager to shake my hand. Some of the bolder women and children stroked my hair and rubbed my arm with their fingers. One woman then looked at her fingers, started visibly, and exclaimed in surprise: the white pigment did not rub off my skin. (Thomas Huxley, visiting the island on board HMS *Rattlesnake* in 1849, the first known visit of Europeans, had a similar experience, writing in his diary that men shouted in surprise when he and a friend took off their shirts and revealed white chests.)

I was just as excited to meet the villagers. They seemed pleased when they were told in the Misima language by the visiting local politicians, whom they knew, that I had been sent by the government to study Sudest customs and that I might come to live in one of the Sudest villages. Contrary to the warnings I had gotten on Misima, the people seemed to be friendly and welcoming, although many were undeniably very shy. Very few of the men and seemingly none of the women could speak any English at all, which indicated their relative lack of contact with the outside world, encouraging for someone wanting to study "traditional" island culture but daunting as well, since it would be very difficult to learn their unwritten language without the aid, at least initially, of bilingual individuals.

Two weeks later, when we finally reached Jelewaga Village, the political education patrol's last stop on the south coast of Sudest Island, we found that Martin had walked across to Tagula Station again on government business. But his wife Nora met us and repeated her husband's invitation. I liked her immediately. A pretty young woman with a merry laugh and a quick mind, she was not from Sudest but from Wagawaga Village on Milne Bay near the southeastern tip of mainland Papua New Guinea. She had lived on Sudest for eight years and was fluent in that language and spoke English as well. Martin and Nora and their children obviously did not constitute a typical Sudest household, but they were locally respected people who were willing to take a strange foreigner into their home for an indefinite period of time. I would be able to communicate with them during the difficult first few months, and they could probably help me in my struggle to learn the Sudest language.

Jelewaga itself seemed a good choice as a research location. It was on the south coast of the island, which is less frequently visited by government, mission, and trading boats, but it was only one long day's walk through the swamps and rain forest or by paddling canoe along the coast from Tagula Station, with its small airstrip, its two-way radio, and its intermittent mail service. Tagula also had the island's only tradestore, run by a local family. Of course I could only reach Tagula during fair weather, but Jelewaga was still less isolated in case of an emergency than the villages we had just visited in eastern

7

Sudest, which were three and four days farther away from contact with the outside world. The Jelewaga area also had one of the largest populations of any census district on the island, according to statistics I had previously seen, even though only about one hundred people lived not only at Jelewaga itself but scattered in dispersed settlements along the coast and inland near their gardens.

The Jelewaga people themselves seemed friendly, and they were clearly excited to meet me. Nora said they were "very happy" when Martin told them prior to my arrival that I might come to live at Jelewaga and study their customs. I asked Nora to tell them that I had decided to settle at Jelewaga, that I was returning to Misima to get my belongings and make some last-minute purchases, and that I would come back to Jelewaga to stay on the first available transport.

At last I was on the boat with all of my field supplies en route to the Sudest village where I would live and work for the next year. As we drew closer to Jelewaga I became increasingly nervous. The boat would anchor on the reef along the shore near the village and leave me there, returning immediately to Tagula Station. What if there was no one to meet me? What if I became seriously ill? How was I going to learn a language with no written texts? What if no one would talk to me, as the Misimans had warned? What would I do when my food supplies ran out (for I had been warned that the small tradestore had great difficulty keeping cargo in stock because of the lack of shipping in the area)? How would I get my mail?

As we passed a promontory covered with dark green vegetation, the coastline indented into a large shallow bay backed by steep mountains. The grassy hill toward which we had been heading for more than an hour, which had seemed to be a peninsula jutting out from the coast, was now revealed to be a small island separated from the main island of Sudest by a half-mile of lagoon. We swung to port to cut between this tiny island and Sudest itself, making for Jelewaga, which lay on a coastal ridge marking the southeastern extension of a large bay. The village was not visible, but the crew members pointed out to me the tops of the coconut palms that mark the settlement. Suddenly the deck erupted in a confusion of shouted commands, and we changed direction, heading out to sea. The captain had changed his mind about trying to thread his way through the dangerous reefs we could see just beneath the turquoise waters of the shallow lagoon. The tide was too low, and he was backtracking to where the passage was deeper.

A break in the mangroves on the tiny offshore island revealed a hamlet built on the sandy beach, but a closer look showed that the houses were falling into ruin and that the place was abandoned. I later learned that a bitter quarrel over land boundaries had been followed by several deaths, which each faction attributed to the sorcery of the other. The inhabitants dispersed to other settlements and left the island to the occasional fishing party, even though colonial documents show that it had been inhabited for the past one hundred years.

After a cautious zigzagging approach over the reef, whose whitish brain corals, spiky blue branch corals, and schools of brightly colored fish swimming in formation were clearly visible only a few feet beneath the lagoon waters, we finally dropped anchor a quarter-mile offshore from Jelewaga. The excited shouts of children waiting on the rocky point that interrupted the mangroves echoed out over the water.

An outrigger canoe headed toward us to help off-load passengers and cargo. I slid gingerly into its narrow hull, and an older man poled us toward land. I waded through the warm water to where Nora was waiting for me on the rocky shore holding her two-year-old daughter, who gazed at me with enormous, worried eyes. Several men and women helped me carry my gear up the hill to Martin and Nora's house, smiling at me and talking among themselves about this turn of events.

My new home was located about a hundred yards up the grassy ridge. We passed a government rest house built by villagers of local materials just above the shore to accommodate visiting officials on their rare "patrols" of the area. A flock of scarlet lories wheeled and chattered raucously in the tall palms behind it as we filed past. As we ascended the ridge a panorama of mountains and bay became visible in the inland direction, but the view of the lagoon to the south was blocked by luxuriant vegetation. The path into the hamlet where Martin and Nora lived, only halfway to Jelewaga proper, a further hundred yards up the ridge, was blocked by an enormous pig, which reluctantly moved out of the way in response to the shouts of its female owner, my new neighbor. The hamlet, named Ghewaghena, or "to the moon," referring to its fine view of the night sky from the central clearing, contained three houses on stilts and assorted outbuildings. A fourth house lay collapsed on the ground, victim of the cyclone that had struck the archipelago two months earlier.

The house was just off the main path underneath a huge mango tree. Gingerly, I climbed the slippery narrow ladder—a notched pole—onto the verandah. This house too had been slightly damaged by the cyclone even though it was only a few years old and strongly built. Several sheets of sago palm bark, lashed with cord made from forest vines onto a log frame to form the wall, had been blown away. There was a hole in the roof where a section of doubled-over sago palm leaf, normally a watertight covering layered onto a wooden frame, had disappeared.

The interior of the house consisted of one main room, a much smaller sleeping area, and a narrow storage area full of clay cooking pots, borders incised with abstract designs, some blackened from the fire and others reddish-brown and never used. The pots were moved to the house rafters, and I moved into the former storage area. The only furniture was a number of beautifully woven pandanus mats, made by Nora and used for sitting, eating, and sleeping, that covered part of the floor of *nipa* (black palm) bark lashed together. A sheet of sago palm bark covered with sand held in place by four logs indicated an unvented fireplace, the family's source of heat and light in the evening as well as a place to cook.

Martin arrived to welcome me and hurried off again to assist his kinspeople. My good luck had continued, for the people of Jelewaga were beginning a feast that day. The guests were arriving from the other Sudest villages, and the settlement was in a ferment of preparation. We walked up the hill to the main village to watch. Jelewaga proper consisted of only seven houses in a grove of coconut, mango, and breadfruit trees on the top of the ridge. In front of it lay the saltwater mangrove swamp on the lagoon shore and behind it a freshwater sago swamp and the grasslands and forested mountain slopes inland.

That day the village was full of people cooking food for the feast. A row of smoke-blackened clay cooking pots, each supported over a fire by three stones, contained boiling yams, sweet potato, taro, bananas, manioc, and sago in a coconut cream sauce. A group of women were building an earth oven of hot stones and leaves to roast more vegetables, tossing the fire-heated stones into place with wooden tongs. Nearby several men carefully stirred pots of ceremonial sago pudding, made with the sweet liquid of green coconuts, with elaborately carved, seven-foot-long paddles used only on these ritual occasions. We were given a basket of uncooked vegetables to take home and offered cooked vegetables to eat. Men and women were rushing around calling to each other, while others, presumably the visitors, sat in the shade under the houses and on the red earth in the center of the settlement talking, laughing, and chewing betel nut.

Nora explained that the major ceremony would take place the next day. The feast was being held to clear all the mourning taboos from the widow, the son, and various in-laws of a man who had died more than twenty years earlier. It was the last and most elaborate in a series of mortuary rituals held after the death of each individual. Usually the last feast, or *zagaya*, is held three to four years after a death, but in this case the son was an only child who had no brothers and sisters to help him in his struggle to accumulate enough valuables to hold the feast.

His mother, her sister, and several other kinswomen were wearing the coarse, ankle-length mourning skirts, and their bodies were completely blackened with burnt coconut husks. With their lips stained blood-red from betel nut chewing, they presented an extraordinary sight to my Western eyes. The widow had worn the mourning skirt for two decades. She had been forbidden to decorate herself, dance, or visit other villages except in full mourning regalia and in quest of goods for the feast. In theory she was supposed to blacken herself daily and forbidden to bathe or to cut her hair until this final feast. I was told that a widower is supposed to follow the same stringent mourning proscriptions, wearing ragged old clothes and growing a beard and long hair.

The feast host, the son of the dead man, had chosen to have modern "string band" music—guitars and ukeleles—and dancing that night rather than traditional dancing accompanied by drumming and singing. The music began about eight o'clock that evening and continued until about seven the next morning. A group of young men played their instruments, which were strung with monofilament fishing line, singing in a variety of island languages. Everybody danced except the mourners, a few people with partners but most without. A few old women solemnly performed what was obviously a traditional dance to the lively music, but most people gave highly individualistic, free-style renditions that would not have looked out of place on any dance floor in the Western world. One little boy accompanied his energetic hip-swiveling with exuberant shouts of "Twees, twees!" (twist).

Most of the women wore their usual coconut-leaf skirts, but many had added cloth blouses for the feast, not out of modesty or shame, I was later told, but as a further form of decoration. The men wore shorts or lengths of brightly colored cloth wound around their waists. A few men put on women's coconut-leaf skirts, tied in the front instead of over the right hip. When I asked why I was simply told, "Because they feel like dancing." The Western clothes came either from the tradestore or were purchased second-hand for a small price at the Catholic Mission on Nimowa Island. T-shirts with pictures of Bruce Lee, the Chinese kung-fu star, or of Mohammed Ali, the African American boxing champion, were popular. One man wore a shirt that read, "Hobie surfboards, Newport Beach, California." Many of the boys and men had elaborate feather arrangements stuck at a jaunty angle in their hair along with the more usual carved wooden hair combs worn by both sexes. A few young girls wore feathers as well. Many people, old and young, wore flowers in their hair and stuck in their armlets. I sat on the ground in the village clearing with a group of women who were watching the dancing, cracking jokes, and laughing uproariously.

Early the next morning the musicians were given gifts of clay cooking pots made on Brooker Island and Chinese-made tradestore enamel-plated metal dishes in gratitude for their contribution to the feast. Even Nora and I received strips of raw pork, "because," she said, " we danced and helped them."

Five pigs were carried to the center of the village the next day and slaughtered, butchered, and distributed raw to all the guests according to household, for every house in Jelewaga was full of visitors. On this second day the widow and other mourning women wore on their heads the intricately woven, soft round coconut-leaf baskets made throughout the Louisiade Archipelago and normally used like purses to hold betel nut paraphernalia, tobacco, and other possessions. Their shoulders were covered by capes of fine coconut-leaf skirt, and they kept their eyes cast down.

Finally, in the afternoon the ceremony called *zilidá* (they lay the mat) or *mwagumwagu* took place. I had been told this was the most important part of the ritual. I thought I would see a solemn presentation of pigs and yams of the kind Reo Fortune describes for Dobu Island. I had attended a mortuary feast on Misima Island, and the customs there were similar to Fortune's account. But what I saw was completely unexpected.

The crowd assembled under the house, a frequent arena for social activities of other, more prosaic kinds. The widow and her "helpers"—her kinswomen plus other affines of the dead man—sat in the center of a circle. One by one men and women produced ceremonial valuables and other objects that they placed in front of the mourners. Greenstone axe blades in elaborately carved 7-shaped wooden handles accumulated in front of the women, and two axe blades in their handles were solemnly leaned against the shoulders of each of the blackened mourners. Orange "shell money" pieces called *daveri*, placed in tiny pouches of woven coconut leaf, were pinned on each woman's head, attached to the baskets that covered their hair by means of wooden combs. I suddenly recognized them as the "Rossel Island shell money" described in W. E. Armstrong's classic study from the 1920s. Long red shell-disc necklaces, or *bagi*, made famous to all anthropology students as the most important type of valuable circulating in the *kula* ring (the interisland exchange system described by Malinowski in 1922), were draped around the women's necks, along with necklaces of small, glass tradestore beads. Ceremonial carved tortoiseshell lime spatulas decorated with discs of shell were inserted in their armlets. Fine new coconut-leaf skirts were draped across their laps. More bagi, daveri, skirts, and a few yams were piled in the center of the circle. The mourning women sat quietly, their heads down and their expressions unchanging. The widow puffed quietly on her pipe. Then a different group of people, all men this time, removed the valuables and carried them outside, where they laid them down in a row upon pandanus sleeping mats. They were publicly counted, and the total was made known to the waiting crowd. I had a sudden feeling of unreality, as if I had stepped through a time portal into the Stone Age. Fifty axe blades of polished greenstone, shell-disc necklaces, and other valuables lay gleaming in the late afternoon sun.

At this point a loud quarrel broke out between the dead man's younger brother, a fifty-year-old man from the north coast, the new owner of all of the valuables, and a white-haired man from a hamlet near Jelewaga who had contributed valuables to assist the widow and her son. After a few minutes of angry shouting and gesticulation between the two men and a few of their supporters, both men stormed off in opposite directions. Concerned, I asked a young, English-speaking man what was happening. He told me not to worry, saying such confrontations frequently occur at Sudest feasts. The men had been arguing over a very long, fine stone axe blade that the dead man's brother had given to his kinsman, the white-haired man, about thirty years earlier. It seemed that he had expected a return of five or six smaller axe blades for it from his kinsman at the present feast but had not received them. Both men had now "gone off to cry" and to pack their belongings and leave, I was told, but other men hurried off to intercede and prevent an open breach. Neither man left Jelewaga after all, and both were smiling and behaving normally an hour later. But the following evening a formal meeting was held at which Martin arbitrated, and after many long hours of discussion the north coast man was given another shell-disc necklace and another stone axe blade as further compensation. If the matter had not been resolved, "somebody would die," people said ominously, for both of the older men were adept at sorcery.

There was more guitar playing, singing, and dancing on this second night until well after midnight. The next morning the north coast man presented the widow, his sister-in-law, with one fine greenstone axe blade "to cut the widow's skirt" and formally end her mourning. All of the women attending the feast then trooped down to the small waterfall and pool below the village for the last phase of the ritual. Kinswomen of the north coast man vigorously scrubbed clean with handfuls of leaves the blackened bodies of the widow and the other women who shared her mourning. Then the erstwhile mourners were dressed in fine new coconut-leaf skirts, which were carefully cut at the knee with a tradestore knife. Their bodies were rubbed with scented coconut oil until they glistened in the morning sun, and their hair was carefully combed and cut. The women cut

headbands out of the bright red labels from A-1 brand canned mackerel, saved for this occasion because of their pleasing color, placed
them on the mourners' heads, and tucked in flowers and sweet
smelling leaves. Shell-disc necklaces and necklaces of glass beads were
hung around their necks. Their faces were painted with circles of
black (burnt coconut husk) on their cheeks and chin accented with
small dots of white (powdered lime), and a band of black dotted with
white was drawn on their foreheads.

The newly resplendent widow and her companions walked slowly up the path to the village followed by the rest of us. They were met
by the young men with their guitars, who burst into song. The
women danced their way to the center of the village in a line and
were joined in dancing for about twenty minutes by the other feast
guests. Finally the dead man's brother, who had been dancing with
everyone else, made a short speech, thanking the crowd for making
the widows happy, and the feast was over. All mourning taboos were
now cleared from the widow, her son, and other in-laws of the
deceased as well as from the village of Jelewaga, which the widow's
brother-in-law had "closed" to singing, drumming, and dancing for
two long decades. The widow could now remarry if she chose. The
guests dispersed to their homes the next day, and two more pigs were
slaughtered especially for Jelewaga residents as a means of thanking
them for their work in preparing for the feast.

As the feast visitors dispersed, the people of Jelewaga and its outlying
hamlets turned their attention back to ordinary pursuits, going to
gardens cut into rain forest clearings, making sago in the swamps,
gathering shellfish on the reef, fishing, and hunting. And as the exhil-
aration of the feast with its crowds of people, aura of suspense, and
dramatic rituals wore off, I no longer felt carried along in my research
by the momentum of events. An alien outsider, I had no ordinary
pursuits, and no one, including me, was sure what I was supposed to
be doing. Martin, who was acting as an unpaid interpreter for the
government officer, departed again for the government station. Nora
was busy with her gardens and her three young children. None of my
other new neighbors could speak to me in English, and I could not
fathom their language beyond a few simple phrases. It sounded to me
like a rush of unreproducible sounds, and I could not figure out

where one word stopped and the next began. When I tried strolling over to a group of people seated in the hamlet clearing at sunset, talking, smoking pipes, and chewing betel nut, they would respond to my initial greeting and fall silent, looking down to avoid my gaze. Since I was obviously a social liability I retreated for long periods inside the house, paralyzed by my own shyness and feelings of failure as an anthropologist.

Once during these first few weeks I asked Nora to take time off to come to a communal garden clearing about two miles away where some of the women were working and interpret for me. Sympathetic to my social isolation, she agreed, bringing Hina, her two-year-old daughter, with us. With Nora along to look after me and talk to me, the women were much more relaxed, laughing and joking as we walked along the muddy path through the forest. I felt like a proper anthropologist again, surveying the garden clearing, recording in my spiral notebook what crops were growing and who was weeding her plot. Sitting on the ground with several women near the garden shelter, a wall-less structure with a sago palm-leaf roof and a platform off the ground for storage and sleeping, I asked Nora to translate the question I had been wanting to ask. In the Trobriand Islands Malinowski had described elaborate festivals taking place after the yam harvest. Were there festivals on Sudest Island after the annual yam harvest? There were a few seconds of silence. "*Goreye*," said Tugu (not her real name). "Yes."

That night when we were sitting by the fire inside the house after the children had fallen asleep, Nora told me that there were no harvest festivals on Sudest Island. "But why did Tugu say yes then?" I asked. "She was afraid because you asked her a question," Nora said, "so she said yes."

After this I was even more demoralized by my anthropological failures and retreated to the house again. Eventually, though, I had to confront the fact that this was my problem. I had crossed the Pacific and come to this remote island for a reason, and my job was to take the initiative and learn their language in order to communicate at all and to learn their customs while being as respectful as I could. It was, obviously, not their job to learn English or to serve as social directors and guides to me. I communicated some of my resolve to Nora, who promptly informed the neighbors, as I asked, that my main *kaiwa* (work) for the indefinite future was to learn their language. No European had ever previously done so, and virtually no one from surrounding islands except those few people who have married into a Sudest community ever learns to speak the island's language, perceived in the region as a difficult one. So my statement was met with approval, and my subsequent halting attempts to practice my few phrases and carry on a conversation were greeted with tolerant amusement.

Dependent primarily on observation in those early weeks, I particularly watched the women around me. As they became more accustomed to my presence they dropped the silent, reserved demeanor I later learned to recognize as the characteristic response to the few times Europeans or the Papua New Guinean government officer-in-charge appeared in the settlements. Quite to the contrary, the women were assertive and self-confident, their voices ringing out across the ridgetop along with loud, frequent bursts of laughter. They spoke up at length to men and women, neighbors and visitors from other hamlets. They also came and went in a bewildering fashion. A woman or a couple I had thought was living permanently in a nearby house would suddenly disappear, the house tied shut with a piece of cord made from a forest vine or occupied by other kinfolk. I would later learn that they were tending gardens or visiting relatives elsewhere on the island. Or someone I had never seen before would take up residence next door, completely at home. Or a woman would leave for a day or two, and I would later encounter her, in the course of some expedition of my own, deep in the bush gathering wild foods or paddling a canoe several miles down the coast.

The children too—girls and boys alike—were notably assertive and self-confident, with older ones often left in charge of small toddlers or babies, feeding them and carrying them around while their parents were miles away. I was deeply impressed the first time I saw an eight-year-old boy caring for his baby sister, a fairly common sight. Men also would often wander around the hamlet carrying a small child. I took one photograph of Paga, my neighbor, carrying his two-year-old daughter in one arm and his sister's year-old daughter in the other.

After I had been on the island a month or so I was invited to accompany a party of women on a trip three miles inland to the tiny hamlet of Etadiwewa, where extensive gardens had been planted on the steep and fertile slopes just below the pass in the central mountain range. It was the northwest monsoon season, and the path, after crossing several creeks that divide the grasslands in back of Jelewaga, dipped down and disappeared into about a half a mile of sago swamp, flooded knee-high with warm, dark brown, sulfurous-smelling water. The swamp felt primeval, with ancient-looking thorny sago palms standing in the water and filtering the sun into a dim greenish light. But I was too preoccupied to appreciate its alien beauty or to take my camera out of my day pack. It was a nightmarish obstacle literally on my path to any kind of success as a fieldworker. Shoes were hopeless, for they got sucked into the deep mud hidden under the water and trapped my feet. The sago bark sheets that had fallen into the swamp everywhere were edged with sharp thorns that cut my feet and legs. There were hidden branches and other obstacles, and I had a hard time keeping my balance, especially since I could not grab onto the thorny palms. Mulia, a thirty-five-year-old woman from an inland hamlet who sometimes stayed in her sister's house next door to me, turned back and, laughing, grabbed my hand, guiding me through the rest of the swamp. She kept up a running commentary directed at the other women, in which I heard several times the word *lumolumo*, "European." She had the other women laughing loudly. Even though I knew she was making jokes about me, I thought I felt friendliness too in her direct and shrewd gaze and the firmness of her hand in mine. But when we finally reached the edge of the swamp, pausing before crossing the broad, shallow, fast-running river draining the uplands, she put out her hand palm up and demanded, "*Topwake.*" Tobacco. Wordlessly, I gave her a stick of the molasses-cured, black twist tobacco that is the islanders' passion and watched as she cut it into sections with her knife and shared it out to the other women. But I was deflated, for I had again been naive in thinking that Mulia was helping me out of altruism and friendliness. The warnings that Sudest people wouldn't speak to you except to demand tobacco seemed confirmed. But, I reasoned, she had done something useful for me in exchange for something she wanted in return, and I couldn't expect anything more.

I returned on the following days to the inland gardens with some of the same women and Mulia held my hand through the swamp in exchange for tobacco. One time, though, as we walked single-file beyond the river under the rain forest canopy, she began talking to me rather than about me. She seemed quite emphatic. "*Unga ghubwa*," she said, gesturing toward the side of the path. Other women took up her refrain, gesturing with arms and chins: "*Unga ghubwa! Unga ghumu!*" What was this *unga* business, I wondered, and what was it they were so urgently trying to tell me? Suddenly I had one of those blinding revelations. *Unga* means, "You say," and they were trying to teach me to speak! "Ghubwa. Ghumu," I repeated obediently. "Gor-eye!" they chorused approvingly, "Yes! Tree. Rock." I rapidly acquired a burst of new vocabulary words—nouns, things you could point to and call out the names of. More important, I had acquired a group of teachers, led by Mulia, who were helping me with my publicly stated work of learning their language.

My language-learning rate and my confidence rose greatly after this point, mainly because I began to assume, correctly, that people were willing to help me as long as I was not too demanding. After a couple of months I asked about a word I kept hearing, "*Budai idai Vanatinai?*" "What means this Vanatinai?" Everyone laughed at me. "This place!" one woman exclaimed. "Vanatinai is where you are." I had finally learned the true name of the island, *Vana*, meaning "place" or "land," and *tinai*, or "mother." It has another meaning, "mainland," that contrasts it to the small coral islets off its coasts and in the Calvados Chain, called *rawa*, or islands. The name Vanatinai had virtually never been written down before (the only exception I know of is five-year resident trader and miner David White, who in 1893 rendered it as Anateena), because nobody from outside the area had ever learned the island language. Even government officers thought the indigenous name for the place was Tagula, which is in fact its name in the language of Misima Island and the western part of the Calvados Chain.

Except for a few brief but absolutely crucial times when I was assisted by Nora or Martin, I did not have a language tutor, interpreter, or field assistant, because there weren't any available. I wrote down the sounds I could distinguish in people's conversations and tried to see if there was any regularity to where they reappeared in various sentences. It was a major breakthrough if I heard a word I knew, very often a noun, or an unga word, as I thought of them from that point on, because then I had a context, however minimal, for puzzling out the possible meaning of the surrounding sounds. Occasionally I was able to reproduce a sound for Martin or Nora and receive an English translation. This was all a painfully slow process, and I did not feel that I could properly understand the flow of conversations until I had been on the island for about eight months. At that point I had a sudden and unexpected breakthrough in comprehension and speaking ability and was henceforth attributed greater fluency than I actually possessed. Since I had learned the speech of Jelewaga, with its distinctive accent and dialect locating speakers as coming from an area with a radius of only a few miles, my speaking the language was all the more startling to people I met later in the year during visits to feasts in other parts of Vanatinai and nearby islands.

As for Mulia, I grew to admire her as one of the most intelligent, knowledgeable, and forthright people on the island. When she gave birth a year later she named her infant son in my honor, in island custom a mark of a specially close relationship.

The business of asking questions and of creating a research style that was compatible with local norms of appropriate personal behavior continued for many months to be a problem for me and for the people I met. Bringing out my tape recorder in order to record someone's speech or naturalistic conversation, which was what my paperback copy of *How to Learn an Unwritten Language* advised, was certain to create a frozen silence until I retreated with the machine. People would agree to be taped speaking or singing or playing a bamboo flute and later not show up. I learned not to ask. Even bringing out my notebook was understandably intimidating when someone was in the process of telling me something interesting, again often freezing the conversation. I tried to train my memory for the details of what people said, which, when successful, enabled me to concentrate on words, meanings, and appropriate responses rather than the struggle to translate or invent a spelling, take notes, and somehow avoid missing the next thing someone said. If there was a key word or phrase or bit of information that I felt I could not remember otherwise, I would get my small notebook out of the woven pandanus-leaf basket I carried with me, island-style, and say, "I'll write that down." Occasionally a person would tell me something significant and then command me, "*Uvaghona!*" "You write that down!" In the evenings, or during daylight if, as frequently happened, we had no kerosene and only firelight at night, I would type out my fieldnotes, trying to recall what I had seen or been told during the day, to the endless fascination of little Hina and the other children (adults more quickly grew accustomed to the marvel of the moving carriage and resulting marks on paper).

The deaf-mute middle-aged woman who lived at Jelewaga and had invented her own sign language, intelligible to her family and neighbors, signed to indicate Europeans by placing the side of her hand against her forehead, like someone peering into the sun or wearing a hat or sunglasses. I had been feeling proud of my ability to do without my notebook when I finally figured out that her sign for me was to place her left hand palm up and hold her right hand over it, accurately imitating my scribbling. But at least I had my own sign, "she who writes," and was not just a generic European.

At one point when I had been on the island many months I became very discouraged with what I saw as the inadequate amount of data I had collected. I castigated myself, thinking that if I were a man I would be more aggressive about going out and getting the data and asking people questions, now that I had the linguistic ability to understand their answers, more or less. Although I don't think I changed my behavior very much, one evening shortly afterward Nora said to me, "Have you noticed that people no longer come to visit us in the evening?" "Yes," I replied. "Do you know why that is?" "No." "It is because they are afraid that you will ask them questions." At first this made me feel even worse, because it showed that I had irritated people and socially isolated the family I lived with, and it made my research efforts seem more hopeless. But after a few days I felt both humbled and liberated by this lesson. Rather than not being aggressive enough and feeling inadequate as a researcher because of what I had seen as my feminine lack of assertiveness, I realized that I had in fact been too aggressive and too American in my internal pressure to get information on some timetable instead of waiting to observe events or listen to others. I stopped being so hard on myself and tried more to adjust my personal style to that of the islanders, waiting for others to speak and not trying to ask inappropriate questions or "get to the point." Eventually, people came back to visit us in the evenings. Although I never felt it possible to do formal interviews or adhere systematically to an interview protocol, I did come to recognize moments in a conversation when it was appropriate and even respectful to ask a question about past events or custom.

Since I was interested in both daily and ceremonial life, in observing what people did with their families and neighbors, and in listening to ordinary conversations, I tried to keep track of people's activities and their plans for a given day. This was no easy matter. People make individual and spontaneous decisions about whether to gather shellfish on the reef, weed the garden, hunt wild pig, or visit a friend in another hamlet based upon mood, weather, and what other people also spontaneously decide to do. Often this meant that I would ask permission to accompany someone based on conversations at the stream below the hamlet while washing dishes early in the morning or a remark I had overheard called to the neighbors from the verandah or beside the house fire. Occasionally a friend would come to get me when she or he thought there was something interesting going on that I might like to see.

But people were understandably unclear just what the resident anthropologist might care about. One morning I noticed that virtually every one of my immediate neighbors and the inhabitants of Jelewaga proper were gone. Beda, one of my woman friends, was near her house chewing betel nut, and I asked her where everyone was. She told me they had all gone several miles inland to make a clearing in the rain forest, cutting down mature trees in an area that had not been touched for two generations. After the downed trees had dried several weeks in the sun they would be fired, and the area would be used to plant a new yam garden. She was on her way there, and I asked if I could come with her. "Yes," she said, apologetically adding what several other people repeated to me when I arrived two hours later: "We did not know that you would like to see this."

I had been worried about inflicting myself on them but decided to take the chance and was glad I did. Beda and I got lost on the way trying to find the faint track leading high up the mountain slope to just below a sacred cliff, and we wandered around under the dimly lit forest canopy. When we finally arrived people actually seemed flattered that I should make the effort to come deep into the interior just to see their communal work. They were amused but pleased that I helped clear brush and peel yams for lunch. After this people made a noticeable effort to invite me along on excursions and work parties.

When the feast season began in October I traveled around Vanatinai and some of the East Calvados islands attending a long string of feasts in the company of different friends who were contributing valuables to them. My neighbors were very impressed, declaring enviously that my kaiwa was going to feasts, and that this was an excellent thing because I got to eat so much pork. They commented approvingly when I gained weight as a result of all that feasting.

It took about two months after I came to live at Jelewaga for me to understand another, extraordinary aspect of some people's perceptions of me. There had been clues earlier but I had missed their significance. The first clue came a month into my fieldwork when I traveled with Jelewaga people five miles across the shallow bay by outrigger paddling canoe to Madawa to attend a mortuary feast. The hamlet was crowded with visitors from all over the island and from the Calvados Chain Islands and Misima who had walked or sailed for days, in some cases, to honor the deceased, a prominent big man. I slept near half a dozen others on a pandanus mat on the verandah of one house whose interior was crowded with sleeping forms. I brushed my hair in the morning under the unavoidable and fascinated gaze of the people, then strangers to me, camped on the verandah of the next house a few feet away. One of them, an old man, watched for a while and then told me to give him the long hairs that had fallen out in my hairbrush (in the island language you do not ask, you demand). Embarrassed, I pretended that I could not understand his words or gestures. He repeated himself. Finally his adult daughter and another woman called loudly to Nora and the other Jelewaga people in our party to tell me to give the old man the hairs in my brush because he wanted them for his garden magic to make his yam vines grow long. Nora, having no choice, translated this statement into English. There was an awkward silence while she and the others looked at me and I stood there frozen. Finally I leaned over and gave him what he wanted. He took the hairs gleefully and tucked them out of sight in the woven, intricately patterned coconut-leaf basket the islanders carry with them. Late at night, when everyone else was asleep, two older women admonished me in low, tense voices, with

Nora translating. "You should never do that again. That old man is a dangerous sorcerer, and he wants to use your hair to kill us all."

Another clue came a few weeks later. I had naively expressed an interest in climbing to the top of Rio, the highest peak on the island, visible when not shrouded in cloud from many parts of the island. I later heard that the spirits of the dead go to Rio *vwatai* (Rio's summit) and join the community of the dead. The clouds you see are the smoke from their fires, wild marsupials are their pigs, and so on. A middle-aged man, visiting the hamlet where I lived one evening asked me, "Why do you Americans always want to climb Rio *vwatai?*"

I knew from searching out every scrap of written information about the island before beginning my fieldwork that a botanical and zoological expedition from the American Museum of Natural History in New York had visited the island and climbed Mt. Rio in the 1950s, collecting specimens. My immediate answer to his question was some elaboration of that to the question about climbing Mt. Everest, "Because it's there." But this was not was not the answer my questioner and my other neighbors were waiting to hear.

I had been asked immediately upon arrival in Jelewaga and other island settlements, "Where are you from?" When I replied, "America," people would murmur knowingly. I did not then understand the significance of this beyond being struck by the fact that they had heard of my "place." This was a startling contrast, in spite of the "ends of the earth" feeling the island had for me, with villagers in the mountains of Bosnia whom I had met a few years earlier, who did not recognize the words America or United States. I correctly concluded that Sudest people knew of America as a result of World War II and the Battle of the Coral Sea.

It was Utu (again, not his real name), who as a young man in 1942 had been conscripted to labor for the Americans at Milne Bay, who finally made me understand. By this time I had enough language facility to carry on basic conversations. Utu came over one evening, along with several other people, to sit around the fire, chew betel nut, and talk with the family and with me. After a while he said what was on his mind. "Maria, where do we go when we die?" Startled, I tried to answer diplomatically using comparative theology, thinking the question might have been precipitated by his hearing some variant of

Christian teachings—there was then no missionary or pastor at Jelewaga. "Some people say the spirits go to Rio vwatai, and some say they go to heaven, and some . . . " I began. He interrupted, "I heard that they turn white and go to America." Everyone fell completely silent. I was stunned, fascinated, and suddenly aware of the significance of earlier events and remarks. Then one woman hissed, "You silly man, why did you say this? Now they will put you in jail!" Utu moaned, "Oh, why did I say this foolish thing?" After that, no one would answer my questions, including the family, and the visitors slipped away into the night.

I gradually learned what some of the older islanders believed I knew all along. I was thought by many people born before World War II to be an ancestor spirit returned from America. America had become known as the land of the dead simultaneously with Rio vwatai. I had come back "to help the place" by my "generosity" with material goods or cargo. In fact, they had concluded that I was the spirit of Taineghubwa (upright forest tree), an elderly big woman who had died three years earlier and who was buried fifty feet away from where I lived, in her hamlet and on her ground. A minority opinion held for a while that I was the spirit of the deceased mother of Thomas, Martin's young clan brother, who came to live with us during the year, but a consensus that I was Taineghubwa eventually emerged in the Jelewaga area. Elderly people from other parts of the island astonished me several times during the year by greeting me as "Miz Mahony." Mrs. Mahony, the only other white woman before me to live on the island, came with her husband in the gold rush of 1888 and remained, a widow, as a trader until the 1920s. My spirit nature was why my hair had such magical power to the old man at Madawa. It was a *muramura*, a relic of the dead, the most potent category of both beneficial and destructive magical paraphernalia, normally a tooth or piece of bone or skull taken secretly from the burial place of a dead relative or long-dead culture hero.

This set of beliefs had made a completely unexpected and inexplicable transition in my thinking, from being an exotic cultural phenomenon of the past reposing in books about other parts of the Pacific from the Kroeber Anthropology Library in Berkeley to being my daily, lived reality. My first reactions were excitement and fascination, along with a determination to learn more. But shortly afterward I found myself very disturbed. Already dealing with inevitable feelings of intense loneliness and isolation despite living at such close quarters with other people, I began to think, self-pityingly, "Here I am, all by myself, and these people don't even think I'm a human being!"

The older people on the island had witnessed the awesome and deadly power of the Americans during the Battle of the Coral Sea, the largest air and sea battle in human history, fought between the Americans to the south and the Japanese to the north of the island, which represented the southernmost advance of the Japanese forces in the Pacific. The young men conscripted to labor for the Allies on the mainland had returned the following year with amazing stories, which I was also told by these same men years later, stories that were very consistent and detailed. The American soldiers and sailors had behaved in remarkably different fashion from the Australian colonial officers and traders of prewar days. They had freely given food, money, tobacco, and clothing—*bigibigi*, things or cargo—to island men and spoken to them in a friendly manner. There had been both black and white soldiers, dressed identically, who sat down and ate together (the U.S. Army was officially segregated until 1949, but apparently people showed better sense in wartime mess tents in Papua). Eating together is a mark of close kinship and trust on Vanatinai because of the extreme fear of poisoning and sorcery. G.I.s and sailors also casually and repeatedly shared food with islanders on the docks. The island men and their elders concluded that the Americans must have been the spirits of their ancestors returned from the land of the dead to help them. They were not surprised when I showed up more than forty years later.

The younger people, born after the war, understood quite clearly that I was just a lumolumo, although a different kind from the Australians and one who lived among islanders. Of course I denied being a spirit and argued with the older people for my ordinary human status. "If I am a spirit from Vanatinai, why can't I speak your language properly?" I asked one man. "That's true," he conceded. Months later, when my language facility in the Jelewaga area dialect had improved so much that I was attributed total fluency, I overheard the same man tell someone else, "You can see that she is a spirit of this place because she speaks our language perfectly." By this point, my desire to belong to the island people was so strong that I said to myself, "Well, they may think I'm an ancestor spirit, but at least I'm *their* spirit!"

These beliefs had some unexpected consequences for my field-work. Both my denials of supernatural status and my requests for information about the spirit world were described to me as my "testing" of the islanders as a representative of the ancestor spirits. Once when I was asking the acknowledged expert on such matters, a seventy-year-old man, about details of the activities of the spirit community on the summit of Rio, he looked into my eyes, smiling, and said with emphasis, "*You* know!"

Even after months of my denials and of friendly relations with island families, I found both outright rejection and doubt of my human nature by some people. One older man who had labored for the Allies in World War II continued to spread the message that I was a returned ancestor spirit to communities all over the island during his numerous trips in quest of ceremonial valuables and to attend mortuary feasts. I traveled to a feast at Rehua, forty miles along the coast to the southeast, on the sailing canoe of another older man. I had previously lived with him and his kinspeople for weeks while they hosted a series of feasts and traveled as guests and contributors to other feasts in the East Calvados Chain. I felt that I had a close and warm relationship with him. The first night at Rehua he and I stayed up until about midnight, sitting cross-legged on pandanus mats around the house fire and talking in low voices while our hosts and the other members of our visiting party slept. "Tell me, Maria," he asked me quietly, "Will you really die as we will?" I was shocked to hear this question from someone with whom I had actually lived and who I thought knew me so well. I replied, to my own surprise, with an adaptation of Shylock's speech from *The Merchant of Venice*, "Yes, I am just like you. If you prick me (*ivwe* means to spear, prick, or cut) I will bleed. I will die the same as you will." He did not look convinced.

My spirit nature was most greatly challenged not by what I said but what I did. I left the island in 1979, and it turned out many people had assumed, contrary to what I said, that I was going to live there forever. I was told by friends when I returned for two months in 1981 that when I had "gone back to my place" most of the elders had decided I was just a lumolumo after all. Leaving forever after brief visits is of course a primary characteristic of the lumolumo.

But the issue was still not resolved in 1987, when I returned again. My old friend, a returned World War II laborer who had been most active in proclaiming my spirit identity all over the island, still routinely referred to me in conversation as *kaka*, spirit. I was still coming back instead of disappearing for good. And one peaceful morning, one of my neighbors, an older man, motioned me over. Everyone else was gone from the hamlet, and there were only pigs snuffling nearby. But he looked cautiously over his shoulder in each direction, then asked me in a whisper, "Maria, is it truth or lie that you are an ancestor spirit?" After nine years I still had to argue for the mundane status of ordinary human being.

The more I learned about Vanatinai people's previous contacts with lumolumo, the more humbled and touched I was by their generosity and, in many cases, by the deep friendship that they eventually extended to me in spite of my white skin. Among the whites who had resided on the island in this century there had been the trader who had ridden the mountain paths on horseback to track down men who owed him money for goods they had gotten on credit, or book, from his tradestore, lashing them with a long whip to force them to pan gold for him. Other traders are remembered for cruel treatment of debtors, such as the one who ordered Papuan employees to tie them to the back of a motor launch and drag them through the lagoon. In the 1950s Harry Pierce, a trader who colonial government reports note was pathologically jealous of his Papuan wife, opened fire from his boat onto a canoe full of men coming to trade with him as he was anchored off Pantava, killing two of them. More recently one of the last white traders on the island used to give people a few sticks of tobacco and a handful of rice in exchange for an ounce of gold dust. One of the last two whites to live on Vanatinai, in the early 1970s, was a thirty-five-year-old Australian man who resided on a remote coconut plantation with a fourteen-year-old girl from another island, forbidding her any contact with either men or women from the villages. The other was an elderly English remittance man who lived alone until his death on an even more remote plantation, sent money by relatives to stay out of England. He would not allow any male Papuans to work his plantation or to buy at his tradestore, only girls and women. He also permitted only hens and no roosters or other male animals at his establishment. The last Australian colonial officer in the area and an American prospector and plantation owner told me of the time that the Englishman had invited the two of them to dinner during a rare visit. He met them at the door that evening by pointing a loaded revolver in their faces and threatening to kill them. They disarmed him and proceeded to dinner.

So these were the whites whom the islanders had encountered before my arrival in newly independent Papua New Guinea. They seemed like a collection from descriptions of the South Seas in the colonial days of a much earlier, more sinister era of relations between whites and Pacific Islanders. The other whites were the occasional Catholic priest from Nimowa Mission who wished to convert them and colonial officers who visited once a year for the census, collecting taxes, judging and jailing violators of laws against sorcery, adultery, and tax delinquency, and issuing orders to build government rest houses, latrines, and regulation cemeteries. The reserve with which I was initially treated and the closed, withdrawn manner of the islanders, described to me previously as unfriendliness to strangers, became much more understandable as I gradually learned about the history of their relations with outsiders, particularly with whites. Their more usual manner with each other, and eventually with me, was direct, assertive, and often warm, exuberant, and kind. Most people watched me carefully for weeks and months before they included me in their conversations and in their lives.

Their perceptions of me were multiple and conflicting. I had an abundance of material goods, or cargo, which some of my neighbors jokingly referred to as my *stoa*, store. I clearly had the alien nature and the privileges of a person with white skin, locally known especially by the recently ended Australian colonial rule of Papua and by the enormous wealth and destructive power of the Americans encountered during the Battle of the Coral Sea and the Battle of Milne Bay. My spirit identity was proclaimed with vigor by a handful of individuals, former World War II-era laborers prominent among them, and strenuously denied by me and by some of my neighbors. Many, including all the younger people, saw me as a woman from America who had come to live at Jelewaga to study custom.

I think that being female helped in my gradual acceptance. In spite of the distant but remembered legacy of Mrs. Mahony, I was freer to negotiate an identity and construct relationships with islanders than a white male might have been. I was not suspected of being a tax collector (like a male anthropologist colleague working elsewhere in the Milne Bay region). I was not as likely to be identified with government officers, planters, traders, or miners—white men who in the recent past had held power and expected deference from islanders. With the exception of the rarely seen nuns living in the Sacred Heart Convent on Nimowa Island, there were few models of what a female lumolumo was like.

The islanders recognized that learning about Vanatinai culture was my work and they approved. One elderly woman told me, "It is good that you are writing down what we say about custom. That way our grandchildren will hear our words after we are dead." After a reflective pause, she added, "So make sure you write them down properly!"

The primary reason for Vanatinai people's understanding and approval of my anthropological project, I think, is their feeling, frequently expressed, that they have deliberately chosen to retain customary forms of ritual and daily life that their neighbors to the northwest, such as the Misima people, have abandoned. My interest in custom matched theirs.

Their retention of custom is not accidental. They have deliberately resisted, over several generations, the pressure from colonial and now national governments, missions, and commercial interests to give up many of their ways of making a living, relating to one another, settling disputes, exchanging wealth with distant partners, and honoring the dead. Outsiders have deplored their lack of interest in cash cropping or working for wages and criticized their "sailing about" to distant islands, devoting enormous amounts of goods and energy to their feasts, believing in spirits, and worrying about sorcery. But the great majority of the islanders, although they explicitly recognize the changes in their lifestyle and have adopted many things they find useful or interesting, believe that customary ways of doing things are inherently good. As they say, "We are proud that we are following *taubwaragha*, the way of the ancestors."

Chapter Two

Fruit of the Motherland

Dominance and Equality

These chapters examine Vanatinai gender relations, comparing women's and men's lives, focusing on changes over time, the life cycles of both sexes, how supernatural power is engendered, and how gender shapes exchange and mortuary ritual. The Vanatinai example of gender relations—the actions of men and women and their ideas about how things are and how they ought to be—offers a dramatic contrast to gender arrangements and ideologies reported from most of New Guinea and most of the world's cultures. Vanatinai is a good place, then, to evaluate prevailing, and sometimes mutually contradictory, theories of gender, power, and social relations.

Gender studies have been a notable presence in debates on anthropological theory and ethnographic practice over the last two decades. Ignored by some, provoking debate and controversy in other quarters, they have influenced anthropological thinking about power and authority, ritual and symbolism, work, social change, and the complex interrelations of individual and society. But most previous anthropological studies of gender roles and ideologies have been primarily studies of women. Few have systematically compared women and men, analyzing gender and age-based symmetries and asymmetries of rights, privileges, and proscriptions. Perhaps because of the challenge of documenting sharply contrasting ideologies of male and female, prominent exceptions have been studies of New Guinea societies.[1] "Sexual antagonism" between men and women has been identified as a fundamental principle in New Guinea Highlands societies since the pioneering work of Kenneth Read (1954).[2] New Guinea ethnographers have also been among the few explicitly studying male gender roles, rather than studying men as normative culture bearers, the fallacy for which feminists have criticized anthropological studies.[3] In this book I join previous New Guinea ethnographers who have focused on gender roles and ideologies as they affect both sexes, but I do so in analyzing a culture in which ideologies of male superiority and domination are absent and where the value and autonomy of all persons is emphasized. On Vanatinai males are not dominant over females in either ideology or practice.

This challenges the position of prominent feminist theorists in anthropology and beyond that male dominance, or sexual asymmetry, is universal and that only its forms and intensity vary.[4] The first problem we come to in evaluating this position in terms of the Vanatinai case is how to define male dominance. The definitions vary greatly, and, not surprisingly, assessments of its universality vary accordingly. Authors favoring materialist approaches focus on control of key resources or means of production, while others refer primarily to the differential access of men versus women to prestigious activities and thus to power over others.[5] For example, Ortner (1974) suggests there are ideological universals in gender symbolism, with women associated with nature, men with "the high ground of culture," and women therefore universally devalued (cf. Lévi-Strauss 1969a). Rosaldo and Atkinson (1975) see a universal symbolic opposition of woman the life-giver and man the life-taker (related to the woman/nature, man/culture opposition), which in all cultures indicates sexual asymmetry. Sanday's (1981:164) definition of male dominance combines material and ideological dimensions, stressing both "exclusion of women from political and economic decision making" and male aggression against women, measured by expectations of male aggressive personality traits, men's houses, wife abuse, institutionalized or regular occurrence of rape, and raiding other groups for wives.[6] I will discuss, in this and the following chapters, the relevance of the Vanatinai ethnographic material to these criteria and their relevance for assessing gender and power cross-culturally.

Few anthropologists have attempted to define or characterize sexual equality. Leacock (1978:247) sees women as "autonomous in egalitarian society" because they hold "decision-making power over their own lives and activities to the same extent that men did over theirs." Lamphere (1977:613) focuses on equal degrees of control over others. Etienne and Leacock (1980:9) discuss societies with "egalitarian relations of production," where the division of labor is entirely by sex, the sexes reciprocally exchange goods and services, and all adults participate directly and equally in production, distribution, and consumption, having equal access to resources. Previous cross-cultural studies have suggested that many of the characteristics of Vanatinai society—small scale, lack of social stratification, matriliny, and a horticultural subsistence base—are frequently associated with societies that are relatively sexually egalitarian (e.g., Whyte 1978, Sanday 1981).[7] Leaving aside the gender dimension, social equality more generally has usually been defined negatively. Egalitarian societies lack centralized authority, systems of rank, stratification other than by age, sex, or personal characteristics, or sharp status divisions. Anthropologists have generally agreed that no society is truly egalitarian in practice or principle, with equal access to power and resources by each individual—access is everywhere restricted by a combination of age, sex, and personal qualities. By implication, then, most influential anthropological constructions of political equality and inequality have implied, without fully analyzing, a universal principle of male dominance.[8]

The status of women in matrilineal societies, the nature of matriliny, and its significance for human social evolution have been subjects of ethnological debate for over a hundred years. Victorian male anthropologists saw matriliny as a survival of an archaic social form dating from a matriarchal past in which women had power over men and women's sexuality was unregulated. Matriarchy and matriliny, they believed, everywhere preceded the more highly evolved patrilineal form of social organization, where descent is traced through men and men have power over women. Since the demise of nineteenth- and early twentieth-century theories of unilinear social evolution, ethnographers have reported considerable female autonomy and influence in specific matrilineal societies in New Guinea, Central Africa, and North America. Nevertheless, the most ambitious and widely read theoretical and comparative analyses of matriliny and female status have stressed male authority over women and focused on male roles such as husband, brother, and mother's brother. Only very recently have anthropologists looked again at matriliny and female status and emphasized the powers and the authority of women.[9]

The Vanatinai case creates an opportunity to take a fresh look at matriliny and gender in light of ethnographic evidence accumulated in recent decades and with perspectives drawn from more recent feminist and anthropological theories. Descent traced through women, female ownership and inheritance of lands and valuables, and a shifting postmarital residence simultaneously shape and reflect the sexual balance of power and authority in various domains of Vanatinai social life and throughout the life course.

Some of the most fruitful recent discussions of gender theory in anthropology have stressed that cultures or societies do not have one unique, monolithic and noncontradictory ideology of gender operating in the thoughts of each person on all occasions.[10] These approaches have appeared in an intellectual climate with a much greater tolerance for contradiction in analyses of social relations and an appreciation of cultural ambiguities, a climate often characterized as poststructuralist or postmodernist, which feminist studies more generally have helped to create. Ortner (1990) speaks of gender hegemonies: prevailing ideologies, whether egalitarian or hierarchical in content, that coexist with and are contradicted by alternative, less pervasive ideologies of gender. Schlegel (1990) distinguishes between a culture's "general," abstract gender ideology and its multiplicity of "specific" gender meanings, again, often contradictory, articulated in "fields of action" such as particular religious rituals or kinds of interpersonal relations.

I find these theoretical emphases on the messy and contradictory nature of gender ideologies and gender-related behaviors to be more accurate reflections of the actions and thoughts of real people throughout the world. They take into account individual variation, the human tolerance for cognitive dissonance and ambiguity, transcultural flows of ideas and practices—both imposed by conquest and freely accepted—and the accretion over time of laws, codes, values, and expectations. They also acknowledge that different categories of persons, in different historical periods and situations, mobilize salient aspects of custom and belief for their own reasons.

34

Having written that, I have to report that in the Vanatinai case both the general, most abstract forms of gender ideology and the majority of specific gender meanings derived from everyday and ritual life are congruent, reflecting an ethic of egalitarian relations between women and men and among all persons. In Ortner's terms, the hegemonic Vanatinai gender ideologies are egalitarian (I see them as multiple, not single). I believe this ideological congruence is a highly significant feature of cultures with a strong tendency toward gender equality. There is little discernible difference on Vanatinai between gender ideologies, or ideas about women and men, held by women versus those held by men. This is unlike the situation where an ideology of male dominance prevails among men and is acted out in many customary practices but is still "contested" by women, as Rena Lederman (1990) puts it in her analysis of the Mendi of New Guinea's Southern Highlands.[11] The contradictory ideologies of gender that do exist on Vanatinai then become all the more interesting and revealing: the nurturing mother who is also a life-destroying witch; the beliefs about menstrual blood, the sexual fluids of men and women, and the growth of yams; the ideal that women and men have equal ritual obligations to obtain ceremonial valuables and the observable fact that more men than women become prominent in ritualized exchange. I focus on these contradictions and their implications in the following chapters.

Gender and Exchange

Vanatinai belongs to what scholars since the late nineteenth century have referred to as the Massim culture area.[12] The most famous portion of the Massim to the outside world is the Trobriand Islands, whose culture was described as it appeared seventy years ago in the extensive writings of Bronislaw Malinowski. In the Massim, with the exception of Goodenough and West Fergusson Islands, descent is matrilineal, and women inherit land and valuables equally with men. The region is characterized by elaborate systems of ceremonial exchange, typically the ritualized exchange of valuables such as shell jewelry and axe blades of polished greenstone between partners on different islands.

A high status of women has long been described as a diagnostic feature of the Massim culture area. But before the 1970s and the restudy by Annette Weiner (1976) of the Trobriand Islands, no ethnographer had offered any systematic description of what this high status consisted of or an analysis of the positions of men and women as they related to ceremonial exchange.[13] Weiner describes how the day after she took up residence in a Trobriand village she was taken to a women's mortuary distribution of banana-leaf skirts and dried banana-leaf bundles. Finding only a brief mention of women's mortuary exchanges and no information on women's wealth items in Malinowski's works, she changed the focus of her research to document this key aspect of Trobriand ceremonial exchange that Malinowski had almost completely overlooked.

On Vanatinai I found that women not only figure prominently in exchange activities but that they participate in the same arena of exchange as men, exchange with both men and women, and compete with men to acquire the same ceremonial valuables. Exchange is largely integrated sexually. Women participate alongside men in all of the many types of intra- and interisland exchanges. Individual women as well as men may gain areawide prestige and renown for their success in accumulating valuables such as shell-disc necklaces, greenstone axe blades, shell currency pieces, and pigs, and in giving them away to other men and women in public acts of ritual generosity.

The exchange activities in which both sexes participate on Vanatinai are the local equivalent of kula. As documented by Malinowski (1922) in the Trobriand Islands, shell-disc necklaces circulate clockwise among male exchange partners on distant islands while armshells circulate counterclockwise. Exchanges on Vanatinai that involve the same shell-disc necklaces and greenstone axe blades that circulate in the kula region to the northwest as well as other valuables (armshells are not used in the Vanatinai region) are the island's most important means of acquiring prestige and influence over others. Women's freedom to enter into these most important and prestigious arenas is a dramatic indicator of the sexually egalitarian nature of Vanatinai culture.

Various authors have suggested either that there is a universal sexual asymmetry in the tendency for men to be prominent in an analytically separable public domain while women's roles remain largely domestic, or that the exclusion of women from public activities and their restriction to a domestic domain is strongly correlated with women's lower status relative to men.[14] As I argue later, the Western dichotomy of public/politicojural versus domestic/private does not apply well on Vanatinai, but, if we use this dualistic, oppositional, and Western-derived framework, women's exchange activities clearly belong to a public rather than a domestic domain.

Ortner and Whitehead (1981) see the public domain as significant for understanding the cultural construction of gender in that it is simultaneously dominated by men and the locus of a culture's prestige structures. They suggest that "cultural notions of the genders and sexuality will vary from culture to culture in accordance with the way in which women, the woman-dominated domestic sphere, and cross-sex relations in general are organized into the base that supports the larger (male) prestige system" (1981:19). The argument that male supremacy is predicated on prestige suggests the primacy of ideological rather than material causes of sexual inequality. Clearly, though, domination of public activities and forms of power that generate and reinforce prestige can result directly from control of the material domain, such as the means of production, or the most highly valued or scarce forms of wealth by males or by certain classes of males.

The writings of Pierre Bourdieu on symbolic capital clarify the relationship of the symbolic power of prestige to the power of the material in a fashion useful for the analysis of gender relations. Bourdieu proposes extending economic calculations to all rare goods, both material and symbolic, rather than viewing them as belonging to separate and opposing domains of social life. He argues that the symbolic capital of honor, distinction, and the indebtedness of others "in the form of the prestige and renown attached to a family and a name is readily convertible back into economic capital." The "strategy of accumulating a capital of honour and prestige" is characteristic of "archaic" economies, he suggests, and a form of credit (1977:179). Gift exchanges such as potlatch, then, are "exhibitions of symbolic capital" (1977:180) where actors spend both time and economic capital to accumulate symbolic capital. The giver gives away an object of value but gains prestige, a reputation for wealth and generosity, and the indebtedness of others. Unless and until they at some future time return labor or wealth to the giver, the debtors are subordinated to the giver by the ostensibly selfless act of the gift. Giving is thus an act of symbolic violence and symbolic domination (1977:178–192).

This perspective reconciles material and ideological approaches to the study of social inequalities in general, and gender inequalities in particular, by encouraging the observer to look at who controls not only economic capital but also the related and convertible symbolic capital of prestige and honor. The principal Vanatinai prestige system is embedded in the ceremonial exchange and mortuary ritual complex, but it is not restricted to men. Participation of island women in this and other arenas of prestige, such as ritual expertise, production of garden surpluses, and the rearing of healthy and hard-working young matrilineage members (a primary concern of both men and women), generates and in turn validates egalitarian Vanatinai gender constructions, as Ortner and Whitehead predict. The prominent positions of women in Vanatinai exchange and other activities outside of household and subsistence indicate as well as reinforce generally egalitarian relations between women and men. Vanatinai women have access to power both through their control of the economic capital of land and the subsistence and surplus production of yams and through their accumulation of symbolic capital in exchange and mortuary ritual.

Gender and Social Relations

I suggest that sexually egalitarian societies tend to place little emphasis upon other forms of social stratification such as class, ranked descent groups, or age-grading.[15] Social stratification is more likely to arise in societies with dense populations. Thus some, but by no means all, low-density, small-scale foraging and horticultural societies are among the most socially and sexually egalitarian societies in the world. Vanatinai has only four persons per square mile of territory. Unlike the densely settled Trobriand Islands, also part of the Massim culture area, Vanatinai has no chiefs or other categories of ascribed rank and no division of lineages into noble and commoner.

Vanatinai and the rest of the Massim are unusual in Melanesia in having no men's houses, no male cult activities, and no initiation ceremonies for either males or females (cf. Allen 1967). The institution of the men's house, where adult men either sleep apart from their wives and children or congregate regularly, limits women's participation in political, economic, and ritual life in much of Melanesia. The men's house, male initiation, and male cult activities concentrate both power over others and social prestige in the hands of adult males and group women, boys, and young children in a subordinate social position.

Characterizing Vanatinai society as egalitarian does not imply that there are no differences among individuals on the island. Some islanders hold more rights to land, food trees, and reef areas than others, and some inherit more ceremonial valuables, pigs, and potential exchange partners from maternal kin or fathers. Some have more kin and more affines who can potentially offer aid, while others are disadvantaged in accruing prestige by chronic poor health.[16]

Nevertheless, Vanatinai society has an egalitarian ethic. It offers every adult, regardless of sex or kin group, the opportunity of excelling at prestigious activities such as participation in traditional exchange or ritual functions essential to health and prosperity. With hard work and the appropriate magical knowledge anyone may achieve the gender-blind title of gia, "giver." This status is not limited to one individual per hamlet or even per household. The multiplicity of *giagia* meets Fried's (1967:52) definitional criterion of egalitarian societies as those in which there are as many positions of valued status as individuals who are capable of filling them.

The result is a continuous competition for status and influence involving a large number of men and women who choose to make the extra effort necessary to acquire prestige among a wide group of peers. This state of competition and flux is inevitable precisely because Vanatinai society is egalitarian and without ascribed positions of status.

The low population density of Vanatinai largely negates the advantage that people with rights to more land hold over others, since the right to garden, hunt, fish, and make sago on particular tracts of land is virtually always granted by the owners to their neighbors within the same district of the island. Low density probably also contributes to an ethic of respect for the individual, since if a serious conflict arises one party has the option of moving to another location. This happens often on Vanatinai. Since a hamlet will dissolve if its population drops, because of conflict, sorcery accusations, and resulting migration, below the minimum necessary to carry out subsistence tasks, people must learn to tolerate each other's idiosyncrasies of behavior and outlook or go their separate ways. The notion of personal autonomy, along with the idea that individuals vary greatly in their personalities and temperaments, is a key aspect of Vanatinai cultural ideology. The most common explanation for markedly unusual behavior is a flat and nonjudgmental statement, "(S)He wants to/doesn't want to," or, "It is her/his way." There is a wide latitude of normal or acceptable behavior. The most significant means for regulating individual behavior, the fear of arousing anger or jealousy in a sorcerer or witch or of violating a taboo attached to a particular place by its guardian spirit, is based on an ideology of individual supernatural power rather than on a social body or code.

In a small population where kin and fictive kin groups largely overlap the community of coresidents, as on Vanatinai, the opinions of women are voiced in public debate, and "domestic" actions of kin group and hamlet are "public" actions.[17] Key decisions affecting the lives and well-being of community members are made locally and as needed. Political authority is not delegated to a restricted number of adult male representatives who convene formally in a distant place for efficiency of communication and social control as in a large-scale society. Children, old people, and women are all more likely to be respected as individuals in a small-scale society, even in cases, unlike Vanatinai, where the predominant ideologies of social relations hold women and children inferior to men and elders.

Perhaps the most striking evidence that Vanatinai is a sexually egalitarian society is the fact that there are both "big women" and "big men," individuals of both sexes who fit the ideal type of the big man outlined by Sahlins (1963). Big men are the principal form of authority in Melanesian societies, which generally lack classes and chiefs. They have been the subject of anthropological debate for the last three decades. Big women are found in a few other Melanesian societies, such as the Kove and Kaulong of New Britain (Chowning 1979) and the Nagovisi of Bougainville (Nash 1987), as well as among the Misima and East and West Calvados peoples northwest of Vanatinai (author's fieldnotes, cf. Battaglia 1991), but the institution of the big man has generally been taken for granted as another manifestation of male dominance among the supposedly egalitarian societies of Melanesia (Lepowsky 1990a).

On Vanatinai any individual, male or female, may choose to exert the extra effort to go beyond the minimum contributions to the mortuary feasts expected of every adult. He or she accumulates ceremonial valuables and other goods both in order to give them away in acts of public generosity and to honor obligations to exchange partners from the local area as well as distant islands. These people are the gia-gia. While there may be more than one gia in a particular hamlet, or even household, there may be none.

A woman may have considerably more prestige and influence than her husband due to her reputation for acquiring and redistributing valuables. There are more men than women who are extremely active in ceremonial exchange, but there are also some women who are far more active in exchange and feasting activities than the majority of men. Women and men exchange valuables with exchange partners of both sexes and compete with each other to obtain the same types of valuables. These include the same shell-disc necklaces that circulate in kula in the islands to the northwest, greenstone axe blades, ceremonial lime spatulas of tortoiseshell or wood, shell currency pieces, pigs, baskets of fine yams, bundles of sago, clay cooking pots, carved wooden platters, pandanus-leaf sleeping mats, and coconut-leaf skirts. The food and household items may be used within the household, but all are essential in large quantities as goods to be exchanged during the island's elaborate series of mortuary feasts.

Vanatinai women may lead expeditions by sailing canoe to distant islands to visit their exchange partners, who are both male and female. They try to convince them to part with valuables, employing the same magic of exchange that men use, typically wearing a magically enhanced scented coconut oil (*bunama*) that may have been boiled with the bone of a deceased relative. This oil makes the wearer so beautiful, whether male or female, that the exchange partner of either sex becomes *negenege* (dizzy with desire) and hastens to give away the desired valuable.

Women as well as men host mortuary feasts, mobilizing kin, affines, and exchange partners to plant extra large yam gardens to feed guests sumptuously, accumulating enormous quantities of sago starch, pigs, clay pots, sleeping mats, and coconut-leaf skirts, and amassing enough ceremonial valuables to make a better showing than other feast hosts have done previously. Women often contribute large quantities of valuables at feasts hosted by kin, affines, and exchange partners. They publicly and ritually receive the valuables given away at these feasts, which go either to a matrilineal kinsperson of the deceased or to the deceased's patrilateral cross-cousin.

Fruit of the Motherland

Vanatinai, called Vanatina in the central and eastern dialects, is the largest island of the Louisiade Archipelago, the chain of islands that separates the Solomon Sea from the Coral Sea. It is also the largest piece of land for two hundred miles. Its people, 2,075 of them in 1978 and about 2,300 in 1987, call themselves Vanatinai *ghunoi*, literally, "fruit of the motherland."[18]

Vanatinai is a rich place, the islanders say. Its reefs and miles of coastal mangrove and sago swamps have for generations been obstacles to European penetration and exploitation, but they represent wealth to the islanders for they sustain life. The shallow lagoon waters, so treacherous to navigate in a motor vessel, harbor enormous numbers of fish ranging in color from a brilliant scarlet to an improbable brown with blue polka-dots. Even deep sea fish such as barracuda swim in the deeper parts of the lagoon, for the barrier reef is ten miles off the south coast. Occasionally whole schools of yellowfin tuna leap out of the water in unison, their golden scales diffracting the sun's rays. Gliding over the lagoon waters in a canoe, you may see turtle, porpoise, dugong, octopus, or shark. Crocodiles live in the estuaries at the mouths of rivers and streams. All of these creatures except the porpoise are hunted and valued as food, but are respected, too, for their spiritual power. Each is a totem of a local clan. They figure in myth, and the crocodile or octopus you see may in fact be a place spirit, the guardian and owner of that sandy bank or patch of reef, and should be left alone. Giant squid and other place spirits live unseen by humans below the waters of dangerous passages and whirlpools.

Vanatinai is long and narrow, about fifty miles by eight to fifteen, with one major mountain range trending northwest to southeast. Its highest point, a distinctive triangular peak visible from many parts of the island, is 2,645-foot Mt. Rio, the domain of Rodyo, the creator spirit, and the home of the spirits of the dead. Vanatinai and the neighboring Calvados Chain Islands to the northwest are encircled by barrier reefs in one of the world's largest lagoons, about 120 miles long. The islands are peaks of a submerged mountain range, a continuation of the Owen Stanley Range of southeastern New Guinea. After a few breaks the southern barrier reef of Sudest Lagoon resumes near the New Guinea mainland as the barrier reef that shelters the south Papuan coast for hundreds of miles. From about May to October the archipelago is swept by the strong and constant southeast trade winds. These die down during November and December, a period of doldrums when there is often stifling, humid heat. Then the northwest monsoon winds begin to blow from about January to April, frequently bringing heavy rains, which total about 120 inches over the year.

The land is surrounded by wide fringing reefs extending as far as a mile or more out to sea, particularly along the deeply indented southern coast, merging with the barrier reef in the island's northeastern section. The fringing reef is mostly exposed at low tide, and fish can be stunned with derris root and scooped out by hand from shallow pools. Enclosures of coral boulders improve on natural depressions. Men also wade in the lagoon and spear fish, sometimes using torches of burning palm fronds at night to attract and blind the fish. Both men and women fish with hook and line from canoes, sometimes remaining all night on the lagoon. Fish nets and fish traps woven of pandanus fiber, observed by early visitors, are no longer made. Both women and men dive for the enormous Tridacna clam and for smaller, even tastier bivalves, including the red-rimmed oysterlike shells from which kula necklaces are made, again by both women and men.

The mangrove swamps and saltwater estuaries of the larger creeks serve as a nursery area for many marine species. They also shelter huge numbers of mangrove oysters, their sharp white shells clinging to the aerial roots emerging at low tide. Women wade into the muck, sinking to their knees, coconut-leaf skirts swishing through black, brackish water, collecting oysters by the dozens and avoiding their razorlike edges. These make a superb stew when boiled in the clay cooking pots with coconut cream and delicate new fern fronds or the tender young leaves of *tagarugu* gathered in the forest. Large blue crabs with oversize front claws wander the mud flats in the mangroves and are collected, with caution, by women and men. People also catch shrimp, eels, and small freshwater fish and shellfish in the upland streams of the island's interior.

The starch extracted from the large stands of sago palms in the extensive freshwater swamps is not only the staple food of the island but one of its major exports, through customary exchange networks, to the smaller, drier Calvados Chain Islands to the northwest. Vanatinai people say that sago pith, the inedible fibers remaining when the starch has been pounded and sluiced out of the trunk of the female palm, allows them to raise large numbers of domestic pigs. Many of their pigs are exchanged as far as Misima and even Ware Island, almost two hundred miles away near the New Guinea mainland, requested by exchange partners for memorial feasts.

The swamps are also home to large numbers of areca palms. The betel nut that they produce, a stimulant chewed with betel pepper and powdered coral lime, is exported by sailing canoe as far as Ware, and it is prized throughout the region for its strength and quality (Lepowsky 1982). The island's steep mountain slopes, rising sharply behind the swamps, are covered with rain forest, with some open areas of sharp-edged *kunai* grass, particularly on the north coast.

The island is thinly settled. Large tracts of land both along the coast and in the interior are uninhabited, although they are used as hunting and gathering preserves. Only about 3 percent of the population was not currently residing on the island in 1978, most of the absentees working or attending school either at Misima Island or on the mainland. This is an unusually low percentage of migrants for independent Papua New Guinea, and it has increased only slightly in recent years.

People live in small coastal villages, comprised of up to ten houses on the ridges behind the mangroves or right on the shore, and in hamlets of two to four houses scattered along the coast and throughout the interior. Large tracts of forest and swamp separate them from one another. The settlements are surrounded by shady groves of coconut, mango, breadfruit, and papaya trees.

The islanders practice shifting cultivation in a markedly less intensive fashion than their Misima neighbors, not fencing their gardens against pigs or staking their yam vines but relying heavily upon private garden magic and public ritual. They plant yams, an annual crop, and the perennial sweet potato, taro, manioc, bananas, pineapples, and sugarcane in gardens located mainly on the fertile slopes of the interior mountain range. Fallow periods last from three to forty or more years. Vanatinai people also gather a wide variety of fruits, nuts, legumes, berries, and greens in the rain forest. Pigs are raised and owned by women and men alike, but they are rarely eaten except at mortuary feasts. Wild pig, crocodile, and dugong are hunted by men. Both men and women hunt opossum, flying fox, and fruit bat by climbing trees in the daytime and sneaking up on or build traps for monitor lizards.

The Vanatinai economy is almost entirely a subsistence one, with an average per capita cash income throughout the 1970s and 1980s of at the most twenty dollars obtained from making copra, diving for shell (blacklip and goldlip pearl shell and trochus), gathering copal gum (used in varnishes and other industrial products), or gathering the seeds of a leguminous plant from the genus Pueraria used to fix nitrogen in the soil and provide ground cover on oil palm plantations in other parts of Papua New Guinea. A handful of men own shotguns, for which they hold licenses, and sell crocodile belly skin to a trader. A varying number of young men have been employed as laborers by the government at Tagula Station. Until the early 1970s sporadic employment was available for a few men as laborers in expatriate-directed goldmining on the north coast.

There had been no whites living on Vanatinai since the early 1970s when I arrived in 1978, and there were none besides myself until 1984, when the first white missionary ever to reside on the island arrived. An American from Oklahoma, he took up residence with his wife and four children, sent by the Summer Institute of Linguistics, an arm of the Wycliffe Bible Translators who operate among indigenous peoples in remote areas from the Amazon to Borneo, to translate the New Testament into the island language. It is one of the last languages in Papua New Guinea to be documented in the mission to produce a printed version of the gospels in every language in the world.

The people of Vanatinai trace their descent through twelve matrilineal clans, called *ghu*. Each possesses a set of totem animals and plants. A visitor is immediately asked, "What is your bird?" (*Len ma budâ?*).[19] Birds are the most important totem emblems. Each clan has one or several totem birds, one or several totem fish or marine animals such as sea tortoise, dugong, or crocodile, a totem snake, a totem tree, and a totem vine used for making cord. The Misima Islanders are not supposed to eat the totem fish of their father's clan, but the people of Vanatinai do not practice any avoidances concerning totem animals or plants. Marriage and sexual intercourse is forbidden within the clan or with people from other islands of the region who have the same bird, although the clan name may be different. Marriage and sexual intercourse are improper with members of the father's clan, but this rule is kept more strictly with the father's own matrilineage, those individuals of the father's clan with whom one can trace a particular kin relationship, as opposed to people of the father's clan from more distant hamlets and islands.

Vanatinai has a Crow kinship system. As among the Crow of North America, the children of a pair of brothers or of sisters call each other brother or sister, while children of a sister and brother are cousins, *ivaiye*, a close relationship throughout life that takes on particular meaning after the death of a father. The tendency of fathers to give valuables and knowledge to their own children rather than their sisters' children because of paternal love is formally compensated for during the mortuary feasts that mark the father's death. Ceremonial valuables are publicly presented to a particular cousin, called the *tau*, who represents the father's matrilineage, culminating a lifetime of exchanges between the dead man's parents' kinfolk.

Women inherit land and use rights over forest and reef areas as well as pigs, household goods, and ceremonial valuables equally with men. These come from their mothers and mothers' brothers. A woman as well as a man may act as tau to either a male or a female cross-cousin, inheriting wealth during the mortuary rituals in the name of her matrilineage, which gave her mother's brother to the lineage of his wife in marriage to sire children for them.

Societies where women own and inherit land, live with their own kin after marriage, and not only produce but allocate culturally valued resources, controlling their distribution beyond the household, tend to treat men and women more equally.[20] These conditions, more likely in a matrilineal society due to its characteristic structures of inheritance, residence, and economic organization, describe Vanatinai and ensure the prominence of women in all aspects of island life. Women control the land and valuables they inherit or possess just as men do. They, along with men, produce staple garden foods such as yams, sweet potato, and taro, and raise pigs, and they have ultimate jurisdiction over the distribution of the fruits of their labors. Women are said by both sexes to be the "owners" or "bosses" (*tanuwagaji*) of the gardens, although men too spend much of their time working in gardens. It is the women of the hamlet who must decide whether in a particular year there is a sufficient surplus of garden produce to exchange with outsiders for other goods such as clay cooking pots or pandanus-leaf sleeping mats or to host a major feast to commemorate a death.

"Wife-centered" postmarital residence has been suggested as a key variable affecting female autonomy. The postmarital rule on Vanatinai is bilocal residence. The ideal arrangement is for a married couple to reside alternately during the year in the natal hamlet of the wife and that of the husband, making gardens on the matrilineage lands of both spouses and assisting the kin of each with subsistence tasks. Each spouse has equivalent rights and obligations when living with affines. A newly married couple resides with the wife's parents for at least several months, and the husband is said to be working for his mother-in-law. Some longer-married couples may choose to reside permanently or most of the time with the kin of either spouse depending upon their personal preference. But, even so, active ties are maintained with the hamlet of the other spouse through visits for subsistence and social purposes.[21]

The shift between residing with the kin of the wife and the kin of the husband allows each spouse the security of living with relatives for at least part of every year. Neither one is expected to give up the opportunity to participate in the important decisions of the natal kin group, and neither spouse by virtue of absence loses the right to use garden land, food trees, and territory belonging to the matrilineage. By living alternately with kin and affine, each spouse is in a good position to cultivate or maintain personal exchange ties with individuals belonging to both groups.

Local matrilineages or subclans are referred to only by their clan affiliation. They hold specific rights of land tenure and use in common. They often, but not always, have one individual who is most influential in subsistence and land-related matters. This person is frequently a man, the *tanokau*, but it may also be a woman, called *yola*. The tanokau or yola advises kin on gardening and other subsistence activities and officiates at the public yam planting ritual. He or she is the recognized authority on matters of land ownership, exchange and custom. It is a position achieved by superior intelligence and ritual knowledge.

The Time of the Ancestors

We cannot make sense of Vanatinai gender constructions without considering the historical contexts of their late twentieth century cultural forms. Cultural innovations and reinterpretations do not begin, for small-scale, non-Western cultures, at the moment of contact with Europeans: they are ongoing and creative processes endemic to all cultures.[22] Vanatinai gender roles and ideologies are not static: they have been formed over time by shifting fields of power relations, technologies, and ideas. These have both reinforced and contested in key ways the notions of gender equality that prevail today. Considering changes over time informs our understandings of the broader contexts of Vanatinai social relations, between the sexes, among islanders, and with outsiders as allies and enemies, exchange partners, and colonial rulers. I present in brief in this section some of the multiple perspectives on the past of Vanatinai that can be gleaned from linguistic and archeological evidence, oral traditions, and the accounts of European visitors, private and official. Each of these traces of the past has been generated by different agendas and conventions of representation, and these need to be kept in mind as we try to discern the interrelations over time of women and men, islanders and visitors.

Vanatinai at first appears curiously unchanged by the six generations of intermittent contact it has had with foreigners from outside the network of islands to which it is linked in exchange. In spite of colonial and national governments, missions, the cash economy, and European technology, the islanders continue to live largely according to the way of the ancestors, growing and foraging for their own food, continuing to exchange ceremonial valuables and other goods with their traditional exchange partners, and holding their elaborate series of mortuary feasts. Nevertheless, the island has endured a tidal wave of change that has profoundly altered its way of life. Vanatinai people have responded to new technologies, new forms of religious ideology, and new economic and political systems in which they are peripheral. They have adapted some ideas and objects of value, modified their customs in response to changing social fields, and resisted strong pressures to change in other ways.[23]

Linguistic, archeological, and oral historical evidence suggests that Vanatinai people are descendants of multiple waves of settlers speaking both non-Austronesian and Austronesian languages, and that the islands were first settled thousands of years before the advent of Austronesian-speaking Lapita peoples to the islands of the southwest Pacific. A varied ancestry and continuing intermarriage with neighboring peoples is also suggested by the great variety in their physical appearance, first remarked on by Captain Owen Stanley and his crew in 1849. They range from very dark-skinned people less than five feet in height, indistinguishable from Rossel Islanders, to taller, brown-skinned folk with long, wavy hair, a characteristic also first recorded by Europeans 140 years ago.

The language of Vanatinai is Austronesian, related to Hawaiian and Malay: this is true of all of Milne Bay Province except for Rossel Island, whose non-Austronesian language is in its own linguistic phylum. There are at least nine dialects on Vanatinai, all mutually intelligible. It would be more accurate to speak of a dialect continuum running the length of the island, since there are no clear-cut linguistic boundaries between dialect areas, and each settlement is locally perceived as having its own recognizable speech. It is possible, though, to distinguish four principal dialect groups in the southwestern, northwestern, central and eastern regions of the island.[24] A significant number of vocabulary words show no cognatic relationship between dialects. Understood and used by sophisticated speakers of other dialects, who sometimes use them among themselves as synonyms, they are frequently not comprehensible to people from other parts of the island.

This startling linguistic diversity in a population of about two thousand people who view themselves as sharing a basic set of customs as Vanatinai ghunoi, the people of Vanatinai, underscores the degree to which districts of a sparsely populated island each formed the core of their own social worlds in precolonial times. Oral histories mirror the linguistic evidence, recounting how people often fought with neighboring districts with which they sometimes traded and occasionally intermarried.

In contrast to the linguistic complexity of Vanatinai, the Misima language is spoken from Misima Island itself to Panaeati and as far southeast in the Calvados Chain as Kuanak Island with only minor local pronunciation differences.[25] Between the Misima language area and Vanatinai live twelve hundred East Calvados Chain Islanders, who speak their own language, frequently called Saisai or Nimowa and consisting of two principal dialects, Saisai and Sabara (Sabarl).[26]

No archeological excavations were undertaken in the Louisiade Archipelago before the 1980s.[27] Dates and history of the islands' original settlement are obscure and must be inferred from evidence uncovered elsewhere in Melanesia. New Guinea was probably settled as long as forty thousand years ago.[28] It is frequently assumed that the speakers of non-Austronesian languages, such as the Rossel Islanders, settled in Western Melanesia prior to the arrival of pottery-making Austronesian speakers. It is possible that the earliest migrants into the Louisiade Archipelago walked most of the distance into the region during the period when the islands were separated only by narrow water gaps from the continent of Sahul or Greater Australia, which included present-day New Guinea.[29]

Linguistic evidence suggests that the first speakers of Austronesian languages may have reached Melanesia as early as six thousand years ago (Pawley and Green 1976:54). This may be corroborated by significant recent excavations in the islands north of New Guinea. The area is now hypothesized to be the "homeland" of the Lapita people, the (presumed) Austronesian-speaking, seafaring, long-distance-trading pottery makers believed to be ancestors of the Polynesians and the Austronesian-speaking island Melanesian populations. Recent excavations at Lapita sites off New Ireland, dating from about thirty-five hundred to two thousand years ago, uncovered shell rings and necklaces reminiscent of those circulating in kula and in the ritualized exchanges of the Louisiade Archipelago today. Similar shell necklaces and armshells have been found on the south Papuan coast along with pottery related to Lapita ware. Austronesian-speaking migrants were probably absorbed by peoples already living in the region, to whom they contributed pottery making, maritime, and trading skills. There may have been further migrations to the south Papuan coast and Trobriand Islands about A.D. 1000, and subse-

quently more localized and specialized economies based heavily on
maritime trade developed, with kula as known from the ethnographic record possibly only about five hundred years old. The evidence shows dramatically changing patterns of trade over centuries,
but interisland exchanges of shell valuables seem to be thousands of
years old in island Melanesia.[30]

Oral tradition on Vanatinai explains that the world and its inhabitants were created by Rodyo (see chapter 4). He lives with his wife
Eurio, several other supernatural beings, and the spirits of the dead in
a village at the summit of Mt. Rio. Members of the clans of Vanatinai that are not represented by the supernaturals dwelling on Mt. Rio
generally trace their origins either to Misima or Rossel.[31] People of
the Wozhoga clan say their ancestors arrived in the Jelewaga area on
the southwest coast from Ware Island, to which they had originally
migrated from the hamlet of Dawin on the Suau Coast of mainland
Papua New Guinea. The myth of their first arrival tells of a woman,
her brother, and her husband. When the two men went inland to
hunt in this fertile, well-watered, uninhabited land, the woman covered their sailing canoe, drawn up on the shore, with palm fronds and
set fire to it, so that the men would not be tempted to return to
known lands from this place of abundance. The large outcropping on
the shore below Jelewaga is the Wozhoga canoe turned to stone.
Wozhoga people still own most of the land stretching for several miles
inland from this landmark. Taineghubwa, the big woman whom
some elders thought me to be in spirit form, was of the Wozhoga clan
and a direct descendant of this female pioneer. The small Bwetha clan
is said to have originated somewhere in the Solomon Islands, where
one woman was caught by a cyclone while fishing in a canoe and
blown westward until she washed ashore near East Point, Rossel
Island. Several generations later a descendant married at Seghe on
Vanatinai, and members of the Bwetha clan are now found scattered
around the island.

During the late precolonial period the islanders lived in hamlets
built in the interior on the tops of the mountain ridges. Relics of
their hamlets and the living descendants of their gardens of tubers are
still visible, and the hamlet names are well remembered. Previously
some hamlets were close to the shore. Oral tradition records a marked
increase in warfare during the decades before the British began to

extend colonial control over the region in 1888. One likely cause was a rise in the population of the small, infertile, drought-ridden islands of both the nearby Calvados Chain and the more distant Engineer Group near the mainland. Another contributing factor was probably an increasing number of rifles traded to the islanders by unscrupulous white traders from the 1860s to the 1880s, plus the capturing of weapons following surprise attacks on Europeans. In the late nineteenth century it was unsafe to dwell along the coasts of Vanatinai, which were habitually raided by Sabara and Brooker Islanders from the Calvados Chain and Tubetube and Kwaraiwa Islanders from the Engineer Group.[32]

Neighboring groups on Vanatinai itself frequently made war on one another, sometimes asking their off-island allies and exchange partners, such as the Grass (Wanim) Islands, for assistance in fighting other groups on Vanatinai and then presenting the allies with ceremonial valuables as compensation. Nevertheless some marriages were contracted between people living in different parts of the island, and people sometimes visited other districts to attend feasts. Patterns of intra- and interisland alliance and enmity seem to have been fairly unstable, although some alliances, like that between Grass (Wanim) Island in the East Calvados and the southwestern portion of Vanatinai where the modern village of Jelewaga is, have endured since precolonial times. Oral histories indicate that visitors from the Engineer Group and the Calvados Chain traded in some districts of Vanatinai and raided in others, or traded in some years and raided at other times. People say that the Brooker (Nogini) Islanders, who were notorious for their attacks on Vanatinai settlements until 1893, still used to exchange their clay cooking pots for Vanatinai sago in precolonial times just as they do today, residing temporarily on the island while their Vanatinai exchange partners prepared the sago.

Islanders say that their forebears relied far less on horticulture for subsistence than today, although they did plant yams, bananas, and the large taro that is called *via*. Sago was the major staple, supplemented by a wide variety of foodstuffs gathered in the forest, particularly the large legume called *kaikai*, which nowadays is eaten mainly on ceremonial occasions. This shift to more intensive cultivation, particularly of New World crops such as sweet potato and manioc introduced to Australasia by Europeans, began in the 1880s but grew more pronounced as recently as the 1940s (Lepowsky 1985a).

First Contacts

One quiet morning while the rest of the family was away from the hamlet and I was alone in the house trying to catch up on writing my fieldnotes, Martin's uncle Sale came down to visit from his home high up on the mountain slope. We sat cross-legged chewing betel nut and exchanging news. Sale rolled a cigarette of Paradise Twist, molasses-cured black tobacco I had bought at the tradestore, in a piece of a three-month-old copy of the Port Moresby *Post-Courier*. Tobacco is the islanders' passion, which one of my neighbors had firmly told me it was my job as a European with money to provide. After a meditative pause Sale said he was going to tell me the story of the first lumolumo to visit Vanatinai.

One day, he said, a double-masted sailing ship anchored in the lagoon. The white-skinned people on board were anxious to obtain gum (copal gum, from a rain forest tree, is still an item of trade locally and was formerly used to caulk and varnish European ships). In exchange for the gum the lumolumo gave the Vanatinai people tobacco and demonstrated to them how to smoke it. The visitors departed, leaving behind a supply of tobacco and some *machisi* [matches] with which to light it. Sale began to chuckle at this point. The islanders, he said, were afraid of being burned by the matches, so they submerged themselves to the neck in the local stream, holding the matches over their heads to practice lighting them.

By 1892 the governor of British New Guinea, Sir William MacGregor, was able to report of the neighboring Rossel Islanders, "They have taken kindly to tobacco, and will consequently be willing to trade" (Haddon 1947:192). The technique of introducing an addictive drug whose supply they controlled has been the most successful one Europeans have ever devised in the islands of southeastern New Guinea for extracting island wealth—gold, pearl shell, copra— and islander labor. Desire for tobacco and for steel tools have for over a hundred years been the primary motivations of Vanatinai people in occasionally working for cash, an activity for which they still, in the late twentieth century, show a marked reluctance. Attempts by Euro pean traders, colonial government officers, and missionaries to pressure them into the roles of laborer, taxpayer, and churchgoer have been met with resistance, and they have been markedly less successful than in areas of New Guinea such as the Highlands whose peoples were only known to Europeans since the 1930s, and which only came under effective colonial control in the 1950s and 1960s (Lepowsky 1991).

By contrast, the islands of the Louisiade Archipelago were first sighted by Europeans in 1606, when Luiz de Torres, coming from the south, was unable to round the eastern tip of Rossel Island. He gave up and sailed westward outside the southern barrier reef of Sudest Lagoon on his way to the "discovery" of New Guinea and of the straits that bear his name. For another two hundred years the forbidding barrier reefs encircling the islands kept other Europeans from entering the lagoon in search of the fresh water and food for which they were desperate. Their ranks including the French explorers de Bougainville in 1768, who named the Iles du Sudest, and D'Entrecasteaux in 1793 (Macgillivray 1852:169–174).

There are no written accounts of the likely first meetings of Vanatinai people with Europeans. The Solomon Sea was frequented by American and European whalers and traders in the 1830s and 1840s.[33] It is likely that some of these vessels landed in the Louisiade Archipelago in search of food and water. The whalers, as well as traders in tortoiseshell, pearl shell, and bêche-de-mer, were secretive about their movements in order to avoid competition for their prized spots for trading, fishing, and obtaining fresh water and food. The memoirs of one Thomas Jefferson Jacobs (1844:74–76, 250) record, though, that the clipper *Margaret Oakley*, out of New York under Captain Benjamin Morrell in search of tortoiseshell and pearl shell, obtained "fruit" on an unspecified Louisiade island in 1834.[34]

The Europeans who first wrote of their visit with the Vanatinai people were the British officers and seamen of HMS *Rattlesnake*, a three-masted frigate lately refitted at Portsmouth Naval Yard after seeing service in the British Opium Wars in southern China. Under the command of Captain Owen Stanley, the *Rattlesnake* was on a four-year mission of empire to chart the approaches to the Torres Strait and find a less hazardous route for military and trading ships sailing between Sydney and Singapore and on to Chinese or Indian ports or back to England. On board as well were the ship's naturalist, John Macgillivray, who wrote the official account of the *Rattlesnake's* four cruises, and the twenty-four-year-old assistant ship's surgeon and assistant naturalist, a sarcastic, opinionated, brilliant young man named Thomas Henry Huxley, whose first scientific paper, on the morphology of the *Medusae*, was written on the *Rattlesnake* and based on his dissection of the fragile invertebrates he caught in townets off the ship's stern. Mailed home by Captain Stanley and published through the intercession of his father, the bishop of Norwich, the paper was the basis of Huxley's subsequent election as a fellow of the Royal Society and of his career as one of the greatest scientists of the nineteenth century. Both Huxley and Captain Stanley kept diaries during the voyage. These three written records, plus the watercolors of island scenes painted by Huxley and by Oswald Brierly, a marine artist invited on the cruise by Captain Stanley, provide a rich and remarkably detailed portrait of these island encounters.

Sailing from Sydney Harbour, the *Rattlesnake* rounded Cape Deliverance on June 13, 1849, made a rendezvous with its tender, the *Bramble*, from which it had been separated during a gale, and unsuccessfully searched the northern barrier reef of Rossel Island for a passage into the sheltered lagoon waters. By the next morning the current had carried the British expedition westward to north of the Sudest barrier reef. A careful search finally revealed a narrow passage in the reef, and the two vessels passed into Sudest Lagoon, leaving the blue waters of open ocean in which 111 fathoms of line had failed to reach bottom just outside the passage and anchoring in fifteen fathoms (Macgillivray 1852:186).

The following day island men approached the European vessels in their sailing canoes armed with spears but offering yams, coconuts, and tortoiseshell in trade. This is one of several hints that Vanatinai people had had prior contact with Europeans, although the men of HMS *Rattlesnake* believed, as Captain Stanley (1849:7) records, that "they can never by any chance have seen Europeans before." Raw tortoiseshell, as opposed to carved tortoiseshell lime spatulas, is not now, or within local historical memory, an interisland exchange commodity. It was eagerly sought though by European and American trading vessels in the Solomon and Coral Seas in the 1830s and

1840s. During this first contact with the British on June 15, the islanders "were very greedy for iron and stole one of the crutches wh. happened to be lying loose . . . they passed it from hand to hand and concealed it at the far end of their canoe . . . " (Huxley 1935:183). Nimowa Island men also stole Thomas Huxley's pistol two days later, although whether they coveted the metal or understood its use as a weapon is not clear. They may have injured themselves with it, as the British read the islanders' "violent gesticulations" and shouted and pantomimed invitations to leave the lagoon (Macgillivray 1852I:193–196, Huxley 1935:187–9). It is possible too that the Vanatinai people and their neighbors had merely heard about Europeans, their guns, their iron, and their tastes in trade goods from their exchange partners on other islands.

Island men also tried to drive the British away by setting fire to the grasslands near where crews were "watering the ship," (Macgillivray 1852I:214), but the *Rattlesnake* remained in the lagoon for almost a month, surveying its coasts and reefs and taking on 78 tons of fresh water from the falls on the Veora River of northern Vanatinai, enough to last them until they reached Cape York in northern Australia (Stanley 1849:17). A considerable trade was carried out with the islanders during this time. The British obtained 368 pounds of yams in exchange for "about seventeen axes and a few knives" at Dedehai Island in a single visit (Macgillivray 1852:229), as well as coconuts, bananas, ornaments, and weapons in exchange for

> strips of calico and pieces of iron hoop. Axes, however, were more prized than any other article, and the exhibition of one was certain to produce great eagerness to procure it, amidst much shouting and cries of kelumai! The purpose to which they applied the iron hoop we found was to substitute it for the pieces of a hard green stone (nephrite) in the heads of their axes and adzes.
>
> (Macgillivray 1852I:200–201)

Kelumo means metal axe, literally European axe, in the Vanatinai language today.

After ten days the women, who had initially kept out of sight, paddled out to the *Rattlesnake* and the *Bramble*, along with their children, to study the visitors and to trade. Captain Owen Stanley (1849:18) writes of one contact about ten miles west of the initial anchorage,

Two boats went in and had a most friendly interview with the Natives who though shy at first soon came down with great confidence, & the women soon followed The Men at first tried to drive them away but the good ladies afsorded their own right and remained sufficiently near, to have a good look at the company & were perfectly contented when some peices of Handkerchief were given them.

Macgillivray (1852I:219–220) also recorded the women's refusal to hide themselves and eagerness to trade in their own right. It was customary in interisland warfare until the early twentieth century for women and children to be taken captive and carried off by enemies (and then usually adopted by an elder or powerful person), and we may guess that this is what the island men feared in 1849.

Captain Stanley (1849:18) further observes, "Some of the Women in the Canoes seemed to have a certain amount of Command; & some respect was shown to them by the Men, but" he continues, "those we have yet seen on Shore have been employed carrying Baskets on their heads." The British visit was in late June and July, the present-day yam harvest season. Then, as now, women were probably "the owners of the garden" and in charge of distribution of yams and other produce for consumption or exchange. The women carrying baskets on their heads were likely not just porters but presenters of their own yams to their new British exchange partners.

Relations between islanders and whites turned sour. Some of the men from the ship, engaged in survey work in smaller boats, were attacked by three canoes of men from Panatinani (Joannet) Island. After what Macgillivray describes as "sham bartering" for iron axes, the islanders tried to capsize the European boats. One sailor was "struck on the head with a stoneheaded axe," and another was speared in the arm. The British fired back with muskets and a twelve-pounder howitzer, and the islanders fled after throwing a few more spears. One canoe, stained with blood, was later captured by the British, who removed its paddles and broke the spears in it, then let it drift toward shore. This is the first unambiguous evidence of the injury or death of a Louisiade Islander at the hands of Europeans. The British regarded the attack as an "act of deliberate treachery," for they recognized some of their attackers (Macgillivray 1852I:234–36).

About ten days later HMS *Rattlesnake* sailed westward to complete the survey of the islands and reefs of the Louisiade Archipelago and make for New Guinea.

The islanders clearly felt the British had remained too long and outlasted the benefits of exchanging food for iron axes. The survey boats were probably lingering too close to their beaches for comfort. The survey work carried out by HMS *Rattlesnake* remains to this day the basis of European nautical charts of the region, and it was the key to opening up these reef-strewn seas and islands to European penetration. The islanders seem prescient in trying to retain control of their homelands and their resources by driving the British surveyors away.[35]

The documents surviving from the 1849 first (or early) contacts with Europeans show the men of Vanatinai and neighboring islands as the makers of initial contacts with these potentially hostile strangers. Armed with spears but also bearing goods for barter, their words in the initial exchanges lost to history, they confronted the invaders fearlessly but cautiously, preferring exchange to a fight. They were also bold and aggressive, taking iron goods from the uninvited strangers who had landed in their section of lagoon rather than waiting to barter during their first contact and at least two other times. (As Macgillivray puts it in a page heading, "Natives shew thievish propensities.") On several occasions they taunted the strangers. Their encounters with the British reveal verbal, pantomimed, and acted-out aggression, courage, and a willingness to defend their territory. They also tried but failed in one instance to keep the women from approaching the white men who had just landed, again uninvited, on the beach of Dedehai Island. The women kept back at first but later traded on their own account and satisfied their curiosity. They struck the British with their poise and by showing "a certain amount of Command."

It is possible that in the mid-nineteenth century, characterized by frequent interisland and interdistrict warfare, there was a greater valorizing on Vanatinai and neighboring islands of personal qualities such as aggression and fearlessness in men than in recent decades and a greater difference between the socialization of males and females. It is the role of warrior, now extinct, that of all occupations was most exclusively male. Its demise may have altered a previously less than fully egalitarian gender balance in favor of women, who already had considerable autonomy.

Encounters on the Coral Sea Frontier

There are few records of visits by whites to the Louisiade in the years between 1849 and the 1880s, but the rich fishing grounds of Sudest Lagoon—now charted—continued to attract European traders seeking tortoiseshell, bêche-de-mer, and pearl shell. Vanatinai people say that during this period a few island men worked on European vessels "just to sailabout." One such local adventurer returned to his village on the north coast of Vanatinai bringing with him a kind of sago known henceforth as "Solomon," after the island group where he obtained it. He planted it in the swamps near his home, from which it gradually spread through exchange, and it is now planted in many parts of Vanatinai and the East Calvados Islands.

A few European bêche-de-mer fishers and pearlers took up temporary residence in the Louisiade in the 1870s and early 1880s, employing local men to work for them. Some brought boat crews and divers with them from other parts of the Pacific, including men from the Solomons and Torres Strait, Chinese, and Malays. Others employed local men for short periods, typically three months, in exchange for metal axes, tobacco, and other trade goods, and Snider rifles and bullets.

There were no laws and no government to restrain the white men on the Coral Sea frontier in those years. Some of these early traders kidnaped local women and fired on and terrorized the local people. In one instance in 1878 the Brooker Islanders of the West Calvados Chain formed an alliance with the Solomon Islanders, killing bêche-de-mer trader John McOrt, three other European men, and eight men from the Torres Strait after McOrt abused two Solomons men in his crew (Bevan 1890:112–113). Two Torres Strait women whose lives were spared were picked up by Special Commissioner John Douglas in 1887 and returned to Australia (Douglas 1888–89). Another party of whites led by W. B. Ingham of Queensland was murdered on Brooker a few months later in 1878 by the same alliance of Brooker and Solomon Islanders (Bevan 1890:113–114). As of 1878 six boatloads of European traders and their crews were murdered by the local inhabitants of the archipelago, according to accounts published in the Brisbane *Courier* by Reverend McFarlane, of the London Missionary Society, who was based on Ware Island (Wawn 1893:185). Captain Forman and his party in the *Annie Brooks* were murdered off Motorina in 1880, and bêche-de-mer trader Frank Gerret at Panapompom in 1885. The bleached skull of McOrt was purchased from his murderer seven years later by a Motorina Island man "for several pigs, canoes, white arm-shells, and hatchet-heads" and hung in its new owner's house (Bevan 1890:110–118).

The white traders and fishers quickly noted that the islanders were avid for rifles and ammunition and otherwise loath to dive for shell or gather bêche-de-mer. A man called Nicholas Minister, variously described as Austrian or American but most often known as Nicholas the Greek, was notorious for his physical abuse of island men, for kidnapping and raping women, and for supplying those who worked for him with guns. Based at Brooker Island, he had bêche-de-mer trading stations on numerous islands in the archipelago. Rifles obtained in trade and those taken as plunder after the successful attacks on whites such as McOrt and Ingham enabled Brooker Islanders and others in the Calvados Chain to increase the scale and the frequency of their raids on Sudest and other islands by the 1880s, as documented by contemporary observers.[36] Vanatinai people, whose island was less often visited by whites, obtained fewer guns than their enemies in the Calvados Chain.

Oral tradition on Vanatinai closely parallels the written accounts of European visitors in the 1880s. Island elders say that in the years before the coming of the government there was a sharp rise in the number of raids on the hamlets and gardens of Vanatinai by the peoples of the Calvados Chain, especially men from Brooker Island and from Sabara, and from Tubetube and Kwaraiwa, 150 miles to the northwest. Significantly, the most frequent raiders came from the smallest, most densely populated coralline islands of poor soil and unreliable water. They came to steal food—yams, bundles of sago, and pigs—as well as to kill, according to Vanatinai oral accounts and British written documents from the 1880s. I would speculate that a rise in population beyond the carrying capacity of these islands, which then as now depended in part on trade with larger islands to sustain themselves, combined with the new availability of European rifles and the added burden of white residents who helped themselves to scarce resources, triggered the increase in raiding in late precolonial times.

As a result, elders say, Vanatinai people abandoned ancient hamlet sites, whose locations and names are well remembered today, along the coast and near streams and fertile garden lands, moving to new places inland, easily defended sites on top of the steep, forested ridges, where they had a good view of any sailing canoes approaching in the lagoon. The visitors would appear off the coast, and sometimes they wanted to exchange their clay pots or greenstone axe blades for Vanatinai sago, yams, betel nut, pigs, or shell-disc necklaces. But every year, especially after the yam harvest in July, parties of these sometime exchange partners would attack, killing people, plundering yam gardens, and stealing pigs. Occasionally they would take women or children away with them, marrying the women and adopting the children.

According to oral history, which is corroborated by European visitors' written accounts, Vanatinai warriors rarely sailed to other islands to make war but primarily defended their own people and made war intermittently with people of other Vanatinai districts. Vanatinai people sometimes successfully fought off attacks by off-islanders in locally famous battles, often after making alliances with exchange partners who would come to their aid.[37] The skulls of victims became ceremonial valuables, often decorated with shell discs or the pigments used as face paints, circulating in exchange for other valuables—like the skull of John McOrt—and displayed in houses and at special feasts. These feasts, called *ghanmaghamaghada* on Vanatinai, honored champion warriors, or *asiara*, for killing enemies, and decorated skulls were exchanged by the asiara for shell-disc necklaces and greenstone axe blades. Sometimes the bodies and brains of defeated enemies were ritually eaten by the feastgoers. The locally famous story of Dulubia, the Kwaraiwa raider defeated about 1910 by the Vanatinai champion Kalinga in alliance with the Wanim people, or Grass Islanders, concludes with a ritual cannibal feast in which Kalinga receives about one hundred valuables—greenstone axe blades and shell necklaces—from Wanim in exchange for the decorated head of Dulubia, and the Wanim people each eat a pearl shell spoonful of Dulubia's brain (Lepowsky 1983:495–497). Dulubia's skull was kept in a shallow cave on Wanim until the early 1970s, when an old woman, angry because it was being used by sorcerers as part of their destructive magic, threw it into the sea.

In ancient times, several elders told me, mortuary feasts were the primary venue at which ceremonial valuables were exchanged, as they are today. These feasts are taubwaragha. But formerly far fewer valuables were necessary to make a generous contribution honoring the dead. Vanatinai people recognize that an inflationary spiral in ceremonial valuables has set in since colonial days. But in the period of intensified fighting shortly before the coming of the lumolumo, feasts honoring champion warriors and featuring the exchange of enemy skulls for valuables were the most frequent public, ritualized exchanges.

Women had prominent roles in warfare and peacemaking, these elders, male and female, further explained. Women participated in all decisions concerning whether to fight and whether to make peace. The signal for both, interpreted according to context, was for a senior woman, or the mother or sister of a warrior, to remove her outer skirt and throw it to the ground. This could either signal an attack or, in the heat of battle, protect an enemy from being killed by placing him under the woman's protection. If her brother subsequently threw his spear, it would be like committing incest. A sister could also finger the tiestrings on her skirt as a signal, saying, "My brother, my skirt." The brother would reply, "My sister's head." Women also knew powerful war magic taught them by their fathers. Sisters accompanied brothers onto the field of battle, carrying extra spears and retrieving the wounded. Nevertheless, only men were and are permitted to kill with spears, whether in hunting or in war, and only men could become asiara.

In 1883 the bêche-de-mer fishers and traders encountered a new form of competition for the labor of the islanders. The sugar plantations of Queensland, Australia had long depended upon Melanesian laborers recruited from the Solomon Islands and the New Hebrides. But in 1884 the Queensland government forbade the Australian and English recruiters to supply firearms to the islanders, who by then were demanding rifles and ammunition for their friends before they would board the vessels (Corris 1968:87).

The recruiters quickly turned their attention to the Louisiade and succeeded in obtaining about five hundred men from the region. D. H. Osborne (1942:34), who settled on Sudest Island in 1901 and later moved to Rossel, writes that this was because the region was in the grips of a "severe drought . . . and the natives of Sudest and Rossel were practically starving." But on subsequent trips after the drought had broken the recruiters were unsuccessful.

They complained that the bêche-de-mer fishers, particularly Nicholas Minister, were trying to protect their own labor supplies by traveling around warning the islanders that they would be killed and eaten in Queensland. But tales of kidnapping and trickery became known not only to islanders, who saw friends dragged onto boats, seized from canoes, or duped into thinking they were going "sailabout" for three months to dive for shell or collect bêche-de-mer. In the Australian colonies and Great Britain public sentiment against the South Seas labor trade led to an investigation by the Queensland Parliament into recruiting practices at which Louisiade men testified. By 1885 the New Guinea waters were closed as a recruiting ground, and more than four hundred men were returned by the Queensland government to southeastern New Guinea, seventy-one of them to Sudest Island along with thirteen packets of trade goods as compensation for recruits who had died overseas.[38]

The returnees brought with them a greater knowledge of the English-Melanesian pidgin called Vanga Lumo, the "language of Europeans," by Vanatinai people.[39] Island men returning from Queensland, their grandchildren say, also brought with them stolen seeds and cuttings of plants they had learned to admire, including manioc, sweet potato, pineapple, "European mango," sugarcane varieties, corn, pumpkin, and other crops. These new food plants gradually spread among island gardens. Manioc and sweet potato, in particular, crops of New World origin brought to Australia by British colonists, became staples of island diet, joining yams and taro boiled in coconut cream as true food, or *ghanika moli*. Easy to grow perennials that did well in sandy soils and drought conditions, they contributed to a major shift in diet and subsistence over the course of a hundred years from greater emphasis on sago, fishing, and gathered wild foods to more reliance on horticulture. The earlier diet, based less heavily on starchy tubers, was probably more varied and nutritious, a significant change in a region where over 90 percent of children under five have been measured as having mild to moderate undernutrition (Lepowsky 1985a, 1991).

This has probably affected the sexual division of labor as well, since women perform more horticultural work than men. Although caring for these perennial crops means more tedious weeding and less time in the more pleasant gleaning of wild foods from forest and shore, the increased emphasis on gardening may have strengthened women's position, as they are, and were, the principal controllers and distributors of garden foods.

But in general the coming of European men during this frontier period probably gave island men greater power and opportunities. A rise in warfare meant more chances for men to exercise their unique avenue to prestige and renown, becoming a champion warrior, which would have been all the more heavily valorized in those dangerous times. Island men had the greatest chances to approach the European men, spears in hand, seeking out trade goods. Some of them also greatly increased their mobility and experience, voluntarily or involuntarily, during their employment by Europeans as bêche-de-mer collectors, divers for pearl shell, crewmen on whaling and trading vessels, and indentured sugarcane workers, returning home with valuable goods and fascinating stories of distant parts.

Gold and Gavamani

In 1888 reports by a young English pearling captain named David White, who had been working the Sudest Lagoon, of a gold-bearing quartz reef on Joannet (Panatinani) Island prompted a prospecting expedition from the port of Cooktown in North Queensland. Failing to find gold on Joannet, the party crossed to Vanatinai (Sudest), where gold was discovered not far from the river where HMS *Rattlesnake* had taken on water forty years earlier. By the end of the year nearly four hundred Australian miners were encamped on the north coast of Vanatinai, a number that almost doubled by the following year. Although the southeastern portion of the island of New Guinea had been a British Protectorate since 1884, it was the gold strike on Sudest Island that caused the whole region, including the Louisiade Archipelago, which had been overlooked in the original protectorate, to be annexed as British New Guinea. The *gavamani* (government) had arrived. A white colonial officer took up residence on Vanatinai for about a year, the only one ever to do so except for the military administrators of World War II who followed the Battle of the Coral Sea.

The miners were never able to discover a motherlode on Sudest, and many of them died of malaria and dysentery. But in the decade from 1888 to 1898 gold worth more than fifty thousand pounds was taken from the island. In 1889 gold was discovered on Misima Island as well, and four hundred miners immediately moved north. By 1891 only thirty-eight white miners remained on Sudest.[40]

Relations between miners and the people of Vanatinai were generally free from violence, although the miners complained of thefts by islanders, and one miner in the Rehua area was killed following a quarrel. His alleged assailants were publicly hanged. Sir William MacGregor, first administrator and lieutenant governor of British New Guinea, who several times visited the island, believed that its people felt the miners offered protection from other islanders such as the Brooker (Utian or Nogini) people, who raided Vanatinai as late as 1893.[41]

The white miners stayed near their streamside diggings, and the islanders remained mostly in their ridge-top hamlets and hillside gardens, carrying goods and trading for food with the miners, who sometimes accused islanders of "pilfering" from them. Some of the whites who visited the island were surprised at the amount of English that the inhabitants spoke. Women generally kept out of sight of the white men, and they refused to sell their sexual favors. Very few mixed-race individuals were born during this period.

The island of Vanatinai and its neighbors lapsed again into obscurity in the early twentieth century. Only a few Europeans remained on the island, some establishing coconut plantations. A piece of land near Rambuso on the northeast coast was purchased about 1910 by a white man for one axe, an eighteen-inch bagi, one large empty bottle, one parcel of trade tobacco, and a bag of rice wrapped in a woven mat (Territory of Papua 1972). It was planted in coconuts. Land for other coconut plantations was bought by Europeans near Rehua (Tambamba), Pamela (Hula), Pantava, and Madawa (Tetena) on the south coast. Only Tetena was still operating in 1978–79, under the supervision of local managers, and it was abandoned by the 1980s.

By the 1890s islanders had overcome white objections and learned to pan for gold in the streams themselves. Europeans maintained a few small tradestores to which the islanders could bring gold dust, blacklip or goldlip pearl or trochus shell, copal gum, or copra and receive credit (locally called "book") for items such as metal axes, bush knives (machetes), cloth, fishhooks, rice, and tobacco. Vanatinai people received a poor rate of exchange from the all of the white traders and they knew it. Some traders also physically abused and threatened their debtors in order to force them to bring in gold dust or tropical commodities.[42] The most prominent trader through the 1920s was an Irish–Australian widow named Elizabeth Mahony who came with her husband in the rush of 1888, the second white woman to live in British New Guinea (the first was Mrs. Lawes, wife of the missionary at Port Moresby). Mrs. Mahony managed a tradestore, ran plantations, and raised her children alone after her husband's death in about 1907. Islanders exchanged gold dust not only for European goods but for necklaces of shell discs, bagi, that Mrs. Mahony imported Rossel Island men to manufacture in order to stimulate trade (Lepowsky 1991, n.d.1).

Australia took over the administration of the former British New Guinea in 1906, after which it was known as the Territory of Papua. Existing records indicate that prior to World War II Vanatinai was officially visited only half a dozen times, even though a yearly head tax was instituted in 1919. The government patrol officers, based at Misima Island, conducted censuses, collected the tax from adult men, and arbitrated local disputes, mainly concerning alleged acts of sorcery.[43] A system of village constables had been instituted as early as the 1890s. These officeholders, all men, varied considerably in the seriousness with which they took the job of reporting colonial law violations to the infrequently appearing white patrol officers. Then, as now, the great majority of disputes were settled by customary means or left unresolved to result in sorcery and countersorcery attempts.

Although the colonial government was under the impression that the Louisiade Archipelago had been completely pacified by 1888, at the time of the first gold strike on Vanatinai, people say that in fact the last raid by Engineer Group Islanders on Vanatinai and East Calvados (Saisai) settlements occurred about 1910 (Lepowsky 1983:495–497), and raids by the Sabara Islanders upon Vanatinai and on Nimowa took place as late as the 1920s. Nevertheless, raids became rare, and the physical mobility of the majority of islanders, especially women and those men who did not go to work for Europeans, was greater than in precolonial days.

World War and Afterward

The Louisiade Archipelago again became a focus of international attention during World War II (Lepowsky 1989a). The Japanese used Panaeati (Deboyne) Lagoon as a seaplane base. Their southward advance toward Australia in 1942 was halted by American and Australian forces in the Battle of the Coral Sea, which took place in the seas and skies south and north of Vanatinai. The wreck of a bomber is still visible on the southeastern coast near Buyawe. There were no local casualties in the fighting, but Vanatinai people still run in terror for cover when the rare low-flying plane passes over their settlements, fearing aerial bombing. As the Japanese advanced on the region, the civilian colonial government and the few white residents were evacuated. A military administration was formed, known as the Australia New Guinea Administrative Unit, or ANGAU. Representatives of ANGAU visited the villages of the Louisiade Archipelago, informing the islanders that they were obliged to send a number of unmarried men to labor for the Allied Forces at Milne Bay on the mainland. Most islanders complied with this demand, and over seven hundred men were recruited from Vanatinai and Misima. There was an uprising at Hebwaun (Bwailahine) Village on Panatinani Island, and a local constable who advocated cooperation with this order was killed by other men who feared that the laborers in Milne Bay would die in the war. The withdrawal of colonial government also triggered other incidents of violence. A Vanatinai man living at another hamlet on Panatinani who had been suspected of sorcery in the death of a Nigaho man was killed at Grass (Wanim) Island by men from some of the East Calvados Islands. The people of Vanatinai, in fear of attack on their own island, fled their villages and hid in the mountains, where they remained for several months.

In 1943 a man named Buriga, from Siagara Village on Misima Island, claimed to have received a message from the spirits of the dead that if the villagers killed all the white and mixed-race people the spirits would sail back to their earthly homes in a ship full of European cargo. He found no support for his prophecy on his home island of Misima and moved to the West Calvados island of Motorina. The Calvados Chain Islanders, who had had less opportunity to obtain material goods from Europeans than the inhabitants of Misima and Vanatinai, were more receptive to this message. In 1943 an ANGAU patrol led by Lt. Mader was ambushed at Motorina Island; eight members of the patrol died in the attack, including Lt. Mader, a local mixed-race man named George Burfitt and six Papua New Guineans from other parts of the country. An old mixed-race man of Filipino ancestry was killed on the passage off Panawina Island in the East Calvados. A total of 151 persons were arrested in connection with these murders, and Buriga hanged himself in his cell shortly before eight of his collaborators were publicly hanged at Bwagaoia, Misima. A large percentage of the adult men from the Calvados Chain Islands served time in jail. Lt. Sidney Smith of ANGAU, who investigated the murders, writes that "every native in the Calvados Chain from Motorina Is. in the west to Nimoa in the east, had decided that Government control had more or less ceased to exist and they could return to their old fashions and kill with impunity." Of one Panawina man who escaped capture for his part in the murders Lt. Smith says, "When he returned to his village he boasted of his deeds and hoisted a flag made out of scraps of calico, saying that the Government had now been killed and they would fly their own flag" (Territory of Papua 1943).

Following these wartime episodes of violence, all of the Louisiade peoples were ordered in 1943 by ANGAU to live only in designated coastal sites where they would be subject to greater government control. This order has never been rescinded, and the nucleated coastal villages of present-day Vanatinai are the result.

After the war laborers returning from Milne Bay spread stories throughout the Vanatinai region of the friendliness of the black and white American soldiers whom they had met while constructing the airfield and the port and carrying supplies in the Milne Bay area. These men still speak of how the black and white soldiers sat down and ate together and of how the Americans habitually gave the Papua New Guineans presents of food and tobacco. Some of the people of Vanatinai decided that the spirits of the dead of their island "turn white and go to America." This relationship between the two places would explain those wartime acts of kindness.

Very few whites returned as traders or planters to Vanatinai after the war. Small-scale Australian-run goldmining operations were carried out sporadically in the Veora River area of the north coast until the early 1970s. In 1947 increased mission activity began in the Vanatinai-Yela (Rossel) area. Although the Misima-Panaeati region to the northwest had fallen under heavy mission influence beginning in 1891, when the Australasian Methodist Missionary Society established a mission station with European and Polynesian teachers on Panaeati, the peoples of the southeastern islands remained mostly pagan until after World War II. The Methodists, known nowadays as the United Church, had briefly established a mission at Rambuso on the north coast of Vanatinai in the 1930s, but after the war Misiman-speaking missionaries from Misima, Panaeati, the Suau Coast, and Tonga established churches in the major coastal settlements of Vanatinai.

The Roman Catholic Mission of the Sacred Heart also came into the area in 1947. The Catholics acquired rights to a piece of land on the north coast of Vanatinai and planned to build a mission station, but they discovered that the Saisai people feared the sorcery of Vanatinai and would not be likely to attend church or send their children to a mission school on that island. Accordingly their mission was built on Nimowa, a small East Calvados island only a few miles across the strait from Vanatinai, in the hope that both ethnic groups could be reached from this site. An Australian priest and several Australian and Papua New Guinean nuns lived on Nimowa in 1978-79. The result has been that the Saisai people have fallen under the influence of the Catholic mission much more than the people of Vanatinai. The Saisai people are virtually all Catholics, and now the second generation of Saisai children is attending the mission primary schools at Nimowa, Hobuk (Panatinani), and Sabara.

The people of Vanatinai are mixed in their religious affiliation, with some villages such as Jelewaga being predominantly Methodist, and others, such as the hamlets of the Rehua area, mainly Catholic. A significant minority of older people do not adhere to either faith. Christians continue to retain indigenous religious beliefs. In 1978 about a third of the school-age children of Vanatinai attended either the Catholic primary schools at Griffin Point or Rehua on Vanatinai or at Nimowa itself or else the United Church primary school at Rambuso. There were no government schools in the entire southeastern Louisiade until 1984, when a primary school was opened by the provincial government at Madawa on the south coast of Vanatinai.

The postwar years brought the southeastern Louisiade under closer government scrutiny. Yearly census and tax collecting patrols were launched from Misima, and the Local Government Council system of government was introduced throughout the region by the mid-1960s. Tagula Government Station was constructed in 1969 on the northwest tip of Vanatinai, and a government officer-in-charge (OIC) took up residence.

Papua New Guinea became an independent nation in 1975, comprised of the former Australian Territory of Papua and the Trust Territory of New Guinea to the north, which came under Australian control after World War I, when it was taken from the Germans, and became a United Nations Trust Territory following World War II.

Today the region is part of Milne Bay Province. Its inhabitants elect representatives to the Provincial Assembly in Alotau as well as sending a member to the National Parliament that sits in Port Moresby. In late 1979 a Louisiade man named Patrick Paulisbo, a schoolteacher whose mother is from Bobaghagha, Vanatinai, became the premier of Milne Bay Province, a position of considerable autonomy in line with a nationwide policy of decentralization of power. In January of 1979 the Yeleyamba Local Government Council was formed, consisting of Yela (Rossel), Vanatinai (called Yamba in Yeletnye, the language of Rossel), and Saisai (the East Calvados Islands). These islands had formerly been part of the Louisiade Local Government Council, but in the early 1970s the people of Yela threatened to secede from not only the Louisiade Council but the then Territory of Papua and join the Solomon Islands, complaining that they sent head-tax money to the Misima-dominated council but did not receive enough from the government in exchange. The Vanatinai and Saisai peoples also felt neglected by the government and wanted aid posts and government schools. The Yeleyamba council was formed in response to these sentiments and the new council chamber, located at Tagula Station, Vanatinai, was opened in early 1979.

Raiding has ended, and and the islanders have successively been on the fringes of two colonial empires and an independent nation-state. European goods such as steel knives, metal fishhooks, cloth, and tobacco are essential possessions. These are purchased at the trade-store near Tagula Station or on rare visits to Misima Island. It is necessary to earn a small amount of money to buy these items, to pay the low primary school fees, and to pay annual council taxes of ten kina (about fifteen dollars) per man aged eighteen to forty-five (two kina for single women and one kina for married women). People therefore occasionally make copra, dive for trochus, goldlip or blacklip pearl shell, shoot crocodile, or gather copal gum or *Pueraria* to obtain money. The Vanatinai people had been notorious for their nonpayment of taxes, and in 1978 some two dozen men were jailed for up to three months for this offense. Vanatinai residents are also jailed for sorcery, which is against the law in Papua New Guinea as it was in colonial times, or for adultery, which is also considered a crime. There is virtually no violent crime on the island.

Islanders in the Vanatinai region also encounter the outside world in the form of an occasional visiting yacht, particularly in the Calvados Chain Islands. A startlingly high number of foreign yachts and even freighters are shipwrecked on the reefs of the Louisiade Archipelago—at least four in 1977–78 (clearly a dangerous year for European vessels on this part of the Coral Sea), including a ten thousand-ton freighter bound from Melbourne, Australia to South Korea that ran aground off Yela.

The lagoon was invaded every year through the 1980s, until the central government tried to protect its territorial waters by aggressively pursuing the poaching Taiwanese fishing vessels whose men dove for crayfish and the giant Tridacna clam and fished for tuna, mackerel, shark (for their fins), and other commercial fish. On Misima in the late 1980s one of the world's largest open-pit goldmines was constructed by an Australian multinational corporation and began operations. But jobs there went to Australian expatriates and to Misimans, and few Vanatinai people have expressed interest in working at the mine in any case. Government and mission intervention into the affairs of Vanatinai people remains minimal, and they continue to live off their lands and reefs, to trade their surpluses, and to hold their elaborate mortuary feasts.

Vanatinai lifestyles remain remarkably—and resolutely—like those of earlier generations. Nevertheless, there have been major cultural changes and adaptations to new technologies, new ideas, and new forms of control of their affairs by outsiders. The degree to which Vanatinai people have retained old ways is not because of lack of contact with Europeans or with the cash economy. Nor it is because Vanatinai is one of the most remote islands in the Pacific—protected from easy exploitation of its resources by treacherous reefs and by the fact that its gold deposits remained stubbornly hidden in its mountainous interior—or because the island's low population has for generations made it a low priority as a mission field. The islanders are militant cultural conservatives who have often resisted external political, economic, and religious systems by maintaining their customs while recognizing and promoting some forms of innovation within them (Lepowsky 1991).

Men, Women, and History

This chapter has outlined the basic principles of Vanatinai social life— the ties between people and the relationships between people and the land and sea from which they draw their food—and surveyed the history of the island's people in order to provide a context for understanding gender and power in this island culture. Vanatinai women today share power with men through their central position in the web of kinship, their ownership of land and valuables and control over the distribution of the fruits of their labors, and their access to wealth, prestige, and influence through systems of ritualized exchange. Cultural life on Vanatinai has undergone many changes over the millennia during which it has been inhabited. Many of the earlier ways are lost to memory and have left no presently known material evidence, although traces of them may be preserved in myth, and inferences may be drawn by islanders or scholars about life in the time of the ancestors.

Vanatinai people say that the central position of women in island life is taubwaragha, which means both "ancient" and "the way of the ancestors." How have the cultural changes they recognize and those documented by European writings over the last 150 years affected women's lives and relations between men and women since the pre-colonial period?

The islanders say that the most significant change in their recent history is the forcible suppression of warfare and raiding by the British and later the Australian colonial governments. Oral historical evidence documents a rise in the frequency of warfare, particularly in raids by Calvados Chain and Engineer Group Islanders, in the years before the coming of the government. The presence of new killing technologies—muskets, Snider rifles, and steel axes—and of European traders and their armed crews demanding food, labor, and marine resources exacerbated existing tensions. Local oral histories recount that this was also a period of increasing population on these small and infertile islands and of political rivalries involving land rights and trading relations.

Even though the last raids were as late as 1943 the more peaceful conditions since the early twentieth century, when raids became rare, resulted in an expansion of interdistrict and interisland trading and exchange and greater freedom of movement for both men and, especially, women, who no longer had to sail with male escorts armed with spears to avoid capture by enemies. It is likely that more individuals of both sexes have been able to participate extensively in exchange activities compared to precolonial times because of the lack of danger of physical attack and the greatly increased number of sailing canoes in the region (themselves items of ceremonial exchange). There has clearly been an increase in the quantity of ceremonial valuables in circulation on Vanatinai and throughout the Massim during this century (see chapter 6).

But did the now extinct male role of asiara, a term applied to exemplary and now legendary warriors—both aggressors who are alleged to have preyed cannibalistically on their own people and defenders who repelled invaders from other islands—mean that in precolonial times women could not compete for status and renown as giagia? Did the relatively more circumscribed opportunities for participation in interisland and interdistrict exchange mean that there were no female giagia in precolonial times? Or was becoming an asiara a completely separate avenue to prestige from that of the giagia, male and female, with whom they shared influence over their kin and neighbors?

The great majority of legendary asiara whose names and stories are told today are men who defended their people against aggressors from other islands.[44] Prowess in warfare was greatly admired in Vanatinai men, but according to local belief today, island fighters were primarily defenders of kin and neighbors and did not seek to attack others or gain territory or goods. People from the various districts on Vanatinai used to raid one another, and they also sometimes intermarried. Today, when their descendants are involved in peaceful exchange relations (but still fear each other's sorcery), raids on other districts are publicly justified and remembered as retaliation for offenses such as fishing without permission on reefs belonging to another matrilineage or assault on a lineage sister by her husband.

Killing for revenge or defense was valued, and it was celebrated by ritual cannibalism and tribute of ceremonial valuables by grateful associates. But, in contrast to peoples of neighboring islands and in dramatic contrast to many of the ethnographically well-known peoples of the great valleys of the New Guinea Highlands and forests of the Highlands fringe area, Vanatinai males of the past are generally praised in the present not for their aggressiveness in attack and plunder but for their ability to defend hamlets. Greater prestige accrued through success in obtaining valuables from an exchange partner because of one's cleverness and magical knowledge, then giving them away publicly in mortuary feasts.

Killing human beings with spears or greenstone axes was a former monopoly of men. This male specialization in defense, coupled with the late precolonial rise in warfare frequency, gave certain men, asiara, an advantage in achieving status and renown. But even during the period in which decorated skulls were the primary venue of exchange, women were prominent not only in the decisions to make war or peace, I was told, but in the skull exchanges that marked the conclusion of a successful battle and cemented alliances. Men were more likely to come forward to meet strangers visiting the island in case they planned to raid instead of trade, as demonstrated during the visit of HMS *Rattlesnake* in 1849. But, even in early times, islanders say that women went on exchange voyages.

Maurice Godelier (1986) distinguishes between what he calls great men and the big men typically described by anthropologists as prominent in Melanesian societies—the category that on Vanatinai includes big women. Big men, in his view, are only one type of great men, the type that achieves power and renown by accumulating and redistributing wealth. Godelier (1986:166) points out, crediting Chowning's (1979) survey of leadership in Melanesia, that "Melanesia has two other avenues of power, namely, war on the one hand and ritual, magic, and sacred lore on the other."[45] Among the Baruya of the Highlands fringe region Godelier documents that the typical Melanesian big man does not exist. Instead there are several types of great men in Baruya society—the great warriors, the great gardeners, the shamans, and the initiation ritual experts.

There is probably no Melanesian society where becoming a big man through wealth redistribution is the only road to social prominence. Another road is, or was, prowess in warfare, probably traditionally believed everywhere in Melanesia to derive not only from physical ability and mental acuity but from the active intercession of ancestor spirits or other supernatural beings. Knowledge is power everywhere in Melanesia. Knowledge of warfare skills and warfare magic is one type of power. Other types are the knowledge of how to kill through sorcery or witchcraft and how to heal through countersorcery, counterwitchcraft, and familiarity with magical spells and the properties of plant substances. Ritual expertise in gardening, exchange, or initiation is yet another.

In the Vanatinai case becoming known as an asiara was an avenue to prestige open to younger men. The asiara would, in Godelier's terms, have been a type of great man. Vanatinai women were not excluded from councils of war or diplomacy or from the battlefield. Still, the role of asiara was available only to men. The role of gia was never the same as that of asiara, and it could be filled by a mature and knowledgeable individual of either sex. There are other kinds of great men and, significantly, great women in Vanatinai society, such as powerful sorcerers, renowned healers, and highly successful gardeners. Sometimes these individuals are also giagia, big men or big women who accumulate and redistribute valuables, but in other cases they are not.

The male advantage resulting from contact with Europeans had begun by at least the 1870s, when island men started to trade with European bêche-de-mer fishers and pearlers, bartering for food and selling their labor as divers and collectors to men from cultures whose ideologies led them to take men only as their exchange partners, the way the islanders saw it, and to deal with women only when they wanted sexual relations, forcible or consensual. The pattern of Europeans dealing with island men as representatives of their people and as sources of commodities and labor continued throughout the colonial era.

Since the early 1950s under the Australian colonial government and, since 1975, the national government of Papua New Guinea, official local authority derives from the local government council. Councillors from Vanatinai have all been male. Women who were nominated, by men, on an occasion I witnessed in 1978 withdrew their names in embarrassment. I was told this was because they do not speak English. Few island women do. A handful of men have learned some English from working elsewhere in Papua New Guinea for a few years. In the local view the local government councillor is a kind of diplomatic host expected to provide hospitality and information to the government officer-in-charge or to other government officials on their rare visits to island communities. All male, these officials were formerly Australians and are now Papua New Guineans from other parts of a country where there are hundreds of different languages. They try to communicate in English, one of the nation's three official languages, since the other two, Pidgin and Motu, are spoken by very few Vanatinai people. Hardly any women have left the island to seek work or schooling, and they feel uncomfortable with visitors from beyond the Louisiade Archipelago and adjacent islands. Many officials are from parts of the country with a strong ideology of male dominance, and they expect to deal with Vanatinai men.

Older men who have never been to school or worked for wages off the island are also uneasy about dealing with visiting officials. The local government councillors are therefore almost entirely men ranging in age from their late twenties to their early forties who are more cosmopolitan than the majority of Vanatinai people. They have often migrated to the mainland for a few years to work and then returned, speaking some English and understanding something of the outside world. Thus the new form of political authority— election to local government council, provincial assembly, or parliament—is effectively open only to younger males with the unusual qualification of having left the island and learned English. This disenfranchises virtually all women and male elders, including those who are giagia.

Local government councillors often perceive themselves as being in direct competition with the giagia. Atypical in having left the island to work for wages, they tend to possess few ceremonial valuables or pigs compared to other adults their age and are conspicuously inactive as a group in traditional exchange activities. In 1978 the Louisiade Local Government Council, whose jurisdiction was then the entire archipelago, passed a rule that mortuary feasts could only be held in December, with November tacitly understood to be a month of preparation that included sailing in search of valuables. Both government officers and local government councillors frequently criticize the islanders, and particularly the people of Vanatinai and the East Calvados for spending "all their time" in "sailabout" and traveling to feasts in distant communities rather than staying home, raising cash crops to pay their head taxes, and participating in government work projects when directed. Another regulation states that every Friday should be spent in government works such as repairing the government rest house each coastal settlement is supposed to maintain; it is almost always ignored. In spite of the new regulation the mortuary feasts of 1978–79 took place from September to April.

In 1987 the Provincial Executive Council, based at Alotau on the mainland of Papua New Guinea, passed a resolution instructing all the local government councils in Milne Bay Province to deal with the increasing problem of domestic and wild pig predations on food gardens. The Yeleyamba Local Government Council met in November 1987 to consider a regulation to limit the number of pigs owned per household: one number suggested was four. Pigs are one of the primary bases of the wealth of the giagia. Since Vanatinai exports pigs, fed on an abundance of sago pith, to islands as far away as Ware, 175 miles to the northwest, in exchange for greenstone axe blades and other valuables, the giagia, men and women, see this movement as another attempt to limit their power and influence by a group of men who are envious because they own very few pigs.

Protestant and Catholic church officials, except for the nuns at the Nimowa Mission, who are locally perceived as being subservient to the priests, are men, and they expect to deal with Vanatinai men. A minority are from Vanatinai. They are recognized as influential community leaders, even by nonchurchgoers, in spite of their youth (they are typically in their late twenties or early thirties). Another largely unenforced local government council regulation states that every Wednesday must be spent working for the mission on such tasks as cutting the grass in front of the pastor's house. Protestant and Catholic missionaries as a group are opposed to what they see as excessive participation in traditional exchange, and many are aware that mortuary feasts are in honor of ancestor spirits. Papua New Guinea's constitution states that it is a Christian nation. Not only the pastors, priests, and lay catechists but also the majority of the government officers and elected officials have been educated in mission schools. The ideological basis of the power and success of the giagia is in their ability to communicate with ancestor spirits to the benefit of themselves and their followers and the detriment of their enemies and rivals. The two forms of gaining authority over the islanders, the customary and the introduced, are often in open conflict with one another.

On Vanatinai the title of gia is awarded to any woman or man who is, as the islanders say, "strong, wise, and generous" enough to build a reputation through traditional exchange and acquisition of supernatural knowledge. The institution of the giagia, in a society with no chiefs, is part of an autonomous cultural tradition that is inherently democratic. It provides an avenue to prestige, renown, and influence over others to any adult, of either sex and from any kin group, who desires to exceed the minimum demands of custom for participation in exchange and mortuary ritual. Introduced avenues to power and influence such as working for cash off-island and returning or becoming a local government councillor or catechist or pastor are effectively closed to women.

There have been dramatic changes on Vanatinai since the voyage of HMS *Rattlesnake*. The most significant in terms of their impacts on gender relations are the suppression of indigenous warfare by British and Australian colonial enterprises, the loss of political autonomy, increased physical mobility, and the imposition of alien systems of law, politics, and religion upon the islanders.

As when the people of Vanatinai were brought under the control of the colonial government, the power of indigenous political and economic systems is being further eroded. The world cash economy and new religious ideologies have increased their influence, and the islanders have become more firmly a part of the nation state of Papua New Guinea. This increasing loss of cultural autonomy is inevitable. But government policies such as introducing systems of elected representation and of appointed administrators may inadvertently have narrowed the access to influence and a public voice by women and older men on Vanatinai.

Eleanor Leacock (1978) and others (e.g., Gailey 1987) have argued that in small-scale societies colonization and the advent of the nation state inevitably result in a diminution of the power and autonomy of women. This is too simplistic. Gender relations, and all power relations, must be situated in the context of the specific external forces that impinged on the society and on women versus men, on specific sequences of local historical changes, and the ways local cultural forms have been affected by transformation, adaptation, and resistance to forces of changes.[46]

Godelier (1986:195) writes that even among the Baruya—whose entire society is organized around the principle of male dominance and female inferiority—colonially imposed pacification and the loss of the male "monopoly of armed violence" has lessened the social distance between male and female. Similarly, it is likely that on sexually egalitarian Vanatinai, where women were prominent in public life and external relations in precolonial times, men's loss due to pacification of the chance to gain prestige by becoming an asiara has given more equality of opportunity to women to achieve renown through other customary means. Women may become a gia, or a respected healer, gardener, or ritual expert. It is through introduced means of achievement, such as becoming a local government councillor or a lay catechist or pastor, that men have a new advantage.

Clearly in some ways every individual on Vanatinai has lost a certain degree of autonomy. Every woman and man alike is now subject to externally imposed laws, compliance with which is supposed to be mandatory, and all face pressure to worship new supernatural beings and to exchange labor for cash for head tax, tithe, and goods at the tradestore. In precolonial times everyone's mobility was circumscribed by the danger of attack, but in theory no one could tell anyone else what to do. The principle of respect for individual autonomy remains extremely strong in Vanatinai culture, and this principle continues to underlie egalitarian social relations—including gender equality—on the island despite externally imposed systems of political, legal, and religious authority.

The islanders have consciously resisted the pressures to refrain from participation in customary avenues to respect, influence, and prestige such as ceremonial exchange, mortuary ritual, and healing. This resistance is overtly a statement of political and cultural autonomy, phrased in terms of the moral correctness of following the way of the ancestors (Lepowsky 1991). It preserves women's autonomy and influence by continuing to valorize participation by all adults, women and men alike, in these customs despite the pressures and allure of new systems of power from which women are excluded. Women, like men, are expected to participate in exchange and to acquire supernatural knowledge, and if they wish, they may try to become known as giagia.

The availability of education and English literacy on Vanatinai has dramatically increased recently, with the opening in 1984 of the first government primary school. In contrast to other parts of Papua New Guinea with customary ideologies of male dominance, parents are sending both their daughters and their sons to the school. The numbers of women who will seek education or employment off-island and then return home will therefore probably also increase in the near future. If they are encouraged and not opposed by government and mission officials, women in the coming years may have a greater opportunity than at present to gain prestige and power not only through traditional means but also through some newer ones, for there is no barrier in Vanatinai philosophy and custom to women having socially recognized power.

Chapter Three

Island Lives

Childbirth

Rara sat on the floor of the little house with her knees spread, wearing only her underskirt of shredded young coconut leaf and gripping the horizontal log bracing the wall in front of her. Each time she felt another labor contraction she gasped and cried, "*E noi!*" O mother! and the women who were attending her would wince in sympathetic pain. Her mother had died only a month earlier. Two of the women, Rara's father's sister and one of Rara's own kinswomen, sat in a row behind her. The first woman locked her hands under Rara's breasts and pushed her toes and the balls of her feet into Rara's lower back, near the base of her spine. The second woman similarly clasped the first under her breasts and pressed her feet into the lower back of the woman in front of her. If the house, built originally to accommodate visitors to a feast, had not been so narrow, the others would have joined the line of seated women. In unison, each woman carefully pressed on the lower back of the woman in front of her every time Rara's contractions came, the last women bracing herself against the far wall of the house.

Rara had already been in labor for six days, and her face was gray with pain and exhaustion. This was her first pregnancy. One of the women gently felt Rara's abdomen and whispered, out of her earshot, that the baby's head was still pointed sideways. Another woman gave her a tea of boiled sweet green leaves to drink to induce the birth. Later, a kinsman brought in a different medicinal tea boiled from the grass called *volevole*. Rara's husband and her father both came in for a while and left, their anxiety clearly visible on their faces. The women continued to pile wood on the already blazing fire, making the one-room house, with its doors and windows tied shut, unbearably hot.

As the line of seated women pressed their feet into each other's backs, sharing the labor of Rara's contractions, one of them, a childless middle-aged woman, said, "Having babies is too hard." Another immediately retorted, "Who will build your fire and cook your food when you are old?" The first woman replied that it did not matter. She herself had no children, she said, because her own mother had eaten a bark with contraceptive properties while she was a nursing baby, and she had drunk this bark with her mother's milk. I asked her whether she had used any of the locally recognized plant contraceptives herself, but she said no.

By the following morning the baby's head was pointing down, and Rara's contractions were at more frequent intervals. She was noticeably weaker. Her father came in and sat down beside her. He chewed a piece of ginger root and muttered a magical spell in a voice too low to be understood by anyone else. Then he carefully spit a fine spray of saliva onto Rara's stomach and back, saying, "Hurry up and come out! What are you waiting for?" The women in the room echoed his words. He continued, "Come out and we'll go make sago!" Sago-making is men's work on Vanatinai, so he seemed to be expecting a grandson.

The husband of one of Rara's kinswoman attendants then entered the house. He muttered a magical spell over a container of water with another piece of ginger root in it. He gave half of the charmed water to Rara to drink and poured the other half on her head. The women then gave her boiled volevole tea to drink.

Rara produced a small amount of amniotic fluid. Shortly afterward another young married kinswoman came in. She sat down and chewed a piece of ginger root, muttering a magical spell. Then she blew on her hands, rubbed Rara's stomach and back, sucked noisily on the small of Rara's back, and spit out a hard, greenish object. The other women leaned forward to look at it. They said this object had been sucked from Rara's body, where it had been obstructing the birth. Now she would be able to give birth without difficulty. They handed the object to me to examine. It had two small protrusions on it and smelled like the ginger the woman had been chewing. It might have been a vertebra that had turned greenish with age. Rara's father took it from me and left the house. I was told he was going to put it in a cold place, perhaps in the crotch of a tree deep in the forest. Meanwhile the young woman magician was retching, from having swallowed ginger, people explained.

The husband of Rara's kinswoman returned and repeated the charming of a section of ginger root that he chewed, spitting carefully on Rara's head and back, saying, "Come out! What are you waiting for? We are all waiting to see you!" Rara's husband came back a while later, chewed ginger root and muttered a magical spell, spit on his wife's body and called, "I am your father. Hurry up and come out! I want to see you!" He turned and left the room.

The baby, a large and healthy boy, slipped into the world half an hour later. Rara (not her real name) recovered, but she has never had a second child. Her abdomen has remained permanently distended from internal damage during her protracted labor.

Women's autonomy and power are revealed over their life courses. Ideas about socializing children, becoming adult, and living in old age are inevitably potent ideologies of gender. They enable us to contrast the roles, beliefs, and customs shaping the lives of females with those affecting males the same age and to focus on the restrictions and opportunities of each sex.

Consideration of sex roles requires the understanding of age roles as well. Sex and age are the primary criteria by which small-scale, technologically simple, supposedly egalitarian societies apportion responsibilities, work, and power, and by which they restrict certain privileges.[1] These two biologically based and culturally elaborated criteria cannot be considered independently. Although this is especially obvious in places where mature males are socially differentiated through initiation or other forms of age-grading from young men, boys, and females of all ages, it is true as well in cultures like Vanatinai that do not heavily stress principles of age and seniority.[2] In the last twenty years of new ethnographies of gender, with some notable exceptions (e.g., Godelier 1986), sex and age are rarely considered simultaneously.

There is no one social fact that can be labeled "the status of women." Nor is there any one key aspect of women's status—personal autonomy, control over the actions of others, ownership of the means of production—that may be compared across cultures to describe, or explain, women's position as fixed or absolute. There are instead many variables representing different dimensions, both material and ideological, of women's power, autonomy, and influence relative to men. Status and social position change in relation to the multiple fields of social and power relations in which they are embedded.

To evaluate the multiple statuses of women and men on Vanatinai, then, we should examine the actions, duties, and privileges characteristic of both sexes from early childhood to old age and the cultural ideologies and expectations associated with each life stage. Are they congruent or markedly different for females and males or as a person grows older? How are gender roles acquired and reinforced? Have historical changes affecting larger fields of social relations caused gender roles and ideologies associated with different life stages to change as well?

Conception, Pregnancy, and Birth

Vanatinai ghunoi see two reasons why the population of their island is so low. The first, they say, is that people are killed by sorcerers. The second reason is that the women of Vanatinai know and use a variety of plant substances as contraceptives. These include at least six kinds of leaves, barks, and roots taken orally, accompanied by the reciting of magical formulas, as well as the liquid of the pitcher plant, which is drunk "the morning after." With some of these a woman may not eat fish, or, it is said, she would conceive. These medicines must be "turned around" by countermagic and the ingestion of a certain bark for a woman later to conceive, a less widely known procedure usually done by a specialist, either female or male.

Some childless women flatly state that children are too much trouble or that they are afraid of the pain and the very real danger of childbirth. They are chided by others, as I heard during Rara's childbirth, and warned that there will be no one to care for them when they are old and helpless. Childless women are criticized by other men and women because they are believed to have chosen their state. More positively, some women have explained to me in private that they have the power to control child spacing, avoid pregnancy, and limit their number of children to one, two, or three. In the Jelewaga area, including outlying hamlets, there were five childless marriages (one polygynous) out of about forty couples in 1978–79.[3]

Children should be spaced several years apart, through abstinence and the use of contraceptives, so that "one is already playing with its friends" before a younger sibling is born. Ludi, the seventy-year-old grandmother who spontaneously advised me about this, pointed out a neighbor's three year old running around the hamlet to illustrate her point. Intercourse is taboo until a child is walking or else, people say, the child will fall sick or even die. This rule is widely violated, and various unhealthy-looking babies are referred to as evidence.

My women friends say that conception occurs only through repeated acts of intercourse with the same man. Intercourse with a variety of men, then, has a contraceptive effect. One young woman explained that this is why she changed her partners frequently. She, like other people, explained to me, in the tone of one giving useful advice to a naive but curious person, that it is not possible to become pregnant after having intercourse with a man only once or twice. I met few teen-aged mothers on Vanatinai. Most first pregnancies seem to occur when women are in their early twenties.[4]

There is occasionally a child with no publicly known father in a hamlet or village. No shame attaches to mother or child, although the children are considered unfortunate to have no father to love and nurture them, and neighbors speculate privately on who he is. Such a child will of course be part of the mother's lineage, just as any child is, and there is no term meaning illegitimate.

Women speak privately of several ways to induce abortion, principally through drinking magically enhanced scraped or squeezed barks in cold water. Drinking extremely hot water is said to be effective. Some people told me there is no custom of infanticide on Vanatinai: one woman said that if she did not want a baby, she would abort it and not carry it to term. Others pointed out several men in their sixties whose mothers had placed them as unwashed newborn infants in garden baskets left in forest trees because they had too many other children to care for. In each case another woman had gone and taken the infant and raised it as her own. Women in the East Calvados

Islands say that unwanted infants were placed in loosely woven coconut-leaf baskets, like those used to carry home betel nut, and thrown into the sea. I was told the name and home community of an adolescent girl from one of the East Calvados Islands who was saved from this fate and adopted after her mother had died in childbirth.

When a Vanatinai woman discovers that she is pregnant, she is supposed to refrain from having intercourse with her husband until after the baby is walking, retiring to sleep on a different mat on the other side of the room from him. Otherwise, it is said that her labor will be prolonged and difficult, as the baby "might feel ashamed to come out because it is dirty" from the semen on its head, which might cause the child to sicken or die.[5]

The principal birth attendants are usually women, but men are not barred from the scene of a childbirth. Both women and men may know different kinds of birth magic. The actual spells that they say to bespell certain substances are their personal secret. As in Rara's case there is often more than one magical practitioner present at a childbirth. It is not customary on Vanatinai for birth attendants to attempt intravaginal examinations or to press directly on the mother's abdomen, for such procedures are regarded as too dangerous to the child.

If the placenta is not expelled spontaneously after a birth, the attendants press gently on the mother's stomach with half coconut shells and recite an appropriate magical spell. The umbilical cord is cut with scissors, a razor blade, or a knife, although sometimes the traditional mangrove oyster shell is used. The infant is washed in warm water, and one attendant warms her hands by the fire and gently presses the baby's head, eyes, nose, and mouth "so that it will see its parents." The infant is placed on a mat. The placenta and cord are put in a basket of woven coconut leaf and placed secretly, usually by the father, in the crotch of a nearby tree, where they will remain until the basket rots away. The new mother is also bathed in warm water. She will sleep by the fire in the hot, dry air of the closed-off house, protected from supernatural attack, to strengthen her body with therapeutic heat.

Women on Vanatinai sometimes say that they prefer girl babies, who will grow up to help them. Men frequently state a preference for girl infants, particularly if their sisters and other kinswomen are pregnant. These girl babies, as adults, will give birth to new members of the man's matrilineage. Fathers and uncles may also say they favor boys, who in future will assist them in their work.

The desire for female infants as well as male, lack of a strong preference for sons, and evidence that both boys and girls have been abandoned in the past to be adopted by others, are significant evidence of prevailing ideologies of gender equality. The more explicit the cultural preference for sons, the lower the value of females, who are at greater risk than their brothers of being killed or neglected as infants and who are subordinated to fathers and husbands as adults.[6]

Childhood

The gender-neutral term *gama* (plural: *gamagai*) is used to describe a child of either sex from the time of birth until after puberty. Use of such an all-inclusive term reflects the overall lack of age-grading and sex differentiation on Vanatinai. Many other New Guinea societies use an elaborate set of terms to distinguish girls and, especially, boys of different ages.[7]

After a child is born the mother and infant must remain inside the house out of the potentially dangerous sight of others for a period of up to four or five months for a firstborn child or for a week or two following the birth of a later offspring. The mother presses on her belly with warmed half-coconut shells to expel the daily "bad blood." She does not work in the garden.

When she goes outside to eliminate she must wear a woven coconut leaf basket on her head and a coconut leaf skirt over her shoulders "so that no one will see her body." This custom is called *zogazoga*, and it is also followed by widows and other mourners after a death and during memorial feasts, the other point in the life cycle when the living are in closest proximity to death and to ancestor spirits. The new mother's husband will not comb his hair or cut his beard during this period of seclusion, customs, again, that are followed after a death. He will sleep in another corner of the room or in another house, for if he did not, the baby would get sick and have a big belly and small arms and legs. Both parents must refrain from eating meat or fish—for four to five months after the birth of a firstborn and for two weeks after the birth of a later offspring.

Sometimes a cord, magically treated, is strung twice around the house where a mother and her firstborn are secluded. This keeps out sorcerers and diseases such as scabies. It is cut at a small feast that takes place four to six months after the birth. The child's hair may also be cut for the first time on this occasion. During this feast, called *iragi*, or "(s)he goes out," pork and vegetable food are given to all the people who helped at the confinement. The kinfolk of the mother give one or two stone axe blades or bagi necklaces to the father in gratitude for his having sired another member of their matrilineage. All restrictions on food and movement are then lifted. This ceremony takes place after the birth of a firstborn, or sometimes after the birth of the first boy and the first girl in a sibling set. A firstborn is called *gamau*, and its parents refer to each other as *yagoau*.

The flow of valuables in the childwealth ceremony is the reverse of the bridewealth situation, when the husband's matrilineage contributes the same types and numbers of valuables—stone axe blades and a bagi—to the wife's matrilineage. Bridewealth on Vanatinai is said to compensate a woman's mother and mother's brother for their efforts in nurturing her and raising her to maturity. The husband's matrilineage does not gain any rights to her labor or claim to her future children. On the contrary, her matrilineage is entitled to brideservice, that is, labor by the groom for his mother-in-law. The childwealth payment, on the other hand, transfers certain rights over her husband to her matrilineage. It compensates the husband and his kin for the child he has helped to generate, which belongs to the wife's matrilineage, and secures the latter's claim to his future offspring born during the marriage.

Babies are named within a few days of a birth, often receiving several names. One is frequently that of a deceased member of their matrilineage, but they are also named after living kinfolk and friends of any age, or new names may be created for them.[8]

Food taboos on Vanatinai are more stringent after the birth of a firstborn, just as the custom of seclusion is more pronounced for a firstborn. The child and its mother seem to be regarded as being especially vulnerable to magical attack, sickness, and death. To protect the child's health, its mother should eat no animal protein foods at all except for clam, which is frequently boiled with wild greens. Some people say that this taboo lasts until the baby is big enough to sleep on its stomach with its arms in front of it and others say until the baby is walking. For a subsequent child most food taboos are lifted after three to four weeks, but mothers should not eat "European" food or "greasy" foods such as crab, eel, opossum, or pork fat until the baby is walking around habitually. A mother's eating pumpkin before then would make the baby's stomach swell. Violating these taboos is said to make the baby sicken or die, and old people frequently berate young mothers for their supposed dietary or sexual lapses when a baby gets sick (Lepowsky 1985b). Women say that they adhere to these customs because "we must respect our children, for we are living very far from hospitals." Several times a day nursing mothers may drink a tea brewed from leaves called *mwaoli* and *wadala* to increase their milk supply. These teas are also drunk by men and women as a general tonic, to reduce hunger, and to make one more able to work.

Babies are breastfed on demand. Semisolid foods are first introduced at about six months, but breastfeeding continues until about the age of three. Weaning is sometimes accomplished by smearing the nipple with ginger.[9] Relatives of babies and young children may perform special magic to make them grow well and be strong. Betel nut is chewed while a magical spell is uttered, and then the magician sprays charmed saliva on the child's head. A woman friend told me that, while this magic is effective, it may have the unwanted side effect of making children "silly," meaning that they may cry frequently and have temper tantrums.

People say that an infant must never be left to cry or "it might become angry and leave us." In other words, it might be so displeased by its treatment that it will die and join the ancestor spirits. This philosophy recognizes the autonomy and personal will of even the youngest members of society. The infant is therefore always picked up and consoled with the breast by its mother, or nuzzled and talked to by its father, matrilineal kin, or older siblings. It is bad for young children as well to cry, and this is why their wishes are often granted. If they are frustrated, even well beyond infancy, it is believed, they might get sick. Children are treated with respect, and their personal idiosyncrasies are tolerated like those of adults.

Childless couples and widowed old people frequently adopt or foster the children of relatives to assist them with the work of daily life.

This practice is referred to as *vaghan*, meaning "give food." Such children may remain with their adopted parents until they are adults, or they may alternate in residence between their adopted and natural parents. Adopted children retain the clan name, totems, and land rights of their natal matrilineage.

Even young children are aware of their social and economic value. One morning the mother of a six-year-old girl complained that she was tired of carrying her and her eight-year-old brother from the main room of the house, where they usually fell asleep on the floor shortly after dinner, into the tiny back room where parents and children normally slept. The little girl immediately retorted, "You had better carry us around without complaining, because we are the ones who will have to carry you around when you are old!"

Children generally begin to walk and talk in the months following their first birthday. They are treated with extreme indulgence by parents, older siblings, other kin, and neighbors. If a young child demands a choice piece of food from the portion of a parent or older sibling, he or she always receives it, and an older brother or sister who is reluctant or unwilling to comply is scolded. But children who find at an early age that almost anything they ask for will be given to them learn a few years later that they themselves must give without complaint to children only slightly younger than themselves.

Children as young as two or three are permitted to play with objects that Westerners consider dangerous, such as sharp knives, burning brands from the fire, or matches. When three-year-old Bunebune demanded the knife with which her mother was peeling yams and sweet potato for dinner, her mother sighed in exasperation but gave it to her, watching her play "peel the yam" for a full fifteen minutes as the sun set. This was even though the mother was tired from working in the garden all day, anxious to finish preparing the food so she could relax and eveyone could eat, and unable to continue making dinner until Bunebune returned the family's only knife. The mother (and I, with my Swiss Army knife) ended up peeling vegetables in the dark, our work lit only by the cooking fire. This permissiveness about relations with objects as well as people tends to produce assertive, confident, and competent children.[10]

Personality differences become apparent at an early age. Some one and two year olds are placid and rarely cry or speak, while others may initiate "conversations," call out to passers-by, or cry frequently. Children are taught very early the valuable social skill of requesting objects from others (cf. Schieffelin 1990). Even a three year old may be sent to the neighbors after the parents carefully rehearse with him or her what to say: "*Unga bwebwe inago ghelezi*" (you say that Daddy asks for betel nut). The earnest efforts of very young children to deliver such messages are considered charming and amusing by adults, but they are received with solemn and respectful attention.

Girl children are prevented by their mothers and female relatives from going naked by about the age of four, and women teach them to keep their genitals covered by their coconut leaf or cloth skirts while playing, sitting, or climbing ladders into a house. A small girl who is carelessly showing her vulva will have her skirts pulled down to cover it by an adult woman, who gently chides, "*Sisiga*" (naughty)! Boys begin to wear shorts or a piece of cloth wound around the waist at age four or five. Children continue to bathe naked in streams and lagoon in mixed groups until about the age of ten.

From the age of about five or six girls are entrusted with a variety of chores by their mothers and other kin. They are taught to carry the family's dishes and utensils (both customary and store-bought) on their heads to a stream below the hamlet and wash them, to fetch water, gather firewood, build the fire, peel vegetables, cook, wash clothing, and to care for their younger brothers and sisters during the day while their parents are working in the gardens or sago groves, fishing, or gathering. They also accompany their mothers or female relatives to the gardens and either care for younger children there or help with weeding or planting.

Boys of the same age and older are more likely to be left alone to play with their peers, and they are frequently found swimming in the sea, hunting for shellfish, fishing near the shore with spears or derris root, a fish poison, and cooking their catch, or foraging in the bush for wild fruits and nuts. Girls too participate in these expeditions. Children learn to share any food they obtain with each other, and they proudly return to the hamlet to give any surplus to their families. But boys are given chores as well. They are rarely made to wash dishes, but they sometimes collect firewood, and they occasionally help their parents in the gardens. Both boys and girls have learned by the age of six or so to build a fire, using an ember obtained from a neighbor, and peel and boil tubers or roast sago pancakes.

Little girls, like little boys, often play on their own rather than working at tasks assigned by adults. They too may be found swimming and playing boisterously in freshwater streams in the interior and in the warm, shallow waters of the lagoon, chasing each other, hunting for shellfish or wild fruits and nuts on their own initiative, or making long series of string figures. Boys and girls may play separately, but mixed groups of children of varying ages often range around the hamlet and surrounding areas. Children are generally left alone to play without adult interference unless they are needed for a specific task.

Boys as well as girls frequently care for younger siblings or the small children of other kin. Boy babysitters have rarely been reported in the cross-cultural record, and the common sight of a boy of eight or ten indulgently caring for his two- or three-year-old sister is evidence that childcare is not something restricted to females on Vanatinai, even though it is a female specialization. Early experience in taking care of small children prepares boys for their later role as father, a role in which the qualities of nurturing and giving are heavily emphasized in Vanatinai ideologies of interpersonal relations. In exchange for his paternal nurture, a man's children compensate his matrilineal heirs with ceremonial valuables in mortuary rituals after he has died.

Girls and boys patiently carry around and watch a younger child scarcely smaller than themselves. Child caretakers are kind and indulgent to their charges. Even older siblings who might complain and resist the demands of a younger child when the parents are present become nurturing and giving when they are entrusted with its sole care. Seven-year-old Warai tried to run off immediately after breakfast when his mother said she wanted him to look after his two-year-old sister while she went to the garden, a task his five-year-old sister had accepted without complaint for several days in a row. But once his mother and the five-year-old had departed, Warai played quietly with his baby sister, carried her around the hamlet, built a fire and cooked sago and coconut pancakes for their lunch, then put her down to sleep on a mat for her afternoon nap.

Mothers often take a very young child to the garden rather than leaving it in the hamlet with a caretaker. An older sibling comes along to watch the baby in the garden shelter, and the mother nurses it when it cries.

Very young children begin to imitate the activities of adults. A naked two-year-old girl collects a few dry twigs and carries them gravely into the hamlet on her head, the normal mode of carrying for women. She presents them as firewood to her mother, who receives them with equal solemnity. She asks her mother for pumpkin seeds to plant in the garden. Some of them sprout and grow. The resulting pumpkins belong to the small girl, and months later she is asked for permission to harvest them for the family dinner. Her mother is proud and privately predicts that the child will be an outstanding gardener in future.

Adults also instruct children in how to perform various tasks when they are slighly older. A five-year-old girl who lives most of the time with her father's mother and the old woman's sister, two elderly widows, regularly prepares meals, gathering firewood, building the fire, peeling the vegetables, and boiling them in a clay cooking pot. She also washes dishes in the stream below the hamlet and helps to weed the garden.

One of the only times I saw a little girl treated differently on the basis of her sex was when a six-year-old girl joined her brother and several older boys in throwing mock spears made of smoothed out, thin branches at a nearby tree trunk. Her mother finally noticed, after about twenty minutes of shouting and loud laughter, and came out of the house. She stood close to her daughter and said, irritably, "Are you a man that you throw spears?" (*Ghomoli gheni ugauye?*). The girl burst into tears and ran into the house, where she hid, crying, for most of an hour.

One of the only activities that Vanatinai women should not perform is throwing spears to kill animals or, formerly, human beings. There is no supernatural sanction for this proscription, but it is considered to be wrong because women should only give life, while men are the ones who take it. This ideological principle, and its contradictions, in a society where women hunt, are believed to have the power to kill through magic, and participated in warfare short of using spears, is discussed in chapter 4.

In 1978–79 only a third of the primary school-age children—those from about nine to fourteen—from the Jelewaga area attended school. At the time there were no government primary schools on the island. The closest school was at Griffin Point, eight miles away on the other side of the island, run by the Catholic Mission based at Nimowa Island and staffed by three young teachers from elsewhere in Papua New Guinea. The school children had to walk to the north coast every Sunday afternoon, wading through the sago swamps, fording several rivers, and hiking up a steep pass in the central mountain range, carrying on their heads their food for the week and a few belongings. They would make the return trip on Friday afternoon, spending Saturday in the gardens with their parents collecting food for the next week. Many parents justifiably said that this was too far to send young children and too long for them to be separated from their parents. Some said that they needed the children to help them at home. Others spoke of the dangers, not only the physical ones of the weekly journey but also of attacks from north coast sorcerers who might bear a grudge against a parent or other relative and take revenge on a vulnerable child away from his or her home district.

A few Jelewaga children attended the primary school on Nimowa Island on the Catholic Mission grounds, whose headmistress was a Papua New Guinean nun. Most children attending Nimowa School returned to the village only once a year during Christmas holidays. The handful of adults in their late twenties and thirties who had been to school for a few years had gone to Nimowa in the 1950s. Martin told me how he watched as the nuns pulled the traditional tortoise-shell earrings from the children's ears when they arrived. Children were forbidden to speak their own language on the mission grounds. When they were caught by the nuns, he said, they were forced to carry and stack heavy coral boulders in the hot sun for hours at a time until their hands bled and their bodies ached. When I asked an elderly nun, who had taught at Nimowa during the 1950s, about this, she said, "We were wrong. I know that now. But," she sighed, "they did learn such beautiful English in those days."

During the 1950s and 1960s there was a rudimentary United Church (Methodist) mission school at Jelewaga run by a resident Misiman pastor. Children were taught to speak in the Misima language so that they could understand the Sunday sermons, to write Misiman, and to read the Misiman Bible. The adolescents and young adults who had attended it for a year or more spoke disparagingly of it to me as being intended purely as a proselytizing device rather than as a source of education. A few children were also sent to the United Church mission school at Rambuso on the northeast coast.

Most of the school children attended for only a few years and then left after learning how to speak, read, and write a little bit of English and to do simple arithmetic. Those who complete Standard 6 take a government examination, and one third of them are selected to attend high schools (government, United Church, or Catholic) located about two hundred miles away in the Milne Bay region. Hardly any students from Vanatinai actually attend secondary schools. During 1978–79 there was only one high school student from the Jelewaga area, a girl, and she left after one year to return home. Even government high schools require an annual school fee of well over two hundred dollars, an impossible sum for almost every Vanatinai parent to obtain.

One prominent big man, whose nine-year-old daughter said he had forbidden her to go to school, told me in 1978 that if a government school was built in the Jelewaga area, he would send the girl to it. The mission school, he said, was too far and too dangerous, and its purpose was not to educate but to turn the children into Catholics.

Martin, as the local government councillor, had tried for many years to have such a school built, but the population of Vanatinai is so low and the number of school age children so small that if a school were built at Jelewaga, it would draw children from the southwest coast villages away from Griffin Point School. The priest and nuns at Nimowa told government officials and parents at a meeting I attended at the mission that opening a government school anywhere on the island would force the closure of Griffin Point and even Nimowa School as the number of students fell below the minimum number required by the government for its financial subsidy. Construction of government schools in the Vanatinai area was actively opposed by the mission on these grounds.

Finally, in 1984, the provincial government opened a primary school at Madawa, five miles from Jelewaga along the south coast, staffed by two dedicated and effective Papuan teachers, both male. It too is a boarding school. The parents must supply their children with food, but they can paddle over by canoe with garden produce in two hours, and relatives come and fish nearby for the children. By 1987 most of the children from Jelewaga and the southwest coast of the island were attending Madawa School, including adolescents who had never been to school before. In contrast to other parts of Papua New Guinea where there is a strong prevailing ideology of male superiority (Godelier 1986, Young 1971a, Brown 1979, Herdt 1990), parents were sending girls and boys in equal numbers. The big man who had said he would send his young daughter to a government primary school kept his word. At age sixteen, she was the star pupil of Standard 4 and hoped to persuade her father to allow her to go to the government high school on the mainland.

The Madawa Primary School is potentially the most significant change on Vanatinai of the past decade. It is dramatically increasing English literacy and may well add substantially to the migration of young people off the island in search of higher education and wage labor and to the following of newer avenues to prestige through jobs and political positions. It may also result in a lessening familiarity and satisfaction with island life among children who have spent the bulk of their time for many years in a boarding school, away from village subsistence and ceremonial life. The majority of schoolchildren will remain on the island as adults. But they will transmit a significantly different version of Vanatinai customs, including ideas about gendered behavior, and a different set of knowledge, values, hopes, and aspirations to their own children.

Gender identity on Vanatinai is primarily formed after puberty. Children of both sexes live substantially similar lives, greatly indulged by adults except when they must defer to the wishes of even younger children, playing together and working alongside parents of both sexes. Both boys and girls learn to nurture and share, and both are expected to want to. They have roughly equal responsibilities, but girls are slightly more closely tied to adults and subsistence tasks. Childrearing is characterized by its extreme permissiveness and by respect for personality differences. Parents tell children what to do, but when children sometimes refuse, a parent may accept this outcome with the expression commonly used to describe the behavior of an adult—"*Ibotewa*" (she/he doesn't want to). With this kind of upbringing Vanatinai girls and boys alike become competent at a young age, confident, autonomous, experienced in caring for and sharing with others, but highly individualized in their personalities and activities.

Youth

There is a specially marked period of gradual transition from childhood, with its lack of personal responsibility for action, and the attainment of full adulthood. At this point in the life cycle male and female persons are referred to by separate terms for the first time. This is the period during which individuals develop a more strongly marked gender identity and experiment with the power of their sexuality.

Construction of personal identity and the building of social competence during this life stage are closely related to the development of a person's sexual power. This period of the life cycle is culturally marked by the terms *zeva*, meaning "youth," for a male and *gamaina*, literally "child female," for a female. These terms are best translated as youth rather than adolescence. They extend from about age fourteen to the early or mid-twenties, often to the time of an individual's first marriage, if this does not rapidly end in divorce, and are contrasted to mature adulthood, when people are referred to as *ghomoli*, man, or *wevo*, woman.

Cultural definitions of youth emphasize the young person's beauty, sexual desirability, and resulting power over others. The young person also has considerable leeway in participation in adult subsistence activities. A youth is expected to be more irresponsible and erratic in work habits than mature adults and to be preoccupied with sexual intrigues. The Vanatinai period of youth bears clear resemblances to the traditional Polynesian adolescent or youth stage of life, *taure'are'a* and cognate terms, in the Marquesas (Kirkpatrick 1983), Tahiti (Levy 1973), and Samoa (Mead 1928). Translated as literally meaning "the time or period of pleasure" in Tahitian and as "wandering youth" in Marquesan, the analogous Polynesian life stage also emphasizing youthful irresponsibility and preoccupation with sexual desire and intrigue as well as the beauty and thus the power over others of young boys and girls. Gladwin and Sarason (1953) and Schneider (1953) describe a similar stage of life on the Micronesian islands of Truk and Yap, respectively.

Closer to Vanatinai and within the Massim region, Malinowski's (1929:51–55) descriptions of "the amorous life of adolescence" in the Trobriand Islands are famous in anthropology and beyond. He describes a named period of youth extending from puberty to marriage and the "happy, free, arcadian existence, devoted to amusement and the pursuit of pleasure" of "the flower of the village," in whose beauty their elders take a possessive pride. The recognition of youth as a separate stage of life and of love affairs as central to it is so developed in the Trobriands that there a "bachelors' house," the *bukumatula*, where young boys and girls cohabit as they choose. Similarly, in the Trobriands of a half century later, Weiner (1976) writes of the power of youthful beauty and their elders' encouragement of it. These examples suggest a widespread pattern among Austronesian Pacific cultures of a recognized period of youth emphasizing sexual activity and beauty and a reluctance to assume the subsistence and ritual responsibilities of mature adults.

A second widespread Pacific Island pattern of a recognized period of youth is a dramatic contrast. It occurs in many cultures of interior New Guinea and in the archipelagoes of Eastern Melanesia such as the Solomons and Vanuatu. Young boys are segregated from girls and women and undergo a rigorous, often years-long, series of initiation rituals. Physical contact with women—especially sexual contact—is believed to be polluting and dangerous to the youth's health, and even his life. The youth lives primarily in a male world.[11]

There are no initiation ceremonies or other rites of passage on Vanatinai for either boys or girls to mark the transition from childhood. A girl whose breasts have begun to develop—to be the size of betel nuts, in the island idiom—begins to called gamaina. A boy is called zeva beginning at around the same age, generally fourteen or fifteen. With no formal transition into adulthood, the time at which one is considered mature varies with individual personality and lifestyle. Marriage and parenthood do not necessarily confer adult status. Early marriages often lead rapidly to divorce, and the young people revert to an earlier lifestyle that they may have been reluctant to give up for the responsibilities and lessened freedom of movement of adult married life.

Nevertheless, young people feel pressures from adults to contribute significantly to the daily quest for food and to household maintenance. At age fourteen or fifteen a girl is expected to work diligently at the same tasks that adult women perform in order to aid her family. She should work regularly in the gardens, feed the pigs, gather shellfish and fish, forage for wild foods, weave baskets and mats, cook, clean, and care for children. Both young men and adults state that the most important quality to look for in a wife is someone who works hard, and young girls who are industrious increase their chances of a desirable marriage in later years.

Boys at the same age are also expected to work hard for their families. They help to clear new gardens, plant crops, make sago, hunt, fish, and assist in house-building. Again, girls and adults say that the best prospective husband is a young man who is a hard worker. I was told, for example, that a certain youth, then in his mid-twenties, had remained unmarried because he is lazy and rarely helps his parents, and that local girls consider him a bad risk. Boys are more likely than girls to be left to their own devices if there is no major project for which their services needed. Girls regularly participate in the tedious work of weeding and maintaining family gardens, but boys frequently spend the day in small groups away from hamlet or garden. They may return in the evening with fish, game, or betel nut or with an account of how they followed the trail of a wild pig for miles but failed to catch it. Individual boys and girls vary in their personalities, activities, and willingness to contribute voluntarily to the work projects organized by adult family members and neighbors.

Sometimes their mothers or the older men and women of a hamlet complain that local youths are not spending enough time working in the gardens and helping their families. On one such occasion my neighbors said that all the young men of the hamlet had neglected garden work and other subsistence-related tasks and instead were off in the forest having spear-throwing contests, throwing mock spears at tree trunks. They were publicly and loudly criticized, especially by one prominent middle-aged woman. Later, one old man laughed about it and said to me nostalgically, "I remember when I was a young man, we always used to practice throwing spears too, and our parents would complain."

Cultural elaborations of the biological fact of menstruation and menarche are particularly revealing of gender ideologies. Many New Guinea societies are well known anthropologically for their strong beliefs in female pollution and the danger to the well-being of people, particularly men, and things of female genital fluids, particularly menstrual blood. The danger imputed to this female substance mirrors and justifies cultural beliefs in female inferiority and the exclusion of women from key ritual and economic domains.[12] Feminist anthropologists have recently argued, though, that cultural beliefs in female pollution and the danger to people and things from menstrual blood may reflect attributions of female power, creative as well as destructive, and therefore should not automatically be construed as evidence of low female status (e.g., Gottlieb 1988).

The relative lack of cultural elaboration on Vanatinai of ideas about menstrual blood and the absence of beliefs in female pollution or danger is striking. Menstruation is called *wakinie*, which is also the adverb meaning "behind." It is probably also related to the word *waghena*, or moon. A girl's first menstrual period is treated no differently from her subsequent ones, and it is not publicly marked in any way.

Women do not work in their gardens or go near a garden while they are menstruating, for it is said that if they did wild pigs, birds, or other animals would devour the garden. When I asked why, I was told that perhaps the animals would smell the blood. This taboo is particularly strict at the planting of a new yam garden, when not only menstruating women but both men and women who have had sexual intercourse within the last couple of days are barred from participating in the communal planting activities. Both male and female genital fluids are in this context believed to be inimical to the future growth of the yam plants. Each represents human fertility and the power to create and nurture an infant. Semen forms a child's bones and menstrual blood the soft tissues of the body. But these human creative powers, both male and female, must be kept away from the newly planted yams.[13] The most important cultigen on Vanatinai, the yam is nourished during a public yam-planting ritual by the agency of a male or female expert appealing to the creative powers of ancestor spirits. The taboo against menstruating women and against men or women who have recently had sexual intercourse bars them not only from the actual planting of yams but from this ritual appeal in the new yam garden to supernatural powers. The generativity of people and of yams, both sometimes referred to anthropomorphically in garden ritual spells, should be kept separate during this crucial period. Other garden crops, and yams when they are already growing, continue to thrive if they are placed in contact with the fluids of human generativity and need not be kept separate from them. A menstruating woman who visits other kinds of gardens does not blight crops. Her blood flow attracts birds and animals to eat them, but the crops are not spoiled or polluted by physical or supernatural properties of menstrual blood or the woman herself.

The days of the menstrual period are usually relaxing ones for women and girls, who speak of them as a pleasant interlude when they are free from garden work. They wear many layers of their oldest coconut leaf or cloth skirts (or a combination) and may spend their time around the hamlet doing a few domestic chores, weaving baskets, or just chewing betel nut. They also make excursions into the forest to look for "mustard" (*dia* or betel pepper) to chew with betel nut, or down to the shore to look for shellfish. The foods they have collected or cooked are shared by fathers, brothers, husbands, and children.

Menstruating women are not secluded or kept away from either men or children. There is no belief that they are polluting or dangerous to other people. They also may have sex with men. This is a dramatic contrast to many interior New Guinea societies, organized around principles of male dominance and female inferiority, in which female genital fluids in general, and menstrual blood in particular, are believed dangerous or even lethal to men.

When I asked whether it was all right to have sex with a man while menstruating, my female friends said, "Of course! Why do you ask?" I answered, weakly, that I had heard that in the New Guinea Highlands, women could not sleep with their husbands while menstruating because they would make the men sick. The women laughed heartily, and one demanded, jokingly, "What kind of 'sickness' do they get? The same kind we have [i.e. menstruation]?"

It is customary for women not to bathe during menstruation, and their first bath afterward marks the end of the time during which they avoid garden work. Except for the taboo against going in or near a garden while menstruating and the taboo against participating in yam planting if one has had sexual intercourse in the previous few days, which applies to both men and women, Vanatinai women are not subject to any taboos on the basis of their sex.[14]

101

Youth is regarded by young and old alike as a relatively carefree time in which it is normal to indulge in intrigues with the opposite sex. Sexual activity on Vanatinai is regarded as a pleasurable activity appropriate for men and women from youth to old age. It is not believed to be dangerous or depleting of vital essence for either men or women, unlike in many parts of Melanesia where ideologies of male dominance are prevalent. The time at which boys and girls become interested in forming romantic and sexual alliances seems to vary with the individual. One twelve-year-old boy amused his family by passionately sighing the name of the object of his affections, an eleven-year-old girl whose older sister had briefly been married to his older brother. But the parents of girls up to the age of about fifteen or sixteen may explicitly forbid their sleeping with boys, saying that they are still too young, or as one mother put it, "too small," implying also the dangers of intercourse and pregnancy for someone physically immature. Parental disapproval of sexual activity may be particularly strong if the girl's lover is a boy of whom they disapprove. These parental prohibitions are usually ineffective.

Neighbors try to figure out which youth has crept into a house in the middle of the night, his breath smelling of ginger from the love magic he has just performed, to awaken a girl quietly and ask for her favors. She may have been forewarned of his visit or may have asked him to come, or he may be completely uninvited and just "trying his luck," as young people say. She may accept him, refuse him quietly so that he may slip away unnoticed, or rouse her sleeping family and the rest of the hamlet with her loud, indignant cries so that the rejected one slinks away in public humiliation, providing amusement to the neighbors for days to come. The accepted lover remains throughout the night, politely ignored by the other sleepers in the house. He slips away just before dawn, when the early riser is likely to spot shadowy figures climbing hastily down a house ladder pole and hurrying away with their heads down, clutching themselves in the damp chill. Remaining in a girl's house in the morning and publicly eating with her constitutes marriage.

Assignations arranged in advance frequently use a go-between such as an older child or a female cousin of the youth to send a verbal message that "X wants you." They may set up a nighttime visit or a daytime rendezvous away from the hamlet at which the go-between will stand guard for the couple against accidental discovery. Girls as well as boys initiate intrigues, generally sending a go-between with an invitation or, if they are confident enough, asking the boy directly.

All success in sexual intrigue at any age is attributed to the possession of effective love magic. Nowadays boys and girls may keep carefully guarded notebooks in which love magic and other magical spells, as for successful hunting, are written. Spells may be learned from friends or from adult relatives. One youth had been taught several powerful spells by his grandfather; he said that their potency was indicated by the fact that his grandfather used to sleep regularly with a fourteen-year-girl when he was in his sixties, an alliance that scandalized his contemporaries. A girl who had slept with a number of youths at a large feast on another island explained to me that her popularity was due to the fact that her uncle had carefully prepared the magically enhanced scented coconut oil with which she had anointed herself. Charmed, scented coconut oil, *bunama*, is used both in love magic and in the magic of exchange. In each case the prospective lover or exchange partner is said to be so overwhelmed with the beauty of the anointed one that he or she is helpless to resist, becomes dizzy with desire, and will give either him or herself or any valuable that the seeker desires.

In the practice called *buwa*, the first time parents or matrilineal kin discover a strange boy or man inside their house in the middle of the night lying asleep on the mat next to an unmarried girl or woman they quietly put a small basket at the head of the sleeping couple. It is filled with items such as shell currency pieces (daveri), mother-of-pearl scrapers (*gile*, a ceremonial valuable), fabric, tradestore plates, silverware, money, or sometimes even shell currency necklaces (bagi) or greenstone axe blades (*tobotobo*). The man, usually waking later in consternation after a deep sleep, takes the basket to his parents and matrilineal kinfolk. He is not supposed to keep these valuables but to return the basket with an equivalent number of the types of valuables that the woman's kin originally placed in it contributed on his behalf by his own kinfolk. These items are distributed among the woman's kin, particularly her mother and mother's brother, and do not go to her. After giving a buwa payment, the man and woman may sleep together without further compensation for as long as is mutually agreeable to the couple.

People stressed to me that buwa is in no way related to marriage or bridewealth. It goes to a woman's kin because they "worked hard to feed her." Lovers of prominent older divorced or widowed women may also give buwa to the woman's kin or to the woman herself, sometimes a shell-disc necklace, a valuable gift that is a source of pride to the woman. Buwa "is paid to the house." It cannot be demanded if a couple meets clandestinely in the forest or on the shore, a strategy that is thus favored by many young men.

"Putting out the basket" for a buwa payment is also a way in which a girl's kin may discourage return visits from a suitor who is not seriously interested in her or whom they do not consider worthy. One disconsolate youth had collected buwa baskets from the families of girls in several different hamlets and was unable to pay on all of these obligations.

Parents may deliberately refrain from "putting out the basket" if they wish to encourage the suit of a particular man or boy. The people of the closely related hamlets of Araida and Pamela in central Vanatinai agreed not to put out baskets for buwa payments when their young people slept with each other, which has the effect of encouraging courtship among the boys and girls of the two communities. One big man who had recently returned from a long exchange voyage assigned the youths who had served as crew to sleep in the same house as his unmarried teen-aged daughter during a feast he sponsored, and he did not put out any baskets when a few of them slept with her.

The East Calvados Islanders do not share this custom of buwa, and their youths who visit Vanatinai during exchange voyages or feasts complain that they feel inhibited about sleeping with local girls because they might be caught and forced to pay. If they do not pay they say they might be victims of sorcery attempts. Buwa payments are occasionally made publicly, particularly at feasts. Early in the morning at one feast the kin of a boy who had slept with a local girl the previous night marched into the girl's hamlet in single file bearing five clay cooking pots, two garden baskets, cloth, and shell currency. People pointed out the boy and girl in question, sitting at opposite ends of the hamlet looking mortified.[15]

It is also customary for men and boys to give love gifts (*mwadai*, literally, "its price") to their paramours. As one girl explained to me, "If you sleep with boys, they might give you some tobacco or money, but if you sleep with big men (giagia), they will give you shell currency necklaces (bagi) and greenstone axe blades (tobotobo)."

There is no ritual or institutional homosexuality on Vanatinai. When after a long period of residence on Vanatinai and adjacent islands I had heard nothing about individual acts of or dispositions toward homosexuality (although I heard of one alleged case of father-daughter incest on another island), I asked some trusted friends if there were any men or women who slept with members of their own sex. They seemed sincerely puzzled and amused at the idea and asked me why anyone would bother when intercourse with the opposite sex was so enjoyable. By contrast, homosexuality is institutionalized for young males in some Papua New Guinea societies with an ethic of male dominance and an extreme ideology of female pollution and belief in the danger of heterosexual activity.[16]

Vanatinai is an area of low population with small, dispersed settlements, and young people frequently find that their choices of sexual and potential marriage partners near home are severely limited by the local definitions of incest. It is taboo for members of the same clan to marry or cohabit, even if they cannot trace any relationship or if they come from different parts of Milne Bay Province. Marriage with members of one's father's clan is also improper, particularly in cases where there are known kin links between the individuals and where they would otherwise be known as cousins (ivaiye). Large memorial feasts (zagaya) therefore provide one of the most important opportunities for young people to meet eligible potential mates with whom they may arrange liaisons and determine their possible compatibility.

Only about 3 percent of the population of Vanatinai—about sixty individuals—reside away from the island. The majority are young men working at unskilled labor for the government or private individuals at Bwagaoia on Misima Island, or at the provincial capital of Alotau on the mainland. Some young men find work as crewmen on government and commercial vessels. A few young people are studying at high schools or at the government vocational school at Bwagaoia or at the Catholic Mission vocational school at Sideia, near Samarai. Only a handful of people have obtained postsecondary training, but their numbers include primary school teachers, university graduates, a government auditor, an instructor in adult education at Lae University of

Technology who formerly worked for the United Nations in Thailand, and students of navigation and of fisheries management.

Most young people remain on the island and in their home communities. A dozen young men are employed at Tagula Station as unskilled laborers, cutting the grass on the airstrip and maintaining the government buildings. In 1978–79 a few others worked at three coconut plantations, one locally owned, on Vanatinai, but these were all defunct by the early 1980s. Several young women work in the convent at the Catholic Mission on Nimowa Island.

When adult men and women go to visit an exchange partner, they make themselves beautiful by decorating themselves with bunama, flowers and aromatic leaves tucked in their hair and their woven armlets, and fine shell-disc necklaces. Augmented by powerful magical spells, their appearance dazzles their exchange partner, whether male or female, who becomes negenege, dizzy with desire, and hastens to give away any ceremonial valuable the visitor requests, even against his or her conscious will. This sexually charged power, expressed in the idiom of seduction, is the key to renown and influence over others through a reputation as a person successful in exchange, accumulating valuables and then publicly giving them away in elaborate mortuary feasts. The power to seduce others into doing what one wants through one's personal aura of beauty and desirability is first learned during youth, the stage of life in which Vanatinai individuals first become fully gendered persons. Boys and girls use their newly acquired physical, mental, and magical power to incite desire in potential sexual partners. As adults they may not only refine their skills of seduction and magic to attract and retain sexual partners, licit and illict, but extend their skills to the metaphorical seduction of exchange partners.

On Vanatinai, as in the Trobriands and the rest of the Massim, Polynesia, and parts of Micronesia, youth is part of a longer period of gradual transition from the irresponsibility of childhood to the sobriety and hard work of adulthood. Industry in the young is admired but not insisted on. Young people are expected to have sexual liaisons, and they go through most available potential spouses until eventually settling down with a compatible one. Marriage is by choice, and early divorce is frequent and not stigmatized. The largely symmetrical opportunities, freedoms, and responsibilities of both sexes on Vanatinai in work responsibilities, courtship, and personal freedom during the period of youth continue into mature adulthood and mirror the egalitarian ethic of Vanatinai culture. This ethic encompasses both males and females, and it emphasizes personal autonomy and the power of individual will, a power first fully exercised in youth.

Adults

The terms for adult man and adult woman, ghomoli and wevo, also mean male and female. There is no clear-cut point of transition into adult status on Vanatinai. Not only do no initiation rites exist but there are no activities forbidden to younger people, and no men's houses or areas of the hamlet are set aside for adult men or women.[17] Young people are considered to be adults once they have entered into a stable marriage. But since people frequently marry several times before they enter into a lasting relationship, recognition of adult status is a gradual process that is only retroactively attributed to the effect of what turned out to be an enduring marriage.

A couple is considered married when they begin to cohabit openly. Instead of slipping away before daybreak, a young man will remain and eat the breakfast that his new wife has cooked. Unmarried couples do not eat together. Young people almost always choose their own mates. Since first marriages often do not endure more than a couple of months or years, a marriage arranged or suggested by parents who, for example, were exchange partners would only be successful if the couple were personally compatible.

Most people marry for the first time in their early twenties. A few individuals choose never to marry, although they may have liaisons from time to time. About 90 percent of marriages on Vanatinai are between people from Vanatinai itself, and there is a tendency toward regional endogamy, as most people choose marriage partners from their own western, central, or eastern section of this fifty mile long island with its several distinctive dialects.[18]

The new husband is expected to spend anywhere from several months to more than a year in brideservice, living with and working for his wife's parents in the garden, making sago, fishing and hunting. He is said during this period to be "working for his mother-in-law." During this time his in-laws evaluate him and decide if he is a good worker. If they find him lazy or uncongenial, they will launch a campaign of criticism against him, complaining to other relatives and neighbors and to his wife. She will ignore any such remarks if she is still passionately attached to him (which others will attribute to the power of his love magic), but if she herself is doubtful about her choice of spouse, familial pressure will likely contribute to a divorce.

Later on in their marriage the couple normally alternates between living with the wife's kin and the husband's, sometimes for part of a year and, in other cases or other phases of life, for several years at a time. They plant gardens on land to which this spouse has rights, assisting others in the hamlet with their gardens, making sago, building or repairing houses, or other tasks, then relocating with their offspring to the natal hamlet of the other spouse and planting gardens there. Couples return to each hamlet to maintain and harvest their gardens. This pattern of bilocal residence is only possible if both spouses come from Vanatinai or a nearby island. Bilocal residence means that both wives and husbands maintain close social ties with their own and their fathers' matrilineages and actively retain their rights to land as well.[19] If the kinfolk of one spouse have access to more ample or desirable land, the couple is likely to spend more time living there or to settle there more or less permanently. But Vanatinai people, who have plenty of land and a low population, are characterized by their residential mobility and fluidity.

The Vanatinai postmarital residence ideal of bilocality contrasts with the pattern found in the closely related cultures of the Misima- and Saisai-speaking islands to the north and west. There the ideal pattern is virilocal residence. The wife goes immediately to live with her new husband's parents, which on Misima and Panaeati is ideally his father's residence.[20] This difference in custom is quite significant as both a reflection and a support of a greater degree of female autonomy on Vanatinai. Schlegel (1972) finds woman-centered residence one of three factors most highly correlated with a stronger position of women in matrilineal societies. Beginning a marriage with the husband coming to live with his wife, working for her mother, as Vanatinai people phrase it, and showing deference to his in-laws, privileges the young wife in contrast to her spending her married life residing with or next to her husband's kin.

When the new husband goes to live with his wife's parents, his kin begin to assemble the ceremonial valuables necessary for the bridewealth, or *vazavó* (literally, toward the woman). It is customary for the groom's parents and matrilineal kin to present the bride's parents and matrilineage, particularly her mother and mother's brother, with a fine bagi and two long greenstone axe blades of the kind called *giazagu*. Ten smaller greenstone axe blades (*tawai* or *bwam*) may be substituted for the two giazagu.

Some long-married husbands have never paid their bridewealth. This may be a source of friction in marital quarrels. Bazi, when she was angry with her husband, to whom she had been married for about fifteen years, used to shout for the whole hamlet to hear, "You never gave my parents any tobotobo for me!" In addition to meaning greenstone axe blades, tobotobo is also a generic term for ceremonial valuables. Her anger derived from her husband's failure to valorize her publicly through the ritual presentation of valuables to her mother and matrilineal kin.[21]

A short bridewealth presentation ceremony typically takes place several months to several years after the couple begins to live together, after it seems evident that the marriage will survive. Bridewealth is often transferred after a young wife becomes pregnant. The man's parents and matrilineal kin kill and cook a pig and cook vegetable food, then present the food and valuables to the wife's kin, ideally to her mother and mother's brother. The valuables have been obtained by activating the exchange relationships of each of the man's parents, his mother's brother, and their matrilineal kin. The woman's parents and maternal uncle will subsequently present baskets of garden produce, especially fine yams that can be used as seed stock, to the husband's matrilineal kin.[22]

The bridewealth necklace and axe blades are valuables that compensate a woman's mother and mother's brother for their labor in nurturing her. After marriage the woman's labor and her companionship will be partially detached from her matrilineage and redirected toward her husband and his kin, and she and her husband will have reciprocally exclusive rights to each other sexually. The husband's labor for the wife's matrilineage, in brideservice and afterward, and his sexual labor in providing the wife's matrilineage with children, will be formally compensated later—after the wife gives birth—in the childwealth payments of ceremonial valuables that flow from the matrilineal kin of the wife to those of the husband.

The two affinal lineages will continue to call on each other as needed, throughout the lives of the married couple and beyond, for labor such as garden clearing and yam planting and for ceremonial valuables to satisfy individual or lineage mortuary ritual obligations. Bridewealth on Vanatinai is merely the opening round in a series of reciprocal affinal exchanges that continues even beyond the deaths of the married couple, ending only with the completion of the mortuary ritual sequence at the deaths of a couple's children.

Sanday's (1981:164–165) definitions of male dominance and gender equality include the presence or absence, respectively, of male violence against women. In Schlegel's (1972) cross-cultural study of matrilineal societies, "absence of punishment of the wife," along with matrilocal residence and "positions held outside the home" are found to be strongly correlated with "high female autonomy." Violence against women on Vanatinai is rare and abhorred. In the 1950s a Pantava man killed his wife and dumped her body in the lagoon. I heard of no cases, past or present, of rape. Wife beating is rare and is strongly disapproved of. In one case about two generations ago a man assaulted his wife and caused a serious head injury. Her kinsmen in retribution killed almost every single member of the husband's lineage, which today consists of only a few people. In 1978–79 one husband hit his wife in the face and broke her jaw after accusing her of infidelity. His action was considered reprehensible.

Husband abuse is also rare, but it too takes place. During the same year of 1978–79 a jealous young wife broke her husband's wrist and burned his chest with a firebrand. In both of these cases village gossip held that the violent spouse had in fact been committing adultery and that the injured spouses were innocent. Both spouse abuse victims remained married for several more years, during which there were no further acts of violence, but both couples were divorced when I returned to the island in 1987. A husband who beats his wife is likely to be the victim of a sorcery attempt by her mother's brother, brother, or father.

Adultery is disapproved of, but if it is discovered it may be ignored or the adulterer may be forgiven by the spouse, although sometimes an angry quarrel ensues. There is no disparity in cultural ideology or actual practice in treatment of male versus female adulterers. A husband has no license to beat an adulterous wife. His only recourses are to resort to love magic to bind her to him or to divorce her, the same options she has. Gossip attributes acts of adultery to both sexes in approximately equal numbers.

Divorce may occur when a couple ceases to cohabit. Either spouse may initiate it and for any reason. If bridewealth has been paid the wife's family frequently discourages the divorce, for they will have to repay the valuables to the husband's family if the couple separates permanently. This is true even if it is he who is at fault or he who chose to leave and take a different wife, because he will need the bridewealth valuables to give to his next wife's family. Since the original bridewealth valuables are usually long gone to satisfy other exchange obligations, the wife's kin would therefore have to collect replacement valuables from their exchange partners. This gives them an incentive to counsel restraint and patience to the couple and is an important reason why bridewealth is only paid in the first place when it looks as if a marriage will be a lasting one. Childwealth is never repaid.

Couples sometimes separate for months or even years following a quarrel, but if they say they are still married, and if they satisfy any obligations to aid their affines, people refer to them as married, and any children that the wife has subsequently are said publicly, if not privately, to have been fathered by the husband. The usual grounds for divorce is suspected or actual infidelity. Other couples divorce because one of the partners is said to be lazy and not fulfilling his or her economic obligations. Children generally remain with the mother after a divorce, but there is no set rule, and sometimes the parents will alternate custody of children.

In the late 1970s there were only two polygynous marriages in the Jelewaga area and two formerly polygynous marriages interrupted by the death of one or more parties. One was a case of sororal polygyny. Even co-wives who are not related are supposed to call each other "my sister" (*gavagu*). Co-wives live in the same house with their husband if they are compatible or in separate houses if they cannot get along. A husband is supposed to have his first wife's consent in order to take another wife, but this consent is not always forthcoming. In one case a local big man, aged about fifty, told his wife of twenty-five years that he planned to marry his mistress, a younger widow from a nearby hamlet, and bring her to live with him. His wife hit him and threatened to leave him if he did, and he subsequently dropped his plans to take a second wife (and broke off his affair). A very few men in past years had as many as five wives at the same time. Only wealthy, energetic, and ambitious men are polygynous, because having two or more wives means taking on two or more sets of affinal obligations.

Marriage on Vanatinai unites more than just two individuals. Whenever the kin of one spouse want to clear a new garden, plant yams, build or repair a house, satisfy exchange obligations, or host or contribute to a memorial feast, they call upon their affines to assist them with labor, vegetable food, pigs, or ceremonial valuables. For this reason young men say that only a hard-working and well-connected youth will marry the daughter of a big man or big woman, because such people will constantly expect their son-in-law and his kin to assist them in the economic and ritual activities that they initiate and participate in. Following a death it is the spouse and his or her kin who bear the brunt of the mourning restrictions and who are obliged to contribute the most heavily to the series of memorial feasts.

The sensitivity of affinal relations is underscored by the custom of name avoidance. People may never speak the name of any of their in-laws, and if their names are also common vocabulary words, as sometimes happens, these words must never be spoken either. Affines may be addressed as "in-law," "X's husband," "Y's wife," "Z's mother" or "Z's father," or simply *"yola na"* or *"amalá na"* ("that woman there" or "that man there").

Marriage with members of the father's lineage is forbidden, as are sexual liaisons (although the latter rule is sometimes violated clandestinely). In other ways the father's matrilineage is treated by his children in a manner analogous to relations with affines. As a sign of respect a father's kin should not be addressed by name. But while people are expected to work hard for a spouse's matrilineage, they expect members of a father's matrilineage to give food, household goods, or ceremonial valuables when asked. Father's kin will be compensated for their generosity after their "child" dies, during mortuary rituals.

Youthful and adult brothers and sisters must also show each other respect, particularly avoiding mentioning sexual matters in one another's presence or leaving the room if a third party unthinkingly begins to discuss a sibling's sexual life. They call each other *logu*, a gender-neutral term meaning cross-sex sibling, rather than by personal name. Brothers and sisters should not walk in front of each other. These rules formalize the mixture of intimacy and avoidance unique to the relation of brother and sister. They support each other throughout life, and a brother is tied to the reproductive outcomes of his sister's sexuality, his matrilineal heirs and symbolic replacements in the next generation. But each sibling's sexual nature is otherwise deeply taboo.

The Sexual Division of Labor

The sexual division of labor for Vanatinai adults, young people, and children features a marked overlap between the tasks considered appropriate for men and for women, as predicted for egalitarian societies.[23] Both Vanatinai women and men tend and harvest yams, the most highly valued cultigen, sweet potato, taro, manioc, banana, and other garden crops, and individuals of both sexes know various forms of garden magic, including the magic used in the annual yam planting ritual.

A woman is referred to by both sexes as "the owner of the garden," or *ghuma tanuwagai*. Women and men together agree on where and when to clear land for a new yam garden and on how big it needs to be for subsistence and exchange purposes. Men cut tall forest trees to clear land for new gardens, but the work party is comprised of men and women, and the women cut the smaller trees and shrubs and supervise the burning of the forest cover. Men normally loosen the soil to form mounds for planting yams using eight foot digging sticks, but I have observed women performing this task. Women generally do the actual preparation and planting of seed yams, and they take the major responsibility for maintaining the gardens.

Both sexes plan the nature and extent of the coming year's gardens and plant them, but women do most of the daily garden maintenance, although certain men too are renowned for their industry in gardening. Food is harvested, usually by individual women, when it is ready. Yams are the only annual crop, and the only root crop which it is possible to store for many months. They are harvested by both women and men along with the appropriate magic and may be stored in small yam houses constructed either in the garden or near the hamlet.

Men weed and harvest gardens according to individual temperament and household needs. Men have primary responsibility for working sago. They do most of the pounding of the sago pith to extract the starch, a major dietary staple, but again the work party is usually mixed, and women supervise the drying of cakes of sago starch over a low fire.

Both women and men forage for a wide variety of wild nuts, legumes, tubers, fruits, and leaves in the rain forest, although women generally spend more time foraging than most men. Foraging, and being in the forest, is considered more enjoyable than weeding gardens in the hot sun.

Both women and men collect shellfish, fish in the lagoon with monofilament line from shore or from a canoe, use derris root to stun and collect fish trapped in shallow pools in the coral, and fish in the inland streams for freshwater fish, prawns, and eel. Men fish with spears in the lagoon at low tide during the day and using torches of dead coconut leaf at night. More rarely, men hunt crocodiles at night with torches and spears, or spear dugong in the lagoon shallows. The amount of time a person spends fishing and collecting shellfish varies tremendously according to whether the individual likes to fish and not according to sex.

Both men and women care for domestic pigs. If a woman owns and raises a pig, it is she who decides whether or not to contribute for a memorial feast or other occasion to satisfy her personal exchange obligations.

Killing human beings with spears or greenstone axes was a former monopoly of men. Hunting with spears, for wild pig, dugong, and crocodile, is also an exclusively male activity. But Vanatinai women hunt as well, without using spears. They hunt opossum, flying foxes, and fruit bats by climbing forest trees or tall coconuts to sneak up on the slow-moving nocturnal marsupials. Women also hunt monitor lizards, which grow to four feet in length, by climbing tall mangrove trees or by setting traps for them.[24]

In many parts of the Pacific, women are not supposed to climb trees, but on Vanatinai women climb not only to hunt but to obtain coconuts or betel nuts. Women fish using a fishing line or derris root, a fish poison. Formerly both sexes fished using nets woven by men of the fibrous aerial root of the wild pandanus palm. Both women and men gather shellfish in streams and along the fringing reef. Both dive in the lagoon for giant Tridacna clams. More rarely women dive for the blacklip or goldlip pearlshell, which may be sold to traders, or for the red-rimmed oysterlike shells made by both men and women into the shell-disc necklaces that circulate throughout the Louisiade Archipelago and the kula ring as far as the Trobriand Islands.

Men do most of the work of building houses. Women participate by collecting sago leaves for roofing and by weaving sago leaves for one type of wall. They must also provide the builders with cooked food. A few men also make outrigger paddling canoes and, more rarely, sailing canoes, but both men and women paddle and sail them. Although men and male youths more frequently make up the crews of sailing canoes, some women are expert sailors and make trips on their own or with other women to gardens and water sources. Both sexes frequently paddle and pole canoes. In the East Calvados Islands, with their strong maritime orientation, women spend most of their time in garden work while men sail to trade, fish, and make sago on nearby islands.

Men carve ceremonial axe handles and lime spatulas of wood and delicate tortoise-shell lime spatulas. Both men and women manufacture shell-disc necklaces. Women weave pandanus sleeping mats, fine coconut-leaf betel nut baskets, and coconut-leaf skirts. All these items circulate in interisland exchange and during mortuary feasts.

Daily cooking, washing, fetching water and firewood, and sweeping are primarily female tasks, but men occasionally perform each of them. Men and women both fetch water and firewood and cook during feasts and other communal occasions such as roofing or yam planting. Men butcher and boil pork, scrape coconut meat, and prepare the boiled sago and green coconut pudding. Women prepare the stone oven for roasting vegetable food.

It is always the woman's job to clean up pig droppings around the hamlet every morning, using a piece of sago bark and a coconut-rib broom. In many cases they are the owners of the pigs. An angry meeting of village men took place to complain when a teacher in the primary school at Griffin Point, who came from another part of Papua New Guinea, assigned both boys and girls to clean up pig droppings from the school grounds, and the job was afterward given only to the girls.

Women are responsible for sweeping the hamlet ground, or *bakubaku*, every morning, for cooking, for fetching water, fetching saltwater (for salting food), gathering firewood, washing dishes and clothes, and caring for children, a responsibility that is often delegated to older siblings or grandparents. Older brothers, fathers, mother's brothers, grandfathers, and other male relatives often play with children and carry them around, but they do this only when they feel like it.

Both men and women are tender and indulgent parents, but the care of young children is primarily the responsibility of women. Because a father and child belong to different lineages, his nurturing is perceived as a gift rather than an obligation of kinship. Men are frequently seen carrying around their offspring or maternal nieces or nephews, and they often take older boys and girls with them to the garden for the day or on gathering expeditions. People explain that the reason why a father's matrilineal kin must be compensated with valuables when someone dies is that the deceased excreted upon the father as an infant and the father cleaned it up uncomplainingly.

Exchange and the Life Cycle

Every individual from young adulthood to old age has obligations to contribute labor, food, pigs, or ceremonial valuables upon certain occasions, particularly to aid kin and affines who may be hosting or attending a mortuary feast. Death comes early to many people on Vanatinai, from infant and child mortality due to malaria, from childbirth, and from infectious diseases such as pneumonia and tuberculosis (Lepowsky 1990c). Genealogies often show that half the offspring of one couple died in infancy or childhood, and young adults and middle-aged people occasionally die suddenly and mysteriously. It is likely therefore that by the time an individual reaches adulthood he or she will have lost several close kin or affines and participated in the years-long series of mourning restrictions and feasts.

Young people begin their exchange careers by producing food-stuffs and household goods for use at feasts, for less spectacular exchange purposes dictated by kin responsibilities, and for home consumption: yams and garden produce, sago, pigs, skirts, mats, and baskets. All of these objects may be generated by the labor of an industrious young man or woman, who by doing so gains a reputation as a hard worker and therefore as a desirable marriage partner.

The unmarried young in their teens and early twenties are also expected to work hard at the many tasks of the zagaya itself. Sometimes their kin or the host of a feast will reward their effort with a valuable such as a greenstone axe blade. Every worker is fed well and given uncooked food to take home afterward. Young adults may request ceremonial valuables from their matrilineal kin, father's kin, or parents' closest exchange partners to contribute to a ritual obligation such as a feast or bridewealth. They will be expected to repay the debt with an equivalent valuable at a later time when asked. Another way in which a young person of either sex enters the ceremonial system is by raising a pig to maturity and contributing it to a feast or in exchange for valuables such as greenstone axe blades.

There is no difference in the obligations of men and women to provide food or valuables upon ceremonial occasions. When an exchange obligation arises, women as well as men may set off in quest of ceremonial valuables, leaving children, husbands, gardens, and household responsibilities behind.

A few adults refuse to participate at all in exchange. Some people of both sexes choose to contribute only the minimum expected by custom. Others strive to give more yams, more bundles of sago, more pigs, and more valuables and to host and organize more feasts for dead kin or affines, earning the title gia. The amount of energy that men and women expend in exchange-related activities is largely a function of individual personality. But the offspring of big men and big women—people with successful exchange careers and generally people with rights to large tracts of good garden land—have an advantage. They will inherit the land, ceremonial valuables, and exchange partners of their parents and matrilineal kin.

They will also closely observe successful exchange activities and their nuances from an early age. The ten-year-old daughter of one big man had already circumnavigated Vanatinai on her father's sailing canoe three times, accompanying him on exchange expeditions and attending feasts. She had also visited several of the East Calvados Islands. By contrast, some middle-aged people from the Jelewaga area had never visited the eastern settlements of the island or any neighboring islands.

A reputation as a big man or big woman is not gained by any one act of generosity in exchange or even by hosting one memorial feast or zagaya. A cycle of personal exchange activities develops as an individual matures and takes on new social responsibilities. By their twenties many young people, married and unmarried, contribute ceremonial valuables as well as foodstuffs to feasts as individuals and develop their personal networks of exchange partners. But people in their thirties to early sixties tend to be most widely known for their wealth, skill, and knowledge about exchange. Not only the mothers but the fathers of young children are inhibited by the fear that envious sorcerers or witches may take revenge by injuring or killing their children. Parents of young children also refrain from extensive exchange activities because of their extra subsistence and childcare obligations.

Women on Vanatinai have the opportunity, if they wish, to build their personal reputations as giagia through exchange activities. If they do not choose to exert the effort, they, like Vanatinai men who do not choose to build their reputations through the exchange of valuables, may gain the respect of their peers by taking good care of their families, growing good gardens, or helping their neighbors through their skill in healing.

Mortuary and other exchanges on Vanatinai are a primary means of gaining prestige and symbolic capital available to both men and women, but it is up to the individual to decide whether regionwide renown and influence is worth the trouble. Experts in exchange, healing, or gardening must be "strong," whether they are male or female: willing to take risks and engage in persistent hard work beyond the demands of subsistence. They must seek out and learn the magic or ritual knowledge without which they will not succeed, exposing not only themselves but their families to the risk of illness or death through the sorcery or witchcraft of envious competitors.

Vanatinai adults of both sexes show a wide range of personality differences, and they occupy their days with a variety of activities, accommodating the demands of subsistence, sharing with others, and maintaining their reputations as strong and reliable kinspeople and neighbors according to their personal desires and preferences. The degree of personal autonomy and privileges of women and men are largely symmetrical in freedom of movement, choosing marriage partners or divorcing them, launching careers as prominent exchangers of valuables, and acquiring supernatural knowledge and power. Their society values autonomy and tolerates idiosyncrasy and variation among women and men. It also values the same qualities of strength, wisdom, and generosity in both sexes.

Elders

I was startled and unnerved the first time I overheard one of my neighbors refer to me, while talking to someone else, as *laisali*, or old woman. The term hardly fit my self-image, and it evoked in me all the pejorative connotations the label has in Euro-American culture: worthless, powerless, desexed, ugly, weak. I understood that my white, corpselike skin and long hair, associated with mourning, had the continuing power to send some small children and at least one elderly woman fleeing from me in terror, and were associated with death and thus old age. (I did not yet realize that I was perceived by some islanders to be the returned spirit of Taineghubwa, who had been called laisali for decades before her death.) Still, my initial shock at being addressed occasionally as laisali in ensuing months (I was also called gamaina, young girl, and wevo or yola, woman, at other times, depending on context) focused my attention on the term's indigenous meanings. It is better translated as female elder. Like its synonym, *mankwés* (or *mankwesi*), it is a polite and honorific term of address and reference and not the great insult it can be, depending on tone of voice and context, in my own society. Both terms were used, I soon discovered by paying attention, to address or refer to prominent women as young as their thirties, although they were used more commonly for women in their forties through eighties. The term for old man, or male elder, *amalaisali*, was similarly used and equivalently respectful. A synonym in common usage, *olman*, old man, derives from Vanatinai Pidgin and had identical connotations. The fact that old woman as well as old man are terms of respect and not of insult on Vanatinai is another marker of its egalitarian gender relations.

There is no cultural discontinuity between the position of the pre-menopausal and postmenopausal woman (Lepowsky 1985a). There is no marked rise for some or all women to a higher or more "manlike" status once a woman has passed the age of childbearing, the way there is in cultures that emphasize the danger of female sexuality to the social order or the polluting qualities of the premenopausal female.[25] The treatment of elderly women on Vanatinai parallels the treatment of elderly men.

The needs of the elderly for food, water, and firewood are provided without complaint by kin and neighbors. Old people are respected for their knowledge and wisdom and for being close to ancestorhood. They may also be feared for their potential retaliation through knowledge of witchcraft or sorcery if their needs are not met, or because of the possibility that after they die and join the other ancestor spirits they might refuse to aid their living descendants who treated them badly in their last years. Widows and widowers must undergo an equally onerous period of mourning that ends after the final memorial feast in honor of the deceased spouse, usually several years later. The deaths of a man and a woman receive equal ritual attention.

People try for as long as possible to continue working at subsistence activities so that they will not be dependent upon their children and others. Both women and men often remain active until their seventies, if their health permits, doing household chores, walking miles over rough terrain and steep mountain paths to gardens, and maintaining ties with kin in other parts of the island. There is no given point at which a person is regarded as old. Big men and women seem to reach the height of their prestige and wealth in their fifties. By their sixties they are more likely to rest on their reputations rather than to undertake many strenuous exchange journeys or attend or host many feasts.

The physical powers of old people may decline, but their magical and practical knowledge is only believed to increase. They may continue to act in such roles as healer or garden magician, and they are consulted in matters of subsistence, custom, and ritual for their opinions and advice. Old people must also be treated respectfully because they have the magical power to harm those around them through sorcery or witchcraft if they are angered. A young married woman who was having difficulty in conceiving told me, for example, that a certain old woman had spitefully placed charmed betel nut skin in her basket so that she could not bear a child. The most widely known and feared sorcerer in the Louisiade Archipelago is a Vanatinai man about seventy years old. For many years, people say privately, he has been teaching his skills to his sister's son.

Old men and women who are unable to do any work may live with one or more of their adult children who provide for their needs. They take a favored place close to the fire and are given the best available food. Their children would be humiliated if they complained of poor or indifferent treatment. The oldest living son of an aged widow rarely visits other hamlets for feasts or exchange purposes, leaving any such obligations to his younger brothers. He says that he and his wife must remain at home to care for his mother until her death. Sometimes old people live in their own house near one of their offspring with perhaps one of their grandchildren or some other young kinsperson to assist them with their daily needs.

Grandparents have a particularly close and indulgent relationship with their grandchildren. They call each other by the reciprocal term *rubugu*, or by the affectionate diminutive *bubu*. Grandparents care for babies and young children while their parents are working. They tell children traditional stories and teach them about the natural world. Grandparents who still garden strive to feed their choicest vegetables and fruit to their grandchildren. They may defend their grandchildren if the parents are irritable or angry with them, scolding the younger adults and telling them to leave the children alone or they might become sick or not grow properly.

Even old people who are not strong enough to garden or fish make themselves useful around the hamlet if they can. Besides caring for children an old woman might prepare meals, gather firewood, or wash dishes and utensils. Old people also keep the fire from going out during the day while the other household members are engaged in subsistence pursuits, which is important since there are usually no matches available and people would otherwise have to use the tedious "fire plow" method of starting a fire, using two pieces of wood of differing hardness, when they returned home in the evening.

Even aged people sometimes participate in ritual events. One old woman who lived with her son and his wife and rarely left the house was especially invited by her kinfolk to assist them in a memorial feast. She and her children were picked up by sailing canoe and taken to Panatinani (Joannet Island), about thirty miles away. The old woman, the last surviving woman of her lineage, played a key role in the mortuary ritual, for it was she who sat down and was ceremonially draped in valuables that were then presented to the heir, the tau, of the deceased in the event called mwagumwagu. She was excited and invigorated by the attention and the responsibility, and it moved her to tell stories of the many feasts she had attended and the exchange journeys she had made in earlier years.

Old people try to make known before their death whom they want to inherit their ceremonial valuables, possessions, pigs, and land. They are afraid that if they do not there may be divisive quarrels which will lead to further deaths through sorcery. When one old man, seriously ill, thought he was dying, he summoned all of his potential heirs. He was not primarily bidding farewell to them from what he thought was his deathbed but was intent on assigning certain valuables to particular individuals and arranging for decades-old debts of greenstone axe blades to be repaid. He later recovered.

The passage of old people to the afterlife only increases their influence among their descendants, for the spirits of immediate ancestors are the source of almost all good fortune. Good relations with spirits are therefore maintained by magical means. Old people who must be cared for by their children or other relatives are treated well not only for sentimental reasons or because of social pressure. If they are not looked after properly at the end of their life, old people will not assist the living after they die and become ancestor spirits, and their negligent children will suffer hunger, sickness, and death.

Gender and the Life Course

As predicted for an egalitarian society, the degree of personal autonomy and influence over others is remarkably parallel for Vanatinai women and men at each point in the life cycle. Customary ideological constructions about females and males as well as their actions are strikingly congruent for each life stage named and separately recognized. Individuals generally gain in power and prestige as they age. Differences in behavior, activities, and personal wealth are largely attributed to individual personality and to knowledge, both practical and magical.

The respect shown the elderly mirrors the respect shown to individuals of both sexes as children and the equal respect accorded women and men. It is underlain by fear of the destructive power of the offended sorcerer or witch. Even if a person does not know destructive magic, one of her or his relatives certainly does. It is safer to mind your own business and let others do what they want. It is also not only morally correct but safer to be helpful and generous to others, even to people who seem to be weak and powerless, like old people and children. Personal appearances are deceiving.

Little girls and boys alike are socialized to be assertive and confident but generous and nurturing. Adults have learned the individual, selfish rewards of sharing and the respect it accrues, and each sex has access to the symbolic capital of prestige. Both men and women can arrange their lives and activities to please themselves, as long as they can withstand the pressures of demands from others to contribute to the food supply in one way or another. The sexual division of labor is not rigid in most areas and and the kinds of work women and men do largely overlap. Both women and men take the sexual initiative, and they have equal rights in marriage and divorce. Female elders are accorded the same respect as elderly males. The life courses of women and men are similar. There is a wider range within each sex of individual variation in experience, character, and social influence than between women and men.

The sexual division of labor on Vanatinai meets criteria predicted for an egalitarian society by featuring a large degree of overlap and of complementarity between the roles and activities of women versus men, female control of valued commodities, and participation by women in prestigious activities in the public domain. It enables women to participate in publicly recognized ways in political, economic, and ritual decision-making. In combination with an ethic of respect for individual autonomy, it also facilitates differences in people's activities. Individual women and men vary in the kinds of work they find congenial or distasteful and are therefore likely to do on a daily or seasonal basis.

Nevertheless, there is a slight but significant degree of gender asymmetry. The activities that are exclusively male, killing human beings and large animals with spears, are high in prestige, while one that is exclusively female, sweeping up the hamlet, is very low in prestige. Giving birth and giving life, on the other hand, are culturally celebrated. Activities that are largely female vary in prestige and significance from making decisions about the distribution of garden surplus to housekeeping and the tedious work of weeding. Childcare has an ambiguous status: highly valued by both sexes in the abstract, with both maternal and paternal nurture ritualized and celebrated, but, again, tedious in everyday practice. As we will see in the following chapters, because of women's specialization in childcare and in life-giving activities more generally, and because of men's identification with the destructive powers of sorcery and killing and their greater freedom from the daily management of the hamlet and garden, more men than women are highly active in ceremonial exchange and mortuary ritual and thus gain area-wide renown and influence.

While cooperation among individuals is extolled and indeed is necessary for continued existence in a small-scale subsistence society, Vanatinai's egalitarian outlook is revealed by the strong cultural emphasis upon personal autonomy and an ethic of respect for the will and the idiosyncrasies of the individual. This respect extends from the treatment of infants to the treatment of the aged and enjoins tolerance of a wide range of character traits and behaviors by women and men of all ages. Respect for others is enforced by the need to cooperate in daily life or have neighbors choose to live elsewhere on the island, but also by strong beliefs in the destructive powers of other persons manifested in sorcery and witchcraft.

Chapter Four

Ancestors and Other Spirits

Long ago, there was a snake (*mwata*) named Bambagho living on Goodenough Island (Mwalatau), near a creek in the kunai grass called Yome. One day, angry over a slight given it by the Mwalatau people, it decided to leave (some people say it was a "Satan snake" that had murdered someone and had been driven off, and others that it found Mwalatau too noisy because of the constant sound of drumming and decided to seek out a new home where there were no drums). The snake departed, sleeping the first night at Sanaroa Island. Then it went to Eyaus on the south coast of Misima Island. It continued to the south coast of Vanatinai and traveled up the large river called Ghekiwidighe, creating its present snakelike bends. The snake found shelter in a cave called Egheterighea on the north side of the island, just underneath the mountain known as Tuage. There it was discovered by an old woman, who fed it secretly. Every morning she would bring it a big plate of *moni* (sago and green coconut pudding), and every morning the snake would in gratitude give her a piece of its excrement. The snake's excrement (*mwata re*) was daveri, orange shell currency. The snake taught the old woman how to exchange ceremonial valuables and gave her the first exchange magic (called *une* or *kune*, cognates to the Trobriand term kula).

The old woman had two grandsons who worked hard to make sago and who were puzzled as to why their bundles of sago kept disappearing (some people say there are thirty youths making sago). The grandsons decided to spy on the old woman. They followed her to the cave and saw her give the snake moni and receive daveri in exchange. Furious, they drove the snake away from the cave with sticks of *maje* and *zhuwe* (two trees that bear edible nuts). It fled to the mangrove-lined shore at a place called Egotú. Just before it left Vanatinai it turned back to the old woman and begged her to fetch its sandalwood bark (*ome*), which it had forgotten in its haste. The snake then dove into the sea using the ome as its "boat" and as protection for its belly. The snake was actually a person afflicted with leprosy (*raibok*). It was attacked on one side by a swordfish and on the other by a shark, for they were attracted by the smell of its sores. As the snake dodged its two adversaries, it created the S-shaped passage in the reef that is still called Snake Passage even by Europeans. The snake reached Piron (Yeina) Island safely. But when it looked back it could still see the mountain of Tuage on Vanatinai. Determined not to stop until it had left behind even the sight of the mountain where it had known unhappiness, it continued to Rossel Island. It went up the large river called Kwejinewe near Saman Village on the south coast. But the way up the river was blocked by two crocodiles with their noses close together. The snake said a magical spell: *Pijo pajo kambajo yonavodu. Nyi wala du* (the second part means "you close your eyes" in Yeletnye, the Rossel language).

The crocodiles closed their eyes and the snake slipped past. The crocodiles then blamed each other for letting it through, and they fought, cutting each other into little pieces. The snake reached the river's headwaters. It is still there today, on Goywo, the peak behind Yongga Bay, and anyone who knows the right magic may go there and see the snake in its true human form.

Koita, a lively, youthful-looking widow in her fifties, told me this myth of the origins of shell valuables, exchange, and exchange magic. It is the most frequently told myth on Vanatinai. Koita's account of it was the most detailed, and people from many places agreed that she was the owner of the myth and the one best qualified to tell it. Her rights of possession as a female elder over the authoritative version of the myth, rare cross-culturally, tell of female stature and authority on Vanatinai.

Koita was born near Tuage, the mountain peak that figures prominently in the myth. As she told me, it is the story of "our snake," the totem snake of her clan, Guau. By the time she recounted it to me, as we sat in the shade near her daughter's house, I had already heard it from other men and women many times in fragments and in different versions. The Vanatinai language is gender-neutral, with no pronouns like he or she to reveal the subject's gender. I was suddenly moved to seek clarification from Koita. "This snake, was it wevo o ghomoli (female or male)?" I asked. "Wevo," she replied, in an unusually impatient tone, as if I should already have known this, which, of course, I should have. Other men and women later confirmed the snake's female nature.

Gender and Supernatural Power

On Vanatinai all sources of human power and influence—wealth, wisdom, skill, moral and physical strength, the loyalty and support of others—derive ultimately from the power of spirit beings. Humans try, with varying degrees of success, to use spiritual powers to achieve their personal goals, approved or disapproved of by the people around them. But spiritual power is often arbitrary, capricious, and unfathomable. Vanatinai beliefs in the potency of ancestor spirits, place spirits, and other supernatural beings, and in the supernaturally derived powers of sorcerers and witches are particularly pervasive, even compared to other Melanesian societies (Lepowsky 1990c:1061).

To understand gender and power on Vanatinai, as revealed by gender ideologies and by the concrete actions of male and female persons, we need to focus on the overlapping domains of thought and social life evoked by the English-language terms religion, magic, and cosmology, and to understand indigenous concepts of sacred and superhuman power. Religious ideologies are particularly potent forces in validating gender relations and the balance of power between men and women in any culture. On Vanatinai supernatural power is manifest in daily life, and human power, influence, and coercion are supernatural in origin. We need to learn, then, which supernaturally based powers are accessible to what persons and how ideas about sacred powers mirror or contradict other aspects of gender relations.

This chapter outlines the indigenous religion of Vanatinai, including notions of the sacred, cosmology and cosmogony, beliefs in supernatural entities and their powers, and magical and ritual practice, both public and private, beneficial and destructive. Vanatinai religion, like other Melanesian religions, cannot be separated from magic. Magical practice, what Malinowski (1954:88) called "the specific art for specific ends," is a form of religious practice or ritual.[1]

Early twentieth-century anthropologists who described parts of the Massim region followed Sir James Frazer (1913) in distinguishing between magic and religion, finding magic prominent and religion rudimentary or even absent. Before launching into a discussion of magic, sorcery, and witchcraft Malinowski (1922:73) notes the invocation of ancestral spirits in Trobriand magic and offerings to spirits in ritual. But he states that "there is nothing of the mutual interaction, of the intimate collaboration between man and spirit, which are the essence of religious cult." Charles Seligman (1910:646), Malinowski's teacher, earlier reported, in his survey ethnography of the Massim, "no cult of a superior being or of the heavenly bodies . . . nor could I discover any definite cult of ancestors or of the spirits of the dead . . . nor any attempt to enter into personal relation with any spiritual beings." Longer residence in a Massim community would, I think, have changed his mind, at least about ancestor spirits and about personal relations with spirits.[2]

The pantheon of Vanatinai contains a wide variety of supernatural beings, believed to exist by everyone on the island including people who speak of themselves as Christians. The islanders communicate through magic and ritual with ancestor spirits and other supernaturals, which in turn intercede in human affairs. Much of Vanatinai religious practice is "a means to or guarantee of material welfare," to use Lawrence and Meggitt's phrase (1965:22) describing a pragmatic focus characteristic of Melanesian religions. Human communications to spirits emphasize precisely what favor the human desires of the supernatural. Magical spells and practices addressed to supernatural beings such as ancestors and place spirits are forms of religious ritual equivalent to European prayers directed to God, the Virgin Mary, or various saints. But Vanatinai religion, like others in Melanesia, is not limited to the pragmatic and goal-directed.

The Supernatural World: Origins

There are two conflicting versions of the Vanatinai myth of who created the world, each of whose partisans insist that it is the correct one.

The first, more commonly told version is that a male supernatural named Rodyo, whose true form is that of a snake, was the creator spirit, making the land, sea, sky, heavenly bodies, people, and all living things. He assigned clans and totem animals and plants to people. His thoughts (*renuanga*) are said to be like a magnet, so that he only needs to think of something and it happens. When he thinks of rain, it rains.

The second, minority version holds that a deity called Alagh or Ghalagh (depending upon dialect) created the world, the heavenly bodies, and human beings. Alagh is also sometimes called Loi. He has white skin. Alagh appointed another deity, Rodyo, who was in the shape of a snake, to be in charge (*tanuwagai*, literally "owner") of the highest peak on Vanatinai, called Rio (or Rion), the spirits of the dead, ceremonial valuables, and sorcery. Alagh had two wives, Ekuneada and Egogona. He at first created only men, but Rodyo was lonely and asked him for a wife. Alagh told Rodyo that he would have to change his shape into that of a man, or else he would frighten the woman, and that is why Rodyo now has the shape of a man instead of a snake. Rodyo's wife is called Eurio (or Eulio). Tauhau, the Duau (Normanby Island) culture hero who originated traditional exchange or kune as well as the first mortuary feast on Duau, is also white-skinned (Róheim 1932:127). The parallels between the white-skinned Alagh providing a wife for the lonely Rodyo and the Biblical God providing a wife for Adam are obvious.[3]

Sanday (1981:33) argues that origin myths and the sex of the creator are particularly significant in describing and validating concepts of power and gender relations. She states that "when the female creative principle dominates or works in conjunction with the male principle, the sexes are either integrated and equal in everyday life . . . or they are separate and equal." On Vanatinai the creator spirit is male. Rodyo, the Vanatinai creator spirit who creates the world by thinking of it, conforms to Sanday's (1981:58) prediction that male creators will be associated with the sky (in this case a cloud-shrouded mountain peak) and create through magic, while female or couple creators create from the body or from other natural substances. If Sanday is correct, then why does an egalitarian society like Vanatinai have a male creator? Or is this gender imbalance in origin beliefs evidence of sexual asymmetry?

The existence of a male creator on Vanatinai does not seem to reflect the influence of Christian missionaries who have worked intermittently on the island since 1947. David White (1893) records that the "Great Chief" named "Rodes" lives on Mt. "Reo" with his wives and gardens and appears "like mist" to the human eye. He also names "Reo" as the home of the spirits of the dead and mentions beliefs in "spirits haunting the creeks, waterfalls and scrub after nightfall," which "after death . . . are able to visit their relations and work them either harm or good."

Some islanders say that at first Rodyo only created men but that he, a male snake, was lonely, and therefore the first woman was made. A snake is associated with this first couple as in the story of Adam and Eve, but on Vanatinai it is the man who is a snake and must change his shape to avoid frightening his new wife. Snakes figure as spirits, clan totem animals, and forms adopted by human sorcerers on Vanatinai. Snake spirits are found throughout the Massim. They are especially numerous on nearby Rossel Island, where the snake is also the most important in the set of linked totems attached to each matrilineage (Armstrong 1923–24, 1928), Duau or Normanby Island, where Róheim (1932:136) mentions a snake ancestress, and Goodenough Island (Young 1983b:61–91), where a snake-human with transformative powers is the hero of the most important myth on the island. Snake spirits are found in widely dispersed parts of Melanesia, such as Manus Island (Mead 1933), among the Daribi of Papua (Wagner 1972:27–30), and among the Arapesh of the Sepik region (Tuzin 1980:45), and they are prominent as well in aboriginal Australia (Mountford 1978).

The myth of the snake Bambagho is the story of how a powerful female supernatural taught a wise, courageous, and generous old woman about ceremonial valuables and the magic with which to obtain them. The valuables themselves, and the rituals in which they are exchanged, are what Vanatinai people describe as their most important customs. The motif of the snake that sheds its skin and becomes a person, or of the supernatural being in human form who dons a snakeskin, is common in Vanatinai myths, as are stories of heroes who shed their scabrous skin and become handsome and powerful men. Similar mythological motifs are found in the northern Massim, reported by Malinowski (1922:306–311, 322–326) for the Trobriand Islands and by Young (1983a and 1983b:61–67, 83) for Goodenough Island.

Snakes are never eaten on Vanatinai, unlike other totem animals, and people exhibit great fear when they come across a snake, making a wide berth around it, although there are said to be no poisonous snakes on the island. The snake on Vanatinai symbolizes, among other things, the afterlife: the snake, which can shed its skin, seems to be immortal (see below). Rodyo, the patron supernatural of the dead, originally had the form of a snake, and he pierces the ears and noses of newly arrived spirits of deceased humans to make them properly snakelike before he will admit them to the land of the dead.

The Vanatinai creation myth is culturally unelaborated, contains few details, and is rarely recounted by the islanders—and not, apparently, because it is a particularly sacred myth. When it is told the narrator usually launches immediately afterward into the story of Alagh, the supernatural who left Rodyo's community taking with him all the valuable goods that now belong to Europeans. Often narrated alone, this cargoistic explanatory myth is obviously more compelling to present-day islanders than the story of Rodyo's creation of the world (Lepowsky 1989b). But the myth I was most frequently told is that of Bambagho.

In Sanday's cross-cultural analysis of 112 creation stories, she finds 50 percent allude to masculine symbolism, 32 percent to mixed male and female, and 18 percent to feminine symbolism. She notes that the largest percentage of "feminine tales" is found in the Insular Pacific region, where there are very few "masculine tales," and comments that the finding of "many feminine origin tales" is consistent with the "ritual focus on female reproductive functions" in this region (1981:60). However, most of the Pacific societies whose rituals are concerned with female reproduction are societies with an explicit ideology of male dominance and female pollution where "ritual emulation by men of female reproductive functions," as Sanday phrases it, seems to symbolize male efforts to control or appropriate female reproductive power. Couple or feminine origin myths in these Pacific societies may therefore symbolize not an egalitarian ideology of gender but male preoccupation with female power and the ritual means through which it may be assimilated by men, who thereby maintain power over women and children.

Although Sanday sees couple creators in mythology as being generally found in more sexually egalitarian societies, as the female creates by giving birth or shaping people, animals or natural objects, many New Guinea Highlands societies with couple creators also feature sexual segregation, concern with female pollution, and an ethic of male dominance (e.g., Glasse 1965:33, Berndt 1965:80, Meggitt 1965:107, Meigs, pers. com., 1983). On the other hand, in the generally sexually egalitarian Massim culture area, there are a variety of origin myths. On Vanatinai there is a male creator, and the world comes into existence through his magical thought. People emerge from a hole in the ground, symbolically analogous to the act of birth, in the matrilineal Trobriand Islands (Malinowski 1922:305) as well as on nearby patrilineal Goodenough Island (Young 1971a:12–13). The people of central and eastern Muyuw, or Woodlark Island, in the northern Massim say that the creator spirit, Geliw, is female. Those in eastern Muyuw say he is male, although throughout the island the world is said to be carried on Geliw's head, a characteristically female mode of carrying on Muyuw (and in most Pacific Island cultures; Damon 1990:249–250). And an androgynous creator named Enak gives birth to "the first mortal ancestor," creating birth, death, and human artifacts on Sabarl Island (Battaglia 1983a:294), one of the Calvados Chain Islands just to the northwest of Vanatinai. But the Bimin Kuskusmin of the Highlands fringe, with a strong ideology of female pollution, also have an androgynous creator (Poole 1981:159). We must therefore be cautious in asserting that a culture's origin mythology directly reflects its gender ideologies.

Origin myths illuminate cultural constructions of gender, but we must examine them in relation to other significant myths and practices in the same culture. We need to focus on the complex and possibly contradictory relationships of mythical motifs to other aspects of gender-related thought and action. Even within the same myth certain motifs may be emphasized by different tellers in different versions. Indigenous exegeses vary among individuals and over time, providing ideological foundations for explaining or validating quite different aspects of the environment or the behavior of humans, animals, or supernatural beings.

Rodyo, the Vanatinai creator spirit, is primarily associated by Vanatinai people today not with his ancient acts of creation but with the spirits of the dead, for he sends his canoe to pick up the spirits of the newly dead and takes them to live in his hamlet on the summit of

Mt. Rio. Rodyo is one of the two supernatural patrons of sorcery. The other, Tamudurere, who lives in the sea, is also male. Sorcery is virtually a male monopoly, replacing killing through warfare as a male activity. All of this is consistent with the Vanatinai belief that women are the givers of life while men are the takers of life.

Cargo and Spirits

Both versions of the story of Rodyo's creation of the world have a corollary that is much more highly elaborated and more frequently told today in slightly differing forms. Alagh, who was a carpenter, disturbed the sleep of Rodyo and the peace of Mt. Rio, where all the deities lived with the spirits of the dead, with his constant hammering and sawing. Rodyo sent Alagh away. Alagh took with him his wife Egogona, his assistant, a supernatural called Kilimboa, and all the noisy implements that Rodyo found so objectionable, including engines, hammers, nails, saws, chickens, cattle, as well as gold and other objects now associated with Europeans. He left behind his other wife, Ekuneada, whose name means "the one of kune."

Alagh took his boat, Buliliti—a motor vessel, not an outrigger canoe—out through the passage in the barrier reef called Buyowa south of Mt. Rio and went to Sydney. Kilimboa continued to England, carrying the gold of Vanatinai in a piece of bamboo. He asked the king of England for land to build a house. The king offered him chairs, tables, spoons, and forks made of silver but he refused them, for all of Kilimboa's household goods were made of gold. The English king was so impressed that he made Kilimboa king in his place and became his servant.

Europeans have all the material possessions or *kago* (cargo) they presently do because Rodyo sent Alagh away. The people of Vanatinai have their own contrasting forms of material wealth, including ceremonial valuables, which English speakers call "Papuan money."

Vanatinai people who tell or hear the story today deeply regret Rodyo's action and Alagh's departure because of his objectionable, European-like noisiness. It has deprived them of their rightful access to what are now European forms of wealth. The unspoken postscript to this story is, of course, that one day Alagh may come sailing back to Vanatinai with the implements he took away with him long ago, which truly belong to this place. Some people told me that the first European visitors to Vanatinai were thought to be Alagh returning to his homeland. Interestingly, while Alagh is the owner, the tanuwagai, of the highly desirable and difficult to attain European wealth, a female being, his second wife, Ekuneada, who remains a place spirit on the summit of Mt. Rio, is a supernatural embodiment of the passionately desired tokens of indigenous wealth and the ceremonial exchanges in which they circulate.

Another supernatural named Witamo left Vanatinai too, in an outrigger canoe named Gharogha with a long prow like those used at Rossel Island and a sail of wild pandanus leaves. He now lives on Iyambau, a mountain on Rossel, according to one story. Another version holds that Witamo traveled not only to Rossel but also to Panaman, Dedehai, the Calvados Islands, Misima, and Duau (Normanby) and that his present whereabouts are unknown. This is why these islands have different customs from Vanatinai. The first story of Witamo says that he had no wife, but the second says that he had two wives and took the first one with him. The other wife was so unhappy at being left behind that she turned into a tree with umbrella-shaped leaves.

The myths of the snake Bambagho, Alagh, and Witamo share motifs of departure by sea and the dispersal of customs and wealth. The supernatural culture bearers are both male and female.

Ancestor Spirits

The summit of Mt. Rio is believed to be the home of the spirits of the Vanatinai dead.[4] Ancestors spirits, called kaka or *latamata*, are generally thought to look benignly on their living descendants and to assist them in all of their endeavors, such as gardening, fishing, hunting, seeking ceremonial valuables, or healing the sick. Ancestors and certain other supernaturals, discussed below, are the source of all good fortune and all wealth. The recent dead whose names and personalities are well remembered are the most important category of ancestor spirits on Vanatinai. Male and female ancestor spirits are equally powerful and are appealed to by the living of both sexes. Relations with ancestors are central to magicoreligious practice.

The belief that ancestor spirits dwell on Mt. Rio is held simultaneously, by elders, with the newer belief that the spirits of the dead turn white and go to America. The latter resonates with the preexisting cargoistic myth of Alagh and his departure for the land of Europeans, nowadays often identified as America rather than England or Sydney, with the material wealth, cargo, that Europeans presently control. The apocalyptic motif—that one day the spirits of the dead will return in a ship full of cargo—is likely influenced by the diffusion of millenarian, fundamentalist Christian preachings as reinterpreted by islanders. But the idea that newer forms of wealth are controlled by ancestor spirits is completely consistent with ancient religious beliefs. As the sources of all good fortune and prosperity, the spirits of the dead or other supernaturals such as Alagh will assist the people of Vanatinai by sending them European cargo (Lepowsky 1989b).

Cargoistic beliefs and cargo cults have been described in many parts of Melanesia during this century, appearing in dramatic and potent forms in Vanuatu (formerly the New Hebrides; Guiart 1951, 1952) and the Solomon Islands (Keesing 1978) and erupting across the length of New Guinea from Dobu to Biak (Fortune 1932:36, Worsley 1968:126–130). The people of Vanatinai do not have a history of active participation in cargo cults, unlike some of their neighbors to the northwest in the Calvados Chain and Misima Islands, activities that were particularly visible and explosive during World War II. Vanatinai people have declined in the last couple of decades as well to participate in a continuing, Misima-based cargo cult. But they say that Alagh and certain ancestor spirits control European cargo and may one day choose, or be persuaded through magical appeals, to return it or direct it to Vanatinai. Some older people who thought I was a returning ancestor spirit emphasized to me and others that I had returned with cargo and was distributing it among the islanders.[5]

Totems

Each of the twelve matrilineal clans on Vanatinai has a unique set of animals and plants to which its members are said to be kin. The precise kinship relation—matrilineal descent, a classificatory sibling-ship—was something no one ever articulated clearly to me in response to my repeated questions. I was told that Rodyo, immediately after creating the world and its inhabitants by thinking of them, assigned clan identities to spirits and human beings and also assigned certain animals and plants to specific clans. But everyone from children to knowledgeable elders was uniformly firm in explaining to me that a particular bird—the scarlet lory, the white heron, the Torres Strait pigeon, the green parrot—is "our bird" (*lema ma*; exclusive *we*, meaning "ours but not yours")—the bird of our clan—as is a particular named type of snake, tree, and so on.

Seligman (1910:9) remarks, "The most characteristic cultural feature of the Massim is the existence of a peculiar form of totemism with matrilineal descent . . . ordinarily these linked totems are a bird, a fish, a snake and a plant . . . special importance is attributed to the bird totem over the greater part of the Massim area. This is perhaps best shown in one of the first questions commonly asked of a stranger: 'What is your bird?' "[6] Almost a century after Charles Seligman visited the Massim the stranger on Vanatinai and the islands northwest of it in the Louisiade Archipelago is still immediately asked, "What is your bird? Len ma budá?" The answer establishes who your kin and potential hosts and allies are and the people with whom you should not have sexual relations. Although clan names vary among the islands of the Massim, there is a great deal of overlap in totem birds, and people with the same bird consider themselves matrilineally related.

The Vanatinai pattern of linked totems matches Seligman's general Massim pattern closely. All twelve clans have at least one animal or plant in each of five categories. The primary Vanatinai totem is a bird, and your clan, ghu, is most often referred to as your bird, ma. As far as I was able to learn, there is no generic term that could be translated as totem.

Some clans have two or three totem birds: for example Guau has the frigate bird, the owl, and the white heron. Each clan also has a particular kind of totem snake, mwata, which is second in importance to the clan bird. The snake is the most important totem on Rossel Island.[7] The third category of Vanatinai totem is called the fish (*bwarogi*), used in its generic meaning of marine animal. Totem fish include barracuda and shark, but also crocodile and sea turtle. The fourth category is the totem tree (*ghubwa*), typically a rain forest tree, sometimes a species that bears edible fruits or nuts. The fifth is the totem vine (*ziazio*), some of which are types used for lashing together houses or canoes.

People are not described as descended from their totems in the creation myths. But there are a few myths that describe animal genitors. For example, in the myth of the hero Mankaputaitai (*man* means "bird" in several Massim languages, a cognate of Vanatinai *ma*), the hero's mother has intercourse with the white heron, a totem bird, and then becomes pregnant. Interestingly, the white heron is father, not matrilineal kinsman, to the hero. The clan of the mother, who has human form, is unspecified in the myth.

Once while walking deep in the interior rain forest, a frigate bird glided above us headed inland, and we caught sight of it in a clearing. Iloga, a Guau man, addressed it, his totem bird, as "*Tinagu*," a formal way of saying "my mother." He continued with a respectful but longing "I would love to drink your soup" (i.e., to eat boiled frigate bird). People should not eat the totem fish of their father's clan, although they may eat their own, in an apparent analogue to affinal avoidance. Violation of this taboo would cause illness.

The categories human, spirit, animal, and plant are not discrete but have permeable boundaries. Members of each category are kin to certain exemplars of the other categories through the system of linked totems. Animals may speak, have supernatural power, or teach human beings spells or songs (as a shark did an old woman at Panaman Island). Spirits in the shape of snakes and birds are petitioned for assistance. Humans transform their bodies into those of snakes, if they know the right magic, and place spirits shift from the shape of a snake or bird to that of a human being. In Vanatinai thought there is no clear division between human and animal world, nor one between human being and spirit.

Silava

Early one morning a few months after I came to live at Jelewaga I met an elderly neighbor on the main path. He told me that a big *waga*, or boat, the same term used for a sailing canoe, had been shipwrecked off Rossel Island. There was, he said, "more food on it than the Rossel people could eat in a year." When I asked what had happened, he answered, with an unmistakable tone of satisfaction, "*Silava* got it." This was the first time I had heard of the supernatural beings called *silava* or *sirava*. They are place spirits that inhabit particular locations in the sea—on coral reefs, in streams, or on land in rock formations or cliffs. They may assume the form of a snake, a bird, a fish, or a giant octopus or other creature, or that of a stone or a log floating on the sea. The places, too, are called silava, translated by English speakers as "sacred."[8]

A silava place is said to be *ghabubu*, a cognate of the Polynesian *tabu* or *tapu* from which Captain Cook and his crew introduced the word taboo into the English language. English speakers on Vanatinai translate ghabubu as either sacred or closed. The hamlet where someone dies and a widowed spouse also become ghabubu until the completion of the mortuary ritual sequence "opens" them.

There are often taboos or proscriptions associated with silava, forbidden behaviors that may result in accidents, drownings, shipwreck, illness of a particular type, or an intense rainstorm or flooding. The boat that ran aground on the reef between Rossel and the uninhabited islet of Loa fell victim to one of the potentially malevolent marine place spirits that inhabit the treacherous passages on either side of Rossel, notorious for their dangerous currents and mountainous seas. Rossel Islanders chew sandalwood bark or ginger while muttering spells, then spray their charmed saliva onto the sea to propitiate the spirit. Loa itself has a particularly strong set of taboos and supernatural beliefs associated with it. It was formerly taboo to women, and men had to employ special esoteric words in the place of ordinary Rossel vocabulary when visiting the island. Uttering the number seven would result in the destruction of the offender and his party by the resident place spirit. Loa is home to a particularly fearsome place spirit named Lab, an octopus that grows to an enormous size and that also appears as a woman in Temewe, land of the dead. Lab controls the southeast tradewind (Armstrong 1928:148–150).

The Filipino crew of the shipwrecked vessel, which turned out to be a ten thousand-ton freighter bound from Australia to Seoul, Korea with a cargo of frozen beef and fuel oil, obviously did not know enough to protect themselves from place spirits. I later heard from Father Kevin English, the Irish-Australian priest who has lived since the 1950s at the Sacred Heart Mission at Jinjo, on Rossel Island, that the ship was eighteen miles off course to the west in the middle of the night and on automatic pilot, while the first mate, supposedly at the helm, was in fact drunk elsewhere in the vessel. Instead of clearing Rossel Lagoon well to the east, following a deep sea route between Australia and the Far East that cuts between New Guinea and the Solomon Islands, the freighter plowed at full speed into the reef, not too far from the treacherous shallow waters near the sacred island of Loa ruled over by the giant octopus. Rotting beef carcasses were dumped in the lagoon by the boat's crew, and we found their bleached white bones, picked clean by sharks, washing up on Vanatinai beaches, fifty miles away, for the next two months. Within days of the spill the lagoon waters off Vanatinai had turned a peculiar, milky color from the oil dumped by the wreck into these pristine waters. The incident confirmed to the islanders the power of silava—that they could seize such an enormous European vessel loaded with cargo.

Armstrong (1923–24, 1928:156–169) describes a category of place spirit called *yaba* on Rossel Island. Yaba also may live in the sea, streams, or in particular rocks, cliffs, caves, or other landscape features. Each yaba on Rossel controls a particular aspect of the natural world or human endeavor, such as a particular wind, rain, sexual desire, sago, or certain categories of illness. When taboos associated with a yaba are violated, the maleficent results are specific to each site. They include crop failure, flood, drought, cyclones, eye inflammation, venereal disease, illness of the lungs, fevers, and insanity. Each yaba is associated with a resident guardian spirit, often in the form of a snake, octopus, or crocodile, and a human "priest" who maintains the yaba with the correct ritual to keep the world functioning properly.

The yaba on Rossel Island seem to differ from the silava of Vanatinai in that the latter do not exert overall control of aspects of the natural or human world. These are the domain of ancestor spirits and the supernaturals called *vivirelavare*, although certain silava cause rain or particular illnesses when violated. There is also no "priest" or human caretaker of Vanatinai silava. I was told that a certain man "took care of" one particular silava (*ijupokiki*, or, in the Vanatinai pidgin called Vanga Lumo, *ilukautinga*, meaning "he looks out for it"). I am uncertain about the nature of this care. Vanatinai people say that even in precolonial times Vanatinai customs differed from those of Rossel reported by Armstrong where a man of rank regularly kept the yaba clean and periodically performed rites to make it function properly. Vanatinai people normally avoid silava. But certain Vanatinai silava may be propitiated by magic, as, for example, in the spell used to alleviate enlargement of the spleen, a symptom of malaria (Lepowsky 1990c). Individual magicians of both sexes go secretly to particular silava to work spells associated with the power of that place.

Silava belong to the category of place spirits found in many parts of New Guinea, called *masalai* in pidgin. Intrusion upon a silava, or, sometimes, speaking at all or speaking a foreign (non-Vanatinai) language while crossing a taboo section of reef or particular stream area may cause rain, flooding, or a darkening of the daytime sky. A person may fall sick with a particular illness associated with that *silava*, such as elephantiasis, sores on the mouth, or malaria. It is usually taboo to take fish or shellfish from a stream or section of reef that is silava on pain of illness or death.[9]

Many of the dozens of silava on Vanatinai and nearby reefs are named. Some assume characteristic forms, such as snakes, octopuses, frogs, or stones. For example, one silava in the headwaters of the Veora River above Gesila Village on the north side of the island is a two-headed snake.[10]

If a language other than Vanatinai ghalingaji, the language of Vanatinai, is spoken near certain silava the consequences vary depending upon the place. In some cases it will begin to rain, and in others a canoe will capsize and the occupants drown. This fate is said to have befallen a canoe full of trespassing Rossel Islanders who were hunting for crocodile across the bay from Jelewaga in a stream that is silava. The rule that only the language of Vanatinai may be spoken may thus be a form of supernatural protectionism to limit access to certain streams or reefs and their wealth to the people of Vanatinai. A similar supernaturally enforced territoriality may operate in Rossel yaba beliefs, such as those about the special esoteric version of Rossel language that should be spoken on Loa.

Certain streams and reefs below Vanatinai villages are silava, and children who play in them or anyone who eats shellfish from them will fall ill, a consequence that might also be predicted by Western concepts of sanitation and the transmission of disease. In one case it is said that clams from a silava reef "will hop around like frogs in the pot" and cause sickness. The disease of elephantiasis seems to be most strongly associated with silava rather than with sorcery or witchcraft like most illnesses, although sores on the mouth and fever (malaria) are common consequences of violations of silava taboos (Lepowsky 1990c).[11]

The gender of silava is not usually emphasized. Individual men and women learn secret magical knowledge through which they can appeal to certain silava—owners of wealth, the fertility of animals and plants, or illness—for specific purposes.

Other Spirits

There are additional categories of supernatural beings on Vanatinai. Beliefs about them are not as systematic as those about ancestor spirits or silava. They are also more rarely referred to publicly.

A major source of good or evil influence in the lives of human beings is the aforementioned category of supernaturals called vivirelavare. They were never born, and they will never die. Each of them has a particular arena of control in human affairs such as health, ceremonial valuables, garden food, or sorcery, of which he or she is the tanuwagai. (Silava, by contrast, are associated with more various phenomena, including winds, storms, and specific diseases).

Vivirelavare are petitioned by human beings who know the correct magic. They are like silava in some of their characteristics, such as the animal forms some assume, and their powers, but many are not fixed in known locations. Ghubughububala, the female being in the form of a Torres Strait pigeon who is the owner of the forest and one of the owners of hunting and hunting magic, lives in an unnamed and unspecified location in the forest. Tamudurere, one of the male supernatural patrons of warfare and sorcery, lives at Warai, a place under the sea outside of the lagoon whose specific location is not common knowledge. The names, types of magic, and arenas of influence of vivirelavare are discussed later in this chapter.

Another category of spirits is variously called *bwarabwarama, ngyau,* or *ghiyoghiyo.* They sometimes make people sick, or they may bring messages from ancestor spirits, assuming the shape of a bird called *manighighi* in the daytime or a firefly at night. In these guises they warn their kin of the approach of either an invisible sorcerer or an ordinary visitor to the hamlet. The spirits themselves are normally invisible. Fireflies, bats, and owls, all nocturnal creatures, may also be spirit familiars of sorcerers or witches.

Lokulokubaji are supernatural beings with pale skin and long hair who live in the forest, in certain stones, trees, or caves, or near the beach. English speakers call them fairies. The one most often mentioned is a female spirit who lives in the island's one lake, below and to the south of the summit of Mt. Rio. She is said to be very beautiful. Several men I know had seen her from a distance when visiting this remote place while hunting. She was sitting in the sun on a rock by the shore of the lake. Upon sighting the men she scooped up her infant into her arms, dove under the waters of the lake, and vanished.

Lokulokubaji cannot be petitioned by humans. They never help people but they sometimes harm them. There is a similar category of spirit beings on Misima Island, where they are known as *bwanbwanleo*. In fact I first learned of this category of spirit beings when I was living at Misima while waiting for a boat to travel to Vanatinai. An elderly Misima man jokingly identified me as a bwanbwanleo. I was later able to learn about the lokulokubaji of Vanatinai by inquiring if there were any bwanbwanleo on the island. Vanatinai people too pointed out that my unnatural white skin and long hair caused me to resemble these beings.

The magical domains of sorcery and witchcraft, associated with the supernatural power of ancestor spirits as well as place spirits such as silava and vivirelavare, are of enormous significance in Vanatinai social life, religion, cosmology, concepts of the person, and constructions of personal power. I discuss them at length in chapter 5.

Culture, Virtue, and the Motif of the Wise Woman

In an article that continues to stimulate debate Sherry Ortner (1974) suggests—based on structural oppositions of nature and culture Ortner argues, with Claude Lévi-Strauss (1969a, 1969b), are universal— that an association of women with nature and men with culture is also universal in human gender ideologies. Ortner (1974:73–74), I should stress, does not contend that men are perceived as exclusively cultural and women exclusively natural, but rather that women are universally seen as "closer to nature than men." The "male" domain of culture is more highly valued, she contends, and thus male dominance itself is universal.

This dichotomy of woman/nature, man/culture does not manifest itself in Vanatinai gender ideology. An association of femaleness with domains that Western analysts, using this structuralist framework, would label as cultural is revealed by Vanatinai mythology. In the Vanatinai worldview nature and culture are not perceived as separate or opposing domains. More generally, Vanatinai myths provide ideological underpinnings for egalitarian gender relations, portraying both sexes as powerful and, often, females as active, strong, wise, and generous.

Vanatinai has a large number of myths explaining origins of particular features of landscape and custom, or mumuga, also referred to as taubwaragha. The most widely told is the myth of Bambagho. Vanatinai people who tell it or hear it often lament the young men's foolish action of driving away the snake who in return for sago pudding gave away something more valuable, shell currency—in the form of seemingly worthless excrement—in the prototypical first exchange. The youths were shortsighted in their anger and selfishness at seeing the fruits of their labor, sago starch, converted into cooked food by their grandmother and fed to a stranger. Sago starch, a white, powdery substance prepared by men, is associated with semen in Vanatinai symbolism. It is morally wrong to hoard both semen and food. Both should be given to others, non-kin, in marriage and mortuary ritual, to build alliances among matrilineages and maintain them through the supreme affinal gift of a child and through affinal compensations after the crisis of death.

The wise and generous old woman symbolizes the moral qualities that are admirable in both individuals and matrilineages. Her giving a valued food to a hungry, needful stranger (and a snake at that) from a distant island was rewarded by the first shell valuables, objects that prototypically circulate between exchange partners from distant districts and other islands. The old woman also received the unexpected gift of knowledge: how to obtain more valuables from human beings and supernaturals through the use of exchange magic.

Because the snake now lives on Rossel, that island now has thousands of shell currency pieces in circulation.[12] Both the myth of the snake Bambagho, who went to Rossel, renowned for its Papuan shell wealth, and the myth of Alagh, who left for the land of Europeans with gold, machinery, and other European wealth, are myths of impoverishment and deprivation of wealth and thus of power rightfully belonging to Vanatinai. In each case the culture hero was driven away, by the grandsons and by Rodyo who angrily asserted their own power and prior ownership of place and resources. This intense preoccupation with inequities of wealth and power is reflected as well in the mythologies of other Massim peoples.

Young (1983a, 1983b) identifies the "theme of the resentful hero" who offers wealth but is rejected and abandons the place where the rejection takes place, as a motif common to the mythology of many parts of the Massim culture area. On patrilineal Goodenough Island, a Massim culture where the dominant ideology explicitly values males over females, a major wealth-producing resentful hero is a male snake named Matabawe.[13] The myth of Matabawe shares several key motifs with the Vanatinai myth of the snake Bambagho. Matabawe lives in a cave. He receives food and gives in exchange for his "tusks," which are in fact ceremonial valuables worn by men and circulating in kula (the boars' tusk necklaces called *doga* in the Trobriands [Malinowski 1922:357]). In the Vanatinai myth there is a motif of sibling rivalry expressed in terms of begrudging food that evokes the grandsons' rage: they see their grandmother feeding the snake and then they chase it from the cave using branches of wild nut trees. On Goodenough Matabawe's human sibling is terrified by the giant snake and spills broth over Matabawe's head, offending the snake and causing it to leave the island altogether. In fact Matabawe cuts a path with his snake's body "through the reef on his way to Muyuwa [Woodlark] or the Louisiades, whence he took all Goodenough's wealth" (Young 1983b:83).

The Vanatinai and Goodenough snake myths are each a remembering in different ways of the snake's mythical journey at its beginning, intermediate destination, and end. The motifs of generosity, nurturing, exchange of food for ceremonial valuables, sibling rivalry, offense, abandonment, and consequent impoverishment remain constant in all versions. But on matrilineal and gender egalitarian Vanatinai the snake protagonist who offers wealth but is driven off the island is female. Similar mythical accounts of a female snake from whose body shell wealth is produced and who also departs resentfully for Rossel Island after being attacked by a human male have been recorded for matrilineal Duau in the southern Massim.[14] The motif of the resentful hero who departs with wealth and who should be persuaded to return is also a powerfully effective vehicle for cargo beliefs, as recent movements have shown in the Louisiade Archipelago and Goodenough Island (Lepowsky 1989b, Young 1971b).

Freudian theories of symbolism and interpretations of dreams, myths, and primary process thinking hold that the snake is a representation of the human phallus. There are potent male snakes in Vanatinai myths, snake husbands who marry women by assuming human form, and these snake beings have clear phallic associations for the tellers and listeners to these myths. But on Vanatinai the motif of the snake, male or female, more generally evokes the immortality of the spirit. The snake does not die—it sheds its old skin and emerges fresh and gleaming like a young human being at a feast whose body glistens with magic oil and who is painted about the face with elaborate abstract designs. Recall that the mythological hero who is disfigured by a loathsome skin disease or by extreme old age and sheds his or her skin is common to the mythology of the Massim region. Associations of snakes in myths with immortality or rejuvenation because of this shedding of the skin are also widespread in the mythology of Amazonia, even where there are snake beings who become lovers or husbands of human women (Hill 1988:17). As in Melanesian and Australian mythologies, the snake in many Amazonian cultures is an ancestor of human beings (cf. Drummond 1981). The phallus itself in any culture may also symbolize immortality: during a man's lifetime it repeatedly dies and is reborn in sexual intercourse, and it creates new life—in a man's children and in their descendants—thwarting death.

In spite of the ritualized expression in the Vanatinai myth of regret that the wealth offered by the snake to Vanatinai went instead to neighboring Rossel, famous not only for shell currency pieces but also for the production of shell-disc necklaces that circulate in kula exchanges as far as the Trobriand Islands, Vanatinai too has thousands of shell currency pieces circulating in exchange. Known as daveri on Vanatinai and *ndap* on Rossel Island, the valuables are used differently on each island but are exchanged between them. They were made famous to scholars as "Rossel Island shell money" by Armstrong (1928), but, as I will demonstrate in later chapters, they are a major, ritually essential ceremonial valuable on Vanatinai as well.

In the Vanatinai myth a female being teaches another female the peaceful exchange with off-islanders of surplus food for ceremonial valuables. Similar exchanges are the most important and valued aspect of Vanatinai custom—taubwaragha, the way of the ancestors. The myth indicates an association of females with custom, in island thought, and with culture, in Western structuralist analysis. It also provides a mythological charter, in Malinowski's (1926) phrase, for the exchange activities of island women, their right to learn the magic of exchange, to own valuables, and to dispose of the surplus production of both men and women. The old woman takes the sago produced by her kinsmen, a semenlike substance, and feeds it to the snake. Two female beings of different matrilineages thus exchange the product of male labor. This is an inversion of the sexual division of labor of female producer and male transactor documented in most ethnographic descriptions of exchange where females are either involved or mentioned at all. The two females are also, by metaphorically exchanging the semen of young men for ceremonial valuables, mirroring the exchange of men in marriage by matrilineages.

After eating her fill of sago/semen, the female snake "gives birth," through excretion, to wealth, but generously gives away her excrement/child, binding the old woman to it in a relationship that combines aspects of kinship and affinity. Exchange partners, or *boda*, meaning person/people, are called by the same term used to refer to close relatives. Perceived by the young, selfish males as the ultimate worthless object, this excrement is supernaturally revealed to the old woman as the ultimate token of value and symbol of custom, shell currency. This element of the myth, of course, echoes the Freudian equation of money or wealth with excrement.[15]

The motif of the wise woman is common in Vanatinai myths. Mothers and sisters assist their kinsmen by giving them the magical knowledge that is the foundation of custom: in this case how to slay tyrannical beasts and giants that menace the islanders, carrying out their heroic male role as asiara and defender. For example, in the myth of the culture hero Mankaputaitai (Lepowsky 1983:493–494) the hero's mother provides him with the magical power and the tactics necessary to vanquish in sequence three human-killing supernatural beasts—a giant pig, an octopus, and an eagle—that have driven away the inhabitants of an island (identified in some versions as Misima). A female culture bearer and a youthful male champion warrior prevail.[16]

When the Rossel Island hero Pindewe comes to Vanatinai at the request of his sister, who has married there, to slay Kawagu, the cannibal giant who is eating all the island's children, the sister knows the war magic to make Pindewe's spears, which she hands to him, invincible. In another tale, a woman knows the witchcraft technique that makes an areca palm shoot into the clouds, taking her sister, who has climbed the palm, with it until she is rescued by a bushfowl, or megapode.

The myth of how human beings first acquired fire tells of a female supernatural named Emuga, who lived in a banana plant at Merawatuwat, near the present-day village of Pamela on the south coast. Emuga was the only being who knew the secret of fire and how to cook food. At that time human beings ate their food raw the way animals do, and their excrement was black, like that of pigs. One day two children, a sister and brother, from a nearby village happened on her. They hid and watched as Emuga placed her food on the ground and cooked it by squatting on the banana plant and shooting fire out of her vagina. When she was not looking the children ran up and stole burning brands from the fire and carried it back to the village. They showed their parents the secret of how to cook food using the fire. From then on, human beings cooked their food, and their excrement was brown instead of black like that of pigs.

Emuga transforms raw food, the diet of animals and precultural human beings, into cooked. In structuralist terms she is transforming nature into primordial culture, the first cooked food, through a natural form of fire that emanates from her genitals (cf. Lévi-Strauss 1969b). The human siblings, by taking fire and bringing it to the village, teach people to separate themselves from animals by their diet, a separation indicated by the natural sign of their excrement. This is physical evidence of a new division between humans as the owners of custom, or, in structuralist terms, as cultural, and animals. Animals have an ambiguous status in this myth, though, for any proposed structuralist opposition. While most animals live in the forest, the natural world in the Western dichotomy, the archetypal animal named in the myth is the pig, *bobo*, a domestic animal that lives primarily in human settlements (wild pigs are called *bobo bwejám*, pigs of the forest). The pig is one of the most significant valuables exchanged according to custom. Its domesticity and its role in exchange would be key attributes of culture rather than nature in a Western, dichotomous framework.

Supernatural beings on Vanatinai often shift between a human and an animal form such as snake or bird, and they typically live in a particular, named locale, such as a mountain peak, rock, or tree. Emuga conforms to this pattern of all place spirits. But instead of living in an enormous hardwood tree in the rain forest, as other place spirits do, Emuga lives in a banana plant, a source of food and a plant that is propagated by humans. There are no wild banana species endemic to Vanatinai, although there are on the New Guinea mainland. Certain varieties of cooking bananas were staples of the ancient diet of Vanatinai (cf. Lepowsky 1985a:111). Emuga's dwelling place, a cultigen that dates from the time of the ancestors, is another indicator of her association with custom. But it, like many other mythological motifs, indicates that custom is both natural and cultural. Although Emuga is animal-like in her dwelling place, a plant rather than a house, she cooks her food as humans will, albeit using a supernatural form of fire from her own genitals. Through her power as a supernatural and through the agency of the two children, she brings custom to human beings. Her name itself means "of custom."[17]

Human beings today go to great lengths to keep a fire banked or embers burning somewhere in a hamlet or village. Often the task of an elderly person left behind while others are at gardens, in the forest, or at the shore, this is said to "keep the place hot" and keep sorcerers away. Fire is kindled immediately, even in the oppressive heat of the northwest monsoon season, whenever people are in residence, either in the house or on the central plaza of the hamlet. Fire is explicitly linked with human sociality and with the village, as opposed to sorcery and the bush. This primary symbol of human cultural life was learned from a female supernatural being.

Emuga's physical form is not explicitly described in the version of the myth I was told, although her femaleness is specified. But humans, and even the spirits of the dead, spend much of their time in villages, or spirit villages, living in houses. Emuga lives perched on a banana plant like a scarlet lory, a fruit-eating bird that is the principal totem of a major matrilineage. Fire, then, is stolen by humans from a supernatural in animal (bird) form, a natural force made cultural in its human appropriation. This is a widespread motif in world mythology: witness, for example, the Central Brazilian myths of how fire is stolen from the jaguar that form the basis of Lévi-Strauss's *The Raw and the Cooked* (1969b). As in the Brazilian myths, due to the agency of human beings, fire and cooking are appropriated from the animal spirit that originally had this exclusive knowledge and power. Since then, both in the Amazon rain forest and on South Pacific islands, the situation has been reversed: humans cook their food and warm themselves with fire while jaguars and scarlet lories eat their food raw and must keep themselves warm. But everywhere in the world fire continues to have a dual nature, domestic in the hearth and wild in lightning strikes and forest fires, the life-giving source of heat and the agency of a painful death by burning.

The motif of fire shooting from the vagina of a supernaturally powerful female being is found elsewhere in the islands of southeastern New Guinea. On Duau, or Normanby Island, Róheim (1948:279–280) was told that fire comes out of a witch's vagina and flies around and that it is the string of light on which she flies herself. It can also be seen as a falling star. Macintyre (1987:217) heard similar descriptions of fire emitted from the armpits and vulva of a witch as she flies across the night sky at Tubetube Island. Macintyre (1987:216) also refers to a Tubetube myth in which children steal fire from their grandmother, who carries it in her vagina, which sounds like a cognate of the Vanatinai myth of Emuga.

Although no one on Vanatinai pointed out to me this resemblance of Emuga to the flying witches of widespread southern Massim tradition, it seems likely that humans, in the form of the sister and brother and their parents in the village, stole the exclusive power of the spirit/animal/witch, the fire that shoots from her vagina. The parents, back in the village, transformed fire into a domestic, beneficial tool to provide human nourishment and warmth as opposed to the potentially destructive and uncontrollable fire of a spirit entity.

All of this mythological evidence supports my contention that there is no explicit or implicit opposition of "natural woman" to "cultural man" in Vanatinai gender ideology. The universality of this dichotomy, suggested by Ortner (1974), has been challenged by ethnographic evidence from a variety of societies (e.g., MacCormick and Strathern 1980). In her discussion of Mt. Hagen, in the New Guinea Highlands, Strathern (1980) disputes the idea of a universal nature-culture symbolic opposition, describing instead a contrast of wild versus domestic that she argues should not be equated with nature-culture. She follows Langness (1976) and others in suggesting that a wild-domestic distinction is widespread in the Highlands and that males are more strongly associated with the wild and females with the domestic.

In Vanatinai worldview nature and culture are not distinct and opposing entities. The closest analogue to nature is *jamjám*, the symbolically powerful domain with the dual meaning of "forest" and "the wild" or "bush." (The related term, *bwejám*, wild, is normally used only to refer to wild pigs. The symbolic opposite of the wild is *gheba*, meaning "hamlet," "village," or "place.") The two domains are not closed and fully separated. Human beings and domesticated pigs dwell primarily in the hamlet, but both wander in the bush. Spirits and other animals dwell primarily in their specific places in the bush, but they wander into hamlets. Ancestor spirits have a spirit hamlet at the summit of Mt. Rio, with wild marsupials as their pigs and wild forest trees as their coconuts. Fire and sociality are at the core of the human settlement. The bush is the domain of power, danger, and solitude.

This jamjám-gheba contrast is similar to the wild-domestic opposition described by Langness and Strathern for the New Guinea Highlands. But unlike in the Highlands cases it includes no explicit contrast of male-wild, female-domestic and no imbalance of power on the male side. Both men and women on Vanatinai travel into the bush to forage and even to hunt and on journeys to distant hamlets. Gardens are anywhere from a quarter-mile to four miles away from the hamlet, and women as well as men routinely walk the forest trails to get to them. Women are not confined to hamlets and gardens by extensive taboos or a rigid gender division of labor. They commonly travel long distances to feasts and for exchange.

The Vanatinai concepts most nearly equivalent to a notion of culture, mumuga, or custom, and taubwaragha, the way of the ancestors, are also symbolically potent. Custom and the way of the ancestors both refer to ancient practices and proper ways of doing things.

Customary practices belong to the domain of the wild as they do to the village. Wild and domestic are continuous and intermingled. The boundary between the human and the animal domains is permeable, and the two are continuous with each other, as they are to some degree with the domains of plants and seemingly inanimate objects such as rocks.[18]

On Vanatinai Rodyo, a snake, creates the world and assigns clans and totems to people. Each matrilineage, whose human members dwell in hamlets, is thus related to a linked set of specific birds, snakes, fish, trees, and vines, beings that inhabit forest and lagoon. Bambagho, another snake, gives the old woman the first ceremonial valuables. Emuga, whose name means "of custom" and who is the first being to cook food, lives in a banana plant like a bird. Trees and rocks are inhabited by place spirits that assume animal forms but can communicate with people. People petition place spirits and ancestor spirits for good fortune or to obtain destructive power. Sorcerers and witches have animal spirit familiars. Sorcerers turn themselves into snakes, and witches fly like birds or use crocodiles as their boats. People and sailing canoes have turned to stone in the mythical past, and their names, locations, and stories are well known today. Floating logs in the sea become animate and try to overturn canoes. Human activities follow custom in bush and village alike. Tracts of forest, swamp, and reef are named, and they are owned by spirits and by clans according to customary entitlements. Custom is not in a symbolic opposition to nature or the wild but to asociality. Finally, custom is not primarily or exclusively either male or female in gender.

Vanatinai men and women credit female ancestors and other female supernaturals with providing human beings with some of the most highly valued aspects of custom, such as the knowledge of how to use fire and how to exchange ceremonial valuables. But despite Emuga's name, culture-bearing is not a monopoly of female supernaturals. Rodyo, the male place spirit who takes the form of a snake and now lives at the summit of Mt. Rio, in a village with the spirits of the dead, did more than create the world. His bestowal of clan identities and totems upon human beings also created the fundamental rules of Vanatinai society: those having to do with kinship ties, incest, and exogamy.

In Vanatinai gender ideology both sexes simultaneously embody the wild and the sociality of hamlet or "place" to the same degree.

Both domains are highly valued. They are intermingled, and both are sources of power. Human beings both cultivate and gather foods and valuables, working in gardens to accumulate a surplus, foraging and hunting, raising pigs for exchange, trading for valuables and creating them through magic. Power and success derive from custom and the way of the ancestors—ancestors and place spirits acting through human magicians and ritual experts who gather magical paraphernalia from graves and forests. In Vanatinai myth both females and males bring key aspects of custom. In ritual, the aspect of human activity that Ortner (1974:72) argues is the epitome of the cultural in portraying human action on "the givens of natural existence," women participate equally with men. In fact, one woman must represent her matrilineage in the climactic moment of the final mortuary feast in order to ensure the reestablishment of social order following the disintegration induced by death. Thus Vanatinai ideology sees women as essential for both cultural and biological reproduction (cf. Weiner 1982).

The Vanatinai case further contradicts the proposition that woman/nature, man/culture is a universal symbolic opposition. But does it indicate that an association of femaleness as well as maleness with what Ortner refers to as "the higher ground of culture," or custom—and sociality in the Vanatinai case—is necessarily associated with egalitarian gender ideologies and roles?

Strong evidence to the contrary comes from the example of the Baruya people on the fringe of the Eastern Highlands of mainland New Guinea. Maurice Godelier (1986) sees an explicit and pervasive ideology of male superiority and the power of Baruya men over women as the dominant factors in all aspects of Baruya behavior and social organization. Yet, in direct contrast to Ortner, he states that "the reason why women in Baruya society are dominated is that they stand far more on the side of culture than that of nature" (Godelier 1986:73). As in the Hagen case documented by Strathern (1980) and as among other interior New Guinea peoples, Baruya women are identified with the more profane and mundane world of the village and the gardens. Men are associated with the forests, where they hunt, travel to make war, and receive from spirits and from forest trees and plants the sacred male powers that make both them and women potent and fertile. To the Baruya men the natural, or wild, male domain is more powerful than the cultural, or domestic, which they share with women. Even childbirth and lactation, the quintessential natural acts of the female, are in Baruya thought the result of the nourishing and fertilizing properties of male semen, which in turn is fortified by the powerful male ancestor spirits, the natural bodies Sun and his younger brother Moon, through a male initiation sequence that lasts two decades or more. (In the more mundane, publicly told version of the myth known to women, Moon is the wife of Sun, ancestor of the Baruya. Only a few male ritual experts know that Moon, who controls the female qualities of coolness and wetness, and who initiates menstruation, is male). The most sacred ritual objects used in male initiations come in pairs, one of each sex, and a closely guarded secret is that the female object is the more powerful. Its guardian is a human male, and its existence is unknown to women. Godelier (1986:94) writes, "In order to dominate, the masculine (the men) must contain the power of the feminine, and to do so, it must first seize that power by expropriating it from the women in whom it originally resides." In the Baruya ideology, organized around the principle of male dominance, the sphere of culture, including even horticulture, the basis of Baruya subsistence, is denigrated because it is associated with women, and the sphere of nature, associated with men, is elevated in religious ideology.

The Baruya explicitly recognize the cultural, creative qualities of females in their myths. Baruya females in one myth invent the bow and arrow and in another the sacred flute, fundamental to the male initiation sequence that justifies and perpetuates male superiority. In ancient times women were the only sex to use these implements, while women today may not even touch, let alone use, a bow and arrow, and a woman would in theory be put to death if she even saw a flute, of whose existence she is supposed to be unaware, thinking its sound the voice of ancestor spirits. But each of these Baruya myths concludes with the story of how men seize and appropriate the women's (cultural) power by taking possession of the sacred object and forbidding it to women. In other myths a woman's corpse produces the first cultivated plants and a woman's head produces the springs that irrigate the salt cane, the basis of the traditional Baruya trade in salt, a male monopoly. But in these myths it is men—in fact, husbands—who kill or decapitate women and collect the unexpected and valuable fruits of their bodies, cultivated edible plants and salt produced through irrigation (Godelier 1986:70–72).

Similar myths of an ancient period of female dominance where women ruled through their control of powerful sacred objects and tools, later taken from them by men who therefore dominate women in the present, are common in warrior societies with a strong ideology of male dominance from the Amazon and Tierra del Fuego (Murphy and Murphy 1974, Bamberger 1974) to New Guinea (Errington and Gewertz 1988). As the Murphys note, these beliefs indicate that "the battle of the sexes" is never resolved, for if women had the power once, they are capable of regaining it at men's expense. Men must therefore expend great effort to keep women in a subordinate position by restricting their activities, barring them from key rituals, secrets, implements, and roles, and promulgating an ideology of male superiority to both sexes.

There are no Vanatinai myths of matriarchy overthrown, and both female and male powers are represented in the supernatural world. The Baruya contrast with the Vanatinai case while sharing an association of the female with culture, or custom, or the world of the village, an association that is not at all exclusive or negative on Vanatinai. The Baruya contrast further in that their myths recount that men violently appropriated the powers of women, and men are associated with a more highly valued domain of nature/the wild. Female/culture/custom associations in the two groups represent drastically different prevailing philosophies of gender, one strongly emphasizing male superiority, and the other gender equality. This difference points to the need to examine in greater detail the cultural contexts and potentially contradictory local meanings of symbolic associations. Even if they are not universal or consistent at all levels of gender ideology in one society, woman/nature, man/culture or woman/domestic, man/wild are indisputably widespread. Untangling their local complexities clarifies the relationship of these symbolically potent aspects of gender ideologies to gender relations overall.

Magical Knowledge and Gendered Power

In Melanesia knowledge, particularly knowledge of magic, ritual, and the supernatural world, is power. Differences among individuals in magical knowledge lead to status differences in Vanatinai social relations. Magical spells and ritual techniques are privately owned commodities normally kept secret. The extent of a person's access to magical knowledge is locally recognized as a sign of her or his power and influence over others. Magical belief and practice, emanating from male and female supernatural beings, further engender human power. Women possess key forms of magical and ritual knowledge, and female supernaturals are prominent and invoked by both sexes.

Some people are born into matrilineages that have more garden and forest lands, more rights to reefs, more sago, betel nut, and coconut palms than others. Others inherit supernatural knowledge from their matrilineal kin or fathers. The knowledge leads to success in all human endeavors, including food production through gardening, hunting, fishing, and gathering, love and marriage, and the maintenance of health. Only some of those wealthy in land possess more magical knowledge than others. It is possible for those who acquire strong magic and who work hard to be successful in exchange, obtaining valuables with which to buy land, to marry well and have healthy children. They will accumulate surpluses of garden food, sago, and pigs with which to make feasts and contribute to their reputations as wealthy and important people. Those with potent magical knowledge also gain influence and respect by helping their neighbors in healing, in garden and other subsistence magic, and by giving them valuables obtained through their superior knowledge of exchange magic. The word for magic, *kukura*, also means "spell," and points to the most essential technique of magical practice, the possession of magical words whose utterance, usually along with the chewing and spitting of certain wild leaves, roots, or barks with special powers, gives magic its efficacy.

The magic of exchange is called une, a cognate of kula. Both women and men may be adepts. Une has several supernatural patrons, or "owners," called tanuwagaji. Bambagho, the female snake who first gave exchange valuables and magic to the generous old woman, was driven away from Vanatinai and so is now an owner of exchange magic on Rossel Island. Two supernatural tanuwagaji of exchange magic still on Vanatinai today are male and one is female. Mwaoni lives on Mt. Rubi, near East Point. He is in charge of ceremonial valuables from Vanatinai and the islands to the north and west.

Rodyo, the male creator spirit from Mt. Rio, is also a patron of exchange magic. So is Ekuneada, wife of Alagh, who still lives on Rio's summit. Another supernatural named Mbasiri used to live at Etubude, on the shore near Western Point. Now he, like Bambagho, lives on Rossel, on Mt. Goywo, the mountain behind Jinjo, or on the reef nearby. He is in charge of *giarova*, the greenstone axe blades from Rossel Island.

All success in obtaining valuables is due to magic, for no one really wants to part with them. Before setting out on an important quest, the leader—either male or female—of an expedition usually prepares the magically enhanced scented coconut oil called bunama, the "food of valuables." The preparer must chew ginger, eat only coconut meat, and drink saltwater. Grated coconut is boiled in a special clay cooking pot never used to boil food. Magically powerful scented roots, bark, or leaves are added to the pot, followed by a relic of a dead kinsperson such as a tooth, a fingernail, a fragment of skull or bone, or a lock of hair. Then a magical spell is recited over the contents. People of both sexes who are requesting valuables wash themselves carefully before entering a village and then apply bunama to their bodies. They also wear their newest and most attractive garments and decorate themselves with flowers and scented leaves tucked into their hair and armlets. A few big men put on trochus shell armlets, a mark of wealth and success in exchange, after performing special magic over them. Visitors try to overwhelm their hosts with their beauty, to make the hosts tremble with desire, so that they "change their hearts" and hurry to give away valuables with which they never intended to part. The relationship between exchange partners, who are frequently of the same sex, is explicitly likened to that between lovers.[19]

A few men and women know magic for finding bagi and greenstone axe blades buried in the ground under trees or in secret locations in the bush. They appeal through magic to the spirits of dead ancestors, who aid them by revealing the locations of valuables in dreams. The valuables themselves were "planted in the ground" in earliest times by Rodyo, or by Mwaoni, who once fell and dropped his tobotobo near Egina on the north coast. Others possess the powerful magic that causes special small greenstone axe blades, tiny daveri, and certain individual pieces of bagi to "give birth" to many larger valuables while locked in the magician's private storage box. One old man told me about the time his floor collapsed under the weight of the new valuables he produced this way.

The primary ingredient in any form of magic for obtaining valuables on Vanatinai is the relic of a dead ancestor, the tooth or piece of bone or hair called a muramura (see chapter 5). This relic aids in communicating with ancestor spirits and in requesting their help. Ancestors are also called upon for protection against the jealous sorcery of others. Anyone who dares to be successful in exchange activities is risking his or her life, for someone, either nearby or in a distant hamlet, is always waiting to humble those proud of their wealth and reputation by inflicting sickness and death on them and their families. Most illnesses are routinely attributed to the envy of some powerful sorcerer. Another elderly man told me how a rival made magic, a form of witchcraft (wadawada), causing sudden wind to capsize his sailing canoe. He and his party nearly drowned, and his precious metal box full of valuables tore loose from its lashings and sank to the bottom of the sea. But no important person would become prominent in exchange without learning how to attack and protect through sorcery or witchcraft.

Another useful kind of magic is mbasiri, "convincing magic," which makes your words persuasive or "hot" and causes the listener to believe you and to do what you want, including to give valuables. Mbasiri is used by the old sorcerer Zeyala in the incident described in the beginning of the following chapter. The supernatural patron of convincing magic is, of course, Mbasiri, who now lives at Rossel Island.[20]

One of the most important kinds of magic is used for planting, growing, and harvesting garden produce, particularly yams. Garden magic is called ngangaya, which means "talk to," as the practitioner talks to the yams. Many women know important kinds of garden magic and virtually every adult knows some. The supernatural "owners" of garden food, appealed to in garden magic, are two female beings called Jinrubi and Eurubi. Their home is Mt. Rubi near the eastern tip of Vanatinai, and they are related to Mwaoni. Jinrubi and Eurubi are euria, or givers of good things. They are often asked through magical spells to bring two baskets of yams from rich islands elsewhere, like Misima, Duau, or Kiriwina, to the garden of the magician.[21] Ancestor spirits are commonly appealed to by their descendants for help in providing prolific gardens and good harvests, using relics of the dead or poignant spells reminding the spirits that their children are hungry. Ancestors are often petitioned as "mother," "father," or "in-law."

Either a woman or a man may preside over the crucial public yam planting ritual that accompanies the planting of a new garden. By contrast, the analogous yam magic in the Trobriand Islands is a monopoly of chiefly male specialists (Malinowski 1935). Yam planting is a communal activity, usually involving a hamlet group plus kin and affines of some of the members. A wide area is cleared by men of large trees, and the small trees and brush are cleared and burned by women. Plots for each participating household are marked with branches. New gardens are usually planted in about October after the end of the southeast tradewind season, or *zegezege*, the time called *zegezege posuye*, or the "nose of the year." Seed yams are removed from the small garden or hamlet yam houses where they have been stored. The garden magician charms a certain type of branch with green leaves on it and brushes it over all the yams. The baskets of yams are then poured over the ground onto some flat green leaves in a central spot in the new garden. The knives or goldlip pearl shells, *gile*, used to cut the seed yams are bespelled by the garden magician, who grates and chews a white root while uttering a charm and then spits on the utensils. Women cut the growing tips off the tops and sides of the yams, and the remainder is cooked in coconut cream to feed the workers. Other women fetch water, which is often some distance away.

The garden magician places a magically enhanced bundle of bark and leaves with special powers into the water in a pouch. She or he squeezes this bundle while muttering a charm and spits onto it in a fine spray. The water, which turns a reddish color, is then poured carefully onto the yam seeds so that all of them become wet. This phase of the ritual is an appeal for rain to make the yam vines grow properly and put forth large tubers. The garden magician then squats, chews certain substances, spits charmed saliva onto some freshly dug dirt, and pushes the dirt in handfuls down onto the pile of yam seeds, continuing to work magical spells.

Meanwhile, men and some of the stronger women have been laboriously making holes in the ground for the yams with long digging sticks. The garden magician continues to chew and spits charmed saliva on one garden basket, and the seed yams are piled first in this basket and then in the rest, ready for planting. The magician takes the first yam seed and plants it while spitting on the spot and muttering magical spells. Finally the women each take a basket of yam seeds and begin to plant them.[22]

There is different magic for each type of garden crop, including those which have only been introduced in the last few generations, such as sweet potato and manioc. Each person knows his or her own magic, learned from a matrilineal kinsperson or father and normally kept secret to preserve its potency. The bark of the trees called *leyava* and *butu* are often burned in gardens to make sweet potato and manioc tubers abundant. People also burn the bark of kaikai trees. They say magical spells while planting the cuttings for their tubers, then leave the garden area alone for a month or more.

The yam harvest takes place in June and July, when the Pleiades, or Gamayawa, have appeared in the eastern sky. Other crops may be planted or harvested at any time of the year. Harvesting, especially of yams, unlike planting, is almost always an individual activity. It is rude, and threatening, to enter another person's garden uninvited. The abundance of your yams might incite envy and incur a sorcery attack. Any visitor to a garden must be given a basket of its produce. The garden is also a place where married couples seek privacy. Their lovemaking in the garden house while resting from work in the heat of the day encourages the growth of plants and is no longer inimical to it. The yam vines are first cleared away with a bush knife to be burned later. Then the gardener digs up some ginger root (*zeyala*) that has been transplanted from the forest for this purpose, adjacent to the yams. She or he sits down and chews ginger root, uttering a magical charm. Then the harvester explosively sprays her or his palms with the charmed ginger and saliva and rubs them on the point of the digging stick, used to dig up the yam tubers.

Food magic is essential for feasts to make sure that guests will be amply fed and the food will not be finished early, bringing shame upon the hosts. This magic, called *rogana*, or "fenced one," causes guests to feel satisfied after eating only a small piece of yam or sago. The name refers to the temporary walls of woven sago leaf that are erected along the stilts under the host's house, within which all of the baskets of food are stored to protect them from prying eyes. Prominent practitioners of rogana include both women and men. They are rewarded with several ceremonial valuables (tobotobo and daveri) by the host after a feast has ended. There is no patron supernatural of rogana. Another type of food magic, *wivwara*, which involves making a small amount of something larger, is under the patronage of Mwa-jemwaje, male supernatural who lives in the forest, and of Mwaoni. Wivwara is also used when butchering pigs at feasts, a male specialty, to ensure enough meat for everyone.

The magical practitioner in charge of the food at a feast may never be seen to eat by others. She or he should remain under the house with the food, directing others as to which baskets of food to take at a particular time. When the feast begins, she or he charms all of the garden produce, sago, coconuts, firewood, and leaves for making the stone oven that has been contributed for the occasion. The practitioner chews ginger and squats on the ground, muttering magical spells and spitting a fine spray of charmed saliva onto certain spots on the leaf-covered ground under the house. Then women assistants pour baskets of garden produce onto these spots. The magician makes a further magical spell over the ginger, spits on all of the food lightly, and the food is covered with inverted garden baskets. The magician squats by the entrance to this fenced-off area, chewing ginger and working further spells, removing the ginger from his or her mouth and placing it carefully at the end of a large, burning log. This fire must not be allowed to go out during the feast. Mourning affinal women, the major contributors of yams and other garden produce at mortuary feasts, are responsible for assisting the magician with food distribution, remaining under the house in shifts. The food magician goes upstairs into the house where bundles of sago are hanging from the rafters and bespells them in the dead of night. During the feast the central ground of the hamlet must not be swept as it usually is every morning or the food magic will be spoiled.

The food roasted in stone ovens, or *ghumughumu*, at feasts is sorted by a circle of seated women for distribution to those attending the feast. This long procedure involves the charming of baskets by the food magician and a taboo against each woman's talking about what kinds of food are left in her basket, which would spoil the magic and cause the food to fall short.

Fishing magic, used by both sexes, is called *bwawi* (*bwa* means water). Special leaves may be rubbed and charmed and placed either in one's basket on a canoe or on one's head. Raré, a male spirit, is the "owner" of fish, marine animals, and fishing magic. He lives in the sea, though in no specific place, and humans appeal to him through magical spells.

Hunting magic, *monamona*, is known by both men and women. It has two supernatural patrons, Tova, the owner of wild pigs and dogs, and Ghubughububala, the owner of the forest. The former is male and the latter is female. Both live in unspecified locations in the forest. One spell, used by men, involves bathing naked and rubbing the body with magically treated plants, which also removes most of the smell of human. In another, men rub their eyes with charmed leaves or apply them to hunting dogs before looking for wild pig. The magic for finding wild nuts or other wild food, *wivwara*, is also used by both sexes. The owner of nuts and wild food is Mwajemwaje. *Mwaje* is a variety of nut that grows on a forest tree. Special magic, used by men and women, for finding copal gum, called *kula*, belongs to Ghubughububala. A *bala* is a Torres Strait pigeon and the totem bird of the Wozhoga clan.

Sago-making spells, called *ghalage*, or "to enlarge," are known by men and women, even though men do the bulk of the work of making sago, the other great dietary staple along with yams. Its owners are two supernaturals, one male and one female, who live in large sago palms. They are both named Kulakulaiva (*kulakula* means "to call out"). The men's cry of "Hwe! Ho!" when they rhythmically pound the sago pith is a magical invocation to these beings. Alagh, who used to live at Varidamo, near Mt. Rio, but left for the land of Europeans, is another patron of sago magic.

Weather magic is the only form of magical knowledge completely reserved for men. Its supernatural patron, to whom appeals are made for rain or wind or to end a storm, is a male called Ghejeghe-je, who lives at Lumutaiwa in the deep sea outside the barrier reef. The men who become rain magicians may or may not also be sorcerers. Rain magicians can work to help their neighbors and make their gardens grow or they can make rain maliciously to spoil a feast or other occasion, as in the case of Zeyala, described in the next chapter. Malicious rain-makers are sorcerers as well, and perhaps the link between weather magic and the magic of destruction explains its association with males and opposition to the female domain, which prevailing Vanatinai ideologies associates with life-giving.[23]

Love magic, *udi*, is known to both men and women and has no supernatural patron. In important workings of udi the practitioner should fast or refrain from eating "cold food" such as fish, drink salt water, and chew ginger while reciting appropriate charms. Love charms use a wide variety of plant ingredients. Bunama, magically enhanced scented coconut oil, with its intoxicatingly sweet smell, is a potent form of love magic, especially when the person wearing it brushes against the person he or she desires. The most powerful kind of bunama is made by boiling a relic, a bone or tooth of a deceased relative or of a long deceased person known to have been successful in love, with the coconut oil, while reciting spells calling on the aid of ancestor spirits. Specific ancestors, rather than place spirits and other supernaturals, are the primary owners of the most serious and secret forms of love magic, the magic of seduction on which exchange magic is modeled. Its possession enables even very old men and women, if they wish (and most do not), to sleep with young people of the opposite sex.

Healing magic, called *zawazawara* (*thawathawara* in some dialects), is known to both sexes. The supernatural owner of illness is a female being called Ediriwo, and the owner of health is another female being named Egoregore, who is appealed to in healing magic and during childbirth. Their home is Mt. Rio, and they are kinswomen of Rodyo. Healing is a form of countersorcery, or, less often, counter-witchcraft (Lepowsky 1990c). It may also involve appealing to place spirits offended by the violation of taboos. Since sorcery is almost always practiced by men, it is striking that both women and men possess powerful healing magic and a wide knowledge of bush medicines. The people of Vanatinai have a vast pharmacopoeia of medicinal plants. These are usually administered after being activated by a magical spell. Indigenous medicines are said to include six or more types of contraceptives, several abortifaecients, and cures for a wide variety of ailments, such as coughs, baldness, bloody bowels, malaria, gonorrhea, and stonefish stings. Research may well reveal that some of these substances are pharmacologically active. The cures for some illnesses, such as venereal disease, consist only of spells worked upon plant substances, with no medication of a physical nature being given to the patient. A knowledge of specific healing techniques is transmitted in secret, normally within the matrilineage, although sometimes a father may teach a child, a grandparent from a different clan may instruct a grandchild, or exchange partners may teach one another.

When someone falls sick it is generally a relative, trusted in-law, or neighbor who attempts to cure the patient. If she or he is not successful, other healers will be asked to apply their skills, for each person's knowledge of curing is different. In difficult cases half a dozen people may treat the patient. For example, one old man fell ill with a serious respiratory complaint, probably after having influenza. He was widely believed to be dying, and he called for his kinfolk to assemble at what he thought was his deathbed from all parts of the island in order to discuss the inheritance of his many ceremonial valuables, pigs, and other property. A number of widely regarded healers, all older men and women, tried to cure him, but he showed no improvement. Finally his nephew, a young married man, asked if he could try too, saying modestly that he was only a "small boy," but that his grandfather, a highly respected aged man and healer who had died the previous year, had taught him certain healing techniques. Shortly after the young man performed his curing ritual, the patient recovered, and so he was credited with saving the old man's life. Just as sorcerers carry their paraphernalia around with them in their betel nut baskets, healers normally carry in their baskets an assortment of medicinal roots, barks, and leaves in case they are needed. Many well-known healers—but not all—are widely believed to be powerful sorcerers or witches who know the appropriate countermagic.

Healing techniques often involves the chewing of ginger or various other roots, barks, and leaves by the curer while almost inaudibly muttering the appropriate magical spell, then forcefully spitting a fine spray of saliva onto the afflicted part of the patient's body. These secret spells call upon ancestor spirits for assistance in driving out illness. The most dramatic form of healing involves the magical removal of a sorcerer's projectile from the patient's body. It was first reported in 1892 by an outside observer, David White, who writes, rather disrespectfully, "Some of the old men are supposed to be able to make rain, and others who understand medicinal plants, take out stones, spears &c. from the sick to cure them. I saw one man take a stone out of another man's head. It was so very clumsily done, it being quite apparent that he had it in his hand all the time, that I was surprised that he could dupe even a child" (White 1893).

The most common present-day technique for removing magical projectiles involves chewing and bespelling ginger and other plant substances and then "sucking" the projectile out of the patient's body, as in the childbirth described in chapter 3. Another technique is to take some *kunai* grass, bespell it, and place it on the afflicted part of the patient's body, at which time the projectile causing the illness, such as a piece of skull or a fish spine, will fall out. This object should be placed in a coconut-shell cup or other container on the top of the house in order to cool the patient's fever. Later it will be buried, hidden, or burned. The nature of the projectile removed is evidence of the identity and motive of the sorcerer responsible.

One of the two most important patron supernaturals of sorcerers and witches is a male being named Tamudurere, who lives at Walai, an unspecified location in the deep sea outside the barrier reef. The other, also male, is Rodyo. War magic is also under the supernatural patronage of Tamudurere. He is analogous to beings with similar names from islands far to the northwest, where he is one of the most potent supernatural figures. The Vanatinai Tamudurere shares with his namesakes associations with the destructive magic of war, sorcery, and witchcraft, but he is a much less central figure on Vanatinai.[24] Rodyo too is invoked in war magic. One type of war magic, *bwauyezovo*, is (or was) practiced only by men. A second type, *inde*, is (or was) also taught to some women, especially firstborn daughters, by their fathers. A father who wanted his son or daughter to be fearless in battle would chew ginger and recite a spell, then urinate in a stream upstream from where his child was bathing, unbeknownst to the child. The father might also drink salt water and chew ginger and defecate the resulting diarrhea upstream. Causing mental illness or suicide and driving pigs into the bush are kinds of magic, known to both sexes, resembling sorcery, all malicious in intent, but Vanatinai elders stress that they are magic (kukura), not sorcery (*ribiroi*). They are also, like some war magic, called bwauyezovo. Their owners are again Tamudurere and Rodyo. Practitioners may drive others insane, causing them to behave foolishly, go around naked, or race around without any rest. The most extreme form causes the victim to commit suicide (*ikebenuanua*), rare on Vanatinai. This kind of magic may also be used out of spite to drive someone else's pigs into the bush, preventing another's participation in a successful exchange (see chapter 5).

Other types of magic with no supernatural patron, used by men and women, include *rogau*, or "the chewing one," the magic for making yourself invisible, a highly useful skill employed by sorcerers to work their nefarious deeds or by any adept to travel long distances such as from one side of the island to the other in just a few minutes. Another type is *gana* ("fence"), the antisorcery magic that involves spitting on doors and windows with mouthfuls of charmed ginger.

Gender and Supernatural Power

For the islanders supernatural power, mediated by knowledge of magic, ritual, sorcery, and witchcraft, underlies all human success and influence over others. This includes knowledge of how to do things properly, in subsistence, in exchange, in social relations—the kind of knowing and wisdom gained through intelligence and long experience. But when the islanders speak of wisdom or knowledge (*garegare*) as a personal quality admired in both women and men, they perceive it as grounded in knowledge of the supernatural domain. Respectful and successful communication with ancestor spirits, place spirits, and other beings leads to a deep understanding of custom, garden plants, creatures of the forest and lagoon, and human nature. The wise person is therefore a productive gardener and gatherer of wild foods, rich in valuables to be given away to others in honor of ancestors and on behalf of living kin, able to resolve disputes, and willing to teach and advise others. The wise person also knows how to kill and destroy, though he or she may show restraint, acting only to protect kin and neighbors.

An explicit emphasis on knowledge—particularly supernatural knowledge—as power is common in Melanesian societies.[25] So is a view of knowledge as a personally owned commodity to be transmitted in private to a chosen heir, sometimes in exchange for tangible compensation such as shell valuables or pigs. What is less common is that key forms of knowledge, and thus of personal power and influence over others, are regularly transmitted, by men and women, to women, as on Vanatinai.

Eleven of the supernaturals discussed here are males and seven are females. Among them is a male creator spirit. A slight but perceptible gender asymmetry in the supernatural balance of power becomes more pronounced when we further consider male predominance in the destructive power of sorcery, discussed in the next chapter. But even though influential male supernaturals outnumber the female, females are the owners of such crucial domains as garden, forest, health, and illness. Even more important, ancestor spirits are the supernatural beings most often called upon for magical aid by both men and women, for beneficial and destructive ends. The mother and other female ancestors are especially likely to look kindly upon their living children.

Women's rightful position in ceremonial exchange, the primary arena of power and prestige in Vanatinai cultural life, is validated by the myth of the first exchange, in which a female supernatural gives a generous old woman the first shell valuables and teaches her their use and the magic of exchange. Another female supernatural is the first to use fire to cook food, the quintessentially cultural act.

Women have access along with men to the supernatural knowledge necessary to gain renown in gardening, in exchange activities, or as a magical practitioner. The wise woman motif found in Vanatinai myths and legends reflects present-day human realities on the island, where women as well as men are esteemed for their abilities and admired or feared for their magical knowledge and power.

Chapter Five

Sorcerers and Witches

It was early January, and the big feast at Isosoro was over. Most of the guests dispersed by foot and by sailing canoe to their homes throughout Vanatinai and the East Calvados Islands. The Rossel Islanders departed in the small motor vessel they had built near their own village. But several canoes set sail across the wide bay to the hamlet of Vanabwadibwadi to attend a smaller feast there. The shallow lagoon waters were choppy and turbulent, and a strong wind was blowing from the southwest. By sunset when we reached the hamlet, built on stilts over the white sandy beach, the wind had reached gale force, and a torrential rain had begun. We spent an uneasy night lying awake as the wind threatened to blow the house down, the stilts and palm bark walls creaking ominously with each new gust. The sea level rose alarmingly, and each wave roared under the house just below the floor.

All the Vanabwadibwadi people, and the visitors who had come to attend the feast, said that an old man named Zeyala had made the rain and wind. Zeyala came from a hamlet farther up the coast, but he had been living at Vanabwadibwadi with his two wives for several years. His second wife was from there. She had died the previous week, and people said that Zeyala had killed her through sorcery. The rain, they said, was falling because "he is crying for his wife." No one could explain to me why he would kill his own wife or why, having killed her, he would then cry for her.

The residents of Vanabwadibwadi were afraid of the old man and wanted him to go live somewhere else. Like eight other Vanatinai men in the past few years, he had spent time in jail for sorcery. His neighbors said that he knew both the sorcery techniques of Vanatinai (ribiroi) and the witchcraft of the Misima and Calvados Chain region (*wadawada*). He had been taught witchcraft by his kinswoman and her husband, both widely believed to be powerful witches, on visits to their home island in the East Calvados.

He also knew the magic for making rain, known only on Vanatinai and Rossel, although a few East Calvados men have learned it from Vanatinai exchange partners. His neighbors told me that another old man there would make rain in order to help his fellow villagers and cause their crops to grow properly. But Zeyala would make rain out of spite if someone refused to give him the bagi or tobotobo he requested, only relenting and stopping the rain when the valuable was handed over. He could make rain, they said, not only locally but at Misima, Alotau, and all over Papua New Guinea.

The big man with whom I was staying said that I should threaten to report Zeyala to the government, which would put him in jail for sorcery. I refused. Exasperated, he asked, "Don't you want the rain to stop?" Thinking I was intimidated by the fear of Zeyala's revenge, he added, "If you would only trick him, things would be fine by now. He won't kill you. He is afraid of you because you are white" (*Zogo ukwanuanga mwarau izovuye. Ma ne iunugi gheni. Imarore gheni u kakavara kaiwai*).

The fierce tropical storm continued. A young visitor from the East Calvados had brought a radio with working batteries, and we learned that a cyclone was raging over much of Papua New Guinea, flooding airstrips and blowing down houses in widely separated parts of the country. I moved to a house located one hundred yards inland on slightly higher ground. The house on the beach where I had been sleeping was cut off from the rest of the settlement when the normally placid lagoon waters swallowed up the beach and surged into the coconut grove behind it. My former hosts said they sat awake in fear all night as the sea rose to level with the house floor and as the house next door, fortunately used only for storing clay cooking pots, was blown down.

Two days later a village meeting was called to discuss the accusations of rain making. Several men made angry speeches about how the feast preparations had been delayed by the storm. A local government councillor from another village who had come to attend the feast threatened to report the problem to the OIC (officer-in-charge) at Tagula Station if the rain was not stopped. The government-sanctioned month for holding feasts, December, was already over. In addition, all the islanders had been notified by their councillors that they were supposed to be in their home villages making sago and accumulating garden produce and pigs for the opening ceremony at the new Yeleyamba Local Government Council Chamber at Tagula, scheduled for the end of January. But the feast at Vanabwadibwadi had not even begun yet, because of the storm, and the guests were trapped at the hamlet by the weather.

Finally, someone directly accused Zeyala of making the rain. Zeyala had previously been sitting quietly with his head down chewing betel nut. Now he spat an emphatic spray of red saliva upon the ground while mumbling something inaudible, magic for enhancing the power and persuasiveness of his words. He heatedly denied having caused the rain. Why, he demanded, should he want to make rain since his wife had just died and he was planning to hold a memorial feast, *ghanrakerake* ("food goes out"), for her the following day. So, if it rained the next day, he said, everyone would know that he had not caused it.

Nobody believed Zeyala. The storm deluged the island for another week. The ghanrakerake for Zeyala's wife was actually held under a house during a break in the rain three days after the meeting at which he was accused. The previous day the mwagumwagu ritual took place, in heavy rain, for the old woman who had died several years previously. The atmosphere among the assembled guests and residents was tense and oppressive. There was much private cursing and swearing at Zeyala as the relentless wind and rain trapped everyone inside the houses for long hours. Some of the women ran away in fear when he appeared on the rain-slicked clay of the hamlet's central plaza.

An old woman from one of the East Calvados Islands had sailed fifty miles to the hamlet with a crew of her young relatives to claim the replacement of two long bagi she had given to an exchange partner. She had made one of them herself. Her debtor had promised to follow her from his home to Vanabwadibwadi. He said he would be given a bagi at the feast there that he would transfer to her. But the storm had prevented him from attending the feast. Nevertheless the old woman privately disagreed with the Vanatinai people, who all blamed Zeyala for the rain and wind, saying, "The rain just came by itself."

Both the inhabitants and the entire region of Milne Bay Province are frequently referred to as Samarai by people from other parts of Papua New Guinea, after the island port that used to be the capital of British New Guinea. Samarai people are famous throughout the country for their knowledge of sorcery and witchcraft. But in Milne Bay Province itself, it is the islands of Sudest (Vanatinai) and Rossel (Yela) that are especially notorious for their powerful and active sorcerers.

Almost all serious illnesses, injuries, and deaths are said by Vanatinai people to be due to sorcery or witchcraft or, more rarely, to violations of place or food taboos (Lepowsky 1985b, 1990c). The individual whose friends, neighbors, exchange partners, and enemies think he or she possesses the knowledge of how to kill or injure through supernatural or subtle physical means also possesses great coercive power over others. Vanatinai representations of sorcery and witchcraft belief and practice illuminate concepts of the person, constructions of male and female, interpersonal relations, and the intersections of gender and power.

Killing other people or causing them illness or misfortune through destructive magic is morally wrong to Vanatinai people. It is also against the law, and has been since the turn of the century. For decades white colonial government officers and Catholic priests have been vocal and active in their opposition to sorcery. So, for an outsider, and especially a lumolumo to learn details about these beliefs and practices is extremely difficult. Europeans are known to claim disbelief in sorcery, although some elders suspect that Europeans secretly control powerful magical knowledge that can lead to either wealth or disaster. Sorcery beliefs are deeply rooted in indigenous religious philosophy, which missionaries are dedicated to eradicating. Government officers express anger at the turmoil and trouble that sorcery accusations cause, and they carry sorcerers off to prison on the mainland. Although everyone fears sorcerers, many people feel sadness and shame that their island is home to such evil people.

Asking questions about sorcery is also threatening. Your motives and intentions are suspect. You might use what you know to kill. I had an ambiguous status. I was white, but I had been living in "the place" for a long time. Many older people thought I was an ancestor spirit, a being who by definition possesses enormous magical knowledge and power. Was I seeking more? Was I testing their knowledge? Knowledge of any magic, including the destructive magic of sorcery and witchcraft, is a personal possession of material value that leads to power over others. As Jeanne Favret-Saada (1980:10–11), who studied witchcraft (*sorcier*) in the French countryside, writes, there is no neutral ethnographic position: "In witchcraft, words wage war. Anyone talking about it is a belligerent, the ethnographer like everyone else. There is no room for uninvolved observers . . . nobody ever talks about witchcraft to gain knowledge but to gain power. The same is true about asking questions."

It would be impossible to live on Vanatinai, learn the language, and not hear about sorcery fears and accusations. I asked other questions, often after much hesitation, but there was much I was never told. Some individuals whom I have known for months and, eventually, years, have sought me out, shown me the relics of their dead relatives and their other magical ingredients, and discussed their spells and techniques. I have changed the names of all people and places in this chapter to protect the privacy and confidentiality of everyone concerned. I am not including many details of sorcery practice, in particular, because I was told them on the condition that I keep them secret. I have tried to describe enough about sorcery and witchcraft to discuss Vanatinai religion, worldview, and concepts of self, person, and other as they shape social life in general and gender relations in particular.

I follow anthropological custom, based especially upon the work of Evans-Pritchard (1937) among the Azande of East Africa, and, more important, indigenous Massim beliefs, in distinguishing Vanatinai sorcery from witchcraft. Sorcery, called ribiroi, is a conscious, malevolent act involving the manipulation of objects and conscious magical techniques. Other anthropologists who have studied Melanesian societies offer similar definitions (e.g., Stephen 1987b:75). Witchcraft, wadawada in the Vanatinai language, is a separate magical tradition in the Massim, but it does not follow the

African-derived definition as neatly. It often does emanate from "an inherent quality," in Evans-Pritchard's phrase, of the witch. In Evans-Pritchard's classic definition acts of witchcraft are unconscious, involuntary, or beyond willful control, and they do not involve the use of spells or paraphernalia (Evans-Pritchard 1937:21, 387). This is sometimes the case on Vanatinai as well. But throughout the Louisiade Archipelago witchcraft techniques may be learned as well as inherited at birth from the mother. A few Vanatinai descriptions of witchcraft involve stealing the victim's image in a reflection or even a photograph. This may be done by the witch's spirit as her or his body sleeps or by a deliberate act. Other local descriptions of witchcraft imply acts of conscious volition. They include the desire to repay debts to other witches by providing victims for a supernatural cannibal feast, or an urge to kill a victim that cannot be restrained even by the admonitions of the spirit of another witch.

One significant difference between sorcery and witchcraft is that I have never met anyone on Vanatinai or the nearby islands of the Calvados Chain and Misima who admits to being a witch. Their neighbors privately describe them as witches. But I have met a number of Vanatinai individuals who not only are accused privately of being sorcerers by their neighbors but who have boasted privately to me themselves of their skill at killing through sorcery, showed me some of their paraphernalia, and discussed their techniques.

Sorcerers on both Vanatinai and neighboring Rossel Island are almost always male. But, significantly, the practice of sorcery on Vanatinai is not closed to women, as it is in other parts of New Guinea such as among the Mekeo of the south Papuan coast (Stephen 1987b) or the Garia of Madang Province (Lawrence 1987). In the late 1970s there was said to be only one living female sorcerer on Vanatinai, a fifty-year-old widow and gia, or big woman, who also knew witchcraft. Three other female sorcerers had died recently. Female sorcerers, like their male counterparts, wear male customary dress—the pandanus loin covering called the *memeyoa*—when they carry out their rituals. The memeyoa is otherwise rarely worn by men nowadays, except occasionally at feasts.

My neighbors recalled seeing a certain woman in her fifties, who died a few years previously, occasionally wearing the memeyoa and wandering by herself in the forest. Both solitude and the forest are associated with sorcery practice. This woman, respected and feared for her deep knowledge of custom, was widely believed to be a sorcerer. Childless herself, she taught some of her techniques and spells to her brother's son. Women assume a male social identity when practicing sorcery, and their sorcery is identical to and just as deadly as that of a man. Men are most closely associated with sorcery throughout the Massim.[1]

The male-dominated sorcery traditions of Vanatinai and Rossel are in distinct contrast to the witchcraft beliefs of their immediate neighbors to the northwest. Witchcraft is called wadawada on Vanatinai, *wadewade* in the Saisai language of the East Calvados Islands, and *olal* in the Misima language. It is said not to be native to Vanatinai, although a number of islanders have learned it, but to come from the Calvados Chain Islands, Misima, and Panaeati. Vanatinai people say that it is also indigenous to more distant regions of Milne Bay Province such as the Milne Bay area of the mainland, the islands near Samarai, the D'Entrecasteaux Islands, the Trobriand Islands, and the Woodlark (Murua) Island area. Most—but not all—of its adepts are said to be women.

Witches can leave their bodies behind, seemingly sleeping or dozing. They travel long distances to attack their victims invisibly, causing them to fall sick and die. This witchcraft tradition, sometimes described as the "flying witches," has been reported by anthropologists in the same region described to me by Vanatinai people, extending for hundreds of miles to an area including the Trobriands (Malinowski 1922), Dobu (Fortune 1932) and Normanby (Róheim 1948) as well as the Milne Bay region of the mainland (Seligman 1910). It is closely related to witchcraft beliefs found as far as a thousand miles away in the Mt. Bosavi region of the Great Papuan Plateau (Schieffelin 1976:127), although these witches are mostly male. It is curious that the region in which this cultural tradition is indigenous should end abruptly in the East Calvados Islands only a few miles across the strait from Vanatinai.

Sorcery

Both sorcery and sorcerers on Vanatinai are called ribiroi, which literally means "poison." More rarely, the Papuan Pidgin term *puripuri* is used. The practice of sorcery itself is more rarely called *susudi*, which is said to derive from the English word sorcery. A sorcerer is also referred to by the cautious and fearful euphemism, *loleh*, which means "person" or "someone." All forms of magic detailed in the last chapter can be used in destructive ways, as with malicious weather magic to spoil a feast or a harvest, sending a rival's pig into the forest when an exchange partner shows up to claim it, or magically stealing someone else's yams, but these destructive magical techniques have their own names and are not labeled sorcery.

In over a decade I have been told about only one death resulting from natural causes rather than sorcery, witchcraft, or, more rarely, taboo violations. This was the death of Ghabe, a man in his eighties who died of old age. People said he was such a good person—a healer (and thus a countersorcerer) who never worked sorcery against anyone else—that no one had ever attacked him through sorcery. His remarkably long life testified to his high moral character. Even though beliefs in the personal rather than natural causation of death and illness are common in New Guinea, there is great variation in the degree to which deaths are attributed to sorcery. For example, the Ningerum of the Western Province (Welsch 1983) and the Huli of the Southern Highlands Province (Frankel 1984, 1986) much more rarely ascribe deaths to sorcery or to supernatural causation. I would argue that this is not only due to longer or more thorough exposure to Christian proselytzing or to colonial and national governments and missions introducing biomedicine in the form of aid posts and hospitals. Indigenous beliefs in sorcery and the supernatural causation of illness were, I believe, far stronger on Vanatinai even in precontact times (Lepowsky 1990c). Even in the Mekeo area, famous along the Papuan coast for its potent sorcery, many more deaths are believed due to natural causes than on Vanatinai (cf. Stephen 1987b).

In every Vanatinai settlement there is at least one individual said to be a sorcerer, or someone who has the power to kill or cause sickness through ritual. Often there are several reputed sorcerers living in one hamlet. Certain Vanatinai sorcerers are widely believed to be particularly malevolent and active, and they are held responsible for a large share of the island's deaths. Such individuals are often accused of extorting others into giving them shell currency, greenstone axe blades, pigs, or whatever valuables they may request. Their often unspoken threat is that if the desired objects are not forthcoming, their owners, or members of their family, will be targets of sorcery attacks. Sorcerers may be desirable as exchange partners because of their wealth, but it is extremely dangerous to arouse their envy or covetousness through one's own renown or success in exchange. The only possible protection is a knowledge of countersorcery.

One particular old man, whom I will call Marai, and his sister's son, who has been taught his uncle's skills, are notorious throughout the Louisiade Archipelago as master sorcerers. During my first year of residence on the island the nephew came home after eighteen months' imprisonment at Bwagaoia, Misima and at Giligili Prison near Alotau for the practice of sorcery, a second offense to which he pleaded guilty. His return from prison, like that of any convicted sorcerer, caused great anxiety among his neighbors, who feared his revenge.

Some men who are said to be sorcerers—a status that can only be achieved by successfully killing someone with magical techniques— have not practiced sorcery for many years but use their knowledge to protect their kinfolk and neighbors from attack by other sorcerers. Deaths on Vanatinai are frequently attributed to the actions of a sorcerer who resides in a different hamlet or region from his victim, although sometimes a sorcerer will attack a neighbor or relative. People say, though, that a sorcerer must obtain the permission of his fellow sorcerer in the victim's own hamlet or district before killing someone. He will then owe the second sorcerer a death in his own area, a supernatural form of exchange. By contrast, in the witchcraft beliefs of the Calvados Chain-Panaeati-Misima area, witches commonly are said to attack their own kin.

The Vanatinai men who are known as sorcerers are often the most influential members of their hamlet. They are therefore also called by the term for "big man" or "big woman," gia, literally "giver," referring to the generosity of big people, who are active and successful in exchange activities and who host memorial feasts at which large quantities of goods are redistributed. The giagia are politically influential, for their economic success arises not only from their intelligence and ambition but also their customary and magical knowledge and thus power over others. A gia is often called "the owner of the village" (gheba tanuwagai). This refers to his—or her—influence and leadership rather than to exclusive ownership of land, which is held communally, although giagia normally activate their rights to more garden land and garden larger areas than their neighbors.

Both male and female giagia are also usually known as healers, and healers are countersorcerers. At least some knowledge of sorcery and countersorcery is a prerequisite to these forms of local leadership and influence. The sorcerer is simultaneously a big man and protector of his kin and neighbors in many parts of New Guinea. He is also the upholder of chiefly authority in those few New Guinea societies with hereditary chiefs.[2]

The giagia of Vanatinai are often the ribiroi, or "poisoners," as well, givers of death rather than nurturers of life. The owner of the village who leads and advises others may also kill his own kin and neighbors or allow them to be killed by his counterparts from other communities. This mirrors a larger paradox of Vanatinai worldview that is found in many parts of Melanesia but is particularly pronounced on Vanatinai. Social life is based upon the ethic of cooperation, generosity, and sharing, and each person is dependent upon others for basic subsistence. But at the same time there is a strong belief in the personal causation of almost all misfortune, including death, illness, drought, excessive rain, or failures in gardening, fishing, or hunting. Most such difficulties are said to be due to the malevolent actions of some individual living on the island or nearby. This belief allows the victims at least the possibility of attempting countermeasures against the perpetrators, such as public accusations, countersorcery, or bringing the alleged sorcerer to court at the government station. Like the Dobuans described by Reo Fortune (1932), Vanatinai people strongly manifest "the paranoid ethos" that Schwartz (1979) argues is characteristic of Melanesian societies.

Sorcery, Influence, and Cultural Change

Both the colonial government and present-day administrators have sought to reduce the power and influence of sorcerers on Vanatinai. Government opposition becomes clearer when the influence of sorcerers in their own and neighboring communities is acknowledged. Sorcerers are often, though not always, big men and/or ritual experts, protectors, and healers of their own kin and neighbors. Although there are big women, female witches and sorcerers, and female ritual experts and healers, men who are widely known as sorcerers often have more influence over their neighbors than anyone else because of the threat, explicit or implicit, of their magical attack.

Several local government councillors, who are generally younger, mission-educated men, have publicly denounced the influence of sorcerers on the island, which they themselves hope to supplant. When a complaint has been lodged against a sorcerer (or other alleged law-breaker), it is normally the local government councillor who has the unpleasant task of escorting the accused to the government station at Tagula to court and possibly to jail. The councillors are fearful that they or their families will be magically attacked in retribution. A few local government councillors have been widely believed to be sorcerers themselves, although the most notorious of these was voted out of office in 1978.

The Catholic Mission at Nimowa has also long deplored the power and influence of Vanatinai sorcerers. They located their headquarters at Nimowa in 1947 instead of the Griffin Point area of Sudest because they feared, probably correctly, that if the mission were on Sudest, the East Calvados Island parents would be afraid to send their children to the mission school. When I returned to the area in 1987 I met a priest from the Mekeo area of Central Province living at Nimowa. His personal mission was a more effective conversion of the Sudest people to Catholicism through his active psychic combat with the power of the Sudest sorcerers, and he was vocal in his hatred for sorcerers. I think it significant that the Mekeo people are also widely known in mainland Papua for their powerful sorcerers and pervasive sorcery beliefs (e.g., Stephen 1987b). Just as the government accurately perceives the competing political power of the sorcerers, the missionary priests, Australian and Papuan, correctly recognize the religious basis of sorcery power, a competing religious ideology they see as false and dangerous.

A few people on Vanatinai say that sorcery was not practiced at all on the island before the beginning of the colonial period in the late nineteenth century, when the incidence of warfare and raiding was sharply reduced. But most maintain strongly that sorcery was indigenous to Vanatinai, agreeing that as fighting became a less accessible means of settling grievances, the practice of sorcery became far more common (cf. Lawrence 1973:219).

Vanatinai people frequently say, "Before we killed with spears and nowadays we kill with sorcery." This statement that physical aggression has been replaced by sorcery suggests that the giagia of precontact days maintained their positions of leadership and influence through their prowess in warfare or by their control of younger warriors. The idea that physical attack has been replaced by sorcery attack helps explain why sorcery is so strongly associated with men.

Peter Lawrence (1987:21) rightly criticizes anthropologists for relying so heavily on functional and "sociopolitical" analyses of sorcery—what it does rather than what it means—and for failing to consider sorcery as an intrinsic part of Melanesian religions. But the idea that sorcery substitutes for physical aggression is a functional argument made by Vanatinai people themselves. Lawrence (1987:33) himself reports that the Garia, whom he began to study in 1949, say something very similar. And by saying that men are the killers, both with spears and with sorcery, Vanatinai men and women alike are making philosophical statements about the nature of the world in general, the power of spirits, and the fundamental nature and tendencies of humans as gendered beings.

During the goldmining days in the last years of the nineteenth century, laborers from the Dobu-Normanby-Fergusson Island areas of the D'Entrecasteaux Archipelago were brought to Vanatinai by the whites. These "Duau" men, as they are usually called locally, are said to have taught Vanatinai people many new sorcery techniques. The "sorcerers of Dobu" described by Reo Fortune in 1932 say that sorcery originated at Duau, which is the eastern district of Normanby Island and the indigenous name in southern Massim languages for the whole island.

The influx of hundreds of white miners to Vanatinai in 1888 and the increased contact with Europeans that followed the gold rush caused the introduction and the further spread of new and deadly infectious diseases such as influenza, pneumonia, bronchitis, whooping cough, dysentery, and tuberculosis (Campbell 1899, Lepowsky 1990c:1055–1056). Vanatinai people explain a remembered rise in illness and death during this period by attributing it to the efficacy of the new forms of sorcery introduced from Duau. A similar tendency to adopt new beliefs about illness causation and, correspondingly, cure from people from other parts of New Guinea during the colonial period has been reported in many parts of the country. Colonial policies inadvertently facilitated new kinds of intercultural contacts by the suppression of warfare and the increased mobility that resulted and by encouraging migrant labor to provide a workforce for European-owned mines and plantations.

Some government officials, expatriates and nationals alike, are sure that sorcerers on Vanatinai kill their victims by actually administering poison, as their name, ribiroi, would indicate. A hundred years ago David White (1893), a sometime pearl and bêche-de-mer fisherman and goldminer who lived on Vanatinai through much of the 1880s, wrote,

> The natives are in constant dread of being poisoned by each other, and on no account would anyone leave the basket in which he carries his lime and betel nut out of his possession, and when anyone dies suspiciously they at once put it down to puri-puri or poison. I have been shown six different plants from which they are said to extract poison, one being, I believe, a species of the Euphorbia.

It is true that islanders know of plant and marine poisons. But the accounts I was given of recent sorcery cases and sorcery techniques suggest that most, if not all, sorcery attacks nowadays are magical attacks. The fact that sorcerers have the capability of poisoning their victims probably lends weight to their threats of magical destruction.[3]

Government officials have fought a long and losing battle against the power of sorcerers on Vanatinai. For over seventy years colonial dispatches were disproportionately concerned with sorcery as a symptom of incomplete control by the government over the islanders. A patrol report submitted to the Territory of Papua in 1911 is the earliest presently existing record of a visit by an Australian colonial officer to Vanatinai, five years after Australia took over control of the Territory of Papua from the British.[4] The 1911 report describes a case of alleged extortion by a sorcerer:

> About 20 different boys waited on me from all parts of the island with complaints about a man named Taunana, whom they are in terror of their lives of [sic], on account of the threats that he has sent out, that he will Puri-Puri plenty of people, sent V.C. [Village Constable] Jimmy and 2 A.C.s [assistant constables] to arrest him, they returned with him 3 p.m. Held N.M. [Native Matters] Court, defendant

admitting that he did frighten the people, and that it was all the fault of his snake. I asked him about his snake, and he informed me that all the time he drank salt water, and that when he was asleep at night, the snake used to come up from the salt water, and whistle in his ear (the defendant then gave me an illustration of how the snake whistled) "when the snake whistled I woke up, and went to where some man was sleeping, and told him that he had to give me something, or else I would talk to my snake." [I] proceeded in the whaleboat about 4 mile up the coast to where the Puri-Puri man Taunana has a house, found a large quantity of Papuan trade [ceremonial valuables], which the defendant Taunana informed me that he got through frightening the people, also giving me the names of the people from whom he had received them from [*sic*], sent for the respective owners of the goods, and returned them to them.

(Territory of Papua, Patrol Reports August 14 and 16, 1911)

Sorcery on Vanatinai is strongly associated with the power of spirit familiars: ancestor spirits, long-dead sorcerers and warriors, and place spirits. These often take the form of a snake. The two supernatural patrons of sorcery, Tamudurere, who lives in the sea, and Rodyo, owner of the dead who lives on Mt. Rio, are snake beings. Sorcerers fast and purge themselves by drinking salt water. Sorcery is also strongly associated with the night and contact with spirits in dreams and visions.

A patrol officer in 1912 mentions, without further comment, that while at Pantava he "held Court and sentenced a native to imprisonment for sorcery." This is the earliest record of the jailing of a Vanatinai sorcerer. The Australians were primarily concerned with the threat to public order and to colonial control that belief in destructive magic and fear of its practitioners created. The patrol reports from 1934 record two cases of murders on Sudest (Vanatinai), the details of which are not specified. One man was given three years at hard labor and the other was judged insane and kept in custody. The colonial officer writes,

In the last named case there was some reason to suspect that the accused had been the victim of an alleged harmful drug—a bark known as OM-E the use of which is very prevalent in Rossel and Sudest Islands, and which of late has also been used in the Misima District. It would appear that when used medicinally the bark has the

180

power of clearing the bronchial tubes, or relieving a severe headache, but when over-indulged in, it gives rise to symptoms of nerve poisoning rather similar to the effects of cocaine or strychnine. It is also supposedly possessed of magical properties. The subject when under its influence is said to be able to receive telepathic tidings from distant places—such as news of the death of close relatives, the resulting grief serving to increase the symptoms mentioned. The writer has seen a subject so convulsed that he had to be held down by three other natives, and on two occasions this year has been threatened by natives suffering from the effects of this drug.

Ome (sandalwood) has important medicinal and magical uses on Vanatinai and Rossel. Vanatinai people recall no recent cases where someone went into convulsions or threatened to attack another person (except for two unusual cases when large quantities of alcohol had been consumed; see Lepowsky 1982). It is possible that the hysterical and aggressive behavior described above was triggered by the unusual presence on the island of a white colonial officer. At that date, according to surviving records, Vanatinai had not been visited by an Australian colonial officer for nine years.

Another alleged case of extortion under threat of sorcery is reported in 1943 following the withdrawal of the civilian colonial government, the cargo cult-inspired attack upon a military patrol, and other incidents of violence that followed. Lt. Smith writes that one Nigaho Island man "in particular seems to have wielded quite a lot of power and was feared by those whom he did not call his friends. I have the names of six natives of small villages on and around Joannet who paid him with axe stones, baggi, and limesticks to ward off his enmity, and I have recovered the axe-stones etc. with the help of his wives, of whom he had four."

He also discusses the case of a Vanatinai man who was killed in the East Calvados Islands along with a local friend. He found it "difficult" to investigate the case, as "(t)here were half-a-dozen explanations, all giving 'purri-purri' as the excuse" (Territory of Papua, Patrol Report no. 2/43, April 3, 1943). Descendants of the principals in this case say that the Vanatinai man became involved in a quarrel over valuables. He was murdered because he was suspected of killing a Nigaho Island man through sorcery (Lepowsky 1989b).

Assistant District Officer C. F. Cowley reports in 1948 that he was told "V.C. KAPAI of HULA village, had formed an 'army' of 10 soldiers, and was going to use sorcery on the Sudest peoples. Other village officials present said KAPAI told them he was the 'boss soldier.' " Kapai and others were said to have talked of "drilling 'soldiers' for an alleged attack on other villages at SUDEST ISLAND." Kapai later "admitted that he had 'yarned' about 'soldiers.' "

Master sorcerers today are alleged to employ *gatu*, or assistants, a word translated by English speakers as soldiers. Using the idiom of military training and attack for sorcery is a continuing legacy of World War II.

Patrol Officer R. Matthews reports on the "Native Situation" in 1951:

> At SUDEST the strong hold that sorcery still has, was again in evidence. A native was brought, sweating with fear, and gravely charged with having caused the recent cyclone by magic. Upon hearing the evidence which was offered, it appeared that the native had, just before the big blow, been making a charm to bring rain for his garden! The coincidence which gave him considerably more than he bargained for, was nevertheless sufficient to make him culpable in the eyes of the rest of his unsophisticated neighbours. As there was no appearance of a mischievous intent in the charge, it was explained that the native could not have brought about the storm, and that any further suggestion of that nature would result in a prosecution under the Native Regulations. The majority of the natives present then said that they had never believed it anyway! It seems that most of SUDEST goes in continual fear of sorcery, except when there is a Government officer actually present when they fear the government just slightly more than the sorcerer. It is seldom possible to make friends with a small child at SUDEST, because they flee to their mothers' arms at the approach of a stranger, in marked contrast to the children of the Calvados Chain and MISIMA.

This incident parallels the case of Zeyala, the alleged sorcerer and cyclone summoner, whom I was urged by his neighbors to report to the government officer for prosecution. Note that in the 1951 case Matthews concluded that there had been no malicious intent and thus did not charge the man under the sorcery laws. Instead he explained his notion of causality as it pertained to weather phenomena and threatened to prosecute the accusers. He may have succeeded in intimidating them, and he remarks on their fear of the coercive power of the government officer, who could, solely on his own authority, charge, find guilty, and imprison a Papuan. But he did not succeed in convincing the islanders of his views on the nature of storms: at least, I found the same ideas a generation later.

A slightly later patrol report by Matthews dated 1951–52 comments, "It is a locally accepted theory that Sudest is the centre of magical power," and discusses two complaints concerning sorcery. A man from Jelewaga

> had threatened to kill a pig. . . . DICK admitted making the threat, but claimed that it was as a reprisal to hints of puri-puri being made by CHARLIE to bring about his death. There was no satisfactory evidence of this, but ample evidence of the prevalence of puri-puri talk, so without taking any action, I warned DICK against such threats, and in general discussion, tried to discount the fear of sorcery. It was apparent that there was much more idle talk than actual practice of puri-puri. The people were advised that action would be taken against anyone of whom complicity in sorcery rites or threats could be actually proven.

The second case involved sorcery threats at a feast at Rewe (Rehua):

> KAPAI of BAUMUMU had threatened to bring about the death of KUKI of GESILA. KAPAI cheerfully admitted this, but pointed out that KUKI was not yet dead, although frightened, so there was really nothing to worry about! I decided to bring KAPAI to BWAGAOIA [Misima] to appear before a Court for Native Matters. KAPAI is one of a group of about half a dozen Sudest natives who are generally conceded, whether justifiably or not is not certain, to be the "strong" magicians of the island. An interesting sidelight on the situation is that when the patrol was at BAUMUMU, an election was held to nominate a councillor, and KAPAI was unanimously elected. I was later told by the councillors of other villages, that many people have migrated away from BAUMUMU to escape from KAPAI'S influence, and that those who remained were well under his control.
>
> (Territory of Papua, Misima Patrol Report no. 4, 1951/52)

A 1952–53 patrol report by another officer comments, "It does not need a long stay at Sudest to realise that sorcery exists in a big way; to realise that it has many of the people terrified." He heard a case of alleged extortion of ceremonial valuables under threat of death:

> TODAU sent his messenger over to SIGILI [another alleged sorcerer] with the message "Why don't the PAMELA people give me (TODAU) payment of some native food, one tomahawk stone, one bagi, and one pig." SIGILI had then gone to PAMELA and said to about 20 of the people—"Word from TODAU that he wants payment of .... [sic] Why are people dying here? It is better to give things <u>back</u> to TODAU. You know that TODAU is a big pourri-pourri man. You must give these things back quickly. People are dying here. We will see what happens then. TODAU is not like myself for I am good to the people." After a lot of questioning it appeared that the goods were owed to TODAU by his nephew a native of PAMELA for whom TODAU had given a feast, but it seems to be the fashion on Sudest that such goods are not repayable under such circumstances. As far as the PAMELA people and the rest of the people on the island were concerned such talk plainly meant—if the PAMELA people don't give these goods quickly to TODAU then a lot of PAMELA people are going to die in the very near future.

Charges that debts in ceremonial valuables have not been paid are among the most frequently cited causes of sorcery threats and sorcery attacks today. This case, if understood correctly by the patrol officer, who relied on interpreters, is interesting for the ambiguous role of the second sorcerer, Sigili, said in the report to come from nearby Pantava (whose inhabitants are closely related to the Pamela people). It is unclear if he is acting primarily out of concern for the welfare of the Pamela citizens or if he is an accomplice of Todau, said to reside at Araida on the north coast. This patrol officer names Todau, Sigili, and Kapai as the "biggest sorcerers" on the island.

A 1954 patrol report comments that "Sudest is the home of sorcery, but as usual, it is very difficult to secure a complaint. The injured party is afraid of sustaining greater injury if he complains." Five years later a colonial offficer remarks that the people of Vanatinai "bask in the unsavory climate of their evil reputation," and notes that a sorcerer from Pantava had threatened to obliterate all of Pantava and Araida if he was not allowed to return from jail at Misima Island, a feat he would accomplish by mobilizing his "soldiers," or assistants (Territory of Papua, Patrol Reports 1959). The following year a patrol officer reports that the islanders always travel in pairs or groups and exhibit a "complete reluctance to travel at night" for fear of sorcery attacks. He records the death of the last "master sorcerer" in 1958, asserting that there is always one such individual, and commenting that the usual sorcery technique is to introduce a foreign object into the victim's body through magic (Territory of Papua, Patrol Reports 1960/61).

Firing magical projectiles remains the most frequently described magical technique. In the late 1970s and the 1980s there was still one individual (and his matrilineal heir), Marai, most renowned and feared for sorcery on Vanatinai and throughout the archipelago. This reputation did not confer political authority on Marai, nor was he known as a prominent exchanger of valuables. People alleged, though, that he and his nephew had stockpiled large quantities of ceremonial valuables acquired through threats and extortion.

The 1962 patrol reports describe a mass migration of the citizenry of the village of Nainhil to a new settlement about ten miles away—in fear of the sorcery of a man named Feelergauge. In 1971 a child disappeared and was never found. A sorcerer alleged to be responsible was reported and imprisoned for three months at Misima. The entire population of his hamlet fled upon his release.

A typed sheet of paper I found in the government station at Tagula dated 1973 and entitled "The Name of Sorcerers Man Around Sudest Island" lists forty individuals. The list omits the names of at least half a dozen more men widely believed by local people in 1978–79 to be sorcerers and fails to mention any of the female sorcerers who were alive and supposedly active in 1973.

As noted in the government patrol reports, another recourse against a sorcerer is migration, which results in the withdrawal of social support from him in the form of a viable community. For example, in the mid-1970s the members of two clans, related by marriage, who lived together in a hamlet on tiny Iyen Island, a half-mile offshore from Jelewaga, quarreled over who had the right to plant a garden on a particular piece of land. Both clans claimed ownership of the disputed area. Shortly afterward there were several tragic deaths of young adults and children in each clan. These were blamed on the sorcery or witchcraft of the opposing clan. At least two of these deaths were apparently due to tuberculosis. Finally the group of brothers and sisters who with their spouses and children comprised one faction decided to move permanently to another island about thirty miles away where their paternal grandmother had land rights. They founded a new hamlet, where they remained as of 1987. Their departure left the other kin group with only three living adults. Unable to sustain a community with such a small number of people to share subsistence tasks, the remaining faction was forced to leave also and to settle in another hamlet where one of them had relatives. The original hamlet remains deserted, even though it is a highly desirable place to live—with reliable water, adequate garden land, and excellent reefs for fishing—and despite the fact that the site had been continuously inhabited since at least the late 1880s when the first British government officers to visit the area noted its existence. However, two old men, both adepts of sorcery and witchcraft, who were principals in the dispute have died recently, and it is possible that the area will be resettled during the next decade by some of the survivors.

Along with quarrels over land rights, disputes involving exchange relations and envy of another's success in exchange are common motives for sorcery accusations. In the case of Zeyala, described earlier, the local consensus was that the old man had spitefully made rain to spoil his neighbors' feast because he was angry about not being given a medium-sized pig that he had requested from another villager. Any person who owns many pigs or ceremonial valuables, who has a reputation as a generous host of memorial feasts, who succeeds in obtaining particularly desirable pieces of shell currency on greenstone axe blades from an exchange partner, or who is an unusually successful gardener must possess the knowledge of sorcery and magic necessary to counter the sorcery attempts of others. This includes women who are known as giagia. It is fairly common for disputes over ceremonial valuables to erupt into sorcery threats at memorial feasts, as described in chapter 1, at which point attempts are usually made by third parties to arbitrate the matter before anyone falls sick or dies.

Anyone who does fall sick in the weeks following his or her participation in a feast will be described as the victim of another's envy. One middle-aged man, Giazagu, contracted pneumonia and nearly died. A month earlier he had made substantial contributions of pigs, garden produce, and ceremonial valuables to two kinsmen in other hamlets who were hosting feasts. He aroused the envy and anger of a sorcerer, whose identity was not clear, by having added so much luster to his reputation as a gia. Giazagu took to his bed and did not sit up, eat, or chew betel nut for many days. I gave him antibiotics, and he made a dramatic recovery. His kinspeople said that this strong medicine was powerful enough to overcome the sorcerer's attack (Lepowsky 1990c:1052).

Sorcerers may also be motivated by sexual jealousy. The young wife of Marai's nephew was socially isolated and clearly depressed and miserable during her husband's imprisonment for sorcery and absence from the island. Even her own kinsmen were afraid to talk to her or assist her in case her husband heard about it later and worked sorcery on them, believing they had made sexual advances to his wife.

Sorcerers are also said to act sometimes over irritation in petty matters. For example, a little boy was playing in the center of the hamlet when he accidentally kicked dirt into the eyes of Marai, who was sitting on the ground and talking with several other men. This thoughtless act by a three year old was said to have caused the old sorcerer to take revenge by making the child fall sick with an illness (tuberculosis) that permanently crippled his spine and nearly killed him. There are also some cases of illness or death for which no one can discern any motive, and it is said that sometimes a sorcerer may act merely out of spite or to try out some newly acquired magical technique.

Sorcery Techniques

The basis of a sorcerer's power, and the basis of all important forms of magical power, is a link with the realm of the spirits. The knowledge of how to achieve this link is secret. Sorcerers derive their power through their successful appeals to the spirits of their own dead kin, the spirits of powerful individuals such as deceased sorcerers or warriors, to certain place spirits, or to the patron supernaturals of sorcery, witchcraft, and warfare, Tamudurere and Rodyo.

Sorcerers make direct magical attacks upon their victims or bespell their victims' personal leavings. Each sorcerer's array of techniques and spells is different. Knowledge of sorcery and, similarly, of other magical practices is transmitted privately from one adult to his or her magical heir. Such knowledge is dissipated by telling it to more than one person. A few forms of magical knowledge—some, but not all, types of hunting and war magic—are specific to men and will lose their power if told to women. Ideally, a knowledge of sorcery techniques should be transmitted within the matrilineage from a mother's brother to a sister's son, or from individuals who refer to each other as uncle and nephew even though their relationship may be more distant. Rarely, a man will teach his sister's daughter. Sometimes, though, such knowledge flows privately from father to one of his sons or even to his firstborn daughter, or from a stepfather to a favored stepson. Women also learn sorcery techniques from lovers in exchange for their sexual favors.

The fact that one is acquiring a knowledge of sorcery must be kept completely secret, or else it is said that other sorcerers, fearful of the incipient power of the apprentice, will kill him. This secrecy also protects the instructing sorcerer and his pupil from the anger of other younger kin who may have desired to obtain this knowledge of sorcery, and the power that results from it, for themselves. A sorcerer is supposed to choose only one heir, generally male, from among his matrilineal descendants. The choice is based upon character and ability rather than upon birth order. An apprentice sorcerer may only complete his training and prove his power by successfully killing someone.

A sorcerer causes illness or death by using certain magical paraphernalia, the mere possession of which is strictly illegal. The most important of these, also used in beneficial forms of magic, is a relic of a dead kinsperson or other individual, the muramura. The verb *mura* means to blow, as onto a fire. A muramura may be a tooth, piece of bone, or lock of hair. Sometimes a relative sitting in night-long vigil beside a corpse will ask his or her deceased mother, father, uncle, or sister for permission to remove the relic for use in magic. Other times a person will wait a few months until the corpse has rotted in the tropical soil of its shallow grave, then use special digging magic to open the grave easily in the middle of a moonless night and take the relic. Muramura are also taken from burial places—graves, caves, or trees—of powerful sorcerers or of long-dead heroes or warriors, the asiara of earlier generations. The taking of relics was formerly associated with the Vanatinai custom of secondary burial (Lepowsky 1989a), and it is a key part of indigenous religious practice.

Some people keep muramura in their houses in a secret place, but they are said to make the house so hot that they may cause children and other vulnerable persons to fall sick. The relics are therefore more often hidden in a secret place in the coolness of the forest.

The most powerful sorcerers regularly carry their muramura with them in their personal baskets along with their ginger, tobacco, and betel nut fixings. This is why it is dangerous to accept betel nut or tobacco from a sorcerer. Even if he does not intend to harm you, it has absorbed the dangerous supernatural heat of his muramura and his other sorcery paraphernalia. Of course, it is also insulting and thus dangerous to refuse, for it implies that you suspect that an offer to share is an attempt to kill you. When a number of sorcerers congregate in one place for a memorial feast, the presence of so many baskets filled with sorcery paraphernalia makes the entire hamlet hot and may cause sickness. That is why it is dangerous to bring children to feasts. Along with his paraphernalia the sorcerer may carry in his basket the personal leavings of his intended victim, such as discarded husks of betel nut, expectorant, or hair.

I was sitting on the floor chewing betel nut with Ivwara while we were attending a feast. He is widely feared for his sorcery powers, although his kinfolk and friends regard him highly. It was the middle of the afternoon, and no one else could see us in the dimly lit room. Ivwara, who by then had known me for many years, unexpectedly began to show me the contents of his personal basket. He handed me a piece of the skull of his mother, whom I had once known, a tooth of his father, and a lock of the hair of his deceased sister. He also brought out other objects he uses for sorcery and for other kinds of magic and explained some of his techniques.

The muramura embodies the protective power of the ancestor or other spirit toward the living magician or sorcerer. This is a power that is used not only for sorcery and destruction. It is essential for beneficial magic and ritual used in domains such as gardening, healing, or exchange. Government authorities do not recognize this distinction.

The other paraphernalia of the sorcerer are also illegal as a collection, for the government regards all of them as evidence of destructive magic even though many of them are used with beneficial intent. These include a variety of roots, particularly ginger and a white aromatic root called *wughulumo,* barks, leaves, and infusions. One powerful ingredient is a curious, hard, white fungus, whose name and habitat I omit here. It is also used in various forms of "convincing magic."

Illness caused by a supernatural attack is called *gida.* When a sorcerer wishes to attack someone, he—or she—must wear only the memeyoa and avoid social and sexual contact with others. He must abstain from eating a normal diet, and consume only boiled or roasted coconut meat. He should visit the lagoon in the middle of the night to drink salt water, which makes him hot and acts as a purgative. He also chews ginger for long periods of time to make himself hot and powerful.

The property of heat is strongly associated with sorcery as well as with various kinds of beneficial magic where the practitioner must especially avoid eating "cold" foods, such as fish. Ginger and wughulumo are regarded as particularly hot and supernaturally potent. Witchcraft, on the other hand, is associated with the coldness of corpses.[5]

Sorcerers know rogau, the magic to make themselves invisible. One of the main reasons people on Vanatinai are afraid to walk around by themselves in the daytime or to go out at night except in groups, during a feast or during a full moon, is that they fear they may accidentally encounter an invisible sorcerer on one of the island paths on his way to the beach to drink salt water or en route to the forest to obtain some plant that he requires. Merely breathing the breath of such a sorcerer, laden as it is with the scent of ginger and other plant substances that he chews to give himself power, is sufficient to make a passer-by fall ill, even if the harmful magic was not intended for him or her.

Sorcerers also have the power to turn themselves into snakes at will. Snakes are never killed or disturbed on Vanatinai. To do so might bring disaster, as they may in reality be either sorcerers or place spirits—silava.

Sorcerers, when they are preparing for an attack, spend days or even weeks alone in the forest chewing ginger, chanting spells, and trying to reach the altered state of consciousness necessary to contact the spirit world with the aid of a muramura in order to bring about their desired destructive ends (cf. Stephens 1987b). Nighttime is the domain of sorcerers. Their invisible presence in a hamlet may be signaled by a dog who howls for no apparent reason or by the cry of a bat (*manuwijiwiji*). Bats are believed to be sorcerers' familiars who accompany them or assist them. When a bat cries in the evening, people call out, "Loleh!" in fearful tones. Anyone who is outside hastily moves into the shelter of a house, and windows are closed and doors tied shut with cord. Fireflies may also make people nervous, especially if there is just one or if one gets into the house. They, too, may be the familiars of sorcerers or witches.

The most common sorcery technique is to "fire" a projectile through magic into the victim's body. A gourd limepot, or sometimes nowadays a matchbox, is bespelled by the sorcerer. It contains a mura-mura, ginger and other roots, barks, leaves, or infusions brewed from plant substances as well as the "bullet," which may be a piece of shell currency, bone, a fishhook, a stone, a nail, or any other hard object, such as a broken bit of plastic or metal of mysterious origin.

The sorcerer makes himself invisible or merely waits for an opportunity to tap the gourd or matchbox sharply, causing the magical projectile to fly invisibly into the victim's body. He may hide beside a forest path or attack during the crowded confusion of a feast, with its night-long dancing and drumming. A sorcerer also fires his deadly magical projectiles through the walls or floors of houses. He can charm a stick or other object along a path and wait for the intended victim to brush against it or bespell a taboo marker of twisted grass and place it in a place the victim is likely to walk, such as along the route to a garden. Sometimes a sorcerer is said to entice his victim into his presence through magic. The unknowing victim will feel pain or sickness in the part of the body that has been struck and will die within days or weeks.

Another method of attack used by sorcerers is to obtain some personal leavings of the intended victim, such as hair, fingernail clippings, expectorant from betel nut chewing, or discarded pieces of betel nut skin. These are then bespelled, and the victim again falls sick or dies within a short period of time. A sorcerer may offer a bespelled betel nut to his unwitting victim in a spurious gesture of friendship, and after chewing it the victim will become sick. For this reason people sometimes warn their loved ones visiting other hamlets or islands to attend feasts or look for ceremonial valuables not to accept betel nut from strangers or from certain known sorcerers and not to throw away their betel nut skins after chewing.[6]

Known sorcerers are believed to be wealthy in pigs and ceremonial valuables from having been paid for their evil deeds by others or from extortion. They do not necessarily redistribute these valuables at feasts to gain reputations as giagia. Some sorcerers are prominent in exchange, and others are not. The latter are the individuals most hated and feared by their neighbors and by other islanders. They are men who prey on others to accumulate wealth and flaunt their disregard for the values of sharing and generosity by refusing to participate even in the public and ritual forms of giving away wealth that build individual renown and power over others.

Sorcerers' assistants, who are usually their apprentices, or "soldiers," carry out magical executions for their masters, who pay them in ceremonial valuables for their work.

Because of the fear of poisoning, only close kin will share food. And the Vanatinai marriage ceremony consists of sharing breakfast. It is not customary for visitors on exchange journeys or at feasts to eat with their hosts. At feasts the guests are given their own separate portions of raw pork and uncooked garden produce and sago, which they cook and eat by themselves, though they also receive shares of cooked sago pudding or sago, yams, and other produce that has been roasted in a stone oven as well as a share of the liquid in which organ meats and bits of pork have been boiled. The cooked food is eaten separately by guests. People who visit on exchange trips are fed cooked food by their hosts, but guests and hosts eat in different parts of the house. By accepting the food, the visitor is putting his or her life in the hosts' hands, a situation that was even more obvious in precolonial days, when hosts formally protected their foreign exchange partners against the spears of other hamlet residents (Lepowsky n.d.1; cf. Malinowski 1922:92). And as David White noted one hundred years ago, Vanatinai people keep careful track of their personal betel nut baskets.

Formal public accusations of sorcery are rare. When they occur the accused sorcerer usually denies the charges. In one instance several years ago I was told that the accused, believed to be responsible for the deaths of a number of young married men on the other side of the island, burst into tears and emotionally denied the accusations. As he is widely said to be a master sorcerer, he was not believed. In the case described at the beginning of this chapter it is noteworthy that the old man Zeyala was publicly accused of maliciously making rain in order to spoil his neighbors' feast, but no one dared say publicly what almost everyone insisted privately, which was that he had killed his own wife through sorcery just the week before.

Several forms of divination are used to determine who is responsible for a death. As noted earlier, if the sorcerer comes to mourn his victim, the corpse's eyes will fly open at his approach or the body will move slightly. The absence of a suspected sorcerer from his victim's burial would also be suspicious. Some people know how to divine the guilty party through a ritual involving a five-leafed plant.

Frequently a victim's kinfolk will be convinced that they know who killed their relative but will continue to have polite and seemingly normal social relations with the alleged sorcerer. However, if one of their number is also an adept of sorcery, he may wait for months or years to elapse and then take revenge by magically attacking and killing the first sorcerer. A sorcerer's illness or demise is almost always attributed to the revenge sorcery or witchcraft of a powerful relative of one of his victims.

Sometimes after a death the relatives of the deceased may attempt to attack physically the sorcerer believed to be responsible. When one man died suddenly his adult son armed himself with a bush knife (machete) and went looking for old Marai, the master sorcerer whom he held responsible. Marai fled his home in the middle of the night. He crossed the island in the dark and appeared trembling with fright at the door, tied shut for the night, of one of his cousins in a remote mountain hamlet. The family's four-year-old son ordered him to go away and leave them alone. Marai pleaded directly and eloquently to his small cousin to shelter him for the night, saying that otherwise the dead man's son would "cut his throat." The family let him in the house. Before dawn the following morning the old sorcerer continued down to the coast and took a canoe to an off-shore island. He remained in hiding there for more than a month, only returning to his home after the son's rage had been allowed to cool.

Sorcery, a primary source of power over others and of coercion, is not barred to Vanatinai women. But knowledge of sorcery and the power that results is almost entirely the domain of men. Some men who are sorcerers are also respected for their knowledge of beneficial magic, but others, like Zeyala, are hated by their neighbors.

The increase in the practice of sorcery on Vanatinai is directly attributed by the islanders to the prohibition against raiding and warfare. These too were the province of men and a means by which certain men could gain the respect of others and become leaders. The virtual male monopoly on knowledge and practice of sorcery suggests its substitution for warfare, a former male monopoly and avenue for ascendancy over others.

Witchcraft

Witches are mainly female. Although people say witches may kill involuntarily, during sleep or while in a dreamlike altered state of consciousness, most verbal descriptions of incidents of witchcraft emphasize the witch's conscious volition. They attack out of envy or malice, like sorcerers, out of sexual jealousy or frustrated desire, or simply out of a craving for human flesh.

They are said to operate mainly at night, when they leave their bodies behind—seemingly sleeping or dozing—while their spirits fly invisibly through the air to the spot, sometimes on a distant island, where they will kill their victims. They magically attack the entrails and induce weakness and lethargy that later will result in sickness or death. Sometimes witches are seen sitting on the roof of a victim's house. They also may entice their victims out of their houses and draw them to a spot where they may be killed. After a victim is buried witches will fly to the grave from many villages, secretly dig up the body, and hold a cannibal feast, with the killer acting as host. The other witches will then have to reciprocate with similar feasts, a supernatural domain of exchange. Some people swear that they have actually witnessed these supernatural feasts. They say that it is the spiritual essence of the victim rather than his or her flesh that is actually consumed.[7]

Witches sometimes travel by "spirit boats" and "spirit planes." On one rare occasion when a plane flew over a village on Vanatinai, the residents were convinced that it was a "spirit plane" transporting a witch. Many people also told me stories of a European boat that appeared off the north coast a few years ago. No one could identify it, and it vanished when the islanders tried to approach it. It too was said to have been a boat belonging to witches. If a crocodile or shark attacks someone, it may be the "spirit boat" of a witch who is actually making the attack. Witches are held responsible for some shipwrecks, for they haunt the sea, particularly at night when they send their spirits out to cut off the lips of sailors with a pearl shell so that they will "talk like dogs" and be unable to find their way home.[8]

According to myth, the Misima village of Ebora, a remote spot on the precipitous western tip of that island reachable only by sea, is the place where witchcraft originated. Misima and nearby Panaeati Island are said to be home to many witches, but nowadays people in the Louisiade Archipelago regard Motorina Island in the West Calvados group, a Misima-speaking island, as the home of the most active and notorious witches. Motorina, a small island, has this unhappy reputation mainly because the only three sailing canoes in the Louisiade lost at sea in the last forty years were all from there. One was traveling from Motorina to Misima across the open sea at the time. Another, I was told, was returning home a generation ago from Vanatinai heavily laden with pigs and other ceremonial valuables obtained for an upcoming feast, but it never arrived.[9]

The last tragedy occurred in November of 1977 when four men set out in the late afternoon to make the dangerous passage from Motorina to Misima to attend a feast. The trip means traveling for about thirty miles between the relative shelter of the Sudest Lagoon barrier reef and the reef guarding the entrance to Bwagaoia Harbor at Misima. This is an open sea channel notorious to sailors of large motor vessels and sailing canoes alike for its treacherous currents and enormous swells. A cyclone came up, and the Motorina canoe capsized about midway between the two islands. Three of the men drowned, but the fourth managed to cling to the outrigger log and drifted a hundred miles north to the small island of Nasikwabu near Murua (Woodlark Island). Some children found him four days later, washed up on the beach and nearly dead.

The survivor was not blamed for his comrades' deaths, which were instead attributed to the witchcraft of their own female kin. When I was visiting Motorina a few months later I was told that at a recent village meeting held to discuss the incident his female cross-cousin, a powerful witch, said that she was present at the shipwreck. She said she told the other witches to save the lives of their kin, but they did not listen. She is credited by her neighbors with saving her kinsman's life. The survivor reported that he heard the witches "whispering" when the sailing canoe overturned. When I saw him he spoke to no one and still seemed to be suffering greatly from shock.

Witches often attack their own kin. One Misima man explained to me that "the relatives are the owners of the dead." They have the right, he said, to kill their own kin just as Europeans have the right to dispose of their own property.[10]

In one case of suspected witchcraft a young boy on Vanatinai was stricken with a serious wasting disease. He was removed from a mission boarding school and taken to a village on the other side of the island by his mother's brother, who disregarded the advice of the local medical orderly that the boy should be sent to the hospital on Misima Island. People on Vanatinai make use of aid posts and hospitals only for a minority of illnesses and only after trying to cure their illnesses with traditional healers. Various theories were advanced in my hearing as to who had caused the illness and why. Some said that, because he was a bright child who had been doing very well in school, he had aroused the jealousy of some powerful sorcerer. Others noted that the boy's mother's brother had recently been involved with another big man in a quarrel concerning the exchange of a pig and a bagi necklace, and said that the boy was a victim of revenge sorcery. Still others suggested that the mother's brother himself had worked sorcery against his own nephew, although no particular motive was advanced. Some people thought that the boy's own mother, a sweet-natured and seemingly grief-stricken woman originally from Misima Island—well-liked, I had thought, by her neighbors—had caused her son's illness, although again no motive was discussed. When I asked why she would want to kill her own son, people looked baffled and said, "We don't know."

A curing ceremony was held in which pieces of bagi and pig's bones were sucked out of the boy's swollen abdomen. The bone was then said to have been fired into the boy's body by the sorcerer with whom the boy's uncle had recently quarreled over the pig and valuables. But people still did not relinquish their suspicion of the boy's mother. When the boy and his father finally left the island by boat on the first leg of their long journey to the government hospital at Alotau on the Papua New Guinea mainland, we went down to the shore to see them off. As the canoe bearing her pathetically wasted son, held in his father's arms, put out into the lagoon toward the waiting boat, her neighbors whispered to me and to each other, "*Irada, irada*" (she is crying)! From that point on the illness was blamed on the sorcerer who had quarreled with the boy's uncle. The boy died a few months later in the hospital at Alotau, where his illness was diagnosed as abdominal cancer.

Although witchcraft is perceived as a foreign magical tradition, Vanatinai women too are suspected and accused of witchcraft, even those who were not previously thought of as adepts. When women are accused, significantly less often than men, of destructive magic after deaths or misfortunes befall the community, they are typically called witches, not sorcerers. One sunny afternoon, a two year old boy I knew well was playing with other children near my house. That evening he developed a high fever, went into convulsions, and by midnight he was dead, probably from cerebral malaria. The first inkling that his neighbors, kinfolk outside his household, and I had of anything wrong was when we were awakened in the middle of the night by the terrifying and heartbreaking ritual wailing of women for the dead. We all dressed hastily and raced to the source of the sound, the house where the little boy, a favorite of everyone, lay dead, surrounded by his relatives. His mother, Iviowa, was paralyzed with grief and shock. The murmured accusations and recriminations began almost immediately. The young mother, separated from her husband, had only a couple of days earlier had a public quarrel with a young divorcée, whom she accused of sleeping with her husband, and she had physically attacked the other woman. The violence had scandalized the community. Now it seemed obvious that in retribution her little boy had been killed by a witchcraft attack, perhaps by the other young woman herself or perhaps by her mother, neither of whom had previously been identified as witches. I even heard Iviowa's father reproach her the next day, during the burial, "You see, I warned you to curb your temper. Now you see what you have caused." Iviowa, who, just afterward, had to be restrained by several men from throwing herself into the little boy's grave, gave no acknowledgment of having heard.

197

Sorcerers on Vanatinai are usually giagia whose success in economic affairs and resulting political influence are regarded as being based upon their superior magical knowledge or links with powerful ancestor spirits. Some of the men and women believed to be witches on Vanatinai and in the islands to the northwest are wealthy and influential big men and big women who are active in exchange and regarded as community leaders. Other alleged witches may be marginal individuals such as one old woman without living descendants whose presence in a hamlet was tolerated only out of a fear of her magical retribution. An important effect of both witchcraft and sorcery beliefs is to ensure decent treatment of old people, for their neighbors are afraid that if they believe themselves to be short of food, firewood, and other necessities they might take revenge using their superior knowledge of sorcery or witchcraft techniques. If old people are not treated properly in their later years, they will refuse after death to aid their descendants in their struggle to succeed in gardening, exchange, and other economic matters. Conversely, an old person who is well looked after will later show his or her gratitude after death by magically helping and protecting younger kinspeople (Lepowsky 1985a).

On Vanatinai chronic illnesses—wasting diseases such as cancers, mental illness, and senility—are usually attributed to witchcraft, as are the resulting deaths. The witch may either either be a local person or one from as far away as Misima Island. One Misima man who had chartered a boat to transport seven pigs from Vanatinai to Misima for an upcoming feast became very sick. People said he had been bewitched by another Misima man living on one of the East Calvados islands who was jealous of him. The victim would walk out of his house at Tagula Station on Vanatinai in the middle of the night as if hypnotized. He was led inside by his distraught family, who were convinced that he was being lured outside by witches to a spot where they could kill him. He was later found wandering in a daze in the mangroves outside a Vanatinai hamlet while on government business. His supervisor wanted to send him home to Misima, but he pleaded to be allowed to stay, for he said that if were sent back, the witches would know he was sick and weak and would kill him. He and his companions all reported seeing a phantom motor vessel off several Vanatinai settlements as well as a phantom sailing canoe, both of which they were sure had been sent by witches for the victim. The man eventually recovered.

Mental illness is generally attributed to witchcraft as opposed to sorcery, although it may also be caused by bwauyezovo magic. While there are several psychotic individuals at Misima Island, it is worth noting that there are no almost no chronic psychotics on Vanatinai. The exceptions are, or were, two old men, now deceased, suffering from senile psychosis, said to be caused by witchcraft. In one case the bewitching was believed to be retribution by someone for the victim's lifetime of sorcery and witchcraft attacks on others. His enemies took satisfaction in his misfortune.

Several younger people have had episodes of mental illness. A young man from another part of Papua New Guinea temporarily living and working on Vanatinai suffered a psychotic episode and had to leave the island. At an earlier celebration and after drinking liquor, he had suddenly become enraged, shouting, "These people want to kill me!" He then threatened to kill the local youths standing next to him if they did not stop playing their guitars and ukeleles. People were upset by this incident, but by the next morning they were laughing about it and blaming it on the fact that he had obviously been drunk. About two months later the young man went berserk for about ten days, screaming and running around, pounding on house walls, and trying to attack his supervisor. First he reported to his friends that he had seen his mother armed with a bush knife, trying to kill him. He later repeatedly said he had seen certain young girls living in the area who came from Misima, Nimowa, and Vanatinai. Finally he began to say that everywhere he went he saw a tall, thin man with a beard, a faded piece of cloth tied around his waist and an old betel nut basket. He could not recognize the man, who kept his face hidden. He would cry out to the man and once tried to jump out a window—a twenty-foot drop into a steep ravine—to reach him, but he was restrained. He believed, as did his friends, that the man was trying to lure him down to the river to kill him. He said that the man kept calling to him and that he felt a coldness starting at his feet and creeping up to the rest of his body. This sensation of coldness and paralysis is typical of reported witchcraft attacks. He would attempt to hit this man but hit himself on the biceps instead. (Merely hitting a witch will cause its spirit to vanish and kill its distant body.)

His friends asked several local Vanatinai sorcerers and healers to cure him, but after examining him they replied that they could not help him, for he was a victim of Misima-style witchcraft, wadawada. The local medical orderly, a Misima man, was then called in. He gave the victim some kind of injection and also magically extracted a piece of rubber and some wire from his back. The victim was then expected to recover, but he did not. This indicated that he had been bewitched by women. The blame then fell upon a young Misima girl living with her family on Vanatinai. She was said to have desired the young man—her obvious attraction to him was later remembered by his friends—but to have been too shy to approach him. Instead, she bewitched him, people said. She was one of the girls who had appeared as an apparition to the victim. People speculated that she had enlisted the aid of the mysterious bearded man and of the other young girls the victim had reported seeing. They might have removed a photograph of him and bespelled it, then placed it under a tree, or in a pot or a cave. The unfortunate victim was taken away to the hospital at Bwagaoia, Misima by the authorities and returned to the island several months later in a seemingly normal condition.

What is striking in this case is how local beliefs concerning witchcraft seemed to shape the psychotic episode. When the young man first exhibited a paranoid reaction to those around him, the episode was laughed off as being the result of drunkenness and was seemingly forgotten (Lepowsky 1982). When the victim reported seeing his own mother trying to murder him, his friends first asked him and some local people whether something could be wrong in his family, but they were told by others that the problem had originated on Vanatinai. It was after this point that the victim reported seeing the young girls and then the sinister bearded man with his basket, which might have been full of sorcery paraphernalia. A beard signifies mourning and, thus, death and the possibility of revenge sorcery. Mourners also wear old clothing. Thinness is associated with the fasting of the sorcerer intent on enhancing his powers before attacking his victim. The young man's being lured outside by figures invisible to others is typical of descriptions of attacks by witches, such as the case recounted earlier of the Misima man bewitched after he transported seven pigs from Vanatinai.

Just as the Misima, Panaeati, and Saisai people are very much afraid of Vanatinai sorcery, the Vanatinai people are frightened of the wadawada of all of their neighbors to the northwest, confiding tales of witchcraft on these islands and cautioning visitors to them to beware of supernatural attack. Since virtually all of the aid post orderlies stationed on Vanatinai from 1978, when the aid posts were opened, have been men from Misima Island, who must heal by giving medicine by mouth and by injection, suspicion of Misima witchcraft has seriously impeded the acceptance by Vanatinai people of biomedical primary care (Lepowsky 1990c). All of the Louisiade Archipelago islanders also fear the sorcery of the Rossel Islanders, which is said to resemble that of Vanatinai.

Sorcery, Witchcraft, and Social Life

The belief that virtually all deaths and major illnesses on Vanatinai are caused by human agents serves as an explanation of misfortune, a device by which the islanders can find meaning and an understanding of why calamities befall them. Knowledge of techniques of countersorcery and healing provide a potential recourse and a means of dealing with disasters.

Knowledge of sorcery or witchcraft is an avenue to personal power and a sense of control over others and over the environment. Although sorcery is generally the prerogative of men, local beliefs in the power of human beings to destroy their neighbors through magical means helps to safeguard the status of old people of both sexes after their physical powers have waned. Since no one can be sure which women know either witchcraft or sorcery and women are sometimes blamed for sickness or death, beliefs in the personal causation of such misfortunes also mean that individual women must be treated fairly or they may retaliate and destroy one. In this way sorcery and witchcraft beliefs on Vanatinai are social equalizers ensuring that people of all ages and both sexes receive the respect of others.

At the same time, the knowledge of certain individuals who are believed to be particularly adept at sorcery or witchcraft provides a means of gaining power over others and often of attaining the status of community leader. The increase in sorcery practices described by Vanatinai people since the colonial period is ascribed by them to the prohibition against warfare and raiding. Sorcery and witchcraft beliefs in this manner channel aggression and physical violence, for the islanders say that there is no need for them to kill others by physically attacking them, since they can easily kill through magical means. Violence of all kinds is extremely rare on Vanatinai, with the last known murders occurring in the 1950s—of a woman by her husband and of two men by a visiting Australian trader in what may have been a psychotic episode. The paranoia generated by sorcery beliefs and the social tension caused by sorcery accusations are disruptive, but they are clearly less so than the intergroup violence common in precolonial times. Sorcery suspicions and accusations feed a spiral of magical counterattacks but only rarely lead to physical violence.

Sorcery and witchcraft beliefs are a form of social control in daily life. The islanders must share food with each other, give away their possessions upon request, and show themselves to be generous in conformity to local ideals of personal conduct or face supernatural retribution. If they commit adultery or steal from others, their main fear is not punishment from government authorities if they are discovered—although adultery too is a crime that may result in a jail term—but illness or death as a result of sorcery or witchcraft attacks. This fear is often expressed aloud as a reason to refrain from such conduct.

Beliefs in the potency of Vanatinai sorcery also serve as a form of protection for the islanders against the encroachments of others. Visitors from other islands or other parts of Vanatinai must be extremely circumspect in their behavior or face retaliation by supernatural attack. Fear of Vanatinai sorcery keeps other islanders from fishing on the island's rich reefs. Government plans in the late 1970s to settle people from the overpopulated islands of Panaeati and Misima on the eastern end of Vanatinai, which has very few inhabitants, failed primarily because of opposition by Vanatinai people and the resulting fear by the potential immigrants of sorcery attacks. Even the Catholic Mission was forced to locate on Nimowa in the Eastern Calvados Islands rather than on Vanatinai because the Saisai people would never have sent their children to a mission school on Vanatinai, for fear of sorcery. The result has been that Vanatinai has come under far less mission influence than have the East Calvados Islands. Similarly, fear of witchcraft keeps Vanatinai visitors careful not to offend their hosts at Misima-language islands or Saisai.

Still, sorcery and witchcraft beliefs on Vanatinai engender an endless cycle of sorcery suspicions and accusations that create schisms among people in small communities who need to cooperate with one another for subsistence and survival. Other anthropologists, notably those working in Africa, have similarly pointed out that witchcraft beliefs may be dysfunctional in that they exacerbate social conflict. On Vanatinai sorcery and witchcraft beliefs keep the island communities in a constant state of anxiety and tension, for every death is seen as a result of the malevolent actions of another human being, usually someone living not far away. It would be dangerous to make a direct accusation, and the usual recourse is a secret counterattack, which may be made not upon the sorcerer or witch but upon a member of his or her family. The paranoia generated by sorcery and witchcraft beliefs is central to Vanatinai worldview and remains with the islanders every day and night of their lives.[11]

Sorcery, Witchcraft, and Gender

Sorcery on Vanatinai is almost entirely the province of males, but even so they do not have a monopoly on sorcery knowledge, for a few women have been adepts. Men and women both say explicitly that women generally do not learn sorcery techniques because they are responsible for the giving of life rather than the taking of it. That is why, they say, women know and practice beneficial forms of magic such as those used for healing (which may be countersorcery) or for growing gardens, and why men are sorcerers and warriors. That is also why women do not hunt with spears. The association of maleness on Vanatinai with death, war, and sorcery is reflected in the fact that the supernatural patrons ("owners") of sorcery, witchcraft, and warfare are male. The owner of healing, Egoregore, is a female being who lives on Mt. Rio, but, on the other hand, the owner of illness is her sister Ediriwo.

Associations of the female with life and the male with death have been suggested as universal in the gender symbolism of human societies, a binary opposition sometimes conflated with a proposed universal symbolic opposition of woman-nature, man-culture. But death is no more cultural than birth. Both are natural, or, more precisely, biological events that are culturally interpreted.[12]

Still, the female-life, male-death association is extremely wide-spread cross-culturally (e.g., Sanday 1981:5, Schlegel 1990). It is hard to imagine a society that would not give symbolic weight to women's biologically ordained role as the sex that gives birth and lactates. And in all known human societies men are the primary, if not the exclusive, defenders of the group and killers of game (Brown 1970a, Brightman n.d.).

On Misima, Panaeati, and the Calvados Chain Islands, the Misima and Saisai language areas to the northwest of Vanatinai, people say that witches, the destroyers of life, are usually women. This inverts the matrilineal ideology of nurture, for the greatest risk of witchcraft attack comes from classificatory mothers, and secondarily mother's brothers, the "owners" of a person. Witches are cannibalistic consumers of the dead rather than givers of food and valuables (cf. Munn 1986). Even though they exchange corpses with one another, they do not produce, but only destroy. Misima area healers who counter-act the power of witchcraft are usually men. These are reversals of Vanatinai concepts of the usual supernatural division of labor by sex.

The Vanatinai ideal that women are life-givers is partly contradict-ed by the fact that even on that island many deaths are attributed to the witchcraft of women both from Vanatinai itself and the islands to the northwest. Similarly, there are many widely known, powerful male witches in the Misima and Saisai language areas. Both men and women on Vanatinai and throughout the Louisiade Archipelago have the power to destroy.

The prevailing Vanatinai gender ideology associating women with life and men with death—and valorizing female life-giving more highly—thus coexists with contradictory indigenous beliefs. These include the destructive power of female witches and of the few female sorcerers and the fact that women do hunt; they just do not hunt wild pigs, dugongs, or crocodiles with spears. And women for-merly knew powerful war magic and participated in diplomatic deci-sions about war and peace, although they delegated the actual killing to young men. Beliefs about the supernatural patrons of death and ill-ness, on the one hand, and healing, fertility, and abundance, on the other, show no clear-cut sexual division of labor among supernatur-al beings. These aspects of Vanatinai sexual meanings are ambiguous, and islanders may interpret and use them differently for their own ideological reasons. While there is a tendency for males to be more strongly associated with destructive powers, especially sorcery and warfare, and females with powers of fertility and nurture, there is no overall division of positive and negative supernatural powers into male and female domains.

Although the individuals who are most greatly feared on Vanatinai are a few men in every part of the island who are known to be sorcerers, every man and woman must be treated circumspectly because one can never be sure who possesses what secret destructive power, or who is under the protection of an adept. In this manner sorcery and witchcraft beliefs protect the position of men and women, young and old alike.

Nevertheless, knowledge of sorcery is one of the primary means by which certain men gain political ascendancy over other men and women, both through fear of their revenge if their wishes are not met and by the fact that "strong" men place their kin and neighbors under their supernatural protection from the attacks of others. Unlike participation in exchange or possession of other forms of magical knowledge, the practice of sorcery is an avenue to power over others, which, though open to Vanatinai women, is rarely used by them. Implicit or, more rarely, explict threat of sorcery attack is the primary means by which some men increase their power in the form of control of resources and of the actions of others at the expense of women as well as other men. In this way sorcery is a likely compensation for the precolonial advantage some men gained through the role of champion warrior, asiara, as an avenue to power and influence over others.

Chapter Six

The Living, the Dead, and
Relations of Value

I had been traveling with some women from around Jelewaga for a day and a half. We had climbed the central mountain range and were descending through mostly uninhabited rain forest to the north coast of Vanatinai when one of them, a sixty-year-old widow, turned back, limping, with a sore foot. The remaining three of us poled a borrowed canoe across the broad estuary of the Veora River, a dangerous place of crocodiles, to a small hamlet where we spent the night with exchange partners of my companions.

In the morning we headed east along a well-worn coastal path that rose and fell through the grassy hills behind the mangrove swamps. It was a sweaty and dusty walk with little shade, but there was compensation in the changing views of the dappled turquoise lagoon and its contrast with the deeper blue beyond the barrier reef, clearly marked by a white edge of breaking surf. The women moved steadily with stately grace despite the baskets of traveling supplies balanced on their heads. Finally, we stopped to bathe in the clear, shaded stream that runs through a grove of sago palms just outside of Vuo. The women rose from the water, tying their newest coconut-leaf skirts over the dripping leaf underskirts in which they had bathed. Ginuba reached into her basket and pulled out a bottle filled with scented coconut oil, bunama, boiled before we left—along with the recitation of a powerful spell—with magical herbs, roots, and the bone of an ancestor. She smoothed the oil on carefully until her body glistened. The women put on the shell-disc necklaces and woven fern-fiber armlets they had been carrying in their baskets. Now, cooled and beautified, we strolled up the hillside path toward the hamlet. The women plucked red hibiscus flowers from a nearby bush and stuck them in their hair and armlets.

Our hosts, a married couple, watched our approach in silence, then greeted us solemnly as we drew near. We sat with them on the verandah, chewing betel nut and exchanging news of kin and neighbors. Nobody said anything about the purpose of our visit. As the sky began to darken they offered us a dinner of wild pig boiled with forest greens and fine, mealy yams boiled in a separate pot with coconut cream. We were served first, the food passed out to us on individual metal tradestore plates, their enamel chipped at the rim from long use. We ate in solitary splendor on the verandah while the host family squatted near the cooking fire toward the back of the house, scooping food from the clay cooking pots with polished pearl shells and metal spoons.

After breakfast the next morning, we chewed betel nut with our hosts. Finally, Ginuba asked them for the replacement of two daveri she had given them when they visited her near Jelewaga several years previously asking for valuables. She needed the valuables now, Ginuba continued, because she was helping (*labe*) a kinsman, a well-known gia. In a few weeks he would hold a large feast to commemorate the death of his brother-in-law, and she wished to contribute. After a few minutes the wife disappeared into the back of the house and returned with one daveri, promising to request another from one of her own exchange partners and bring it to the feast herself. We said our good-byes and continued our walk up the coast.

At the next hamlet the women asked an old man for the replacement of a tobotobo, a large greenstone axe blade he had gotten years earlier at Jelewaga from the woman who had turned back with a sore foot. Her case was weakened by her absence. The man claimed that he had only one tobotobo, which he had already promised to somebody else. When we reported this conversation several days later, the woman snorted and said forcefully, "*Ikwan*" (He is lying)!

By the time we returned to Jelewaga we had visited six different hamlets. In each a member of our party asked her exchange partner for valuables, either as replacements for ones previously given or to initiate a new exchange so she could contribute valuables at the upcoming feast. Half the exchange partners gave the women nothing, claiming either that they had no valuables or that they would look for some and take them to their partners at the feast (which they did not do, it turned out). The final count of valuables obtained on the expedition was one tortoiseshell ceremonial lime spatula decorated with red shell discs (*wonamo jilevia*), equal in value to a greenstone axe blade, and five daveri.

Apart from distant administrators or locally elected government councillors, whose dictates are often ignored, there are no chiefs or formal leaders on Vanatinai with the authority to tell any other adult what to do. Individual power and influence over others is the result of knowledge, skill, enterprise, and ambition. The strong person successfully channels the power of supernatural beings such as ancestor spirits and place spirits. Supernaturally derived individual power is manifested by a reputation as sorcerer or witch or as a healer, and in former times it accompanied the male role of asiara.

In twentieth-century Vanatinai, as, elders say, in precolonial times, the primary avenue to power, prestige, and influence for women and men alike is to use hard work, skill, alliances with kin, affines, neighbors, and exchange partners, and supernatural power to earn the name of gia. A gia accumulates and then gives away large quantities of food and valuables. This is done in part through mobilizing the labor of kin, affines, and neighbors to produce huge quantities of yams, sago, and pigs. But additional foodstuffs plus locally manufactured household goods and, especially, ceremonial valuables are primarily accumulated through ritualized exchanges. Exchange partners may be close kin or neighbors, but a reputation for wealth and generosity comes only from exchange with partners in distant communities and on other islands. Women as well as men participate in ceremonial exchange, the most successful gaining regionwide fame.

Many Vanatinai people told me that ceremonial exchange and mortuary ritual are their most important customs. They are the core of the way of the ancestors, of both personal and cultural identity, significant and compelling representations of personhood and customary scripts for enacting relations of value.

Through exchange, personal power is projected beyond the confines of the body and home place, animating the objects exchanged and the ties between partners, and often outliving the individual. The self is continually redefined in relation to others of both sexes and many places, spirits as well as human beings (cf. Munn 1986, Battaglia 1990). Ritualized exchanges—rich in gender symbolism—are cultural performances in which men and women, living and dead enact contradictory themes: rivalry and generosity, devouring and nurturing, decomposition and regeneration.

Ceremonial Exchange

The islands of the Louisiade Archipelago are linked to each other and to many other islands such as Ware, Tubetube, Duau (Normanby), and Murua (Woodlark) in an elaborate system of exchange that overlaps and articulates with the kula first described to outsiders by Malinowski (1922), subsequently described by many others. Vanatinai, and each ethnolinguistic group of the Massim, has its own distinctive forms of ceremonial exchange. In the southern Massim, including Vanatinai, exchange centers on mortuary rituals. The sequence of mortuary feasts, their customs, and their rules of exchange are unique to each place.[1]

Malinowski (1922) immortalized the *"kula* ring" of clockwise circulating necklaces and counterclockwise circulating armshells, each accompanied by other goods, a pattern confirmed by modern kula researchers working in the Trobriand Islands, Gawa, and Woodlark (Muyuw) in the northern Massim and on Tubetube Island in the southern Massim. In the extreme southern and southeastern islands of the Massim, including Vanatinai, there is no "ring" or set pattern of exchange and, I was told, there never has been.[2]

Louisiade Archipelago peoples do not use armshells as valuables at all. The *Conus* shells from which they are manufactured are plentiful in the lagoon, and the shells themselves are occasionally given as gifts on exchange voyages to the peoples to the north and west (Woodlark and nearby small islands as well as Ware Island), who are known to desire them.

Both today and in Malinowski's time most of the shell-disc necklaces circulating in kula and other Massim exchange links have been manufactured on Rossel, Vanatinai, and the East Calvados islands. The necklaces and other ceremonial valuables, such as polished greenstone axe blades and lime spatulas of carved tortoiseshell or wood decorated with shell discs, travel throughout the archipelago along the network of exchange relationships formed by each individual. They are sought and used for different ritual reasons in each area.[3] On Vanatinai ceremonial valuables are known by the generic name of *ghune*, or une in some dialects, a cognate of kula in the Kilivila (Trobriand) language.[4] The act of traveling—by foot, canoe, or motor vessel—to another hamlet or island in quest of valuables is called *ghiva* or *gaugau* on Vanatinai and *hipe* or *lobutu* in the Saisai language of the East Calvados Islands.

Gender and Exchange

There is another striking difference between the kula exchanges documented by Malinowski and others and the ritualized exchanges of the Vanatinai and East Calvados islands besides absence of a ring of exchange and disinterest in decorated *Conus* armshells. Women participate fully and equally in the same exchange system as men. They travel by sailing canoe to distant islands, sometimes as organizers and leaders of their own expeditions. They have both male and female exchange partners, both within walking distance and among peoples speaking different languages. These may be matrilineal kin, members of the father's matrilineage, or completely unrelated individuals with whom the woman has developed an exchange relationship. Both adult men and adult women are obligated to contribute valuables to mortuary feasts and for other reasons, and both may strive to become known as gia. Elders say the participation of women in Vanatinai exchange dates from ancient times.

In the Trobriand Islands, as documented for the first time by Weiner (1976), and on Panaeati and Misima Islands in the northern Louisiade Archipelago (Berde 1974) women have their own separate domain of exchange. In both cases it is essential to the series of mortuary ritual events following the death of each individual. Women have their own valuables—skirts in the Trobriands and yams on Panaeati and Misima—that they generate by their own labor and give during mortuary rituals to other women in honor of the deceased. They rarely participate in exchanges of shell wealth.

Trobriand kula as described by both Malinowski and Weiner is, in Malinowski's (1922:280) phrase, "essentially a man's type of activity." Both Malinowski and Fortune (1932) state categorically that women from the Trobriands and Dobu do not to take part in kula voyages or exchanges. Other recent researchers in the northern Massim have confirmed that kula is overwhelmingly male, but have documented some instances of women's participation.[5] On Tubetube, a southern Massim island important in kula that also has exchange ties to the Louisiade Archipelago and that, like Vanatinai, exhibits a high degree of gender equality, Martha Macintyre (1983, 1987:210, 1988:185) reports that women regularly participate in kula and other exchanges involving ceremonial valuables. An earlier account by Róheim (1950:184) corroborates this for nearby Duau, or Normanby Island. Moving farther to the southeast, Vanatinai and East Calvados women are fully integrated into the ritualized exchange system, competing directly with men for the same valuables and for prestige and renown.

The gia role of Vanatinai closely conforms to the model of the Melanesian big man described in Marshall Sahlins's (1963) classic article, as the Vanatinai role too is based on force of character, public "giveaways," "public verbal suasion," the ongoing cultivation of "personal loyalty," and the establishment and mobilization of a network of supporters in order to build renown. But the ethnographic evidence from Vanatinai and, in fact, from all of the islands of the Louisiade Archipelago except for Rossel, suggests that Sahlins's model of the Melanesian big man should be expanded to include big women in these and a few other cases.[6] The big women of Vanatinai are the female giagia.

The power and prestige of giagia, both female and male, develop because they consistently strive to obtain more ceremonial valuables and other exchange commodities, give more valuables away to exchange partners, host more memorial feasts, and give away more valuables at ceremonial occasions hosted by others than the minimum that Vanatinai custom demands of every adult. There are more men than there are women who are commonly referred to as giagia, and more men than women act as hosts of memorial feasts for dead kin and affines. But some women are far more heavily involved in exchange activities than the average man on Vanatinai, and virtually every adult woman as well as every adult man participates in exchange to some degree.

The account of a five-day journey to the north coast of Vanatinai by three Jelewaga area women in quest of ceremonial valuables illustrates the customs associated with these expeditions to distant hamlets and islands. Women follow the same procedures as men while seeking valuables, except that people say if a man receives a sexual invitation while on such a journey, it will "spoil his luck" if he refuses, while a married woman is supposed to refuse to sleep with other men and should "behave like a married woman."

The Vanatinai people call an exchange partner *loboda,* which literally means "my person" or "my kinsperson." Partners are frequently no relation to each other, but many exchanges are made with partners of either sex who are kinspeople, members of one's father's clan, or affines. Sometimes a man will send his wife by herself to ask his exchange partners for valuables, or a woman will send her husband. More often individuals undertake exchange journeys on their own behalf.

There are many women active in exchange, leaving their children, households, and gardens behind and walking, paddling, or sailing with other interested people to distant villages seeking valuables or attending a feast and offering contributions to the host. It is most often men and women who are middle-aged and whose children are grown or adolescent who are active in exchange. Small children not only need care but are vulnerable targets for the sorcery attacks of a rival envious of a parent's success in exchange and growing reputation. Some of the women most prominent in exchange are widows who have lost their husbands in middle age.

Sometimes husbands accompany their wives in order to assist them on a ghiva expedition. The wife in such cases is recognized as the active party in the exchange. Early in my stay on Vanatinai I walked into a coastal hamlet with friends and saw an unfamiliar sailing canoe anchored at a break in the mangroves (each canoe has a uniquely carved splashboard and prow and sometimes a distinctive paint job). "Whose canoe is that?" a friend asked. The couple who lived there looked up from the freshwater eel and sago they were roasting over hot stones near their verandah. "Ghayawa's and Wona's," they answered, referring to a married couple from about thirty miles away whom I had not yet met. "Is Wona seeking valuables?" I asked, referring to the husband and revealing my less than conscious assumptions. "No," the woman replied, "Ghayawa is seeking valuables. Wona is following her" (Ghayawa *ighiva*. Wona *imuyai*).

Ghayawa, I soon learned, is widely known as a gia. It turned out that she was leading a small party consisting of her husband and two of her young kinsmen, sailing up the south coast of Vanatinai to request ceremonial valuables and pigs from her personal exchange partners. Her husband is also well known in the region for his activities in exchange, but her reputation is bigger. About six months later she and her brother hosted a zagaya, the culminating mortuary feast, at which they distributed valuables to the matrilineal heirs and patrilateral cross-cousins of their father, who had died a few years previously. It was to collect valuables for the feast that Ghayawa was making this and other exchange voyages to communities on half a dozen different islands.

On another occasion I asked an old woman if she had ever been on a ghiva expedition. She drew herself up proudly and said that she had. When her father died she was the only surviving child, and her mother, too, was dead. Dressed in a long mourning skirt, or *yogeyoge,* and with her face and body blackened with burnt coconut husk, she had taken her husband's sailing canoe and gone to Boboghagha (Western Point Village) and then to Araida and Jolanden on the north coast of Vanatinai in search of ceremonial valuables to make a memorial feast for her father. When I asked her if her husband had come too, she replied, "Imuyai" (He followed me). Most of the people she visited were her own kinspeople. Then she came home to Edaikorighea, near Jelewaga, rested and sailed east to Pamela. She said she was given so many bagi, tobotobo, daveri, and ceremonial lime spatulas that she could no longer remember the number. She and her eldest son organized the final memorial feast (zagaya) for her father, and the valuables were given to his patrilateral heir, or tau, who in this case was another woman, his father's sister's daughter.

Participation by women in customary forms of exchange has been underreported cross-culturally in the anthropological literature. As Annette Weiner (1976) shows for the Trobriand case, where women's exchanges of banana-leaf skirts and bundles are essential ritual events, this underreporting of women's exchanges seriously distorts anthropological understanding of the actual power and influence of women in the many societies in which ceremonial exchanges and trade bring wealth, power, or prestige.

Women are prominent in exchange in most of the Massim, although often in their own separate domain of exchange. Berde (1974) describes the role of the Misima language-speaking Panaeati Island women in the memorial feast called hagali, where they ritually present baskets of fine yams to the father's sister's child of a deceased spouse or affine. As on Vanatinai, some women from the East Calvados Islands participate extensively in the same kinds of exchanges as men, leading expeditions, hosting mortuary feasts, and holding key exchange partnerships with men and women (Battaglia 1983b, 1990 and author's field research). Sabarl women regularly trade the high-quality lime they manufacture, used in chewing betel nut, for baskets of yams from other islands, a subsistence trade that they carried out in precolonial times as well, when Sabarl men were notorious raiders of other islands (Battaglia 1990:141–146).

Even in the New Guinea Highlands, which anthropologists usually describe as an area where men monopolize public and ceremonial activities and where the prevailing gender ideology is male supremacist, Feil (1978:275) says that Enga "women have the right to allocate the pigs they have raised and to have a share in *tee* decision making" (*tee* are public, large-scale pig exchanges) and take a prominent role in the all-important private negotiations concerning pig prestations that the husband will later make publicly. Lederman (1986, 1990) documents women's active participation in exchange networks among the strongly patrilineal Mendi of the Southern Highlands. A few decades ago, in spite of the constants threat of enemy raids, Mendi women traveled many days away from home to exchange pigs and salt with male and female partners.[7]

Seeking Wealth on Vanatinai

The big men and big women of Vanatinai are more likely than other adults to travel to other islands to ghiva or to attend mortuary feasts. They usually go to the East Calvados Chain, especially Panaman, Dedehai, Grass, Joannet, and Nimowa. They also sail along the Calvados Chain all the way to Brooker Island, stopping to ghiva at all the islands en route. Rossel, separated from Vanatinai by a treacherous passage between two lagoons feared even by captains of motor vessels, is infrequently visited. Vanatinai sailors also, infrequently, leave the enormous Sudest Lagoon to cross to Panaeati or Misima. More rarely still, they launch expeditions to Ware, 175 miles away, or to Duau.

There are tendencies for certain islands to be net exporters of certain goods and importers of others. On Vanatinai exchange partners are more likely to give necklaces, pigs, yams, sago, and betel nut and to receive axe blades, smoked clam, clay pots, carved hardwood platters, and powdered lime. But the direction of all of these exchanges is often reversed in individual cases depending upon the desires and resources of the two partners. Other items of exchange include pandanus-leaf sleeping mats, coconut-leaf skirts, woven garden baskets and personal baskets, ebony lime spatulas, lime gourds with fern-fiber stoppers decorated with a pig's tusk, magical or medicinal barks, face paint, lightweight outrigger logs from Duau, and outrigger sailing canoes from Panaeati Island (Lepowsky 1983 and n.d.1).

The primary impetus for an exchange journey for a Vanatinai person is an obligation to make a contribution of valuables, goods, or foodstuffs to a kinsperson, affine, or exchange partner at an upcoming mortuary feast. People also go on exchange journeys to request valuables for bridewealth, childwealth, gifts to lovers, payments to buy or rent a paddling canoe or sailing canoe, land purchases, payments to house builders or sorcerers, or compensation payments.

Malinowski (1961:86) wrote that "the kula is not done under stress of any need, since its main aim is to exchange articles which are of no practical use." This is not the case in the Louisiade Archipelago. Here the ceremonial valuables that change hands have a distinctly "practical use": they are an essential form of currency, and they must be obtained by all adults in order to satisfy the demands of custom in a wide variety of situations. Even on Kiriwina kula has a practical use, and valuables are essential forms of ritual currency tied to exchanges within and between Kiriwina communities and to social and ritual obligations (Lepowsky 1983, n.d.1).[8]

Exchange partners of the Vanatinai people, who live on the small, drought-prone, and infertile islands of the Calvados Chain and Ware, sail frequently to Vanatinai to obtain sago, yams, and betel nut, bringing clay pots from Brooker, Panaeati, and Ware. The exchange of foodstuffs is frequently intermingled with the exchange of ceremonial valuables, rendering ceremonial exchange all the more distinctly "practical" in solidifying ties that may literally save the lives of people living on overpopulated and ecologically marginal islands in times of natural disaster. Small island exchange partners are major conduits for valuables between Vanatinai and more distant islands to the north and west.

The earliest descriptions of shell-disc necklaces and greenstone axe blades on Vanatinai come from the accounts of Huxley (1935:191–192) and Macgillivray (1852:200–201, 215–216) on the 1849 visit of HMS *Rattlesnake*.[9] Ceremonial valuables were formerly used by grateful allies to pay the asiara, who had defeated enemies, and by the defeated to sue for peace. In fact, I was told that the exchange of valuables with people from other islands first began as a peacemaking ceremony.[10] I was also told that bagi, the shell-disc necklaces prized throughout the region, originated as decorated human skulls. A piece of white helmet shell now replaces the skull to form the pendant, called the "head" of the necklace.

Bagi are made by both men and women on Vanatinai and in the neighboring East Calvados Islands, using a wood and string hand-operated pump drill and a grinding stone. Bagi making seems to be a male specialization on Rossel Island. Bagi made in the Louisiade Archipelago circulate as far away as the Trobriand Islands. Vanatinai men specialize in carving the ceremonial lime spatulas of wood or tortoiseshell, called *ghenagá* and wonamo jilevia, respectively.

Tobotobo, greenstone (hornfels) axe blades polished to a glassy smoothness, are too large and thin ever to have been used to chop down trees. They are prized for their beauty as well as their exchange value. Elders say emphatically that tobotobo were not made by human beings but grow in certain favored streams "the way shells grow in the sea," nurtured by the magical spells known only to people of those places. One of these locations, whose name is well known on Vanatinai, is Suloga, on Murua, or Woodlark Island. The Suloga stone quarry became inactive about 1870 (Malinowski 1934, Damon 1990). Malinowski believed it to be the only source of axe blades in the Massim. Vanatinai people tell me this is not so, nor was it true in earlier times. Another source of axe blades known on

Vanatinai is a stream at a place called Dawin, at Suau on the South Papuan coast.[11] A third source is on Rossel Island, where the rare, dark green blades called *giarova* (literally, "give"—Rossel) come from. I was taught to recognize the white striations that distinguish the blades from Dawin from the Suloga and Rossel blades and given a wide array of terms that describe different categories of axe blades (Lepowsky 1983). Tobotobo is also a generic term for ceremonial valuables. The axe blades are normally presented in elaborately carved 7-shaped wooden handles that typically have a bird's head at the apex. Carved by Vanatinai men, they too are items of exchange.

The small, curved, and worn orange shell pieces called daveri are another major valuable on Vanatinai. They are essential for mortuary ritual exchanges. As described earlier, daveri are the same as the ndap made famous in economic anthropology by W. E. Armstrong (1928) as "Rossel Island shell money"; they are also Vanatinai shell money. Their ritual uses and systems of valuation are quite different on the two islands: on Rossel they are essential for elaborate bridewealth payments and their circulation is largely restricted to male elders. Daveri are the oldest valuables, given to the wise old woman at Tuage by the female snake Bambagho along with the first magic of exchange. Elders say that "true" daveri are ancient and not shaped by human beings but by snake spirits. People recognize the bright orange shell in its natural form as it lies on the coral reef, and some people are known to have made "false" daveri out of shell, but these are easily recognized and have little value. One young man told me how he had once made a daveri from a shell he found while diving. When he showed it to an elderly kinsman, the man flew into a rage and knocked it to the ground, shattering it.[12]

People requesting valuables, male and female, old and young, make themselves beautiful. It is customary to wear your finest skirt or clothing and to decorate yourself with armlets, flowers, or bright colored or scented leaves unless you are in mourning. The wearing of mourning garb is itself a persuasive technique, for it reminds the exchange partner that you must have valuables to honor the deceased's spirit at a mortuary feast and and free yourself from mourning taboos.

Vanatinai people say that no exchange partner would willingly give up valuables unless under the influence of a magical spell. It is customary for a man or woman seeking valuables to bathe and apply bunama, imbued during its making (by either sex) with magical powers through careful techniques of manufacture and the recitation of magical spells.

The idiom of seduction shapes exchange magic and ideologies of human behavior and causality. The persuasive force of the person is extended to the object of desire, the valuable, and to its possessor. The theory is that, as in love magic, the exchange partner will be dazzled and made dizzy with desire (negenege) by the beauty of the visitor and give away valuables that he or she normally would wish to retain. An exchange is metaphorically a sexual encounter, the gift of valuables substituting for the genitals of the seduced lover.

It is impolite to request valuables until just before you are ready to depart in the morning. The valuables are handed privately to the requesting exchange partner. The requesting party either asks for the repayment of a previously given valuable or initiates a new exchange, requesting a valuable or pig, usually citing a particular need, as to contribute to a mortuary feast, and promising to repay when asked with an object equivalent in value.

Giving valuables to others places them in your debt until the valuables are repaid. But, like all credit arrangements, it is a risk. Some exchange partners never repay, but if this becomes known, no one will trust them in future. Fear of retaliatory sorcery or witchcraft often helps to ensure the return of an equivalent valuable.

Sometimes an exchange is concluded on one occasion, as, for example, when a pig is carried off by visitors after the owner has been given a long bagi and perhaps a greenstone axe blade or two. But delayed exchange is much more common. Often a visitor travels to a Vanatinai village from a distant island in search of a pig or a bagi owed him or her from an earlier occasion and is forced to live for days or weeks with the partner's family while the partner sets off on his or her own expedition to nearby villages and islands in order to locate the desired item.

Some people take advantage of their partners. The old Nigaho Island woman described at the beginning of the last chapter made three unsuccessful one-hundred-mile round-trip voyages by sailing canoe to Rehua on Vanatinai to recover the replacement of two long bagi she herself had made and given to a Vanatinai exchange partner several years earlier. Formerly, her only recourse would have been either to persuade her allies to raid her partner's village or to practice sorcery or witchcraft against him. Her young nieces and nephews talked about reporting him to the government officer in charge at Tagula Station, in hopes of frightening him into paying his debt, but they never did.

Ceremonial exchange is an essential part of indigenous religion on Vanatinai, particularly as it involves mortuary rituals. Though it is flexible and has changed dramatically since early prehistoric times, it is remarkably resilient (Lepowsky n.d.1). Ceremonial exchange has withstood strong pressures against it by colonial officers, missionaries, and white traders over several generations. The basis of taubwaragha, its continuing practice is a form of resistance to powerful and coercive systems of domination by outsiders (Lepowsky 1991). Ritualized exchanges are key symbols of cultural identity and autonomy for Vanatinai people and many of their island neighbors. It is therefore all the more significant that the way of the ancestors provides avenues to wealth, power, and renown for women as well as men.

Vanatinai is a small-scale society in which the Western dichotomy of domestic and public domains does not apply well. Household or kin group decisions often have a wider political impact. The most important forms of ritualized exchanges, which may take individuals on journeys of hundreds of miles, frequently satisfy obligations of matrilineal kinship and affinity and are both public and domestic. But exchange on Vanatinai belongs to the public domain in the senses in which feminist anthropologists have debated and defined it. Exchange involves physical mobility, personal ties, visibility well beyond the household, wealth, power, and fame. Vanatinai women have equal opportunities of access to the symbolic capital of prestige derived from success in exchange. This simultaneously reflects and reinforces the power of individual women, corroborating and supporting ideologies of female power and gender equivalence.

Mortuary Ritual: Death and Exchange

Death on Vanatinai triggers a complex array of culturally ordained responses among the survivors. Each deceased person should be honored by a series of increasingly elaborate memorial feasts. These clear the taboos and restrictions that a death lays upon kinfolk, affines, and hamlet groups. The whole sequence of feasts normally takes several years to complete. It is no exaggeration to say that cultural and economic life on the island revolves around the demands of mortuary ritual. A surplus of garden produce, sago, and pigs must be produced in order to host mortuary feasts or to make contributions to the feasts of exchange partners. The requirements of an upcoming feast are the major stimulus for intra- and interisland exchange activities. Surviving spouses and children face years of mourning restrictions and obligations until the final feast is held, and it frequently happens that another death will occur before this point or shortly thereafter, plunging the unhappy survivors back into mourning.

This cultural emphasis upon mortuary ritual, characteristic of Massim societies, is found as well among many groups of Austronesian speakers in coastal Melanesia, island Southeast Asia, and even distant Madagascar.[13] On Vanatinai, as in these other Austronesian societies, the importance of mortuary ritual mirrors the central place of ancestor spirits in religious life. The spirits of the dead, and in particular the recently dead whose names and social identities are remembered by the living, aid and protect their descendants. They are called upon in public ritual—such as during the planting of the new yam gardens—and in private magic to make crops ample, fish abundant, exchange journeys rewarding, and love affairs successful. They are asked to keep their living relatives healthy and to warn them of the approach of invisible sorcerers. Sorcerers ask the spirits of their own dead kin for magical assistance in inflicting sickness and death upon other islanders.

Death on Vanatinai involves the entire network of people with whom the deceased was linked—through matrilineal kinship, patrilateral ties, marriage, hamlet coresidence, friendship, and exchange partnership—in the mortuary ritual sequence, drawing them together in an evanescent group. Social relations often endure longer than the lifetimes of those who initiated them. Mortuary customs force the survivors to work together to organize feasts over a period of several years, despite the suspicions of sorcery that usually arise after a death. Often the demands of mortuary ritual lead to various members of the deceased's social network forming new direct exchange relationships or even further marriage alliances with each other. Mortuary ritual beliefs and practices, central to Vanatinai custom, reveal kin and affinal relations, the meaning and significance of exchange ties, supernatural power and its relation to human beings, individual ambition and personality, and cultural constructions of the gendered person.

Mortuary ritual and the interisland exchange of valuables that supports it are the primary avenues to personal power and prestige on Vanatinai and the islands to the northwest. If Vanatinai society, and Massim societies in general, are in fact relatively egalitarian in their treatment of the sexes, this equality should be reflected in mortuary ritual: in the treatment accorded male and female dead, in the customary roles and restrictions of widows and widowers, and in the activities of men and women in carrying out the mortuary feast sequence.[14] And, in fact, this is the case on Vanatinai: the deaths of men and women are marked by equally elaborate mourning and by the identical memorial feast sequence. The burden of mourning obligations for survivors is also the same for men and for women.

Although the nature of the mortuary ritual sequence, the directions of exchanges, and the types of valuables required is unique for each culture within the Massim region, the feast sequences of Vanatinai, and of the nearby East Calvados islands (which follow different customary rules), with their emphases upon the ceremonial prestations of mourning affines to matrilineal or patrilateral connections of the deceased, fit into a widespread Massim cultural pattern of almost aggressive giving between affines during mortuary exchanges.[15] Women play prominent and public roles in mortuary ritual on Vanatinai and in the neighboring East Calvados (cf. Battaglia 1990). Both Vanatinai and East Calvados women contribute skirts, as in the Trobriands (Weiner 1976), and yams, as at Panaeati and Misima Islands in the northern Louisiades, to mortuary exchanges. But they do so in smaller quantities than in these other islands, where skirts or yams are the primary female valuables, produced by female labor. Vanatinai and East Calvados women also weave and present finely woven coconut-leaf baskets, garden baskets, and sleeping mats of wild pandanus leaf.

But Vanatinai women's primary exchange obligations are the same as men's. They are expected to obtain and present ceremonial valuables such as greenstone axe blades and shell necklaces when one of their kinspeople or affines dies or when valuables are requested from them by one of their exchange partners. Women as well as men may strive to build their reputations by accumulating and then giving away ceremonial valuables and by hosting or contributing heavily to feasts.

The sequence of mortuary feasts (see table) lasts anywhere from one to twenty-five years after a death. Feasts involve up to hundreds of people from distant communities and islands. All contribute via their personal exchange partners to public, ritualized exchanges among the lineages of the deceased, affines, and deceased's father. The exchanges include large quantities of ceremonial valuables of different kinds, pigs, yams, sago starch, clay pots, coconut-leaf skirts, baskets, and other goods. Burial initiates exchanges of the living with the dead and continues exchanges that took place during the life of the deceased. It is followed within days or weeks by a dramatic feast called *jivia,* in which valuables are exchanged and the deceased's kin ritually feed the mourning spouse or representatives of the father's lineage. A widow or widower is released from taboos against leaving the hamlet, bathing, or shaving by a *velaloga* feast, held two weeks to two months later. Within six months or so of the jivia, the feast called ghanarakerake, or "food goes out," is held to remove taboos on the house and hamlet of the deceased. At an optional feast, *vearada,* "for crying," held about a year after the death, kin of the deceased offer pork and vegetable foods to those who cried at the burial. Except in the case of an infant, whose feast sequence usually ends with the jivia, each death must honored in a final feast, the largest of all, called zagaya, usually after about three years of intensive preparation. Afterward all taboos are lifted from people and places, and widows and widowers are free to make themselves beautiful, court, and remarry.

The Burial: Exchanging with the Dead

We waded the shallow river, climbing the steep, slippery path up the last forested hill to the hamlet where the old woman had died the day before. I had last seen her a few weeks earlier, on my way back from Etadiwewa, farther up the mountain. She was a painfully thin woman in a frayed coconut-leaf skirt, squatting in the hamlet plaza near her house coughing a deep, wracking cough. I thought then that she probably had tuberculosis. She was the mother of a friend my own age, and she smiled and motioned me over. I squatted next to her and tried to answer the stream of questions she directed to me about life

Feast Sequence on Vanatinai

Feast Name	Time after Death	Valuables Exchanged	Direction of Exchange	Taboos Lifted (Affinal Mourners)	Taboos Lifted (Community)
Jivia	3 days to 2 weeks	Daveri; Gile; Tobotobo; Plates; Mirror; Sago; Garden produce	Tau, Kin→Affines; Affines→Kin, Tau	May feed self; May leave hamlet (not spouse); May eat animal foods	May exchange pigs and valuables; May store, prepare, eat food in deceased's house if pig killed
Velaloga	2 weeks to 2 months	Tobotobo; Daveri; Sago; Garden produce	Affines→Kin, Tau	May leave hamlet (spouse); May bathe (spouse); May shave (spouse)	None
Ghanrakerake	2 weeks to 6 months	Tobotobo; Daveri; Ceremonial lime spatulas; Sago; Garden produce	Affines→Kin, Tau	None	May store, prepare, eat food in house
Vearada (optional)	1 year	Pigs; Sago; Garden produce	Kin→Community	None	None
Zagaya (Bigibigi, Mwaguvajo, Moni, Kiowak, Ngabubobo)	1–25 years	Bagi; Tobotobo; Ceremonial lime spatulas; Daveri; Pigs; Sago; Yams; Garden produce; Skirts; Clay pots; Mats; Baskets	Affines→Kin; Kin→Affines; Kin + Affines→Tau; Tau→Spouse	May wash, cut hair, decorate body, wear new clothes; May dance, travel, court; May remarry; May leave spouse's hamlet; May eat father's pigs, sago, coconuts, betel, garden produce	May drum, sing, dance

in America and what I was doing here. We had heard the night before that she was dead.

Now, as we came within earshot of the settlement, my companions began the customary wailing for the dead. Their voices rose and fell in mournful counterpoint, crying her name, or "my mother," "my sister," "my in-law," "my grandmother."

We emerged suddenly into the bright sunlight of the hamlet clearing. Dozens of men and women were already sitting on the red clay soil and in the shade under the houses talking and chewing betel nut. They looked up to see who else had come to mourn. If the person who had killed her through sorcery dared to come, the eyes of the corpse would fly open, so everyone talks about who is conspicuously absent from a burial. The Jelewaga people, still wailing for the dead woman, filed directly into her son's house and prostrated themselves around the corpse.

The old woman lay on her back on a litter made of logs lashed together and covered with sago leaves. A large pandanus mat and a sheet of plastic were underneath her body, and her head rested on a pillow. A gaily colored cloth skirt and a white embroidered blouse had been draped on top of her body, but she was actually wearing skirts of coconut leaf, as she had when she lived. A fine, bright orange daveri rested on her forehead, and two more daveri in their delicate pouches of woven coconut leaf had been placed in her hands, along with a two-kina banknote. Four women, actual or classificatory daughters-in-law, armed with coconut-rib brooms, a fifth with a branch of croton leaves, kept a vigil against the flies that continually tried to land on her body. When they killed a fly, they picked it up and put it in a matchbox resting alongside the corpse.

The old woman had complained in the morning of feeling ill and then died a day later. Her close kin, her daughter-in-law, and hamlet neighbors had stayed awake all night mourning for her. They were joined in the morning by people from hamlets and villages up to ten miles distant, who had walked for hours after hearing the news of her death. The mourners explained to me they had come to cry for her, which helps her son and her other surviving kin.

My friends included some close relatives of the dead woman. Wailing and crying, some of them hugged her grief-stricken younger son around the waist as they stared at the lifeless body of their kinswoman. Women fell to their knees and cried with their heads upon one another's backs. Her son and later one of her kinsmen sat down beside the dead woman and spoke to her in a low, emotional voice.

Affinal women did most of the formal, dirgelike wailing and tending of the corpse. Most of the men and some of the women, who had already cried over the dead woman, sat outside in small groups, sharing betel nut and conversing quietly. Several women, kin to the deceased, tended a row of clay cooking pots in the hamlet plaza full of boiling root vegetables in coconut cream. The food would later be served to the mourners.

Inside the house the principal mourners did not wail continuously but paused now and then to chew betel nut. The occasional arrival of new mourners was marked by wailing that could be heard to grow louder as they approached the hamlet. They would come immediately into the house and fling themselves down in paroxysms of grief, triggering fresh bouts of wailing by the exhausted ones already inside.

The dead woman's daughter-in-law, who with her husband had shared her home with the older woman and cared for her in her last illness, stayed inside the house. Beginning at the moment the death became known to others and continuing until the final mortuary feast had been completed, she would be the principal affinal mourner, representing her matrilineage, for the old woman had left no widowed husband to fill that role.

The daughter-in-law only emerged once to urinate in the nearby forest, accompanied by her husband's kinswoman, wearing a long mourning skirt made of wide strips of coconut leaf, her shoulders covered with a sleeping mat woven of wild pandanus leaves, and her face blackened with charcoal. She was not allowed to feed herself. Her in-laws would place food in her mouth until the first mortuary feast, the jivia, took place several days after the burial.

About midday the dead woman's son removed the daveri, money, white blouse, and skirt from her body. He and some of his kinswomen anointed her with coconut oil scented with sweet-smelling leaves and roots. They painted her face as if for a feast with burnt coconut husk and powdered coral lime, drawing black lines topped with white dots under her hairline, above her eyebrows, diagonally across the center of each cheek and vertically on her chin.

They placed flowers in her hair, and her son placed a short shell-disc necklace (*samakupo*) around her neck. A dead person should be made beautiful by the living for the journey to meet the other spirits with whom he or she will dwell.

A kinsman of the dead woman, a gia, regarded as a leader of her matrilineage, strode through the hamlet dragging a very long shell-disc necklace in the dirt behind him, the distinctive sound of its pearl shell pendants clacking against each other drawing all eyes to his passage. He climbed into the house and flung the bagi down upon the dead woman's chest. Her son was later seen wearing it, for it was a gift to him for caring for his mother before and after her death.

Shell currency is generally removed from a corpse shortly before the burial, but, my friends explained, the image of the valuables remains behind "like a photograph" and adorns the spirit in its passage to the summit of Mt. Rio, the land of the dead. The valuables given to the dead in this manner at a burial, they told me, are part of an exchange between the living and the dead. The spirit of the dead person is later expected to aid its kin through magic in obtaining valuables from other human beings in return for the valuables presented at the burial.

Finally a few of her kinsmen covered the dead woman with a wild pandanus sleeping mat. They carried her on her litter through the crowd of wailing mourners, whose laments reached a climax of grief, across the hamlet thirty feet to a six-foot grave adjacent to that of her husband, who had died several years previously. Her son stood nearby weeping. Standing in the grave, her kinsmen cut the handles off the litter and weighed her body down with it. Three green coconuts were placed in the grave for her spirit to drink on its passage to the land of the dead. The men shoveled the reddish soil into the deep hole, and the three standing in the grave carefully smoothed it over the litter-covered corpse, climbing out of the pit as it began to fill with dirt. A smooth mound of soil was formed over the grave. There was no Christian ritual at any point in the burial.

Ancestors

The dead, whether they were beloved or feared in life, continue to have social relations with the living. Rodyo, the snake being who lives on Mt. Rio, sends his canoe, Maigoigo, to pick up their spirits in a clockwise journey around Vanatinai. They climb the mountain from the north coast, weeping for the kinfolk they have left behind, and they are met halfway by the spirits of their dead kindred, who comfort them, telling them they are moving on to another life, and lead them to the summit of Mt. Rio. There they will dwell in a spirit village, with spirit gardens, coconuts, and pigs. These look like wild plants and animals to mortals. The clouds and mist that frequently shroud the triangular peak are really the smoke of their cooking fires.

The spirits of the dead help and protect their living kin. One of my neighbors addressed the spirit of his dead mother, who was buried nearby, when he and his family were leaving their house, asking her to "keep the house hot" to ward off sorcerers. People said you could hear the sound of the spirit scraping coconut for dinner and rattling dishes even though the house was empty (although I never could). An old woman I knew, now dead herself, used to talk to the spirit of her dead husband, asking him to warn her—by talking or scratching—if any invisible sorcerers entered the hamlet. Spirits also send warnings in the daytime through the cry of the bird called manighighi, which always indicates the arrival of a visitor, or at night by means of a firefly.

Ghosts on Vanatinai are usually regarded as beneficent by their living kin, who have little fear that these spirits will harm them if they were on good terms while alive. Still, people may be frightened upon seeing a ghost, and they avoid graves, because the spirit is aware of visitors. I was sitting with a friend inside a house at night once when he saw somebody in a white shirt sitting on the verandah with head averted. When he went out, the figure disappeared. I did not see it. In subdued tones, he told me that it was a spirit. I asked him why he seemed afraid, since he and others had previously told me that spirits did not hurt people. He said it was because he now expected to hear that someone in the area would die shortly. We heard a few days later that an old man, a distant cousin of his, had died, several days previously, in another hamlet. When we heard the news, my friend turned to me and said, "You see, that was his spirit on the verandah." Spirits, like sorcerers, can be kept away by chewing ginger while reciting a magical spell and spitting into the corners of the room.

The spirits of dead kinfolk are magical allies of their descendants in the struggle of the living to obtain enough food and to remain healthy. They are appealed to through magic and ritual. They send messages or advice through dreams on matters such as where to dive to obtain an especially fine pearl shell (gile) to make into a valuable or where to find a bagi in the forest, placed there by spirits in answer to a magical petition.

During the usual day and night before a corpse is buried close kin may discreetly obtain a relic, a muramura, from the body. When a parent, mother's brother, or other close relative dies, a man or woman may go privately to where the corpse is laid out and speak to it, asking permission to cut a lock of hair, to remove a tooth, or later on after the body has decayed, to obtain another bone, such as a jawbone, and requesting the future aid of the deceased. A tooth is pulled out before burial, but other bones will be secured months later by secretly digging up the grave at night with the assistance of special digging magic. Muramura are sometimes described as a "memory" of the deceased. They are objects of great power, but they are also objects that evoke intense emotions of love and grief. They are used by their owners either for beneficial magic or for sorcery. Muramura taken from century-old battlegrounds or gravesites such as shallow caves are sometimes secretly given to others, who will then owe the giver a favor in exchange.

Mourning

Vanatinai mourning customs are the same for women and for men. Mourning restrictions or proscriptions are generically called ghabubu, taboo. The bulk of the taboos resulting from a death fall not upon the matrilineal kin of the deceased but upon the surviving spouse and upon other affines such as sons and daughters-in-law and the spouses of the dead person's nieces and nephews. Matrilineal kin are the ones who have suffered the loss. They must be compensated through the mourning work and ritual prestations of affines for the deceased's person, labor, and wealth during a lifetime of affinal gifts and exchanges.

If there is no widow, as in the death of a woman or of an old widower or a child, one woman from a lineage linked in marriage to the deceased's lineage must serve as principal female mourner. People say that "there must be a woman to sit down in the mwagumwagu," the culminating mortuary ritual (see chapter 7).

The roles of a deceased father's children are structurally similar, but not identical, to those of his affines. Children support and join their widowed mother in her mourning work. But if he was a widower, a maternal nephew's wife, a son-in-law's sister, or some other affine serves as principal female mourner, not his daughter. An adult daughter, and an adult son, are likely to host one or more mortuary feasts, whether or not their mother is alive, and their spouses become mourners.

Immediately after a death occurs mourning affines must remain in their houses, blacken their bodies, refrain from washing or cutting their hair or beard, and wear old clothing. Women don an ankle-length coconut-leaf mourning skirt, the yogeyoge. Until the jivia is made they will only leave their houses to eliminate, accompanied and physically led by a kinsperson of the deceased. They must cover their bodies with pandanus-leaf sleeping mats or coconut-leaf skirts slung over their shoulders and finely woven coconut-leaf baskets placed over their heads. This ritual covering of the body so that it may not be seen by others is called zogazoga, and is the same as that practiced after giving birth, described in chapter 3. After the burial the affinal mourners will present the skirts, mats, cloth, or baskets they have used since the death as zogazoga to the patrilateral or matrilineal heir of the deceased, who receives the ceremonial valuables presented at the jivia. The mourners must walk slowly with their eyes down and their arms crossed over their chests. They are forbidden to feed themselves during the period before the jivia is held or to touch their own hands to their mouths. Dependent for their lives upon the aggrieved kin of the deceased, they must be fed like infants by the deceased's kin, who place mouthfuls of food to their lips. They may not cook, fetch water or firewood, or go to their gardens.[16]

Widows and widowers alike as well as other close affinal mourners blacken their bodies with charcoal made from burnt coconut husks, unless they are nursing mothers who would cause supernatural harm to their children. This blackening is called "eating charcoal (*ghan nyiba*)." Interestingly, both black and white are associated with death, white with corpselike pallor and the fine "white" mats (actually a light tan) or white store-bought clothes in which a corpse may be laid out. Blackening the body signifies the identification of the mourner with the corpse and the mourner's state of social death.

The widowed spouse or principal mourner eats death to become, for the duration of the mourning, a replacement for the dead: an equivalent human valuable, a compensation, a hostage to the deceased's kin and patrilateral relations. In precolonial times the affinal mourner, I was told, could have been killed by the deceased's matrilineage as a compensation homicide for the deceased. The affinal lineage, to avoid this murderous wrath, sometimes killed an enemy, or some other, hapless person, and presented the body to the deceased's lineage at a mortuary feast to be ritually prepared and eaten.[17] This was in compensation to the matrilineage of the deceased for its corpse. Nowadays (and often in the past, elders said, when I questioned them further) a large pig is sacrificed by affines and eaten by the deceased's matrilineage at a feast as a substitute for a human victim. The metaphorical eating of death was clear as well in precolonial mortuary practices, where the charcoal pigment was mixed with the exudations of the decaying corpse and smeared on the mourner's body (White 1893). Mourners who eat the charcoal of death stand for the corpse. They are possessions of the deceased's matrilineage, whose members, in formal, possessive tones, call mourners "our widow" and "our widower," but they are not part of it.

The mourner is in turn symbolically eaten at the final mortuary feast by the patrilateral heir of the deceased. After this final ritual of incorporation, the mourners will be bathed, by those who ate them, in life-giving fresh water, beautified, and freed of taboos and affinal ties: they are reconstituted as fertile human beings and reborn at the pleasure of the heirs of the deceased.

Widows and widowers remain in seclusion until the second memorial feast, the velaloga, is held. They should not travel away from the hamlet except on exchange journeys to obtain ceremonial valuables, pigs, or vegetable food for the final memorial feast, the zagaya. Widows and widowers alike should work especially hard alongside their affines to produce an adequate surplus of garden food and sago in order to hold the zagaya. During the years before the final feast is held, widows and widowers only watch from the sidelines while others dance or take lovers, for they may only participate again in normal social life after all mourning restrictions have been lifted by the exchanges of the final zagaya.[18]

A widower, or *sibawa*, is identifiable by his beard, grown by Vanatinai men only as a sign of mourning to be shaved after the final mortuary feast has taken place. Other affinal mourners such as sons-in-law or brothers-in-law of the deceased also wear beards and old clothes and are likewise referred to as widowers. They too blacken their faces and bodies with burnt coconut husk until the velaloga feast. The actual widower may choose to continue this special practice for many months after the death of his wife as a sign of his special affection for her. One middle-aged widower told me he continued to blacken himself after the velaloga was held because he and his wife always got along well and never fought with each other. The sibawa and other affinal male mourners will again blacken their bodies for the duration of the final feast, at the close of which they will be ritually bathed, dressed in new clothes and decorated by the heirs of the deceased to mark the close of the mourning period.

The term for widow, *wabwi*, is similarly extended to other female affinal mourners, such as daughters-in-law or sisters-in-law, who share the ritual duties and restrictions of the actual spouse. The wabwi are easily distinguishable by their dress: the actual widow wears the ankle-length yogeyoge; the other mourning female affines wear yogeyoge cut several inches above the ankles. After the final mortuary feast their skirts will be ceremonially cut by the heirs of the deceased and they, like the sibawa, will be bathed, dressed, and decorated to mark their reentry into normal social life. Wabwi should blacken their bodies and refrain from cutting their hair or bathing, ideally until the final zagaya is held. In reality both widows and widowers normally begin to bathe again after the second feast, or velaloga, a month or two after the death. They blacken themselves when there are visitors in the hamlet, when they travel on exchange journeys to obtain valuables for the feasts, or when they are feeling particularly sad. At the last memorial feast they again wear full mourning regalia.

After a father dies daughters and sons also follow these mourning proscriptions, blackening their bodies, wearing the shorter yogeyoge or old clothing, growing a beard and not cutting the hair. They are particularly likely to blacken themselves when on exchange journeys to obtain valuables to offer at the final feast in their father's memory.

When a father dies, or one of his matrilineal kin, his children may not eat food from garden lands belonging to him or his matrilineage, sago, betel, or coconuts from his palms or those of his kin, or pork from any pig belonging to him or his kin. A father's death abruptly halts and reverses the normal, ongoing nurturing of his children with food and valuables by his matrilineage, their collective "fathers," except during the ceremonial feeding of mortuary ritual. These taboos are not lifted until the last feast has been made in memory of the dead man several years later, when substantial quantities of cere-monial valuables, vegetable food, sago, and pig are normally present-ed—ritually fed—by his children and their widowed mother to the father's matrilineal heir, the eaters of the feast (cf. Hertz 1907:38).

When the father dies the burden of mourning is primarily borne by the children's spouses. Formerly, daughters- and sons-in-law would have to go into mourning when any member of the father-in-law's matrilineage died, but nowadays the mourning obligation is only incurred when the father-in-law himself dies.

After a death the house where the deceased normally lived is placed under a special taboo. No food may be stored, cooked, or eaten within it until the jivia. The entire hamlet where the deceased either lived or died may also be placed under a taboo by his or her kin so that it is forbidden to beat a drum, sing, dance, or play guitar there until the final feast.

The persons or places that are restricted by these various mourn-ing proscriptions are all taboo. The restrictions are lifted sequentially as mourners and their allies ritually transfer valuables to the heirs of the deceased at each of the series of feasts. Affines of the deceased work to contribute the largest share of valuables in order to free their matrilineal kinspeople, the widowed spouse and principal mourners, from the onerous mourning restrictions.

Mortuary ritual on Vanatinai, and perhaps throughout the Massim, is an elaborate series of compensation payments made on behalf of a surviving spouse by the spouse's matrilineal kin and other mourners to the heirs of the deceased. In a place where most deaths are believed to be the result of sorcery or witchcraft, all members of the social net-work of the deceased need to demonstrate that they share the loss with the matrilineal kin of the deceased and did not will the death or benefit materially from it through an abrupt cessation of affinal obligations or other exchange relations. Formal mourning and wailing are a gift of emotional identification with the close kin of the deceased. Contributing food, pigs, and ceremonial valuables to mortuary feasts maintains social ties of exchange initiated by the deceased or his or her parents and demonstrates the willingness of affines, kin, and exchange partners to compensate the heirs for their loss.

The Owner of the Feast

At each mortuary feast in the ritual sequence there are two primary figures, the host, called "the owner of the feast," zagaya tanuwagai, and the principal heir, the matrilineal kinsperson or patrilateral relative of the deceased designated by kinfolk to receive the bulk of the valuables presented at that particular feast. Both the host and the principal heir may be either a woman or a man, regardless of the sex of the deceased.

The owner of a feast obtains this duty and privilege after consultation—and sometimes argument—with kinfolk. Generally there is a different host and sometimes a different principal heir at each feast in the sequence. Widows, widowers, or adult children of a deceased father, individually or as a sibling set, should host the final feast, according to custom, and often do. But it may also be hosted by a distant affine or even by the deceased's brother or other matrilineal kinsperson.

The kin and affines of the deceased often gather in council within a few weeks of a death in order to work out who shall host which feast. Surviving spouses, children, and those kinfolk who were emotionally closest have the strongest claim on the opportunity to honor the one whom they have lost and, for affines, to compensate the heirs. Hosts must provide large quantities of yams, sago, pigs, ceremonial valuables, and many other goods. They will end up giving away large quantities of wealth to the heirs and feeding the feast participants lavishly. They will have to call on everyone who owes them valuables and favors for contributions and labor. But this is how you gain a reputation as a gia. And those who receive valuables should make an even better return to your lineage and to you personally when, inevitably, they have to host or contribute to a feast themselves, or else everyone will know that you have exceeded them in generosity. Volunteering to host a feast, especially for more distant relations or affines, is a primary avenue to prestige. Women are most likely to host feasts when they are widowed—often along with one or more of their adult children—and when their fathers have died. It is more common for a small subset of middle-aged and older men, rather than women, to relentlessly pursue the opportunities to make feasts honoring more distant connections.[19]

Heirs of the Dead

The principal heir at the final feast, and sometimes at the smaller feasts that precede it, is ideally a patrilateral cross-cousin of the deceased (see figures 1 and 2). This person, the tau, was chosen by the father of the deceased, shortly after the child was born, from among the father's own matrilineal kin to stand in a special exchange and heir relationship to his child.

If the tau dies before his or her "child," which often happens, as the tau may be several years or even a generation older, a new one is chosen from among the father's matrilineal kin. A tau is ideally a cross-cousin, but in many cases a father's sister or brother or more distant matrilineal kinsperson may be appointed. Sometimes matrilineal kinfolk request to be appointed tau of a kinsman's child as a mark of their special affection or respect for the father, and there may be several claimants to the honor, a situation that the father must handle tactfully.

The tau is chosen without regard to gender, so that two women or a man and a woman may be in a tau relationship to each other. Even a female tau is frequently called "my father" (*ramagu*), for she is a patrilateral relative, and the tau in turn refers to "my child" (*narugu*). The "father" will in turn have a tau and heir chosen from among his or her own patrilateral kinsfolk by his or her own father. Tau relationships therefore represent a series of patrilateral links in an otherwise strongly matrilineal area.[20]

A good tau is supposed to contribute—to feed—garden produce, pigs, ceremonial valuables, and tradestore goods upon request to the "child" throughout the latter's lifetime without as strong an expectation of return of equivalent items when needed as that from normal exchange partners. For when the "child" dies the tau should receive all of the valuables contributed at mortuary feasts in the "child's" memory. After the final feast for a dead father, or one of his kinspeople, his children may, by virtue of this contribution of valuables to the tau, the father's father's matrilineal heir, eat pig, coconut, betel, sago, or garden produce belonging to the father's matrilineage or patrilateral kin. This is because they have aided the father's lineage in satisfying its debt to that of the father's father. The tau relationship thus not only binds members of a matrilineage to the offspring of their male members, who are collectively their "children," but also maintains social and economic relationships between members of matrilineages originally brought into an exchange relationship by a marriage in the grandparental generation. The matrilineage of the father's father must be compensated by means of valuables presented to the father's tau

Figure 1

Flow of Valuables at the Zagaya of a Woman

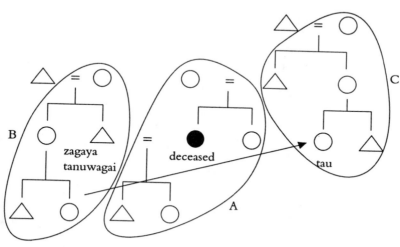

A = matrilineage of deceased

B = matrilineage of zagaya tanuwagai

C = matrilineage of tau

↑ = primary direction of valuables presented at zagaya

upon his death.[21] One friend explained that by presenting valuables to the dead person's tau, "we are thanking their lineage for marrying the deceased's mother."

Some people contribute much more to their "child" in their role as tau during their lifetime than others. If a tau has given generously of all manner of goods and valuables for many years, he or she will have an undisputed right to receive the valuables at the "child's" mortuary feasts. If a tau never or rarely aided his or her "child," she or he may not receive any valuables at all, although he or she may be compensated privately with valuables beforehand.

In some cases a powerful matrilineal kinsperson of the deceased will make it publicly known that he or she expects to be the principal heir as compensation for a lifetime of aiding the deceased in finding the pigs, foodstuffs, and ceremonial valuables necessary to fulfill ritual obligations. This custom is called *vowo*. This claim may either

Figure 2

Flow of Valuables at the Zagaya of a Man

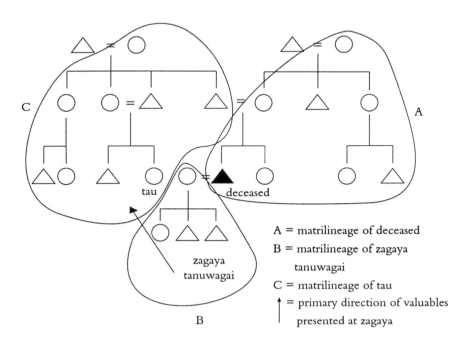

A = matrilineage of deceased
B = matrilineage of zagaya
    tanuwagai
C = matrilineage of tau
↑ = primary direction of valuables
    presented at zagaya

be made shortly after the death or it may be made years later, shortly before or during the final feast, causing consternation and fear among the feast organizers. Defiance of the demand would put the associates of the deceased at risk of being killed by the sorcery of the claimant: those who demand to inherit from their matrilineal kin are almost always men who are known as powerful sorcerers. If the claim is made early enough, other surviving kin and affines who are organizing the feast sequence will arrange to obtain enough valuables to give in memory of the deceased to each individual with a valid claim, often including both the tau and the matrilineal kin of the deceased. Sometimes such claims may be disposed of by arranging for valuables to be given to the kinsperson at one of the earlier feasts, but this strategy may backfire as the claimant later demands further compensation.

A kinsperson may only make a claim at the last minute, just before or during a feast when the host and organizers have no time to locate extra valuables to satisfy the unexpected demand. A feast might be postponed or its conclusion delayed while the host lineage members frantically try to obtain more ceremonial valuables from their personal exchange partners. If they refuse or are unsuccessful, the claimant is likely to boycott the feast altogether and brood at home, placing a cloud of fear and anxiety over it, for the participants recognize that such an open breach in social relations may lead in the near future to attempts at sorcery by the aggrieved party.

People sometimes say privately of occasions when a matrilineal kinsperson of the deceased is the principal heir at the final mortuary feast that the organizers are "making a mistake" and not following Vanatinai custom, but such instances are quite common, occurring in five out of eighteen final feasts that I witnessed. All five were male matrilineal kin of the deceased, or classificatory brothers. In this ritual arena, then, some ambitious men who are feared for their sorcery skills use their power to the disadvantage of women, other men, and the father's matrilineage members to gain valuables and force a public acknowledgment of their alleged prior generosity to the deceased. In nine out of eighteen final feasts, or zagaya, the principal heir was, in fact, the tau of the deceased and a patrilateral cross-cousin. Four of the nine were women, all of whom inherited from deceased male cross-cousins on behalf of their own mothers' brothers, fathers to the deceased.[22]

The custom of tau, both in ideology and in practice, is gender egalitarian. It is a major avenue, for both women and men, for obtaining ceremonial valuables as representatives of their matrilineages. These are compensation for goods, knowledge, and valuables that mothers' brothers, as fathers, gave to their children as tokens of love and nurturance. They also compensate for what the tau has given freely to the child during life. Although these valuable things rightfully belonged to the father's matrilineage, fathers and their lineage mates, collectively known as fathers, should be nurturing and generous to their children. The fathers, female and male, are compensated through their designated heir, the tau, after the death of the child, when the tau is ritually fed valuables in honor of the deceased by the owners of the feasts, the deceased's affines or kinfolk.

Eating the Fruit of the Dead

The principal heir of each mortuary feast, whether it is the tau or a kinsperson of the deceased, is called *ighan zagaya*, which means, "he or she who eats the feast" or ighan ghunoi, literally, "she or he who eats its fruit." This means, I was told, "the fruit of the corpse." All the valuables ritually exchanged at mortuary feasts are the fruit of the dead. This includes the person of the widow or widower and the woman designated to represent her matrilineage as principal affinal mourner, whose bodies are draped in valuables and presented along with them. Mourners and valuables are all said to be "like the corpse."

The customary rule is that the tau, a person of the deceased's father's lineage, not the deceased's lineage, symbolically incorporates the mourners and objects of value that come from the corpse. These are compensation for the paternal nurture of the deceased: ceremonial equivalents and replacements for the persons—children—and valuables that the deceased's matrilineage received from the father, or consumed, beginning with his marriage to the deceased's mother. The actual corpse of the deceased, and its spirit, continue to be part of its own matrilineage.

The one who eats the fruit of the dead ritually eats the corpselike affinal mourners but has the power to give them a new life. The tau

238

and the matrilineal kin of the deceased feed the mourners to sustain them in the weeks after the death and, at the conclusion of the final feast, wash the pigments of death from their bodies. They decorate them, making them as beautiful as any youth or girl and as much a symbol of fertility and the continuity of life. And they lead them to dance before matrilineal and patrilateral relatives of the deceased, liberating them from all taboos and freeing them to resume their lives. This is compensation for their honoring mourning taboos and for their feeding of ceremonial valuables, the fruit of the corpse, to the heirs of the deceased.

The living nurture one another with these representations of the flesh of the dead. Objects of value and people who stand for the corpse are ritually eaten, and death is challenged by being symbolically transformed into the food of life. The exchange of valuables and foods among people of lineages linked to the deceased publicly denies the entropy of death and honors the spirit and personhood of the deceased through ritual nurture—through life-giving. Those who eat the feast, ideally the fathers of the deceased as represented by the tau, symbolically incorporate—take into their bodies—the corpse and the deceased's personal force. They also incorporate the affinal mourners and the valuables that have survived the deceased and sprung from its body. This is a ritual reversal of the nurturance the fathers gave the deceased during life.

There is a coded message of subversion in the ritual as well, an ideology of patrilaterality in a matrilineal culture. The mourning affines, while not the same as the corpse, are "like the corpse," as a father's children are like him but part of another matrilineage. The mourners and ceremonial valuables are the fruit, ghunoi, of the dead that stands for the dead. Ghunoi means both "fruit" and "essence." Mourners and valuables are symbolically reincorporated by the deceased father's matrilineal kin, who, by eating its fruit, publicly claim the essence of the corpse, even though the corpse belongs to its own matrilineage.

Social relations among the people who feed one another were ties formed by the deceased in life. They have been dangerously threatened by death and the powerful and volatile emotions of grief, anger, and fear it generates in a charged field of sorcery suspicions and anxiety. The ritual necessity to eat the fruit of the dead preserves and temporarily reinforces these ties, until the kin and patrilateral heirs of the deceased have been compensated for their grief and anger by valuables and by observing the mourning of the affines. After the final feast mourners and heirs are finally free to choose whether to sever all relations or to rebuild their ties in new ways.

Nilla feeds papaya to a wild sea eagle.

Visitors arrive from Panaeati Island.

Two families board sailing canoes for a
journey to the East Calvados Islands.

A couple welcomes exchange partners. The woman is pregnant.

Paga walks through the hamlet with his daughter *(right)* and his sister's daughter. Malabwaga, his mother, watches.

Bwanaiwe weaves a coconut-leaf basket.

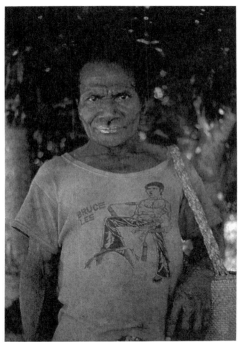

Uncle Sale.

Boys tend a clay cooking pot of vegetables boiling in coconut cream as adults clear a new garden. The boy on the left is minding his baby sister.

Rossel Island woman and child attend a Vanatinai feast.

A woman prepares sago and the wild legume called kaikai for roasting as her baby sleeps.

Making shell-disc necklaces with a wood and string pump drill.

A woman displays her finest greenstone axe blade in its carved
wooden ceremonial handle.

Young men at the Grass Island feast on the family sailing canoe.

Friends at a feast. Koita *(right)* is from Vanatinai and Florence is from Panabari. They communicate in the Saisai language.

Arriving at the feast.

The woman who is tau removes an axe blade propped against the widow's stepmother during the mwagumwagu ritual. The widow is seated on the right.

A young widow in full mourning regalia carries a platter of sago to the oven for roasting in preparation for the mwagumwagu.

After the mwagumwagu the widow is given a fine new skirt by her husband's cousins, and they cut off the last of her long mourning skirt.

Men wearing women's skirts perform a war dance with mock spears during a feast. The wooden drums of monitor lizard skin are specially decorated with "wings" of pandanus palm leaf.

The widow and her young son on a visit after the feast. She is now free to decorate herself, travel, court, and remarry.

Chapter Seven

Fruit of the Dead

Jivia

The jivia was held eight days after the old man was buried. The small upland hamlet was crowded with about a hundred people when we arrived at mid-morning. A few people, unable to attend the burial or visit the hamlet previously and pay their respects, wailed on their knees inside his grandson's house or else underneath it for about fifteen minutes and then joined the other visitors, who were mostly sitting around talking, laughing, and joking. The two wives of the dead man's sister's son wore full mourning regalia: their faces and bodies were daubed black with burnt coconut husk, and they wore finely woven coconut-leaf baskets inverted on their heads and coconut-leaf skirts around their shoulders as well as the long coarse mourning skirts.

A line of clay pots balanced on tripods of upright stones contained the ceremonial foods: sago pudding made with green coconut milk, garden produce with coconut cream, and pork. Some of the visiting women supervised the roasting of large quantities of yams, sweet potatoes, manioc, plantains, and sago in the aboveground stone ovens. Most of the visitors had brought baskets of garden produce or sago to contribute, and close kin and affines of the deceased had worked hard to dig up most of the food in their gardens and to make enough sago for ritual presentation.

In the early afternoon women brought two large baskets of roasted vegetables and sago inside the grandson's house, where the old man had lived and died. The vegetables were carefully resorted and arranged in baskets by a circle of women, using special sorting magic and a procedure that assures that everyone eats some of other people's food, a way of ritually negating the fear of sorcery and poison by exposing everyone to equal risk. One man carried in a large bowl of sago pudding.

The closest kinspeople and affines of the deceased collected in the dim interior of the house. Women and men, mostly kin to the deceased, brought out a total of five large and beautifully polished black-lip pearl shells, or gile. Some were decorated with large red, flat circles of shell strung in a line from one corner.

One at a time females, ranging in age from seventy to the six-year-old great-granddaughter of the deceased, sat down on the floor. And one at a time other men and women dipped one of the shell spoons into the roasted sago, using their hands to break a piece off the sago loaf, and dipped the same spoon into the sago pudding. Each one brought the pearl shell close to her or his own mouth, opening it slightly as if about to eat, then placed the food-laden shell spoon in the mouth of a seated female mourner, who chewed and swallowed the sago. The "feeders" and the "eaters" rotated, each "eater" being ritually fed in this manner by several people in turn and then moving away to be replaced by a new female "eater." The male and female "feeders" also moved outside to be replaced by someone else after ritually feeding one or more persons, always feigning bringing the food to their own mouths first but then giving it away.

After the ritual feeding had been concluded all of the "feeders" passed around a small tradestore mirror and gazed into it. The mirror, the shell spoon, and five or six new "bowl-dishes" from the tradestore were all placed on top of the larger basket of roasted vegetables and sago, which was then presented to the son of the deceased's sister.[1] The smaller basket was presented to the dead man's daughter's son's wife, who had shared her home with him and who had cared for him in his last illness.

Shortly afterward another pot of sago pudding and basket of roasted sago were brought into a nearby house. Those who had been ritually fed became the "feeders" themselves and placed food in the mouths of the women who had just done the same for them. The first group of "feeders" were mourners related by marriage to the dead man who were giving food to the matrilineal kin of the deceased. In the second phase of ritual feeding the kinspeople of the deceased fed the mourning affines.

Large and especially fine greenstone axe blades in their carved ceremonial wooden handles were then produced one at a time by various men and women and leaned against the backs of the two seated wives of the sister's son, the principal affinal mourners. Kin and affines alike brought out many more axe blades, placing them inside the house. The valuables were carried outside one by one and laid out under the house next door on some coconut leaves to be surveyed by the rest of the visiting mourners, who had waited outside and had not witnessed the actual ritual.

The axe blades were formally presented to the two wives, to whom people referred as the "widows" (the actual wife of the dead man had died many years before). The first wife then presented the six axe blades she had just received to the deceased's daughter's son's wife, and the second wife presented the ten axe blades she had been given to her own husband. He had contributed most of the first wife's six himself, and her family and other affines of the deceased had contributed most of the ten that went to him.

Three of the sister's son's pigs were butchered on a specially constructed platform by the men, while the women sat in a rough circle in the center of the hamlet, carefully tossing the roasted vegetables and sago from baskets held in their laps into more baskets and trade-store bowls placed on palm fronds in the center of the circle. The sorting process took about an hour, after which the women passed the baskets of roasted vegetable—theoretically equal in quantity and in types of food included—one at a time to the men, who lined them up in a double row on more palm fronds. A man or youth then carried first a basket of food to each household and then a hunk of raw pork. Some boiled pork, the organ meats plus bits of meat attached to masses of fat, was also passed around to every household. Finally, we all ate cooked pork, vegetables, and sago, sitting separately in family groups.

Most of the visitors headed home afterward, for it was already late in the afternoon, the women bearing large baskets of roasted vegetable and sago on their heads. They had arrived in the morning carrying roughly equivalent contributions of uncooked vegetables or sago.

Jivia is the first ritual honoring the deceased to take place after the burial, anywhere from three days to about two weeks later. It is an emotionally charged event. Participants are immersed in the grief, anger, and fear generated by the death and its repercussions among the living. Affinal mourners, dramatically segregated from normal social life by their blackened and covered bodies and the rigorous seclusion taboos, are under the close scrutiny of the deceased's kin and patrilateral relations.

The central ritual act of a jivia, whose name means "break," as in the breaking of the sago loaf, is the feeding of the deceased's matrilineal kin by his or her affines, followed by the matrikin's feeding of the affines. Men as well as women from the matrilineage of the deceased participate in this ritual feeding, but there must be at least one woman to formally represent the matrilineage.

The ritual feeding releases the mourning affines from many of the most onerous taboos: not leaving the house (except for the spouse of the deceased, who must make the velaloga feast to lift this taboo), not cooking food, and not taking food with their own hands. In theory the deceased's kin could, until then, feed the mourners poison or let them starve, out of anger and as compensation. Until the jivia, all affinal mourners, not just widowed spouses, blacken their bodies daily with burnt coconut husk.

The affines of the deceased, assisted by their own kin and exchange partners, present greenstone axe blades, pearl shells, and sometimes orange shell currency pieces to either a kinsperson of the deceased or a patrilateral relative chosen to "eat the feast" (ighan zagaya) or to "eat its fruit" (ighan ghunoi) at the jivia. The mourners themselves are presented to the person who eats the feast along with the valuables that decorate their bodies (and in the old days they could have been literally killed and eaten at this point). The person who eats the feast gives several equivalent valuables to the mourning affines. The lifting of taboos is ritually indicated by the eater of the feast grating coconut and squeezing a bit of coconut oil on the heads of the mourners, then passing a carved wooden comb once or twice through their hair.[2]

The jivia held for a woman is equivalent in size and elaborateness to that held for a man. The number of participants and of ceremonial valuables exchanged depends on the individual's place in the community during life and on the resources and energies of the survivors and principal mourners.

It is necessary for women to participate in the jivia in a variety of roles. They contribute sizable quantities of produce from their own gardens, they boil and roast garden produce and sago for ritual use and for distribution afterward to principal mourners and other visitors, they may host a jivia, or contribute pigs or valuables on behalf of their matrilineages. They are essential mourners of the dead, observing rigorous mourning taboos, and they are ritually fed by men and women in an affinal relationship to the deceased during the jivia as representatives of the deceased's matrilineage.

Men also work in gardens and contribute garden produce through their wives, sisters, and mothers, who carry it and present it to the hosts. Men bring sago they have worked, prepare ceremonial sago pudding, host and organize jivia, contribute pigs and tobotobo, butcher pigs, distribute raw pork and cooked vegetables and sago, and participate with women in the ritual feeding of the deceased's female matrilineal kin.

Both sexes contribute in public and significant ways to the jivia, participating in a complementary fashion in the same ritual arena. This contrasts with the situation in many other parts of Melanesia and elsewhere in the world where women may produce the objects used in ritual or exchange (for example by growing crops or raising pigs) but are excluded from public participation in key ritual activities, the province of adult men.

The social ties between kin and affines of the deceased are ritualized in food giving and sharing during the dangerous and emotion-charged period shortly after the death. They might otherwise dissolve with the death of the pivotal individual or turn to enmity in the face of private or public sorcery accusations. The sharing of food, as noted earlier, is an intimate act on Vanatinai. Unrelated people do not normally eat together, and affines avoid sitting and eating together even when they live in the same house, saying they would be "ashamed" to do so and that such an avoidance is a sign of respect. In-laws might cook their food together, but, for example, a daughter-in-law and her children are likely to eat in a different part of the house or else after a husband's mother or mother's brother. Eating together publicly constitutes marriage.

To share food with someone is a mark of trust. Sorcerers bespell or poison food, causing sickness or death. The ritual feeding and sharing of food at the jivia are therefore remarkable as a reversal of normal practices. In fact, because of the mourning taboo against principal mourners' touching their own hands to their mouths, they must be hand-fed by the deceased's kin, who thereby act in a fashion analogous to a parent feeding a small child. These roles are reversed in one phase of the ritual feeding of the jivia itself, where the affines feign placing choice mouthfuls of roasted sago loaf and sago pudding to their own lips and then deny themselves, giving food away and hand-feeding the kin of the deceased. Kin and affines alike emphasize through ritual their enduring, mutually dependent and trusting relationship despite the death, publicly addressing the tension and mistrust that any death, with its implications of successful sorcery, brings to the social network of the deceased.[3]

Velaloga

A special feast called velaloga, or "for walking," is held about two weeks to two months after a death when the deceased is survived by a spouse. It removes the taboo restricting a widow or widower and other principal affinal mourners to their houses. Afterward, they can work in their gardens, but they should not travel except to seek valuables to contribute in memory of the deceased at future feasts.

First a surplus of garden produce and of sago must be accumulated by the close kin of the surviving spouse to feed guests. Even though mourning widowers are not supposed to leave the hamlet until this feast is held, they may occasionally be seen, daubed with black mourning pigment, making sago in a nearby swamp.

The mourning affines must also present greenstone axe blades and shell currency pieces to the matrilineal kin of the deceased. They request them from nearby kin or exchange partners of the surviving spouse, for whom it would be difficult to refuse this direct request from a widow(er); if the request for valuables does not meet with success in neighboring hamlets, a relative of the widow(er) will have to travel to more distant communities in the hopes of successfully activating an exchange connection and requesting a valuable, for the surviving spouse is still restricted to the hamlet.

Just as sago pudding, vegetables boiled in coconut cream, and roasted sago loaf are associated with the jivia, a food called kaikai is essential for the velaloga. It is a bean pod from an enormous wild legume that must first be leached of poison, pounded with a stone mortar and pestle of prehistoric origin, and then roasted on a potsherd. The bean is alternated with layers of sago starch, then wrapped in green leaves and roasted in a stone oven.[4] Women do the gathering and the laborious preparation.

Velaloga are generally smaller feasts than the jivia. One I attended, for example, had only twenty participants, compared to one hundred at the jivia for an equally prominent person. Baskets of roasted kaikai and garden vegetables are presented by affinal women to a representative of the deceased's matrilineal kin, and individual affines present ceremonial valuables to them. The matrilineal kin then escort the mourning spouse and others mourners to the stream, where they wash off the charcoal smeared over their bodies for the first time since the death.

Afterwards, they are free to bathe and to leave the hamlet for subsistence. But they must honor the remaining mourning taboos and not visit other hamlets except on journeys in quest of ceremonial valuables for the spouse's mortuary feasts. Violation of these taboos, such as being caught with a lover, would risk death, formerly by murder and today by sorcery or witchcraft. One young widower, still in mourning after about a year, suffered a mysterious partial paralysis (perhaps from polio). Local opinion, which he shared, was that he had been bewitched by his deceased wife's mother in revenge for his having a sexual intrigue with a young unmarried woman.

Still wearing the yogeyoge or old clothes and (for men) beards, mourners must not decorate themselves with coconut oil, armlets, or leglets, or wear flowers or scented leaves, and they should not comb or cut their hair. All of these forms of self-beautification signal desire to attract someone or something, a lover or a valuable, and the possible use of magic to achieve this desire. Mourners should attract valuables by the starkness of their mourning garb, evocative of death, loss, and need, and their sexuality is taboo.

Whether or not they blacken their bodies daily is nowadays a matter of personal choice from this point until they resume full mourning regalia at the final feast. My neighbor, a middle-aged widow whose husband had died several years previously, would put on the black mourning pigment when she left her home area and, she said, on the days when she woke up feeling particularly depressed about her husband's death.

The most significant aspect of the velaloga for the analysis of gender on Vanatinai is the parallel treatment accorded to men and women. The sex of the deceased and of the surviving spouse does not alter in any way the substance or the elaborateness of the ritual. Widows and widowers must bear equally onerous mourning taboos, and kin and affines of both sexes are required to participate in the preparations for and the carrying out of the velaloga ritual, just as they are in the earlier jivia.

Ghanrakerake

The old man's ghanrakerake, the feast whose name means "food goes out," was held in a remote inland hamlet across the mountain from the house where he had died and where his jivia had taken place. His sister's daughter's husband had decided to "close" or taboo one of the three houses in the hamlet to all food-related activities, for the old man had always slept in that house on frequent visits before his final illness.

I crossed the island to attend the ghanrakerake with Gaiba, an older widow who was the dead man's sister's daughter, sister to the wife of the man who was hosting the feast. As she was a daughter of the deceased, she did not bring any garden produce or other contributions to the feast but came prepared to help with the cooking of food for the guests.

After a walk of several hours and a long hot climb over the pass in the central mountain range, we came to an upland plateau, startling a flock of green parrots, uncommon on the coast. We bathed in the cool forest stream below the hamlet. Gaiba produced two "sides" of bagi necklace from the basket she had been carrying on her head. She put one around her own neck and loaned the other to me to wear for the duration of the feast. It is customary for visitors who are not affines in mourning to decorate themselves and to look as attractive as possible. Thus resplendent, we made our entrance into the hamlet.

There had been about a hundred people at the old man's jivia, but we found only twenty adults sitting on the ground, chewing betel nut and superintending five clay cooking pots, each on its stone tripod, full of boiling yams, sweet potato, and other vegetables in coconut cream. Some of the women were building the ghumughumu, or stone oven, to cook sago and garden produce. Meanwhile Zhuwa, the host, sister's daughter's husband to the deceased, built a fire under a clay pot full of fat freshwater prawns and eels.

The house that had been closed by the old man's death was roped off with twine made from wild pandanus fiber, just as I had seen the house where a new mother and her firstborn infant were living roped off with magically fortified twine to keep away sorcerers and sickness. People were staying in the house, ducking under the twine to get in and out, but it was taboo until after the feast was over to bring food into it.

Several of the people who had figured prominently in the old man's jivia were not present for this feast, including a sister's son and his two wives, the old man's own son, and his grandson and grand-daughter-in-law, with whom he had lived at the time of his death. The valuables in this feast were to come only from those related by marriage to the dead man, including people descended from males of his matrilineage, who contribute valuables in a fashion analogous to affines of the deceased. The person who would eat the fruit of the dead man was another sister's son, who had not attended the jivia.

Late in the afternoon most of the adults assembled in Zhuwa's house. The sister's son and his wife sat outside on the ground by themselves, but one kinsman of the deceased came inside to watch the affines make their contributions. One by one people produced a total of ten ceremonial valuables from the depths of their baskets: six greenstone axe blades, two ceremonial lime spatulas, and two orange shell currency pieces in their woven coconut-leaf pouches.

Mumuga, a woman in her fifties, widow of the dead man's sister's son, was the major contributor, giving one axe blade, one lime spatula, and one shell currency piece. Others who gave valuables included her brother, the host, and a man who contributed in memory of his father's mother's brother. The axe blades were placed in their carved ceremonial handles. Then the affines gathered up all the valuables and carried them outside, putting them down carefully at the feet of the dead man's sister's son and his wife, who were gazing impassively in another direction. Casually the recipients turned their heads and put the valuables away in their own baskets, later storing the baskets inside the old man's former house. The host cut the twine around the taboo house.

The hosts fed us roasted and boiled vegetables and sago and boiled prawns and eel. We also got roasted and uncooked vegetables to carry home in our baskets. Some people departed immediately, but those, like us, who had come from farther away, spent the night and left the next morning.

Ghanrakerake is the third feast in the mortuary ritual sequence, the second feast held after a burial when there is no surviving spouse, two weeks to six months after the burial. The name, "Food Goes Out," indicates that this feast clears the taboo against storing, cooking, or consuming food in a house formerly used by the deceased. This house is not the one in which the death occurred, for which the food taboos are cleared by the jivia, but one in a different hamlet, a place where the deceased used to spend time. Since postmarital residence is bilocal and people tend to make gardens in two or more locations, there is usually a second house that belonged to the deceased or in which he or she regularly stayed. This house is declared closed or taboo (ghabubu) out of respect for the deceased until hamlet residents hold the ghanrakerake.

As in the velaloga ritual the principal flow of valuables in this feast is from mourning affines of the deceased to the matrilineal kin or to the tau. It is normally smaller in scale than either the jivia or the final feast, the zagaya: it takes place neither during the first flush of grief over a death nor at the climax of all mortuary ritual several years later. But about twice as many ceremonial valuables are usually presented at a ghanrakerake as at a velaloga. It is the giving of greenstone axe blades and other valuables and not the physical cutting of the twine that "clears" the deceased's house of the taboo on food storage, preparation, or consumption.

Having a series of feasts in memory of the death of one person gives an opportunity for different kin and affines to receive and give valuables at each feast; thus, the feast sponsors hope, satisfying the demands of all parties concerned for a share in the inheritance—the fruit—of the deceased.

Women and men alike host the ghanrakerake and eat its fruit, and the feast is the same if the deceased is male or female. It is worth noting that the major contributor of valuables to the feast I describe was not the owner of the feast, the male host, but a woman who is known as a gia and a wise woman. She thereby either diminished her own personal store of ceremonial wealth or activated one of her exchange connections, requesting a valuable outright or asking for the return of a valuable equivalent to one that she previously had given to her partner. By doing so she reinforced her reputation for wealth, generosity, and respect for the spirits of the dead.

Vearada

Sometimes the kin of the deceased decide to hold a small feast called vearada about a year after a death. It is not an essential part of the mortuary ritual sequence. The name, "for crying," indicates that the feast is for feeding pork to those who cried for the deceased at the burial. There are no ceremonial valuables exchanged at a vearada, and it clears no mourning taboos. The kinfolk kill one or several of their pigs or pigs they have obtained from exchange partners. They also make generous amounts of sago and contribute garden produce, cooking the vegetables and pork for the guests, who assemble to eat and then depart, usually the same day.

There is normally a hiatus of anywhere from one year to a whole generation in mortuary ritual activity following the completion of these preliminary feasts and before the final and most elaborate feast, the zagaya, is held to lift all remaining mourning taboos upon individuals and communities that result from a death.

Zagaya

The sailing canoe skimmed across the shallow bay bearing passengers to the feast, including an unhappy looking sow with her trotters tied to a pole. There was an unusual assembly of finely carved and painted sailing canoes lying just off the normally deserted mouth of the small estuary leading to the hamlet. The crew of Grass Islanders named them all: they came from four different islands. Our own vessel, newly purchased from its Panaeati Island builders by a Grass Island man, poled cautiously up a narrow estuary thrown into dim green shade by white-barked mangroves rising forty feet on either side from a tangle of submarine and aerial roots. More sailing canoes were anchored off a muddy landing about one hundred feet inland.

We were warmly greeted by our hosts, the brothers Taradi and Bagodi, *giagia* well known throughout the archipelago, and taken to the house where we would stay. It was already full of feast visitors reclining on their sleeping mats and sitting cross-legged, chewing betel nut, and catching up on each other's news. The wide verandah offered a fine view of the activities on the red clay of the hamlet's central area.

The hamlet's normal quiet was broken by an animated crowd of about two hundred visitors from most of the communities of Vanatinai and from the islands of the East Calvados. New arrivals continued to pour in. Lines of women proudly bore heavy baskets and large, carved wooden platters full of garden produce on their heads. Men carried an end of poles weighted down with pig or rows of heavy sago bundles. These are the formal in-law presentations called *muli*. Gifts of pig were announced by a young man of the party blowing on a conch shell. One of the women who would eat the feast carried her contribution of produce in a basket blackened with smoke to signify its role in a ritual of mourning. Most of the produce was taken to an area underneath the house next door to us, temporarily screened from public view by walls of woven sago leaf attached to the house posts. Hundreds of double bundles of sago hung on either side of the two poles running the length of our house.

After a dinner of fine yams boiled in coconut cream some people retired early. Others stayed up until two in the morning, talking and laughing around fires built on house verandahs and in the central plaza. I was awakened from a deep sleep about four-thirty in the morning by a woman whispering to me to move so that someone could "make the sago." I shifted my sleeping mat from underneath one end of a long pole from which bundles of sago were hanging, surprised that anyone planned to start cooking at this dark and silent hour.

Then I saw the dim figure of a woman moving down the pole, clasping the outsides of each bundle, spitting softly but explosively on it and muttering something almost inaudible. I realized that I was witnessing the chief food magician charming the sago to make it last throughout the *zagaya* and satisfy all the guests. It was Igaregare, a woman I knew well. This hour in the dead of night—while all others slumbered unaware—was the customary time for the magic. I was told later that she also charmed the sago stored in other houses, the mountains of garden produce, the firewood, the coconuts, and the leaves collected for use in the stone oven. This also enabled her to make an accurate mental inventory of available resources. During the whole of the feast no one will ever see her eat. Several days later I saw a young man sent to fetch bundles of sago start to grab the last bundle on one end of the pole, which had been left hanging alone while all its neighbors had been taken and used. Two women immediately called out, "No, not that one!" and the young man quickly took his hands off it with an embarrassed smile, moving down the pole to other bundles. If the bundles at each end are used, the food magic will be spoiled.

The hamlet awoke before dawn to the rhythmic sound of coconut being scraped for use in the communal breakfast of three huge clay pots of boiled vegetables—yams, sweet potato, taro, plantains, and pumpkin—and five clay pots of white rice. All of the principal mourners had carefully daubed their bodies with burnt coconut husk, including Bagodi, who was mourning his wife's brother. The widows wore the long mourning skirts, plus newly woven coconut-leaf baskets over their heads and new short skirts of coconut leaf as cloaks over their shoulders. The black pigment, and their lowered gaze, erased the force of their personalities as it obscured their features. Strangers to me at that time, I thought they were all much older than I was.

That evening there was a meeting in the central plaza. Several respected men and women, including the senior owner of the feast, asked people not to quarrel over the exchange of valuables during the feast if they were dissatisfied with what they received and not to make sorcery attempts against others. Marai, the most notorious sorcerer in the Louisiade Archipelago, then got up and made a long speech in the Vanatinai language, adding phrases in Saisai, Misima, and English and convulsing the assembly with nervous laughter at his jokes. He asked people not to be afraid of him, as he said he no longer practiced sorcery but only worked in his garden. He assured everyone that nobody would "walk around in the night" during this feast, a reference to sorcerers, because "I am a sorcerer and I know." He was warning his rivals and reassuring the guests in order to help his kin, the owners of the feast, by placing the entire feast under his magical protection.

The next morning five more pigs were slaughtered, singed, and butchered by men using their skill and their special magic to extend the pork enough to provide a surfeit for the assembled guests. Three large clay pots of sago pudding, moni, were carefully prepared by men using seven-foot-long ornately carved wooden paddles, made and used only to blend sago starch and green coconut milk in this ceremonial pudding.

Meanwhile, dozens of women concentrated on building two stone ovens for roasting yams, sweet potato, manioc, plantains, and the tasty chunks of leaf-wrapped sago and grated coconut that are a special feast food. The rounded river stones were heated in the fire and then expertly tossed with wooden tongs upon a bed of tender broad forest leaves. The stones were covered with more leaves and then a layer of vegetables, a third layer of leaves, another of heated stones, more leaves, more vegetables, a final covering of leaves, and then the emptied garden baskets upside-down on top to anchor it in place. The women chewed betel nut and waited for the food to cook.

Taradi and Bagodi spent most of the day inside the house where they store their ceremonial valuables. Men and women filed in and out, presenting their greenstone axe blades (tobotobo), shell-disc necklaces (bagi), and other valuables to the owners of the feast, who would give them formally later to those who would eat the feast.

Others climbed inside to offer their valuables to the hosts for the immediate exchange of equivalent ones. People who in this manner offer a valuable or a pig to the host in exchange for the immediate return of an identical valuable from him or her are still "helping." The exchange permits both parties to use the newly obtained valuables to present to members of the lineage from which they received the original valuable.[5] With the house doors tied shut, in private, the two host brothers and their closest associates laid out on a pandanus mat all the valuables that would be ritually presented later, taking care that equivalent amounts would go in honor of each of the three dead men whose zagaya were being celebrated.

Finally, in the late afternoon a clay pot full of sago pudding and another full of garden produce cooked in coconut cream (*tamja*) were carried to a spot on the central plaza and set down upon a tripod of three stones. A large blackened basket piled high in a carefully stacked pyramid with the finest yams, sweet potato, and taro was carried out of the hidden area under the house where the produce was stored and placed near the clay pots. A friend explained that since the first dead man was a Grass Islander, the hosts were partially adapting the ritual presentation to Saisai customs, particularly by including the basket containing the pyramid of produce, or *sowasowa*, to be used later for seed by the people who "eat the feast."

A piece of red cloth and some new tradestore enameled metal dishes plus some spoons were carried out and placed near the pots of food. The widow and her stepmother, Taradi and Bagodi's sister, sat down by the pots, their bodies blackened, wearing the full mourning regalia of a basket as a cap and new coconut-leaf skirts as cloaks over their shoulders overlapping their long mourning skirts. Both women chewed betel nut and looked down silently at the ground. This was the start of the central zagaya ritual, the mwagumwagu. The name refers to the mourners' sitting down to be publicly presented to the heir of the deceased along with ceremonial valuables and other goods.

Taradi, Bagodi, and their closest associates, male and female, strode one by one across the central plaza, each carrying a valuable from the house to a place on or near the seated mourners. Two tobotobo in their 7-shaped carved ceremonial handles were leaned against the backs of each woman, and one more was laid across each leaf-covered pot of food. Others were placed in front of the seated women. Daveri in their woven coconut-leaf pouches were pinned with wooden combs to the basket covering each woman's head, and one more daveri was placed on top of each woman's head underneath the basket. A fine bagi was looped around the neck of the widow. A wonamo jilevia, or ceremonial lime spatula of tortoiseshell, was tucked into the widow's armlet.

Then Lowaida, the dead man's father's sister's daughter and tau, who was sitting silently nearby with her family, walked over to the widow and removed the bagi, replacing it around the widow's neck with another even finer and redder bagi. Swiftly Taradi and Bagodi carried all the valuables, except for the bagi given by Lowaida, from on and near the seated women and placed them in front of Lowaida in the small baskets that had been on the "widows' " heads. Lowaida immediately got up again and placed three small tobotobo and one large one that bore the individual name of Waramata (after an uninhabited islet near Panaeati) near the mourners. The big tobotobo was to (symbolically) cut the widow's skirt, although the four tobotobo would actually go to Taradi as partial compensation for the wealth he was giving away to release the young widow, his sister's stepdaughter, from her mourning.

Lowaida watched, chewing betel nut and speaking little, as her husband and kin carefully laid out on the ground and counted all the valuables they had received, then put them away in her personal baskets. A casual observer might think that the voluble husband was the one receiving all the wealth, but it is an undignified and shameful violation of ritual protocol for the person who eats the feast, male or female, to show too overt an interest in the wealth he or she receives in compensation for the loss of the deceased. The total number of valuables presented to the dead man's tau, Lowaida, was announced by her husband to the crowd of spectators: one bagi, thirteen tobotobo, one wonamo jilevia, four daveri, and four kina.[6]

Taradi and Bagodi removed the new coconut-leaf skirts from the mourning women and presented them to Lowaida, who got up again and came over to the "widows." Using a polished pearl shell spoon, she scooped up some coconut oil from the top of the pot of sago pudding and poured it onto the widow's head, letting it run down her blackened face and back, releasing her from the taboo against oiling and beautifying her body.

The widow finally stood up. Using another decorated pearl shell, she dipped it into the sago pudding and then into the pot of vegetables cooked in coconut cream. In a ritual detail that echoes the jivia, the first mortuary feast, she feigned taking the food in her own mouth and then placed it instead in the mouth of Lowaida's small son, and the little boy chewed and swallowed the food. Then Lowaida's kin and husband carried all of the remaining items, the pots of food, the huge pile of vegetables—which had to be carried away in two baskets—the cloth, the dishes and the spoons, into the house where she was staying.

Very quickly the second ceremony began, the culminating ritual honoring a different death. Another pot of moni and another pot of tamja were set down in a different place in the center of the hamlet. This time there was no pyramid of seed vegetables and there were no tradestore goods presented. Bagodi and, again, his sister sat down near the pots, bodies blackened and baskets covering their bowed heads. This mwagumwagu was in memory of Bagodi's wife's brother. Bagodi's teen-aged son, Vuti, was, under his father's guidance, organizing his first mwagumwagu. He, Taradi, and other close kin carried out valuables one by one, leaning tobotobo against the mourners' backs, across the pots of food and in a row in front of the mourners, pinning daveri to the baskets on their heads, and winding a long bagi around the neck of each seated woman. The valuables were quickly removed and placed in front of Waghena, father's sister's daughter's daughter and tau of the deceased, and her husband. The two seated mourners got up, as neither was the actual widowed spouse, and Bagodi strode into his house. His son and his helpers then carried three more tobotobo to Waghena. Bagodi dramatically dragged across the hamlet clearing a bagi that was five feet long on each side, the pearl shell pendants on its base clacking noisily together in the dust, and deposited it with a flourish in front of Waghena. Vuti began to weep as he presented the last two tobotobo, for the ceremony had brought back his sorrow at the death several years earlier of his beloved maternal uncle. Touched by his tears, some of his elders began to cry too.

Waghena's husband announced the total count of valuables to the waiting crowd: two bagi, nine tobotobo, one wonamo jilevia, four daveri, and four kina. He then called out that if they had some valuables to give back to the mourners they would have done so but that they had nothing. I was told later that upon their arrival at the zagaya they had privately given Taradi one bagi, three tobotobo, and three daveri.

Almost immediately the third and final mwagumwagu began on the other side of the hamlet clearing. This one honored the deceased husband of Keminana, Taradi and Bagodi's mother's sister's daughter, their sister in local kinship reckoning. Keminana, her sister, and her two daughters—all ritually blackened, except for the older daughter, a nursing mother, and wearing full mourning regalia—sat down near the last pot of sago pudding and another pot of vegetables cooked in coconut cream. The two brothers and their male assistants placed tobotobo in their handles along the backs of both Keminana and her older daughter and one each against her sister and younger daughter, plus one more tobotobo across the tops of each of the pots of food. More tobotobo were set in a line in front of the women. Daveri were pinned to the basket on each woman's head with a wooden comb, and a second daveri was hidden on each woman's head underneath the basket. A wonamo jilevia was inserted into Keminana's armlet, a fine bagi was wound around her neck, and another was placed around the neck of her older daughter.

Meanwhile Taradi strode over to the dead man's father's sister's son and tau, and personally presented him with a special tobotobo, a polished stone axe blade almost black in color. Taradi called out its personal name, "Bougainville." He and his helpers then removed all of the ritually displayed valuables and piled them in front of the tau and his kinspeople, the daveri and bagi nested in the intricately woven baskets that had been on the mourning women's heads. The tau stood up to present his own tobotobo to Keminana, the widow, to "cut her skirt" and formally end her mourning. He returned to his place and laid out and counted the valuables he had received, announcing the total number to the spectators: one bagi, eleven tobotobo, one wonamo jilevia, eight daveri, and six kina. His young kinswoman scooped some coconut oil from the top of the sago pudding with a polished pearl shell and poured it on Keminana's head. All four of the mourning women then ritually fed her in turn, using pearl shell spoons to pick up mouthfuls of sago pudding and cooked vegetable and feigning putting the food in their own mouths first.

As the sun set a crowd of women sat in an irregular circle in the hamlet clearing, sorting roasted vegetables from the stone oven into equivalent amounts, each woman tossing yams through the air from the basket she held on her lap to fill up empty baskets at the center of the circle, talking loudly, and laughing at ribald jokes. But it was still a serious business, the women shielding their baskets from their neighbors' view and arguing about the proper division. The woman next to me explained that the chief food magician had said a magical spell over each basket to cause the yams and other produce to multiply enough to feed all the guests generously and still have an impressive surplus. In addition some of the women said their own individual spells on the baskets they held. It was almost completely dark by the time we had finished the *dogo*, or sorting. A different man in turn then carried each basket to a different individual or family group for dinner. Portions of raw pork were passed out by the men to representatives of every family and important individual attending the feast, and the smell of boiling pork began to fill the hamlet.

That night most of the visitors danced in the hamlet clearing until sunrise to the music of guitars and ukeleles, for the taboo against playing music, dancing, and singing had been "cleared" by the day's rituals. The feast owners had deferred to their younger relatives and agreed to the new music of imported instruments. The customary dancing at feasts is an all-night affair of drumming and singing, called *rausi*, performed by male drummers and singers of both sexes, while women dance, or *sobu*, in a counterclockwise direction around the drummers. The songs are in a half a dozen different languages whose origins stretch from Vanatinai to Duau, diffusing along exchange routes, and there are new ones telling of love, death, adventure, and other universal themes. People still rausi and sobu at about half of Vanatinai feasts.

The principal mourners did not join in the dancing. Some of the middle-aged men put on women's coconut-leaf skirts, tying them in front, while they danced, customary attire for male dancers for reasons no one could ever explain to me. Young people, and a few not so young, slipped off into the shadows to meet their lovers in prearranged rendezvous.

Many of the guests left the next morning, carrying away gifts of new garden baskets piled high with uncooked garden produce, the equivalent in most cases to what they had originally contributed to the feast from their own gardens. The others remained to participate in the last phase of the ritual. The principal mourners, the tau and their kin, and the usual crowd of spectators walked inland to two deep pools on the river. The men took the upstream spot and the women the downstream, and the smiling tau told the mourners to bathe their soot-blackened bodies. I was startled to see, as her face emerged from its covering of charcoal, that Mwaniku, the widow in the first mwagumwagu, was not old, as I had thought, but in her early twenties. Afterward the tau (or their kinspeople) of the same sex cut the mourners' hair for the first time since the deaths they were honoring. Bagodi's beard was shaved, and he was given new woven fern-fiber armlets to wear. Waghena's husband took some bright green and white leaves, held them briefly in the fire, chewed ginger and other magical substances, muttering inaudibly, then sprayed his charmed saliva on the leaves. He gave them to Bagodi to tuck into his armlets, a form of love magic.

The tau and their female helpers tied fine new coconut-leaf skirts around the hips of the mourners, draping them over the coarse, ankle-length yogeyoge. Using tradestore knives, the tau then carefully trimmed all of the skirts to just below the knee. The widows were radiant as the last long pieces of their mourning skirts fluttered to the ground.

The bodies of all of the erstwhile mourners were anointed with scented, magically enhanced coconut oil, and their faces were painted by the tau and helpers. Lines of black, made from the soot burned on clay cooking pots, overlaid with dots of white, made from coral lime, and in one case yellow made from a forest plant, streaked their cheeks and foreheads. They were given new fern-fiber armlets and headbands made of strips of the bright red labels from cans of A1 Brand mackerel. Brightly colored leaves and flowers were tucked into their armlets and headbands. The mourners were given bagi to wear (their own, I was told later, except for Mwaniku, who wore the bagi her husband's tau had given her the day before), as well as many necklaces of tiny tradestore glass beads. Finally the tau led the newly resplendent mourners back to the hamlet where, in an anticlimax, they went back to work preparing food for the remaining feast guests.

That night some of the visitors from Grass Island and Vanatinai gathered in the large house where we were staying to sing traditional songs from Vanatinai, Misima, and Saisai accompanied by slowly beating on a lime gourd with a wooden lime spatula. Some were songs of mourning for the dead called *nuaroru* or *kakalék*, among other names, on Vanatinai (kaka means spirit) and *kahin*, or "cry" in both the Saisai and Misima languages. Others were love songs or pieces newly composed in traditional style about recent experiences, such as a song about an old man's first plane trip, which took him to the hospital at Port Moresby. Koita later told me that by singing nuaroru, "we sing with the spirit" (*la va wozinga woye kaka*).

Some time after midnight the tau and their kinspeople led the widows and other former mourners by the hand one by one into the hamlet clearing and told them to dance to the guitars, ukeleles, and singing of the young men, the first time in the years since the deaths marked by the zagaya that they had been permitted to dance and to enjoy themselves publicly. Mwaniku was on the verge of crying with joy and sorrow. After about two o'clock the host families fed rice boiled in coconut cream and sweetened tea to the dancers and the musicians, who played one more song before everyone went to bed.

The next morning most of the remaining guests left on foot and by sailing canoe, laden down with baskets of garden produce. Before one of the tau departed she gave one of her young kinsmen a toboto-bo from among the many she had received, in gratitude for his exceptionally hard work during the zagaya grating mountains of coconut, carrying firewood, fetching water, distributing food, and running errands whenever asked. The young man's proud sister told me that this was the first tobotobo that her twenty-year-old brother had ever possessed.

The hamlet was littered with a week's worth of betel nut skins, coconut husks, and other debris. The magic that makes the food last throughout the zagaya would be spoiled if the hamlet grounds received their customary morning sweeping. The women finally began to sweep up the mess with their coconut-rib brooms as the food magician herself emerged triumphantly from her days of seclusion under the house where the food was stored. She was privately given tobotobo and daveri by her kinsmen, the hosts, in compensation for her labor. The substantial amount of sago and garden produce that remained would be transported to the upcoming feast on Grass Island to be hosted by an exchange partner.

The largest and final memorial feast held on Vanatinai after the death of each individual is called zagaya in the Western dialects and thagaya in the Central and Eastern dialects of the island. These are also the generic terms for feast.[7] Zagaya usually occur about three to five years after a death. The actual time at which it takes place depends on many factors. It may occur as soon as a few months after a death or as long as twenty-five years later, depending upon the wishes and the resources of the survivors. While a lack of valuables is the usual reason why a zagaya might not be held for many years, prolonging the onerous mourning duties of a spouse and others, having access to sufficient quantities of ceremonial valuables, pigs, and foodstuffs does not necessarily mean that the memorial feast sequence will be speedily concluded. Big men and big women who could hold a zagaya several months after a death often delay this final feast for a number of years because, as one man explained, if they did not, "their in-laws could not keep up with them." They could not provide the hosts with sufficient quantities of valuables to maintain the affines' own reputations, they could not hold future zagaya on an equally accelerated schedule, and they would be ashamed and angry at this implicit challenge to their wealth, connections, and generosity.

Every Vanatinai zagaya is in some ways unique, a product of the precise time in local history at which it takes place, its location, participants' memories of the deceased, and the personalities of the hosts, principal mourners, and most important guests in attendance. And each event shapes subsequent feasts: their participants, the valuables exchanged, hoarded, or unavailable, the quarrels or courtships that develop. The zagaya exchanges of valuables and foodstuffs among lineages and among individuals, as the culmination of exchange relationships begun at the marriage of the deceased's parents, reflect this long and particular history.

Organizing Zagaya

Preparations for holding a zagaya begin years in advance. The principal organizers must accumulate ceremonial valuables, declining to give them to exchange partners requesting them for other purposes, and pigs must be raised and fattened to an imposing size. Often the host of an upcoming feast places a taboo sign, called a *ghivi*, on the outskirts of the hamlet, to close it, as people say. This massive construction of wood, palm leaf, and pig jaws warns other islanders that all the hamlet pigs and valuables are reserved for the planned zagaya. If they anger the residents by coming to ask them for valuables for other purposes, they can expect supernatural retaliation.

Large tracts of extra garden land must be cleared and planted to provide food for the feast visitors, many of whom will remain in the hamlet for weeks before, during, and after the feast. The women of the hamlet decide after the harvest in June and July whether the host lineage and its assisting affines have produced a sufficient surplus of vegetable food to hold the zagaya. As the "owner of the garden" (ghuma tanuwagai), decisions on the disposition of garden produce rest with the senior woman. If there is any doubt about the adequacy of garden supplies the feast is postponed until the following year, for it would bring great shame upon the hosts if there were not enough food to satisfy the crowds of expected guests.[8] Several planned zagaya on Vanatinai were postponed by hamlet women on the grounds of insufficient garden produce during the drought year of 1978.

August or September, after the yam harvest has been successfully completed, is the usual time for those who wish to contribute valuables to an upcoming zagaya to travel to other communities or other islands on a ghiva expedition. Close matrilineal kin of the deceased, their spouses and spouses' kin, the widowed spouse of the deceased and his or her kin, and adult children of a deceased father are all expected to make major contributions at the zagaya no matter who has been named owner of the feast or whether one of the contributor's own kin will eat the feast. There is no particular amount or type of contribution set by custom for any one category of donor, but the close affines of the feast owner normally assist him or her by obtaining and presenting one or several pigs and/or one or several important ceremonial valuables such as bagi, tobotobo, or ceremonial lime spatulas.

Ghiva expeditions actually take place at any time of the year at the convenience of the seeker, his or her exchange partner(s), and the weather. A prudent individual anticipates future needs for valuables and allows plenty of time to travel to the partner's home community and make the request. Often exchange partners wish to provide a valuable either to cancel an earlier debt or to initiate a new exchange but do not have a suitable one on hand and they must travel in turn to their own exchange partners to request one. A common tactic is for the exchange partner to tell the requestor that he or she will bring the valuable or pig to the zagaya itself, as in the case described at the beginning of the last chapter. Good exchange partners do in fact arrive at feasts with the valuables in question, but often the zagaya tanuwagai is overheard swearing with rage at a partner's duplicity in not even attending the feast. The betrayed party may take revenge through sorcery or by a public challenge, an *uraura*, to the absent exchange partner. Requests for valuables made under pressure of an impending exchange obligation such as an upcoming zagaya are most likely to be successful. The exchange partners of the kin, affines, neighbors, and friends of someone who is sponsoring a feast in the near future expect to be visited and asked for valuables. Plans for a zagaya in this manner involve an ever widening network of individuals linked by personal exchange relationships. This network of exchange links activated by zagaya preparations often extends to islands throughout the Louisiade Archipelago, and even beyond it, to Ware and Duau.

Once sufficient supplies of garden produce, pigs, and ceremonial valuables have been stockpiled or promised, the host of an upcoming zagaya calls upon his or her closest kin, affines, and friends to gather in the hamlet where the feast will be held and help with the final phase of preparations. They will normally remain for several weeks working for the host, and they must be fed well. It is customary for one or several pigs to be killed by the host especially to feed these workers either before the zagaya begins or after it is over and the other guests have gone home.

During this period of preparation small guest houses may be built to accommodate the expected visitors, or existing buildings may be repaired. An open wooden platform is sometimes constructed for slaughtering pigs. The chest-high area under one house is screened from public view by temporary walls made of pieces of sago leaf, woven by women, attached to the house poles. This area will be used to store the food used at the feast and must be shielded from prying eyes to protect the strength of the food magic. The construction jobs are performed by men.

Large quantities of sago starch must be produced both for essential ceremonial uses at the zagaya and merely to feed the guests. This too involves several weeks of work. If the sago grove being used is not close to the hamlet, the workers may camp nearby until the job is done. Before one zagaya on Vanatinai in 1978 twenty five hundred double bundles of sago starch wrapped in sago leaf were produced, each half a bundle weighing approximately one pound, and almost all were consumed at the feast. Both men and women work at different phases of the sago-making operation.

Other preparations include the weaving of fine coconut-leaf baskets and making of new coconut-leaf skirts, the gathering of firewood and large quantities of ripe coconuts, and the accumulation of piles of small round river stones and piles of broad and tender green leaves to be used in making the stone ovens for roasting feast foods. These tasks are generally performed by the women of the host hamlet and their kinswomen, who come days or weeks early to help, assisted by young people of both sexes. Both men and women clean their bagi and other valuables, oiling them with coconut oil to make them especially beautiful for their ritual presentation.

Zagaya are generally held during the season following the annual yam harvest in June and July, allowing time for the lengthy necessary preparations. On Vanatinai in 1978–79 zagaya were held from September to as late as April, with none occurring from May to August. This was in spite of the regulation passed by the Louisiade Local Government Council that all feasts in the archipelago must take place in December, with November understood to be a time of exchange journeys and feast preparations.

Several dozen zagaya are held every year in the Vanatinai–East Calvados region. Often a particular one may not take place until one or more others have been completed, as a major contributor expects to "eat the feast," or obtain valuables from an exchange partner who has "eaten the feast," at an earlier zagaya and then present these valuables at another later one. In this manner many ceremonial valuables pass through numerous hands at zagaya held in a wide variety of communities throughout the area in the space of only a few weeks or months. Observers wishing to know when a certain zagaya will occur learn that the feast at X hamlet can only be held after the successful completion of those at Y and Z cause pigs and ceremonial valuables to flow to the zagaya tanuwagai at X or to his or her closest exchange partners and associates.

One whole series of zagaya planned on Vanatinai and several East Calvados Islands was delayed until Ijau, a dignified widow and big woman from Vanatinai, could be transported by a sailing canoe from Grass Island. She had been attending a big feast and was awaiting the conclusion of another feast at Panabari Island to free a sailing canoe to take her some fifty miles to her home. She would then pick up an enormous tusked pig she planned to present to an exchange partner for use at a feast he was hosting on Vanatinai. The subsequent feasts in other communities could not be held until this planned Vanatinai feast released large quantities of ceremonial valuables to a number of people who would then contribute them elsewhere. I only became aware that all these feasts were being held up because of Ijau and her famous pig because I hoped to attend all of them before my long overdue return to the United States. But the scheduled commencement of any of the feasts, which would occur one after the other, seemed to be receding into the indefinite future. It took me several days of questioning many of the people gathered for the Grass Island feast before the reason became clear.

Almost all zagaya on Vanatinai include at least one party of guests and contributors from the East Calvados Islands, or Saisai, and most Saisai feasts are attended by at least a few people from Vanatinai. Guests from the Misima language area—the West Calvados Islands, Panaeati, and Misima itself—are normally found at larger zagaya in Vanatinai and Saisai, and their hosts conversely will attend mortuary feasts, or hagali, at Misima and nearby islands. Travel between the Misima area and Vanatinai may be either by sailing canoe or by motor vessel. It is rarer to find people from Rossel Island (Yela or Rova) at zagaya on Vanatinai, although at two different zagaya in 1978–79 I met several who were attending because one of their kinspeople was married to someone from Vanatinai and living on that island.[9] A few Vanatinai and Saisai zagaya are attended by exchange partners from outside the Louisiade Archipelago, mainly Ware Islanders, who travel four to five days by sailing canoe to contribute their greenstone axe blades and Ware clay cooking pots. Their Saisai and Vanatinai exchange partners, male and female, are then invited to mortuary feasts, or *soi*, held on Ware, to which the Louisiade people bring pigs, bagi, betel nut, and bundles of sago.

Everyone who attends a zagaya at Vanatinai or Saisai is expected to contribute, even those who will eat the feast. Those who are unable to present pig or ceremonial valuables to the hosts will at least bring a basket full of garden produce or bundles of sago, and all except for the closest kin and spouse of the person who eats the feast will work hard at the innumerable tasks connected with feeding hundreds of people several times a day and organizing the zagaya ritual.

People in their late thirties and forties who wish to build their reputations as giagia are likely to be most heavily involved in exchange activities and to attend and contribute generously to the largest number of mortuary feasts each year. They are the ones I saw repeatedly at feasts held on many islands and all parts of Vanatinai. Established giagia in their fifties and sixties often hoard their pigs and their ceremonial valuables and attend only the zagaya hosted by close associates, to which they contribute handsomely.

The roles of women and men in the mortuary feast preparations and ceremonies have equal ritual weight and, in fact, it is essential for at least one woman to represent the affinal matrilineage in public acts of mourning and ritual respect for the dead. Through their ritual roles women are guardians of social continuity, life-givers both through childbirth and the social rebirth of mortuary rites.

Ritual Work

Mortuary ritual is a catharsis and a channel for the powerful, painful, and dangerous emotions of grief, despair, anger, and fear evoked by death and the ensuing suspicions of sorcery (cf. Schieffelin 1976, Rosaldo 1984). Vanatinai people speak of crying for the dead as a form of work by which the mourners help the kinfolk of the deceased, those whose grief is assumed (except when one is suspected of sorcery) because they have lost one of their own. Mourners should be compensated for this emotional work (cf. Hochschild 1983). Mourning affines who have observed rigorous taboos and contributed generously at feasts have honored the dead and should be liberated by the heirs of the deceased.

The Vanatinai mortuary feast sequence is a direct communication with the ancestor spirits. People told me the spirit of the deceased observes the ritual proceedings and the numbers of valuables presented to its heir at each feast, just as it sees and hears the activities of its descendants when it chooses. Islanders explain, "We make zagaya because we respect our dead." Mortuary feasts, they say, are "the memory" of the deceased. The dead must be properly honored by survivors' following of appropriate mourning taboos, the customary sequence of feasts, and the transfer of substantial quantities of ceremonial valuables and other goods. Otherwise the ancestors as a group will retaliate for the insult to one of their number by visiting all manner of misfortune upon the living of Vanatinai, their children. The valuables presented at the zagaya and at all preceding mortuary ritual occasions, including the burial, are exchanges between the living and the dead. If the sequence of feasts is properly performed all mourning taboos are cleared from people and places without fear of supernatural retribution, and the ancestor spirits will provide good gardens, good fishing, good health, success in exchange, and all other material benefits to those who have paid their respects to the dead. In particular the deceased whose memory is being honored will assist descendants in all aspects of their lives in return for the valuables presented at the feasts.

The first pig killed at a zagaya is said to go to Tamudurere, one of the two supernatural patron of sorcery, witchcraft, and warfare. He would become angry if not offered a pig and kill others besides the deceased. The death of this pig, a substitute for a human sacrifice, appeases Tamudurere, protecting the living by compensating him for his voracious desire to kill another human being. This belief parallels the idea that a large pig must be killed by the affinal lineage in place of a human sacrifice of their kinsperson, the widowed spouse, or a substitute victim.

Some of the pigs carried to a zagaya to be given to the owners of the feast are replaced by the hosts with other live pigs, and the exchange partners carry them home afterward. Others are killed and their meat distributed to feast guests. The owner of a pig, and those who have fed it, cannot eat it and will eat the meat from others' pigs. The prize pigs given at feasts have often been named and lovingly cared for by their owners, and it is not unusual at a jivia or zagaya to see the owner crying for the death of her or his pig, sacrificed to honor the deceased.

The exchanges of foodstuffs, pigs, and ceremonial valuables between human beings at zagaya and other mortuary feasts have material as well as religious consequences. The necessity of contributing to or organizing feasts stimulates people to clear more garden land, grow more yams and other produce, make more sago and raise more pigs than they would if it were not for the almost constant demands for a surplus of all of these goods beyond the level of mere subsistence generated by the mortuary feast sequence.

Zagaya are an outstanding opportunity for young people and divorced or widowed individuals to meet eligible potential marriage partners in an area of low population density where the number of unmarried people living nearby who are not either members of one's own or one's father's clan, and thus prohibited marriage partners, is very low. People often describe how they first met their spouses at a zagaya. New marriage ties in turn create a new set of affinal exchanges between those originally brought into contact by their ties to the deceased, the host, or other principals in the zagaya. New exchange relationships or further activity on existing exchange partnerships are also created by propinquity at a zagaya, as one person asks another for a pig or a greenstone axe blade for some future need.

Although giving in excess of what was previously received is more prestigious, because it demonstrates greater wealth and generosity, there is often an exchange of equivalent goods at feasts rather than a net gain by one party. The exchange in these cases is an end in itself (cf. Malinowski 1922, Mauss 1925). Relationships that are maintained partially through the exchange of yams for yams, pig for pig, or tobotobo for tobotobo have an obvious pragmatic value for the eventual redistribution of other, surplus goods and for potential ties in case of economic disaster. The people of Vanatinai tend to have a surplus of sago, betel, garden produce, and pig, while the Saisai people may have greater access to clay pots from Brooker, Panaeati, or Ware Islands, sailing canoes from Panaeati, and smoked fish or clam meat. Direct exchanges of these goods are often arranged between individuals. In the case of a drought or a cyclone the Saisai people, who are more vulnerable to both on their generally low, dry, and infertile islands, will appeal for help to their Vanatinai exchange partners. The latter give them food, secure in the knowledge that the indebted ones will repay them by later gifts as appropriate through their generally greater access to the valuables that circulate on the trade routes of the Massim.

Those who give valuables at mortuary feasts compensate the matrilineage and patrilateral relatives of the deceased, demonstrating that affinal lineages, in particular, have not benefited from the death, for they are publicly giving away a large proportion of their wealth in a gift called, like affinal exchanges during life, muli. Muli is "like a fight," although it is impolite and dangerous to refer openly to this, a competition between two affinal lineages to demonstrate publicly their greater wealth and generosity.[10]

After the spousal mourning taboos have been cleared by the completion of the zagaya, the widow(er) is free either to leave the hamlet of the deceased or to remain with use rights to garden land. Title to land may be given in exchange for substantial payments of ceremonial valuables, garden produce, sago, and pig, which usually continue for a number of years. Generous affinal contributions at zagaya may advance the cause of land purchase, but they do not result in alienation of land from the deceased's matrilineage. A large final separate payment explicitly for this purpose is occasionally made at some later time, but most widowed spouses return to their own matrilineage hamlets and garden lands.

During both the jivia and the mwagumwagu, the climactic ritual of the zagaya, the three lineages most closely linked to the deceased, her or his own, that of the spouse, and that of the deceased's father, ritually feed one another special foods that stand for the corpse, feigning taking it from their own mouths to do so. They feed the fruit of the dead to one another throughout the mortuary ritual sequence in the form of cooked foods, seed yams, pigs, ceremonial valuables, and the persons of the principal mourners.[11]

Since most deaths on Vanatinai are attributed to sorcery and witchcraft, a death strains existing social relationships by more than just the removal of the deceased from the social field. The fact that spouses and other affines bear the brunt of mourning taboos that must be cleared by substantial presentations of valuables mirrors suspicions of affinal complicity in a death. The public ritual payment of valuables by affines and others recompenses the kin of the deceased and forces virtually all members of the social network of the deceased to continue peaceable relationships with one another until the final mortuary feast. Exchange relationships too are the fruit of the dead eaten by the living through mortuary ritual.

The institution of zagaya means that social relationships not only endure beyond the lifetime of an individual but are intensified at a death, as ritual exchange obligations must be fulfilled. Exchange relationships themselves are a form of capital used by Vanatinai area big men and big women. They generate further material and symbolic capital: valuables, wealth, prestige, and fame. The zagaya is the primary staging area at which this occurs, in front of an absorbed and attentive audience. The principals publicly demonstrate the ability to marshal large numbers of people and their labor as well as sizable quantities of garden produce, sago, pigs, household goods, and ceremonial valuables. They flaunt their wealth and generosity by giving away all of these goods, earning the title of giagia. The zagaya is a proving ground for individual reputations. Successful zagaya tanuwagaji are respected, listened to, and sometimes feared for their obvious practical and thus their supernatural knowledge, clearly signified by a good zagaya.

There is a paradox, then, in the idea that giving away valuables is a sacrifice and a form of compensation to the kin of the deceased. In practice by giving away valuables you become known as a wealthy and important person. The hoarder of valuables is criticized, and the ostentatiously generous person is admired. The deliberate display and public, aggressive presentation of wealth to others enriches by putting others in your debt.

Gender and Mortuary Ritual

The two instances on Vanatinai when women have exclusive ritual roles are ceremonial performances of fertility and maternity: woman as mother of firstborn and woman as mother of the matrilineage.[12] The occasions are the birth of a firstborn child, described in chapter 3, and the death of a spouse or affine. In birth and in death the Vanatinai philosophy of gender that woman is life-giver is ritually performed and culturally elaborated. The new mother and the principal female mourner both symbolize the strength of matrilineal fertility and continuity in the face of death, whose power they engage and overcome through ritual practice.

Birth and death are key transition points when matrilineal fertility and continuity are threatened. The islanders know that firstborn infants have a higher mortality rate than others. The new mother goes into a ritual seclusion analogous to that of a widowed spouse, sacrificing her freedom and mobility temporarily to protect her child from harm. Not only sorcerers of unknown identity but her husband's matrilineal kin may be jealous. She has given birth to a child whom their kinsman will help to grow but who does not belong to them. Her matrilineal kin compensate her husband's kin with valuables. This childwealth is part of the ongoing exchange between affines initiated by bridewealth. The wife is then socially reborn in her new status as mother and returns to normal life. The mother acts for the social good: the survival of the infant represents the future of the matrilineage.

At the death of a spouse or a person related by marriage a woman of the affinal matrilineage must represent her kin group and their mourning by undergoing a form of temporary social death. Like the new mother of a firstborn, she remains in the house, leaving only to eliminate and then covering her head and shoulders with a coconut-leaf skirt. She wears the ankle-length mourning skirt and blackens her body with charcoal. She is not allowed to touch her hands to her lips and must be fed by the kin of the deceased until the first mortuary feast is made, when she is released from this strict seclusion. When a husband dies his wife is the principal mourner who represents the affinal matrilineage. When a wife dies her husband undergoes this same form and period of mourning, but he is joined in mourning by one of his kinswomen.

Undertaking this mourning is widely regarded as an honor and a means of accruing prestige for one's matrilineage. The female (and male) mourners and their exchange partners accumulate ceremonial valuables, pigs, and foodstuffs to present to the kin of the deceased and to the person who represents the matrilineage of the deceased's father, clearing their mourning taboos at the final mortuary feast. In the process they build their own reputation and that of their matrilineage for moral probity, for wealth and connections, and for generosity.

The principal female mourner suffers a symbolic death and falls under the power of the deceased's kin. Vanatinai custom places suspicion on spouses and affines of having caused a death or being relieved at it. Affinal relations are marked overtly by respect and covertly by tension and competition. The mourning spouse and/or principal female mourner are hostages of the deceased's kin during the liminal period until the final feast in exchange for the loss of a lineage member.

At this final feast the kinswomen of the deceased, or the father's kinswomen, present the female affinal mourners with new coconut-leaf skirts. The mourning women give new skirts to the kin of the deceased or his or her father. The skirts celebrate renewed female and matrilineal fertility. The potential renewal of affinal exchanges of men between matrilineages, possible after the lifting of mortuary taboos on courtship and marriage for affinal mourners, means the potential paternal gift of new children to a matrilineage, which cannot grow by itself. The ritual exchange of skirts is a metaphor of the continuity of life in the face of death and sorcery.

Vanatinai people say "there must be a woman to sit down" at the key ritual of the final feast, the mwagumwagu, when ceremonial valuables are publicly transferred to the heirs of the deceased. Those who "sit down" at the mwagumwagu are also ceremonially handed over to the heirs, who will lead them to the water to be bathed, dressed, and liberated from all mourning taboos. The widow and widower and the other affinal mourners, including the host of the memorial feast, or his or her representatives, are those who have the duty and the honor of observing all mourning restrictions for several years. They work hard to mobilize a generous contribution to the feast and then "sit down" at the mwagumwagu, placing themselves and all accompanying valuables in the hands of the heirs of the deceased. They could, in theory, be killed, or they could be freed if they have sufficiently honored the dead and compensated the living. They stand for their entire matrilineage and its economic contributions to the feast by sitting down in the mwagumwagu. While the mourning taboos and obligations may be onerous, following them diligently and making a substantial contribution of pigs, vegetable food, sago, and ceremonial valuables throughout the feast sequence are primary means of increasing personal prestige and the prestige of the matrilineage. The hosts and contributors to feasts are regarded as working to liberate their kin or exchange partners from mourning restrictions.

At least one woman will have to follow all mourning taboos for a period of years on behalf of her entire matrilineage to show its respect for the deceased. While an outsider might regard the stringent mourning restrictions for this woman as evidence of lower female status, the people of Vanatinai believe that only a woman can stand for her kin group in this crucial ritual process. She will bring honor to them by demonstrating publicly that her matrilineage and their exchange partners have shown proper respect for the dead and have contributed generously of their labor and their possessions.

Bridewealth does not lead to a permanent asymmetry between affinal lineages, something that in turn might lead to a power imbalance in the status of husband and wife (cf. Divale and Harris 1976:523–524). The lineage of the wife and of the husband, and each spouse as an individual, has the right to make equivalent demands on the labor, yams, pigs, and ceremonial valuables of the affines as needed throughout the lifetime of the marriage partners. When one of them dies, these affinal ties of exchange are intensified and ritualized in the mortuary feasts from burial to zagaya. After both have died and their mortuary ritual sequences are completed, neither the husband's lineage nor the wife's should have gained or given more than the other. Although in practice affinal lineages may compete to give more than the other, this is not tied to whether their kinsperson was the deceased wife or the husband.

Vanatinai people do not perceive marriage as the giving of a woman to another lineage (contra Lévi-Strauss 1969a). A lineage gives one of its men in marriage to sire children for another matrilineage, although he still belongs to his own kin. In exchange for his children, his labor, and the valuables he gives to his wife, children, and affines, his lineage expects compensation. When he dies, his wife's lineage, including the man's children, lavishly compensate the man's lineage and his tau, his own father's matrilineal heir, for their father's nurturance and his years of generosity to his affines, his wife, and, especially, his children. A man's giving to the wife's lineage began with bridewealth. For his patrilateral relations it began a generation earlier with the bridewealth the deceased's father gave to the mother's (the deceased's) lineage. By the end of the mortuary ritual sequence the deceased's wife's lineage has given more than it received. Of course, all the roles are reversed when a wife dies. Her husband's lineage then lavishly compensates her kin and her tau. Muli, affinal gifts, are both groomwealth and bridewealth. On Vanatinai and throughout the Louisiade Archipelago the father's matrilineage eats the fruit of the dead as a compensation, a replacement, for the father, whose issue, labor, and valuables enlarged and enriched the matrilineage of the deceased and his mother.[13]

Women as well as men host zagaya, the final and largest memorial feast, in honor of their fathers or of deceased affines. Frequently a sibling set will jointly host a feast. The majority of zagaya are referred to as being hosted by men, but there are a few women who are famous for the lavish mortuary feasts they have organized in honor of deceased fathers or affines. Female giagia prominent in ceremonial exchange are generally women whose children are already grown. Some are widows in their fifties, like Ijau, the woman with the famous pig, still vigorous and active but with the accumulated wisdom and relationships of a mature person. Late middle age is a prime period of life for male giagia as well.

Ghayawa, the woman I met traveling with her husband in search of valuables for the mortuary feast of her father, is well known in the communities of Vanatinai and Saisai as a big woman. Only in her late thirties at the time of my first fieldwork, her small children had died some years earlier, and she had adopted the young son of her divorced sister, by then a youth of about sixteen. At the zagaya described earlier, Ghayawa had given a fine shell-disc necklace and three long greenstone axe blades to her exchange partner, one of the owners of the feast. Now she expected him to support her with valuables at her father's feast.

Ghayawa cohosted the feast with her much older brother, a quiet and well-liked man not particularly active in exchange, but people referred to her as the owner of the feast. The feast attracted guests from all around Vanatinai, most of the East Calvados islands, and from Panaeati, a region encompassing about 150 miles. Her reputation, and that of her matrilineage, was increased by her large and well-managed ritual presentations and by her generous feeding of pork, yams, and sago to the guests. She and the others in her hamlet killed four of their own pigs. A lineage brother of her husband contributed one more, her tau (her father's sister's son) and an unrelated exchange partner another each, and some of her affines brought four more as muli, carrying them from their sailing canoes into the hamlet in a procession led by a youth blowing a conch shell, along with baskets of yams and poles hung with bundles of sago starch.

Ghayawa staged four separate mwagumwagu. In three of them her husband, as closest mourning affine of her widowed father, sat down along with his aged female kinswoman, the principal female mourner, to be draped in valuables. Ghayawa, her kinfolk, her affines, and her exchange partners presented three different heirs of her deceased father with a total of three shell-disc necklaces, forty-nine greenstone axe blades, five shell currency pieces, two wooden ceremonial lime spatulas, two tortoiseshell ceremonial lime spatulas, and eighteen kina in paper money, in addition to skirts, mats, pots, and other customary wealth. The largest share went to a daughter of her father's sister, his tau and principal eater of the fruit of the dead. Other shares went to a father's sister's son and to a father's clan brother. In the fourth mwagumwagu Ghayawa herself sat down, wearing a calf-length mourning skirt, her head and body covered, to be draped in valuables, including another shell-disc necklace, three greenstone axe blades, and one shell currency piece. This was to clear the mourning she was honoring for a kinsman of her husband, and the eater of this part of the feast was one of the dead man's lineage "brothers." He gave her a tortoiseshell ceremonial lime spatula back in exchange "to cut her mourning skirt." A few days after the feast for her father was over, Ghayawa led a party from her hamlet to another mortuary feast at which she was a major contributor of valuables.

Even when men are the owners of the feast they must have the active participation and counsel of their wives, sisters, mothers, and other female associates. Women control the yam supply, in ideology and usually in practice. Certain women are recognized as food magicians. They are asked by the owners of feasts to use their organizational skills and magical knowledge to ensure that the owners gain fame for generosity instead of the shame of publicly running out of food and they must be compensated with ceremonial valuables.

Women create much of the wealth essential for mortuary ritual exchange, and they and their male associates exchange this wealth to women and men in other ritual roles. The wealth for which women are responsible includes yams and other garden produce, generated largely by women's labor and under women's supervision; it also includes decorated coconut-leaf skirts, intricately woven, dyed coconut-leaf baskets, garden baskets, pandanus-leaf sleeping mats, and the clay pots made and exchanged by the women of Brooker Island. All of these objects have roles in the ritual events, and they must be produced in large quantities. Forms of wealth used in mortuary ritual generated by male labor but contributed by both sexes include sago starch (primarily produced by men), long carved sago-stirring paddles, wooden combs, fern-fiber armlets into which valuables and magical herbs will be tucked, the small coconut-leaf pouches that hold daveri, and carved wooden handles used ceremonially to hold greenstone axe blades. Both women and men raise and, as individuals, contribute pigs.

In many of the island cultures of the Massim farther to the north and west, women's exchanges in mortuary ritual of either yams or skirts, objects they have generated by their own labor, are much more highly elaborated than on Vanatinai.[14] On Vanatinai, as in these other island cultures, there must be a plenitude of highest quality yams and other garden produce to feed guests and to give a basketful to each departing guest. Yams are essential to holding a feast, but they are not the focus of the ritual. In the mwagumwagu, instead of an elaborate pyramid of seed yams, there is one yam, not perfect, but often old and moldy. If possible, it comes from the garden of the deceased. It too is presented to those who eat the feast.

Annette Weiner (1976) has documented the enormous Trobriand Island mortuary exchanges of banana-leaf skirts and bundles, objects of value made by and exchanged among women in honor of the deceased. As with yams, the element of skirt exchanges among women is present in the Vanatinai zagaya, and it is in fact ritually essential. But it is far less highly elaborated than in the Trobriands. Vanatinai widows and female affinal mourners make beautiful coconut-leaf skirts, suitable for dancing, prior to the zagaya. The mourners, female and male, drape one of these fine new skirts over their shoulders as cloaks during the ritual. These body coverings that signify mourning are given, along with ceremonial valuables and the persons of the mourners, to those who eat the feast. They become transformed into dancing skirts worn by women (and by men as they dance) that proclaim matrilineage fertility.

In the Misima-Panaeati area yams are women's wealth, as are skirts in the Trobriand Islands. On Vanatinai, where women participate in the same domains of exchange as men, accumulating and giving away shell-disc necklaces and greenstone axe blades as well as skirts and yams, there is no such clear-cut distinction between male and female valuables and forms of exchange.

Vanatinai women eat the fruit of the dead as patrilateral heirs, or tau, about half the time. This role involves a widening network of exchange ties. When a person, female or male, eats a feast, she or he must bring valuables, foodstuffs, and other goods for those who will be giving, the kin and affines of the deceased. After publicly receiving a large quantity of valuables during the ritual, the person who eats the feast can expect immediate requests for specific ones. Often a tau leaves a feast having already given away all the valuables she or he has received, either to feast guests or to creditors who have come for that purpose. The eater of the feast is then poorer in wealth but richer in reputation for generosity, and she or he has placed many people into a relationship of indebtedness to be activated as needed in future.

All adult women and men are obliged to contribute ceremonial valuables as well as pigs, sago, and garden produce to feasts in honor of their kin, affines, and neighbors. They go on exchange journeys in quest of these valuables, traveling the length of Vanatinai and sometimes visiting other islands by sailing canoe. They act as individuals, seeking contributions on the basis of the closeness of their relationship to the deceased or to the host of the future memorial feast, and they have their own personal set of exchange partners. Certain women surpass the exchange activity and the volume of contributions to feasts of most men. And, by exceeding the minimum demanded by custom of every adult, women as well as men build reputations as giagia, people with the knowledge, persuasiveness, and generosity to accumulate valuables and give them away.

Mortuary ritual on Vanatinai, especially the final feast, the zagaya, is a stage for the enactment of a moral philosophy: honoring the ancestors, following taubwaragha—the way of the ancestors—and giving to others. It is also a public stage for the performance of personal and gender identity. Mourning women, representing their matrilineage as life-givers, undergo a symbolic death and rebirth to counteract the power of death, embodying the nurture and fertility of the fruit of the corpse. Death, associated with maleness—male sorcerers, warriors, and supernaturals—is transformed into life by the ritual work of the principal female mourner.

Ceremonial exchange on Vanatinai reveals relations of power among gendered persons (cf. Strathern 1988). But these relations do not separate men from women or provide a ritual articulation of male superiority. The durable wealth of shell-disc necklaces and greenstone axe blades, individually named and spreading the names of previous owners through space and across time in a regional system of ritualized exchange (cf. Munn 1986), is not exclusively male wealth on Vanatinai.

The giagia are dually gendered. They are androgynous in that, male and female, they are potent through their possession of wealth and their magical knowledge of increase and destruction, and fertile and maternal through their growing and feeding of wealth objects and persons, the fruit of the corpse, to patrilateral heirs or kin of the deceased. The corpse too becomes androgynous at death, reverting to being a child—a life stage not yet fully gendered—of its matrilineal fathers, male and female. The widowed spouse too is desexualized through mourning taboos and enforced celibacy, symbolically identified with the deceased (cf. Hertz 1907). The corpse evokes maleness through its representation of sorcery and of death itself and femaleness through its representation of the matrilineage that gave birth to it and by bearing fruit.

Ritualized exchange on Vanatinai embodies the shifting dynamics of power relations among individuals and among lineages. It reflects ideological contradictions: exchanges should be reciprocal and, eventually, over a lifetime and beyond, equal. Yet exchange is a medium for building power and renown, through publicly giving away more than others, for the person and, in mortuary ritual, for the matrilineage as well. Exchange and mortuary ritual play out intertwined themes of gender and power but not the enactment of male superiority or the unambiguous separation of male persons or qualities from female. Instead they ritually mirror ideals of gender equivalence and the interdependence both of male and female persons and of matrilineages. Maintaining these balances depends on individual desires, labors, and willingness to accumulate and give away wealth at the same rate as others. Exchange therefore also mirrors the competition for influence and fame that is inevitable precisely because there is no formal hierarchy of authority and privilege, either of some men over others or of men over women.

The moral qualities of the good woman and the good man overlap on Vanatinai. Each should be strong, wise, and generous. These qualities are most dramatically enacted in the staging of a successful zagaya. A person who is strong can mobilize enough labor, foods, and valuables to hold a feast. This cannot be done without the wisdom to manage resources and people well, for which the knowledge of how to appeal to ancestral and supernatural power is essential. And the epitome of the generous person is the gia, who gives away more than she or he receives to honor the ancestors and compensate the living. The performances of the owners of the feast, those who eat the feast, the mourners, and their exchange partners, are carefully scrutinized, judged, and reported throughout the archipelago and beyond when feast participants sail home. The renown or shame of women and men who have participated in mortuary rituals or failed to do so will spread to distant islands, attached to words and to objects of value from the feasts.

Chapter Eight

Gender and Power

Vanatinai customs are generally egalitarian in both philosophy and practice. Women and men have equivalent rights to and control of the means of production, the products of their own labor, and the products of others. Both sexes have access to the symbolic capital of prestige, most visibly through participation in ceremonial exchange and mortuary ritual. Ideologies of male superiority or right of authority over women are notably absent, and ideologies of gender equivalence are clearly articulated. Multiple levels of gender ideologies are largely, but not entirely, congruent. Ideologies in turn are largely congruent with practice and individual actions in expressing gender equivalence, complementarity, and overlap.

There are nevertheless significant differences in social influence and prestige among persons. These are mutable, and they fluctuate over the lifetime of the individual. But Vanatinai social relations are egalitarian overall, and sexually egalitarian in particular, in that at each stage in the life cycle all persons, female and male, have equivalent autonomy and control over their own actions, opportunity to achieve both publicly and privately acknowledged influence and power over the actions of others, and access to valued goods, wealth, and prestige. The quality of generosity, highly valued in both sexes, is explicitly modeled after parental nurture. Women are not viewed as polluting or dangerous to themselves or others in their persons, bodily fluids, or sexuality.

Vanatinai sociality is organized around the principle of personal autonomy. There are no chiefs, and nobody has the right to tell

281

another adult what to do. This philosophy also results in some extremely permissive childrearing and a strong degree of tolerance for the idiosyncrasies of other people's behavior. While working together, sharing, and generosity are admirable, they are strictly voluntary. The selfish and antisocial person might be ostracized, and others will not give to him or her. If kinfolk, in-laws, or neighbors disagree, even with a powerful and influential big man or big woman, they have the option, frequently taken, of moving to another hamlet where they have ties and can expect access to land for gardening and foraging. Land is communally held by matrilineages, but each person has multiple rights to request and be given space to make a garden on land held by others, such as the mother's father's matrilineage. Respect and tolerance for the will and idiosyncrasies of individuals is reinforced by fear of their potential knowledge of witchcraft or sorcery.

Anthropological discussions of women, men, and society over the last one hundred years have been framed largely in terms of "the status of women," presumably unvarying and shared by all women in all social situations. Male dominance and female subordination have thus until recently been perceived as easily identified and often as human universals. If women are indeed universally subordinate, this implies a universal primary cause: hence the search for a single underlying reason for male dominance and female subordination, either material or ideological.

More recent writings in feminist anthropology have stressed multiple and contested gender statuses and ideologies and the impacts of historical forces, variable and changing social contexts, and conflicting gender ideologies. Ambiguity and contradiction, both within and between levels of ideology and social practice, give both women and men room to assert their value and exercise power. Unlike in many cultures where men stress women's innate inferiority, gender relations on Vanatinai are not contested, or antagonistic: there are no male versus female ideologies which vary markedly or directly contradict each other. Vanatinai mythological motifs, beliefs about supernatural power, cultural ideals of the sexual division of labor and of the qualities inherent to men and women, and the customary freedoms and restrictions upon each sex at different points in the life course all provide ideological underpinnings of sexual equality.

Since the 1970s writings on the anthropology of women, in evaluating degrees of female power and influence, have frequently focused on the disparity between the "ideal" sex role pattern of a culture, often based on an ideology of male dominance, publicly proclaimed or enacted by men, and often by women as well, and the "real" one, manifested by the actual behavior of individuals. This approach seeks to uncover female social participation, overt or covert, official or unofficial, in key events and decisions and to learn how women negotiate their social positions. The focus on social and individual "action" or "practice" is prominent more generally in cultural anthropological theory of recent years. Feminist analyses of contradictions between gender ideologies of female inferiority and the realities of women's and men's daily lives—the actual balance of power in household and community—have helped to make this focus on the actual behavior of individuals a wider theoretical concern.[1]

In the Vanatinai case gender ideologies in their multiple levels and contexts emphasize the value of women and provide a mythological charter for the degree of personal autonomy and freedom of choice manifested in real women's lives. Gender ideologies are remarkably similar (though not completely, as I discuss below) as they are manifested situationally, in philosophical statements by women and men, in the ideal pattern of the sexual division of labor, in taboos and proscriptions, myth, cosmology, magic, ritual, the supernatural balance of power, and in the codifications of custom. Women are not characterized as weak or inferior. Women and men are valorized for the same qualities of strength, wisdom, and generosity. If possessed of these qualities an individual woman or man will act in ways which bring prestige not only to the actor but to the kin and residence groups to which she or he belongs.

Nevertheless, there is no single relationship between the sexes on Vanatinai. Power relations and relative influence vary with the individuals, sets of roles, situations, and historical moments involved. Gender ideologies embodied in myths, beliefs, prescriptions for role-appropriate behavior, and personal statements sometimes contradict each other or are contradicted by the behavior of individuals.

As Ortner (1984) points out, a great deal of recent social science theory emphasizes "the centrality of domination" and the analysis of "asymmetrical social relations," in which one group has more power than the other, as the key to understanding a social system. A focus upon asymmetry and domination also tends to presuppose its universality as a totalizing system of belief and practice and thus to distort analyses of gender roles and ideologies in places with egalitarian relations.

Gender Ideologies

In some societies of the New Guinea Highlands and Highlands fringe where gender opposition is marked, gender constructions are conceptualized as changeable or transitional, dependent in part upon human actions, such as participating in rituals of initiation or adhering to gender-based food taboos.[2] On Vanatinai gender is ascribed at birth and remains immutable. Each sex follows its own developmental path and its prescribed part in begetting and giving birth to new people. The life cycle is not punctuated by critical periods such as puberty, marriage, or menopause when ritual action may be taken to change or validate male or female status. Passage through the life cycle from one age-sex category to the next is a gradual process across blurred boundaries.

Vanatinai also differs from cultural systems of New Guinea and elsewhere with marked gender opposition in not sharing their tendency to project a dualistic symbolism upon the environment. When the domains and activities of males and females show considerable overlap, there is less cultural logic in categorizing the world into objects and actions with male versus female qualities. Although some aspects of the social and natural world are so categorized on Vanatinai, such dualistic symbolism is much less pervasive than in many other Melanesian groups.[3]

The different levels of gender ideology on Vanatinai match real sex role patterns and the power, prestige, and autonomy enacted in the daily lives of individuals. I believe this is significant. I have suggested that sexually egalitarian societies show a greater degree of congruence among gender ideologies as they are manifested in the words and behavior of men and women in practice.

Societies with an explicit or visible ideology of male dominance are far more likely to exhibit contradictions. These may be among situational gender ideologies, public statements versus private behavior,

male and female versions of gender ideologies, and ideology in contrast to practice. The ritual expressions of male dominance versus the
more complementary and egalitarian relations between husbands and
wives in daily life documented by Donald Tuzin (1980) and Anna
Meigs (1990) for two New Guinea societies, the Ilahita Arapesh and
the Hua, respectively, are good examples. So is the contradiction
Susan Carol Rogers (1975) found between public expressions of male
dominance and male control of positions of formal authority in rural
France versus the actual decision-making power of women and their
control over the activities of men. This was extreme enough to lead
her to speak of "the myth of male dominance." Feminist scholars
from Europe and America writing in the last few years about contradictions between gender ideology and practice and between levels of
ideology have surely been influenced by their own lives in their own
countries, where ideologies of gender and racial equality reflected in
some laws and pronouncements are contradicted by other laws, customs, and widely held beliefs, and where the events of daily life regularly contradict any ideals of the equality of women, minorities, and
the poor.

One of the most significant contradictions that is found in Vanatinai gender ideologies is between the often stated ideal of woman as
life-giver and the belief that women kill through witchcraft and,
more rarely and in male dress, as sorcerers. Images of woman as
mother can be multivalent and oppositional, charged with emotions
of love and horror. The witch subverts the ideal of the nurturing and
life-giving mother and matrilineage. She kills and eats her victims,
who are prototypically her own children or the offspring of her
matrilineage. The witch commits the ultimate antisocial act in
devouring them rather than feeding them (cf. Munn 1986). Interestingly, she sometimes exchanges victims with other witches at supernatural cannibal feasts, deferring consumption in the expectation of
delayed return and giving away her dead as the ultimate possessions
and tokens of wealth to be consumed by others. In Vanatinai custom
witchcraft comes from somewhere else, the islands to the northwest,
and it is the women of other places who are more likely to attack their
own kinfolk. But this belief coexists with the attribution of witchcraft powers to many Vanatinai women, both prominent and weak,
elders and unmarried young.

Both sorcery and witchcraft are projections of the person, intrusions onto the autonomy of others. The witch can leave the boundaries of her body behind and fly great distances to attack, invading the victim's body and eating the entrails. The sorcerer cloaks his body with invisibility magic, or transforms himself into a snake, and uses traveling magic to transport himself almost instantly to another part of the island. He fires projectiles into the bodies of others or invades a victim's body with poison. Both kill for the joy of feeling their own power. Theirs is the ultimate personal autonomy played out in the imposition of individual will upon another. Nancy Munn (1986:233) writes that "Gawans experience the individualistic egalitarianism of their society, *as* domination, in the shape of the witch." On Vanatinai as well the emphasis on personal autonomy and the strength of individual will, in a society with no indigenous formal authority, is played out as the coercion of individual sorcerer or witch. Despite statements that women give life and men death, both male and female, father and mother are simultaneously symbols of nurture and of destruction.

The role of life-giver is further at odds with descriptions of women as hunters of small animals and with women's participation in earlier generations in war magic, the field of battle, and decisions to make war as well as to make peace or give compensation. This is epitomized in the ultimate signal to start a battle: a woman untying and throwing her outer skirt on the ground between male antagonists. Nevertheless, in prevailing gender ideologies, men are, and were, far more closely associated with death and violence, through warfare, hunting, and sorcery, epitomized by the phallic male symbols of the hurled spear of the warrior and hunter and the magical projectile of the sorcerer.

Men's power as killers and destroyers gives them an advantage in ceremonial exchange and mortuary ritual. They can directly or implicitly threaten recalcitrant partners or successful rivals with sorcery and death. More men than women are feared for their knowledge of destructive magic. When Vanatinai people follow what they state is their own custom of having the father's sister's child of the deceased eat the feast and inherit wealth, this individual is female about half the time. In the cases I observed where someone from the deceased's matrilineage ate the feast, that person was always a man, and one known as a powerful sorcerer who claimed that the deceased owed him valuables.

More men than women are widely known for their wealth of ceremonial valuables and their involvement in exchange and mortuary ritual. Still, Vanatinai is an equal opportunity society where this avenue to prestige and renown is open to both sexes. A few women are well known throughout the archipelago for their exceptional wealth, generosity, and participation in ritualized exchanges. All adult women as well as men are expected to participate in exchange to a certain minimum, particularly when a father, spouse, or close affine dies. Besides the opportunity to be the owner or the eater of a feast, women have an essential ritual role as life-givers, the role of principal female mourner who represents her matrilineage in the ritual work of compensating death to ensure the continuity of life.

Women have a complementary power base as life-givers in other spheres that counterbalances the asymmetry of men's tendency to be more heavily involved in exchange, an advantage that results in part from male powers to bring death. The most exclusive is of course the fact that women give birth to children. These children enrich and enlarge the kin group of the mother and her mothers, sisters, and brothers, ensuring the continuity and the life of the matrilineage itself. Her role of nurturer is highly valued, and the idiom of nurturing or feeding is applied as well to fathers, maternal uncles, and those who give ceremonial valuables to others. In ideological pronouncements she is called, by men and women alike, the owner of the garden, even though garden land is communally held by the matrilineage, and individual plots are usually worked with husbands or unmarried brothers. She is, in verbalized ideology of custom, the giver of yams, the ghanika moli, or true food, with which all human beings are nurtured, whether she grew them or her husband or brother. She is likely to raise pigs, which she exchanges or sacrifices at feasts. She is prominent in the life-giving work of healing, a form of countersorcery. And life-giving, Vanatinai people say, is more highly valued than the life-taking associated with male warfare and sorcery.

Vanatinai people continue to enact a moral philosophy of honoring ancestor spirits. Their ritual work is personal and gender identity performed, counterbalancing the power of death by nurturing the living through ritual eating of the fruit of the dead, the valuables and persons that stand for the corpse. It is a ritual form for both sexes of the life-giving role most highly valued and philosophically linked to women.

An overview of the life courses of males and females on Vanatinai and the ideologies of gender associated with them reveals two more potential sources of contradiction to prevailing ideologies of gender equivalence. One seems clear to an outside observer: men may have more than one wife, if they are strong enough to fulfill multiple affinal obligations and if the co-wives consent to enter into or remain in the marriage. Women may not have two husbands. Even though polygyny is rare, and women need not, and do not necessarily, agree to it, it is a customary and continuing form of marriage and an indication of gender asymmetries. A big man may distribute his procreative power and the strength of his affinal labor and personal wealth to two or more spouses and matrilineages, enlarging his influence and his reputation as a *gia*. Women may not.

Ideologies of gender associated with menstruation are more ambiguous. One myth, recounted rarely and in private as a humorous story, tells how a male spirit being has intercourse with a married woman. They are discovered by the outraged husband, who attacks their conjoined genitals. The male's severed genitals become the giant clam (*Tridacna*), which they are said to resemble, and the woman begins to bleed from her vagina in the first menstruation. This myth, with its motif of mutilation of the genitals of both lovers as punishment for their illicit sex, implies a negative association of menstruation with castration, male and female (cf. Stephens 1967). But it is recounted in tones of amusement rather than awe.

Vanatinai menstrual taboos, such as those prohibiting the menstruating woman from visiting or working in a garden and, especially, from participating in the communal planting of yams, are multivalent cultural markers of female power. The symbolic complexity and multiple meanings of such taboos have been emphasized in recent writings on the anthropology of menstruation (cf. Buckley and Gottlieb 1988, Gottlieb 1988). Earlier anthropological constructions have emphasized the relation of menstrual taboos to ideologies of female pollution and thus, directly, of female inferiority or gender asymmetry. In the Vanatinai case there is no ideology of contamination through physical contact with the menstruating woman, who continues to forage, prepare food, and have sexual intercourse. Both men and women who have had intercourse in the last few days are barred from the new yam planting, and the genital fluids of both sexes are inimical, at this earliest and most crucial stage, to the growth of yams. (Later on, marital intercourse in the garden will help the yams to flourish.) Vanatinai menstrual taboos, which bar women from what islanders see as the most tedious form of subsistence labor, weeding gardens, are not regarded by women as a burden or curse but as a welcome interlude of relative leisure. Their predominant cultural meaning may be the ritual separation of the sacred power of female, and human, fertility and regeneration of life from that of plants, especially yams, whose parallels to humans are indicated by anthropomorphizing them in ritual spells. Menstrual taboos further mark woman as the giver of life to human beings.

The Sexual Division of Labor

Vanatinai custom is characterized by a marked degree of overlap in the sexual division of labor between what men normally do and what women do. This kind of overlap has been suggested as a primary material basis of gender equality, with the mingling of the sexes in the tasks of daily life working against the rise of male dominance.

Still, sorcerers are almost all male. Witches have less social power on Vanatinai and are blamed for only a small fraction of deaths and misfortunes. Only men build houses or canoes or chop down large trees for construction or clearing garden lands. Women are forbidden by custom to hunt, fish, or make war with spears, although they may hunt for possum and monitor lizard by climbing trees or setting traps and catching them and use a variety of other fishing methods. Despite the suppression of warfare men retain greater control of the powers that come with violence or the coercive threat of violent death.

Some Vanatinai women perceive an inequity in the performance of domestic chores. Almost all adult women are "working wives," who come home tired in the evening, often carrying both a young child in their arms and a heavy basket of yams or other produce on their heads for distances of up to three miles. They sometimes complain to their husbands or to each other that, "We come home after working in the garden all day, and we still have to fetch water, look for firewood, do the cooking and cleaning up and look after the children while all men do is sit on the verandah and chew betel nut!" The men usually retort that these are the work of women. Here is an example of contested gender roles.[4]

Men are tender and loving to their children and often carry them around or take them along on their activities, but they do this only when they feel like it, and childcare is the primary responsibility of a mother, who must delegate it to an older sibling or a kinswoman if she cannot take care of the child herself. Women are also supposed to sweep the house and the hamlet ground every morning and to pick up pig excrement with a sago-bark "shovel" and a coconut-rib broom.

When speaking of their many responsibilities, women say, "Vanatinai women have to be very strong." Rosaldo (1974) sees participation of men in domestic activities such childrearing and cleaning as a sign of high female status, as does Bacdayan (1977), an argument reminiscent of Western feminists' analyses of the politics of housework. Vanatinai men are less involved in these activities than are the Ilongot and Western Bontoc men of the Philippines whom Rosaldo and Bacdayan describe. While the roles of Vanatinai men and women overlap, they do not overlap completely.

Vanatinai is not a perfectly egalitarian society, either in terms of a lack of difference in the status and power of individuals or in the relations between men and women. Women in young and middle adulthood are likely to spend more time on childcare and supervision of gardens and less on building reputations as prominent transactors of ceremonial valuables. The average woman spends more of her time sweeping up the pig excrement that dots the hamlet from the unfenced domestic pigs wandering through it. The average man spends more time hunting wild boar in the rain forest with his spear (although some men do not like to hunt). His hunting is more highly valued and accorded more prestige by both sexes than her daily maintenance of hamlet cleanliness and household order. The sexual division of labor on Vanatinai is slightly asymmetrical, despite the tremendous overlap in the roles of men and women and the freedom that an individual of either sex has to spend more time on particular activities—gardening, foraging, fishing, caring for children, traveling in quest of ceremonial valuables—and to minimize others.

Yet the average Vanatinai woman owns many of the pigs she cleans up after, and she presents them publicly during mortuary rituals and exchanges them with other men and women for shell-disc necklaces, long axe blades of polished greenstone, and other valuables. She then gains status, prestige, and influence over the affairs of others, just as men do and as any adult does who chooses to make the effort to raise pigs, grow large yam gardens, and acquire and distribute ceremonial valuables. Women who achieve prominence and distribute wealth, and thus gain an enhanced ability to mobilize the labor of others, are highly respected by both sexes. An overview of the life course and the sexual division of labor on Vanatinai reveals a striking lack of cultural restrictions upon the autonomy of women as well as men and the openness of island society to a wide variety of lifestyles.

Gender and History

Since the arrival of the ancestors the permeable boundaries of the motherland's beaches have been swept by regional and global flows of persons, objects, and ideas over time and through space. These are the conditions in which Vanatinai gender relations as we see them today have been formed and transformed. We cannot consider them as part of a discretely bounded and wholly coherent social universe. They are localized and temporally specific artifacts that are components of ethnoscapes, ever changing landscapes of persons and beliefs, charged with the changing valences of complicated power relations (cf. Appadurai 1990, 1991). Vanatinai people explicitly recognize a basic unity of custom and language among the fruit of the motherland. At the same time they point to variations of belief and speech from one district on the island to another, explain that exchange partners from other islands regularly participate in the rituals that are the core of the way of the ancestors, and analyze the changes that have taken place, both before and after the coming of the Europeans, in their most crucial rituals.

Island customs are notably resilient and resistant to externally imposed changes. At the same time they are innovative and adaptive, working out new solutions to the problems posed by new forms of power and desires for new forms of wealth. Key changes in the Vanatinai region include increases and decreases in the frequency of warfare and raiding, the build-up of population (closely related to warfare patterns in the precolonial period), resulting scarcity of resources on smaller islands, new technologies and forms of wealth, the introduction of new forms of religious ideology with the advent of missionization, and the imposition of colonial and then national political authority upon previously autonomous island peoples.

Vanatinai has lost one source of gender asymmetry, the male opportunity in earlier generations to obtain power and influence through a reputation as a champion fighter, or asiara. In spite of major involvement by women in warfare and diplomacy, only men—a few younger men—could gain respect, fame, and power by becoming known as champion.

A male monopoly on warfare cross-culturally has been hypothesized as a factor leading to a prevailing ideology of male superiority and a concomitant lower status for women. A contrasting approach argues that, for example, in the cases of the matrilineal Iroquois and Cherokee, the absence of many men for long periods during battles was a factor contributing to the power and influence of women.[5] Vanatinai warfare, as remembered today and as recorded in the 1880s by European visitors, was characterized by the male defense of people and property from raiders, not heroic attacks on others. In Vanatinai historical memory men killed other men to protect their families, just as they kill animals to nurture women and children and thus, paradoxically, to give life (cf. Brightman 1993b).

Both women and men are brought up to have assertive personalities. But physical violence against women—and men—is abhorred and occurs only rarely today. I have never heard of a case of rape. One of the last battles on the island took place as retaliation for a man's attack on his wife. Descendants mention the justifications of compensation and revenge but deplore the uncontrolled violence of earlier times. It is of course highly likely that male physical aggression was more highly valued in precolonial times, when warriors with spears defended land and people against attack and led raids against enemy districts. The admiration still evoked today by the word *asiara* is probably a muted echo of what it was.

The former male monopoly on warfare on Vanatinai probably did lead to certain kinds of influence within kin or hamlet groups being reserved for certain men, the asiara, in precolonial times. Some of the influence formerly wielded by the asiara, the feared warrior whose success and skill was based on his supernatural power, is now held by the (male) sorcerer.

The pacification imposed by British and Australian colonial authorities between 1888 and 1942 thus may have led to greater equality of opportunity for women to achieve renown and influence through taking prominent roles in ceremonial exchanges and mortuary ritual. There was no competing role of asiara for which they were not eligible. Women may also have benefited even more than men from the increased mobility for everyone made possible by pacification, a mobility that resulted in an expansion of interisland travel and exchange.

The Vanatinai case corroborates the importance of documenting local circumstances in evaluating the impact of historical changes upon gender ideologies and the material position of women. Contrary to Leacock (1978) and other writers, there is no automatic lowering of female autonomy in all aspects of the life of a small-scale society with the intrusion of colonialism or a centralized state. In some ways, in some places, women may gain advantages relative to men. At the same time everyone in the society may suffer the threat of violence, be coerced by outsiders, and lose autonomy and freedom of movement or behavior.

The impact on women's authority and influence of the absorption of Vanatinai into colonial and national polities has probably been negative overall. The new political and religious systems emphasize hierarchical authority controlled by distant male outsiders, with a few local adult males chosen to exercise control over the rest of the population as local government councillors, policemen and pastors. Colonial and national men coming to the island have expected to talk, in English, and delegate authority to other men, not bare-breasted women wearing coconut-leaf skirts. The new systems have their own ideologies of gender that more highly valorize men and that expect men and women to occupy spheres of activity that are more separate than is customary on Vanatinai. And the new systems directly oppose the Vanatinai ethic of egalitarian relations among autonomous individuals and exclude women from the new positions of authority.

Vanatinai people say that the prominent position of women in daily and ceremonial life is taubwaragha, the way of the ancestors.

The observations of Captain Owen Stanley in 1849 substantiate this. I have documented profound changes in island custom in subsistence practices, in forms of ceremonial exchange and ritual, and in systems of power and authority. These have had varying and conflicting impacts on the power and autonomy of women as a category of persons. Nevertheless, ways of producing food, exchanging valuables, and exerting influence over others as a gia are still taubwaragha despite local recognition that changes have occurred (Lepowsky 1991). Adhering to the way of the ancestors has for several generations often been a conscious act of resistance in the face of pressure from government, mission, and commercial interests. This resistance includes defending the power and influence of women: to own land and distribute goods, to acquire customary and magical knowledge, to travel, exchange, and host feasts, and to speak out forcefully in public about community concerns.

Why have Vanatinai people been successful to a large degree in their resistance and their cultural conservatism? Their physical circumstances have helped. They live on a remote island surrounded by treacherous reefs, a mountain guarded by large tracts of swampland. The island, though rich in resources, is hard for outsiders to exploit. Nobody could ever find the motherlode of the gold, transport and shipping of tropical commodities are difficult, and there have been few white residents in this century. Beginning a century ago Vanatinai men and women could pan for gold if they wanted to trade for steel tools and other new needs and wants rather than migrate to sell their labor. Colonial suppression of warfare and the resulting efflorescence of interisland ceremonial exchange and of mortuary ritual provided enhanced opportunities for men and women such as the people of Vanatinai to find satisfaction in the way of the ancestors and the kinds of social relations it embodies. They were affected by colonial policies but far away from the controlling presence of colonial officers and missionaries.

Material and Ideological Bases of Equality

Does equality or inequality, including between men and women, result from material or ideological causes? We cannot say whether an idea preceded or followed specific economic and social circumstances. Does the idea give rise to the act, or does the act generate an ideology that justifies it or mystifies it?

If they are congruent ideology and practice reinforce one another. And if multiple levels of ideology are in accord social forms are more likely to remain unchallenged and fundamentally unchanged. Where levels of ideology, or ideology and practice, are at odds, the circumstances of social life are more likely to be challenged by those who seek a reordering of social privileges justified according to an alternative interpretation of ideology. When social life embodies these kinds of contradictions, the categories of people in power—aristocrats, the rich, men—spend a great deal of energy maintaining their power. They protect their material resources, subdue the disenfranchised with public or private violence, coercion, and repression, and try to control public and private expressions of ideologies of political and religious power.

On Vanatinai, where there is no ideology of male dominance, the material conditions for gender equality are present. Women—and their brothers—control the means of production. Women own land, and they inherit land, pigs, and valuables from their mothers, their mothers' brothers, and sometimes from their fathers equally with men. They have the ultimate decison-making power over the distribution of staple foods that belong jointly to their kinsmen and that their kinsmen or husbands have helped labor to grow. They are integrated into the prestige economy, the ritualized exchanges of ceremonial valuables. Ideological expressions, such as the common saying that the woman is the owner of the garden, or the well-known myth of the first exchange between two female beings, validate material conditions.

I do not believe it would be possible to have a gender egalitarian society, where prevailing expressions of gender ideology were egalitarian or valorized both sexes to the same degree, without material control by women of land, means of subsistence, or wealth equivalent to that of men. This control would encompass anything from foraging rights, skills, tools, and practical and sacred knowledge to access to high-paying, prestigious jobs and the knowledge and connections it takes to get them. Equal control of the means of production, then, is one necessary precondition of gender equality. Vanatinai women's major disadvantage is their lack of access to a key tool instrumental in gaining power and prestige, the spear. Control of the means of production is potentially greater in a matrilineal society.

Matriliny and Gender

Vanatinai women are by definition central to the kin group, the most significant social unit on the island. They have equal rights to post-marital residence with their own kin and to inheritance, use, and distribution of land and other valuable resources. This is a situation in which female autonomy and cultural ideals of the value of women are likely to be high. By contrast, a patrilineal social structure inherently places women at a disadvantage in terms of rights, roles, and privileges and thus probably in terms of autonomy and control over their own actions and those of others.

Matrilineal descent need not result in a sexually egalitarian society or even in significant female autonomy and influence. Matrilineal societies vary tremendously. They include foragers such as the Crow, Haida, Tlingit, and Tsimshian of North America and the Tiwi of Australia, but most matrilineal peoples are small-scale horticulturalists such as the Bemba, Ndembu, and Tonga of Central Africa, the Iroquois, Cherokee, and Hopi of North America, and the Vanatinai people and their neighbors in Melanesia. Some are large in scale and part of larger, ranked social systems and polities, such as the Minangkabau of Indonesia, the Nayar of India, and the Ashanti of Africa.

In some matrilineal societies, such as the Ashanti and the Minangkabau, females and males from high-ranking groups serve as leaders. Others are unstratified, but only males occupy positions of authority. Still other unstratified matrilineal societies have both males and females in positions of authority: these may be the same kinds of positions, as on Vanatinai, or they may be classified by gender as among the Hopi or Iroquois.

Matrilineal societies in which social stratification and rank are absent as organizing principles, such as Vanatinai, are more likely to be gender egalitarian. High-ranking women in matrilineal and patrilineal societies alike may have their own gender-segregated sphere of power and authority over other women, or authority over lower ranked men.[6] But an overall egalitarian ethos is most conducive to gender equality. A strong emphasis on age and seniority seems to have a similarly negative effect on female autonomy, as among the matrilineal Tiwi and in the patrilineal societies of Australia.

Matrilineal societies have disparate gender philosophies. Within Melanesia itself they have a great range in gender ideology and gender roles, even though all their members are small-scale subsistence horticulturalists living in similar coastal and island environments. In the matrilineal societies of the Massim matrilineage members are dispersed by a variety of postmarital residence rules, and uxorilocality is absent. A rudimentary form of chieftainship, with matrilineage ranking and hereditary leadership, has emerged in the Trobriands, particularly in the north of Kiriwina. On matrilineal Rossel Island, adjacent to but not part of the Massim, there is a virtual male gerontocracy, with senior males monopolizing wealth and controlling the marriages of junior males and women. Elsewhere in the Massim big men and, on some islands, big women activate real or fictive ties of matrilineal kinship among widely dispersed individuals, and there are elaborate ceremonial exchange systems, including kula.

Melanesian matrilineal polities range from those where women are central to a larger number where women are excluded through the mechanisms of male societies, chiefdoms, and big men systems (cf. Allen 1984). In some women have a strong position, participate in key rituals, and possess significant supernatural knowledge but are excluded from leadership roles, as in the Trobriands (Malinowski 1922, 1929), or from key ritual domains, as in Lesu (Powdermaker 1933). Other matrilineal Melanesian societies with husband-centered residence, like those in Vanuatu, develop male secret societies. They, like most of the best-known patrilineal Melanesian societies, have strong ideologies of male superiority and female inferiority that also manifest themselves in the presence of men's houses, elaborate beliefs in female pollution, and male control of the most significant forms of ancestral and supernatural power.

Matrilineal descent provides the preconditions favorable to the development of female political and economic power, but it does not ensure it. In the cases of Vanatinai, the Nagovisi, the Minangkabau, and the Hopi, matriliny, woman-centered postmarital residence (or the absence of a virilocal residence rule), female autonomy, extradomestic positions of authority, and ideologies of gender that highly value women seem closely connected. Nevertheless matriliny by itself does not necessarily indicate, or generate, gender equality. As earlier comparative studies of matrilineal societies have emphasized, in many cases brothers or husbands control the land, valuables, and persons of sisters and wives (Schneider and Gough 1961, Schlegel 1972).

The ethnographic example of Vanatinai cannot solve the puzzle of the origins of social and gender inequality but it can indicate some of the conditions in which one egalitarian society exists. These include material bases of equality through equivalent control by all adults of rights to land and reef and to distribution of their products, a largely overlapping and unspecialized division of labor, and congruent ideologies that equivalently valorize males and females and that underlie the equal rights of all adults to seek knowledge and power through customary means.

Forty years ago Audrey Richards (1950), based on her work in central Africa, described what she called the "matrilineal puzzle": the struggle for authority over the wife and children between the coresident husband and the wife's brother and other matrilineal kin. In David Schneider's (1961:21–22) discussion of this structural tension he distinguishes two aspects of the father-child bonds that threaten the authority of the matrilineage, authority and positive affect. This is useful for looking at Massim versions of the matrilineal puzzle and their cultural solutions.

The authority of one adult over another is minimized on Vanatinai as in most Massim societies, the primary exception being the Trobriand Islands with their chiefly clans. The father poses a threat to his own matrilineage through his ties to his children. This is not because he tries to exert authority over them but because he wants to love and nurture them. The nurturing father is a major theme in most matrilineal cultures of the Massim.[7] His love is objectified by the food he produces through his labor and brings to his children and their mother, by the use rights he allows them on his lineage land, and by the magical knowledge and ceremonial valuables he gives to them during his life. In island symbolism these are all things that he feeds to his children. His matrilineage must be compensated for this objectified love and nurturance after his death through mortuary ritual exchanges. These flow from children to "fathers" in the persons of the deceased's father's matrilineal heirs, typically his nieces and nephews, reversing the direction of the valuables that were tokens of the father's nurture. Strathern (1988:238) points out that in Trobriand culture the food the nurturing father gives his children is treated like a wealth item. This is also true on Vanatinai, whether the father feeds yams—not a masculine product and symbol as in the Trobriands—or sago or wild pig to his children. Because this food given by the father is wealth, his children must compensate his matrilineage for it. They do this in mortuary exchanges that redress the balance—out of respect for the integrity of the father's matrilineage that nourished them—in their solution to the matrilineal puzzle.[8]

Gender Ideologies and Practice in Daily Life

In Melanesian societies the power of knowing is privately owned and transmitted, often through ties of kinship, to heirs or younger supporters. It comes not simply from acquiring skills or the experience and the wisdom of mature years but is fundamentally a spiritual power that derives from ancestors and other spirit forces.

In gender-segregated societies, such as those that characterize most of Melanesia, this spiritual knowledge power is segregated as well into a male domain through male initiations or the institutions of men's houses or male religious cults. Most esoteric knowledge—and the power over others that derives from it—is available to Vanatinai women if they can find a kinsperson or someone else willing to teach it to them. There are neither exclusively male nor female collectivities on Vanatinai nor characteristically male versus female domains or patterns of sociality (cf. Strathern 1988:76).

Decisions taken collectively by Vanatinai women and men within one household, hamlet, or lineage are political ones that reverberate well beyond the local group, sometimes literally hundreds of miles beyond. A hundred years ago they included decisions of war and peace. Today they include the ritualized work of kinship, more particularly of the matrilineage, in mortuary ritual. Mortuary feasts, and the interisland and interhamlet exchanges of ceremonial valuables that support them, memorialize the marriages that tied three matrilineages together, that of the deceased, the deceased's father, and the widowed spouse. Honoring these ties of alliance, contracted by individuals but supported by their kin, and threatened by the dissolution of death, is the major work of island politics.

Vanatinai social collectivities, such as lineages, hamlet coresidents, speakers of a Vanatinai dialect, or exchange partners, are unbounded. You are born to Guau clan, but you are not obliged to activate or strengthen reciprocal ties with specific individuals in your lineage or to incur your neighbor's gratitude and indebtedness. You can move away: you can always find other Guau, even on distant islands (or people with the same bird). Or else you can activate land rights that come from some other connection and develop ties of coresidence, fictive kinship, affinity, and exchange with others, who are likely to exchange with you eventually if you give generously of your labor and wealth.

The small scale, fluidity (cf. Collier and Rosaldo 1981), and mobility of social life on Vanatinai, especially in combination with matriliny, are conducive of egalitarian social relations between men and women and old and young. They promote an ethic of respect for the individual, which must be integrated with the ethic of cooperation essential for survival in a subsistence economy. People must work out conflict through face to face negotiation, or existing social ties will be broken by migration, divorce, or death through sorcery or witchcraft.

Women on Vanatinai are physically mobile, traveling with their families to live with their own kin and then the kin of their spouse, making journeys in quest of valuables, and attending mortuary feasts. They are said to have traveled for these reasons even in precolonial times when the threat of attack was a constant danger. The generally greater physical mobility of men in human societies is a significant factor in sexual asymmetries of power, as it is men who generally negotiate and regulate relationships with outside groups (cf. Ardener 1975:6).

Vanatinai women's mobility is not restricted by ideology or by taboo, and women build their own far-ranging personal networks of social relationships. Links in these networks may be activated as needed by the woman to the benefit of her kin or hamlet group. Women are confined little by taboos or community pressures. They travel, choose their own marriage partners or lovers, divorce at will, or develop reputations as wealthy and generous individuals active in exchange.

Big Men, Big Women, and Chiefs

Vanatinai giagia, male and female, match Sahlins's (1963) classic description of the Melanesian big man, except that the role of gia is gender-blind. There has been renewed interest among anthropologists in recent years in the big man form of political authority.[9] The Vanatinai case of the female and male giagia offers an intriguing perspective.

In the Massim, except for the Trobriand Islands, the most influential individuals are those who are most successful in exchange and who gain a reputation for public generosity by hosting or contributing significantly to mortuary feasts. Any individual on Vanatinai, male or female, may try to become known as a gia by choosing to exert the extra effort to go beyond the minimum contributions to the mortuary feasts expected of every adult. He or she accumulates ceremonial valuables and other goods both in order to give them away in acts of public generosity and to honor obligations to exchange partners from the local area as well as distant islands. There may be more than one gia in a particular hamlet, or even household, or there may be none. A woman may have considerably more prestige and influence than her husband because of her reputation for acquiring and redistributing valuables. While there are more men than women who are extremely active in exchange, there are some women who are far more active than the majority of men.

Giagia of either sex are only leaders in temporary circumstances and if others wish to follow, as when they host a feast, lead an exchange expedition, or organize the planting of a communal yam garden. Decisions are made by consensus, and the giagia of both sexes influence others through their powers of persuasion, their reputations for ability, and their knowledge, both of beneficial magic and ritual and of sorcery or witchcraft.

On Vanatinai some lineages own more land, routinely allowing others to subsist on their territory. In exchange their senior men and women are entitled to a token annual tribute of greenstone axe blades and other goods, which in fact is rarely collected. If population density were to reach the same high levels as in the Trobriands I suspect that rights of land ownership and usufruct would be far more tightly controlled. Lineages holding significant larger tracts of land, often those identified in myth as belonging to the clans of autochthonous

301

or first settler ancestors, would receive more formal and regular tribute of ceremonial valuables and foodstuffs. Eventually they would more closely resemble the higher ranked Trobriand subclans. It is also possible that growing social stratification and the rise of formal positions of hereditary authority would generate a gender hierarchy whereby even women of high-ranking lineages, like Trobriand women, could not become chiefs.

Images of Gender and Power

Strathern (1988) suggests that anthropologists should focus on indigenous constructions of male versus female sociality. With the demise of warfare and the uniquely male role of the asiara, the most characteristically and exclusively male image on Vanatinai today is of the solitary and antisocial sorcerer, alone at a secret place in the forest or shore, fasting, drinking a saltwater purge, collecting plants, and uttering his spells over the relics of an ancestor. True, if the sorcerer is your close relative or neighbor, you may say that he only performs the countersorcery of healing or attacks rival sorcerers who threaten his own kin, just as the asiara, with notable exceptions, is generally remembered as defender of the hearth against outside invaders. But Vanatinai people live in constant dread of sorcery, as David White wrote in 1893, and the sorcerer is the epitome of maleness, the taker of life.

Women, as I have already shown, are construed as life-givers, nurturing children and yams, and feeding the heirs of the deceased in mortuary ritual. One of the only occasions on which an all-female group assembles is during mortuary feasts, particularly the final zagaya. Women from the ages of about eighteen to seventy file into the hamlet carrying baskets of yams and garden produce on their heads. Under the supervision of the chief food magician, often a senior woman, they store their baskets under a house whose stilts are covered with palm leaves and magical spells to shield it from curious eyes. The food is roasted each day by a party of women in a stone oven, then piled again into separate garden baskets and carried to a central place on the hamlet ground. Twenty or more women sit in a rough circle, holding their baskets on their outstretched legs. The chief magician, and some of the women, have privately said magical spells over the baskets, prayers to the ancestors for abundance enough to feed others generously and enlarge the names of individuals and matrilineages. For what seems—to a visiting American participant—to be an extremely long period of time, they sit there, talking loudly, laughing, and chewing betel nut as each woman tosses one roasted tuber at a time into an inner set of baskets, carved wooden platters, and enameled tradestore bowls. The idea is to divide all the food evenly for presentation to feast guests. But, even more important, it is to commingle the life-giving products of each woman's garden.

Each lineage will eat yams from the ground of others, putting aside the fear of sorcery and poisoning that is associated with the sharing of food—even, and especially, during the tension of a mortuary feast, where death is sorcery manifested. Each woman is a separate actor, holding what are symbolically her yams (the ones she brought are in fact already mixed under the supervision of the food magician in the storage area and the stone ovens). She protects her own reputation for strength and generosity through magical appeals for the multiplication of the garden produce she holds, shielding her basket from her neighbor's eyes so no one will see if it is nearly empty, avoiding giving away the last tuber. But she acts on behalf of her matrilineage and its ideals of generosity, transforming the symbolically male antinurture of poison and sorcery personified by the corpse of the deceased into a maternal gift of life and renewal.

As elsewhere in Melanesia, the individual actor on Vanatinai in social and, especially, ritual context is a metaphor for other persons. She or he is both singular and plural, acting as an individual and as an embodiment of collectivities of persons (cf. Strathern 1990, Wagner 1991). The mourning spouse personifies his or her matrilineage and simultaneously the corpse of the deceased. The tau who eats the feast stands for the matrilineage of the deceased's father and, even when biologically female, is symbolically male and specifically paternal. The owner of the feast personifies his or her entire matrilineage, and so, especially, does the woman who sits down in the mwagumwagu, who is both biologically and symbolically female.

The corpse is androgynous, associated through death and sorcery with males but maternally nourishing the living through its fruit: food, ceremonial valuables, and the persons of the widowed spouses and principal female mourners who stand for their matrilineages. It is itself the fruit of a lifetime of nurturance by its own matrilineage and that of the father. The images of female nurturing and male poisoning are contradicted by other levels of Vanatinai gender ideology. Women kill as witches. Men nurture as fathers and as giagia, givers of wealth objects. In Vanatinai philosophy human beings are multivalent and unpredictable.

Individuals, as gendered persons, are woven into an unbounded, outwardly ramifying web of relations with others: they are mothers, husbands, daughters-in-law, cross-cousins, neighbors, and exchange partners. But they are autonomous beings, the only ones to know their own thoughts. You can try to influence another person, turn her or his thoughts toward you, through requests, verbal persuasion, the power of your grief or anger, or the suasions of magic and seduction. But, ultimately, male or female, people will do what they want, whether that is to give or withhold, nurture or kill.

On Vanatinai power and influence over the actions of others are gained by achievement and demonstrated superior knowledge and skill, whether in the realm of gardening, exchange, healing, or sorcery. Those who accumulate a surplus of resources are expected to be generous and share with their neighbors or face the threat of the sorcery or witchcraft of the envious. Both women and men are free to build their careers through exchange. On the other hand both women and men are free *not* to strive toward renown as giagia but to work for their own families or simply to mind their own business. They can also achieve the respect of their peers, if they seek it at all, as loving parents, responsible and hard-working lineage mates and affines, good gardeners, hunters, or fishers, or skilled healers, carvers, or weavers.

Mead (1935) observes that societies vary in the degree to which "temperament types" or "approved social personalities" considered suitable for each sex or a particular age category differ from each other. On Vanatinai there is wide variation in temperament and behavior among islanders of the same sex and age. The large amount of overlap between the roles of men and women on Vanatinai leads to a great deal of role flexibility, allowing both individual men and women the freedom to specialize in the activities they personally enjoy, value, are good at performing, or feel like doing at a particular time. There is considerable freedom of choice in shaping individual lifestyles.

An ethic of personal autonomy, one not restricted to the powerful, is a key precondition of social equality. Every individual on Vanatinai from the smallest child to an aged man or woman possesses a large degree of autonomy. Idiosyncrasies of personality and character are generally tolerated and respected. When you ask why someone does or does not do something, your friends will say, emphatically and expressively, "We [inclusive we: you and I both] don't know," "It is something of theirs" [their way], or, "She doesn't want to." Islanders say that it is not possible to know why a person behaves a certain way or what thoughts generate an action. Persisting in a demand to "know" publicly the thoughts of others is dangerous, threatening, and invasive. Vanatinai people share, in part, the perspectives identified with postmodern discussions of the limits of ethnographic representation: it is impossible to know another person's thoughts or feelings. If you try they are likely to deceive you to protect their own privacy or their own interests. Your knowing is unique to you. It is your private property that you transmit only at your own volition, as when you teach magical spells to a daughter or sister's son.[10]

The prevailing social sanction is also individualistic: the threat of somebody else's sorcery or witchcraft if you do not do what they want or if you arouse envy or jealousy. But Vanatinai cultural ideologies stress the strength of individual will in the face of the coercive pressures of custom, threat of sorcery, and demands to share. This leads to a Melanesian paradox: the ethic of personal autonomy is in direct conflict to the ethic of giving and sharing so highly valued on Vanatinai, as in most Melanesian cultures. Nobody can make you share, short of stealing from you or killing you if you refuse them. You have to want to give: your nurture, your labor, your valuables, and your person. This is where persuasion comes in. It comes from the pressure of other people, the force of shame, and magical seduction made potent by supernatural agency. Vanatinai custom supplies a final, persuasive argument to resolve this paradox: by giving, you not only strengthen your lineage and build its good name, you make yourself richer and more powerful by placing others in your debt.

What can people in other parts of the world learn from the principles of sexual equality in Vanatinai custom and philosophy? Small scale facilitates Vanatinai people's emphasis on face-to-face negotiations of interpersonal conflicts without the delegation of political authority to a small group of middle-aged male elites. It also leaves room for an ethic of respect for the will of the individual regardless of age or sex. A culture that is egalitarian and nonhierarchical overall is more likely to have egalitarian relations between men and women.

Males and females on Vanatinai have equivalent autonomy at each life cycle stage. As adults they have similar opportunities to influence the actions of others. There is a large amount of overlap between the roles and activities of women and men, with women occupying public, prestige-generating roles. Women share control of the production and the distribution of valued goods, and they inherit property. Women as well as men participate in the exchange of valuables, they organize feasts, they officiate at important rituals such as those for yam planting or healing, they counsel their kinfolk, they speak out and are listened to in public meetings, they possess valuable magical knowledge, and they work side by side in most subsistence activities. Women's role as nurturing parent is highly valued and is the dominant metaphor for the generous men and women who gain renown and influence over others by accumulating and then giving away valuable goods.

But these same characteristics of respect for individual autonomy, role overlap, and public participation of women in key subsistence and prestige domains of social life are also possible in large-scale industrial and agricultural societies. The Vanatinai example suggests that sexual equality is facilitated by an overall ethic of respect for and equal treatment of all categories of individuals, the decentralization of political power, and inclusion of all categories of persons (for example, women and ethnic minorities) in public positions of authority and influence. It requires greater role overlap through increased integration of the workforce, increased control by women and minorities of valued goods—property, income, and educational credentials— and increased recognition of the social value of parental care. The example of Vanatinai shows that the subjugation of women by men is not a human universal, and it is not inevitable. Sex role patterns and gender ideologies are closely related to overall social systems of power and prestige. Where these systems stress personal autonomy and egalitarian social relations among all adults, minimizing the formal authority of one person over another, gender equality is possible.

Notes

2. Fruit of the Motherland

1. See, for example, Mead (1935), Meggitt (1964), Langness (1967), Poole (1981), Godelier (1986).

2. See also Brown and Buchbinder (1976), Herdt and Poole (1982), Strathern (1988:43–65).

3. For example, Herdt (1981) and Godelier (1986). Studies of the male role in Melanesia tend to focus on male initiation, e.g., Allen (1967) and Herdt (1981, 1982b).

4. See de Beauvoir (1953), Rosaldo (1974, 1980), and Ortner (1974), but see Ortner (1990) for a nonuniversalistic perspective.

5. Sacks (1974, explicitly following Engels 1891), Brown (1975), and Leacock (1978:252) stress the material bases of gender relations. Rosaldo (1974) and Ortner (1974) emphasize ideological factors, and Friedl (1975:164) and Ortner and Whitehead (1981) particularly emphasize access to prestige. Sanday (1981:163–179) reviews definitions of male dominance.

6. Similarly, Langness (1967) attributes the sexual antagonism and denigration of women characteristic of New Guinea Highlands societies to the prevalence of warfare and Meigs (1990) relates the "chauvinistic" ideology of Hua men to the male role as warriors. Divale and Harris (1976) see institutionalized warfare and a corollary cultural emphasis on male aggression as the primary cause of the "male supremacist complex.' "

7. See Atkinson (1982), Strathern (1987), Mukhopadhyay and Higgins (1988) for discussions of the concept of sexual equality and the problems of definition. Lamphere (1977:616) criticizes what she calls the "complementary but equal"argument suggested by Schlegel for the Hopi and Briggs for the Inuit, where males and females control different, but not larger, spheres consisting of "their persons, property, or activities."Sanday (1981:170) points out that definitions of equality may refer either to "sameness"or "interdependence and balance"and suggests using the term "sexual symmetry."Her definition of sexual equality is the converse of her definition of male dominance, or, when "males do not display aggression against women and women exercise political and economic authority or power"(Sanday 1981:165).

8. See Fortes and Evans-Pritchard (1940), Sahlins (1958), Flanagan (1989), Flanagan and Rayner (1988).

9. Bachofen (1861), Morgan (1877), Rivers (1914), and Briffault (1931) are influential early discussions of matriliny and matriarchy. Perspectives based on fieldwork in matrilineal societies include Lowie (1919), Malinowski (1929), Fortune (1932), Powdermaker (1933), Richards (1956), Colson (1958), Wallace (1972:28–30), and Brown (1970a). Richards (1950), Schneider and Gough (1961), and Schlegel (1972) are theoretical and comparative analyses of matriliny. The most recent ethnographic and theoretical accounts of matrilineal societies are Nash (1987), Peletz (1988), Fogelson (1990), Lepowsky (1990a), Petersen (1982), Sanday (1990a), and Schlegel (1990).

10. Anthropologists have written of a unitary status of women in given societies for the last century (e.g., Mason 1895, Evans-Pritchard 1965). See Strathern (1987, 1988), Mukhopadhyay and Higgins (1988), Sanday (1990b), Lederman (1990), Meigs (1990), Ortner (1990), and Schlegel (1990) for important challenges. Strathern (1988) has gone further, pointing out that the concept of society is itself an artificial construct of Western intellectuals. She refers instead to sociality, the human drive to form relationships and maintain cohesion among people and to collectivities of persons. If there is no society there can be no singular set of gender roles or ideologies. Abu-Lughod (1991) argues that the concept of culture, like the earlier anthropological concept of race, unavoidably invokes boundedness, internal consistency, and the difference between discrete cultural units, and thus reifies unequal power relations among different categories of people, such as colonizers and colonized, male and female. She suggests that anthropologists therefore need to "write against culture,"stressing discourse and practice, historical and translocal connections, and "ethnographies of the particular"that relate the lived experiences of named subjects. Ortner's (1990) emphasis on hegemonic and counterhegemonic gender ideologies is a similar attempt to go beyond the unity of belief, value, and practice implied by the culture concept.

11. Yolanda and Robert Murphy (1974) earlier described a similar ideological "battle of the sexes"among the Mundurucú of the Brazilian Amazon.

12. See Hamy (1888), Haddon (1894), Seligman (1909, 1910). First used in 1847 by Marist missionaries living on Woodlark Island, the term appears to be a corruption of the name of Misima Island (Affleck 1983).

13. See Malinowski (1929:28), Reo Fortune (1932:257), Haddon (1894:255), Armstrong (1928:100), Young (1971a:54), and Chowning (1973a:30). Malinowski himself, who once issued a criticism of ethnographers who repeat without documentation "generalities and stock phrases such as that . . . 'the status of the wife is high' " (1962:18), is the only partial exception. In *The Sexual Life of Savages in North-Western Melanesia* he includes a brief chapter on "The Status of Women in Native Society,"in which he discusses the position of women in the descent group, the customs applying to women of rank, and "women's share in magic" and ceremonial activities among the Trobriand Islanders of the Northern Massim (1929:28–49).

14. Rosaldo (1974), Sanday (1973, 1974), Hammond and Jablow (1973), Sacks (1974), Bacdayan (1977), and Leacock (1978).

15. Cf. Leacock (1978) and Etienne and Leacock (1980).

16. Morauta (1981) correctly points out that status inequalities in lowland Papua New Guinea societies have often been underreported by ethnographers.

17. See discussions in Sanday (1973), Schlegel (1977:9), and Leacock (1978:147).

18. In the Misima language, and in the Sabarl dialect of the Saisai language, the island is called Tagula, the name by which it sometimes appears on maps and nautical charts. Tagula was also the name given to the government station built in 1969 on the island's western tip. The East Calvados, or Saisai, Islanders of Wanim (Grass), eastern Panatinani, Dedehai, and Nimowa call it Tagule, and the Rossel Islanders to the northeast know it as Yamba. The earliest published usage of the name Tagula that I have found is in a map drawn by labor recruiter William Wawn (1893: opposite p. 359), in which the island is labeled "Sudest Island (Tagula)."Wawn (1893:315) had engaged interpreters from Grass Island, in the East Calvados, and presumably obtained the name from them.

19. This totemic set was described as "linked totems"by Charles Seligman in 1910 in his remarkable, pioneering survey of Massim cultures. The precise number and kinds of totems vary considerably among the cultures of the region. As on Vanatinai in the majority of Massim cultures a bird totem is most important. On nearby Rossel Island, which also has linked totems, the snake is most significant (Armstrong 1928 and author's field research). The Vanatinai snake totem is second in importance to the bird totem(s).

20. See, for example, Brown (1970a), Hammond and Jablow (1973), Sanday (1974), Friedl (1975).

21. See Richards (1950), Ember and Ember (1971), Schlegel (1972), and Divale and Harris (1976) on the significance of wife-centered residence. A similar pattern of bilocal residence was reported by Reo Fortune (1932) for Dobu Island, also part of the Massim culture area, where couples reside in alternate years with the lineage mates of each spouse.

22. Cf. Rosaldo (1980), Wolf (1982), Vansina (1990), Wagner (1975), and Barth (1987).

23. For a fuller discussion see Lepowsky (1991).

24. The people of Boboghagha Village on the extreme western tip of the island speak their own separate language, which cannot be understood by their neighbors. Vanga Vanazhibwa means "language of the place of zh,"a characteristic phoneme of this dialect, spoken at Jelewaga and other settlements on the southwestern coast. Unless otherwise indicated, all words in the vernacular used hereafter will be from the Vanga Vanazhibwa dialect of Vanga Vanatinai. A closely related dialect is spoken in the northwest coast hamlets of Embambalia, Mitin, and Nainhil. Vanga Veora, named after the Veora River of the north coast, which separates this dialect area from the hamlets to the west, is spoken at Taragia and Gesila on the north coast and Madawa on the south, although Madawa's speech is said to be transitional. Vanga Pamela is spoken at Araida on the north coast and Pamela and Pantava (Ghebira) on the south. All these people came from a large, now extinct settlement named Ragule (from which the Misima word Tagula is said to be derived), located in the interior near Mt. Rio. The eastern dialect, or Vanga Rehua, is spoken at Rambuso, Wimba, and Seghe on the north coast and Buyawe, Rehua, and Njuru on the south, with the speech of Bwamumu being transitional between Vanga Pamela and Vanga Rehua. Other dialects that originated in now deserted parts of the island, such as the extreme southwest coast, are spoken today by only a few older people.

25. Misima is also spoken on Alcester (Nasikwabu) Island, seventy miles northwest of Misima, and on Ole and Tewatewa Islands in the Engineer Group, ninety miles west of Misima, settled from Alcester Island (Henderson and Henderson n.d.).

26. The number of cognate words between the Nimowa and Vanatinai languages is only 28 percent, and it is only 16 percent between the languages of Vanatinai and Misima. All the other languages of Milne Bay Province islands including the Misima language are said to constitute a "chained family,"with cognate relationships of 28 percent to 67 percent (Henderson and Henderson n.d.:47). The linguistic evidence thus suggests that the AN languages of the southeastern Louisiade Archipelago have had a long time to diverge from other AN languages of Milne Bay Province. The cognate relationship between the language of Vanatinai and the non-Austronesian Rossel Island language is only 6 percent. The Rossel language, Yeletnye, has a radically different grammatical structure and phonology.

27. Recently archeological research was carried out by Geoffrey Irwin (letter to author, 1989) on Misima Island.

28. Cf. Birdsell (1977). There are few dated sites presently known in lowland or island areas that offer conclusive evidence of preceramic settlement in lowland Melanesia. The earliest, a recent and dramatic find in the islands north of mainland New Guinea, which involves worked obsidian, dates to 11,000 B.P. (Allen, Flannery, Gosden, Jones, and White 1988).

29. During the last glaciation the average shoreline in the area was about fifty meters below present levels, and at about 20,000 B.P. the sea level may have reached 150 meters below current averages (Birdsell 1977:115).

30. See J. Allen (1977, 1984), Egloff (1978), Bellwood (1979), Irwin (1981), Spriggs (1984), and Kirch (1987, 1988, 1990). Changing patterns of interisland exchange are discussed in Lepowsky (n.d.1).

31. As in the myths of Vanatinai supernaturals who migrated from Vanatinai to Rossel (see chapter 4), Armstrong (1928:xxiv) recounts a Rossel myth wherein Wonajö, the supreme deity of Rossel, invites a dark-skinned snake god named Mbasi from Sudest to visit him. Mbasi arrives in a sailing canoe (*lia nö*), which was not previously known on the island, "bringing with him the sun, moon, pig, dog and taro."The Rossel Islanders are also said to be Mbasi's descendants by "Konjini, an oviparous fair-skinned girl of Rossel."These myths are mirrored by Vanatinai oral histories of long-standing alliances and ties of marriages between the two islands. Vanatinai people told me that Rossel Island (which they call Rova) used to be inhabited by people from Vanatinai, who spoke Vanga Vanatinai. But one day very dark-skinned invaders appeared in "double canoes,"killed all of Rova's inhabitants and settled on the island in their place. The present-day people of Rova are the descendants of these invaders. A myth from Boboghagha, or Western Point Village, Vanatinai, resembles the Rossel myth and suggests the ancient links between the two island peoples. A place spirit in the form of a sacred stone named Mbasiri migrated from the hill near Western Point called Etubude to Rossel Island to a spot on the reef between Jinjo and East Point. It remains there to this day as a small stone that moves up and down on the reef with the tide and is never submerged. When it left Mbasiri took with it the former language of Boboghagha, which became the present-day language of Rossel. Mbasiri changed places with another sacred stone named Fuzeri, which used to be at the same spot on the Rossel reef and is now at Etubude. Fuzeri brought with it from Rossel the present-day language of Boboghagha. Mbasiri is not said to be a snake in the Boboghagha myth, but place spirits often take the form of snakes. There is no mention of Mbasiri bringing the sun and

other objects or of his being the progenitor of the Rossel people in the Boboghagha version. Witamo, a supernatural who in a Vanatinai myth migrates to Rossel, assumes the form of a snake. Also, a female snake named Bambagho, which came originally from Goodenough Island, migrated to Rossel from Vanatinai (see chapter 4).

32. See Bevan (1890:112–117), Douglas (1888–89:8–10), Forbes (1886).

33. See Hunter (1839:38, 1840:301); for a fuller discussion see Lepowsky (n.d.2).

34. Some islanders say that before the Europeans came the islands of the Louisiade Archipelago were occasionally visited by both Malay and Chinese vessels. Malay ships are known to have been engaged in trade with the aborigines of the north Australian coast for bêche-de-mer (sea cucumber or trepang) during the centuries before the European colonial period and to have visited the northern coast of mainland New Guinea. It is possible that this trade extended into the Louisiade, as the shallow lagoon waters there are rich in bêche-de-mer, which even today brings a good price in Chinese ports.

35. The writings of Foucault (1979) on surveillance, the panopticon, and state control are highly relevant to the *Rattlesnake*'s charting and mapping as the first and basic mission of imperial power in these Australasian waters.

36. See Forbes (1886), Douglas (1888–89), Bevan (1890:112–123).

37. The labor recruiter Wawn (1893:321–322) describes how in 1884 at Rehua, on the south coast of Sudest, his interpreter from Teste (Wari or Ware) Island met his brother, who had been adopted twelve years earlier after all the adults in his party had been killed and eaten. The man immediately signed on as a laborer. It was unclear to Wawn why the Wari people had sailed 150 miles: to trade or to raid or to have an adventure.

38. See Douglas (1887), Price and Baker (1976:116); cf. Nelson (1976:8).

39. Vanga Lumo seems to have originated in the Louisiade in the 1870s and 1880s through contact with English-speaking traders and their polyglot crews. Contemporary documents indicate that it was more English-based than present-day Melanesian pidgins. Vanga Lumo today is spoken only by a few elderly men and women, primarily because by the 1970s there were no longer any white residents on the island. Songs in Vanga Lumo and singing styles still used today, particularly in the Rehua area of southeastern Vanatinai, are also said to have been learned in nineteenth-century Queensland. By now the language has become relexified compared to the late nineteenth century, with greater numbers of words from Vanatinai dialects, and is no longer intelligible without study to an English speaker. But the Vanatinai language has also incorporated as synonyms a significant number of English-based words, some used in daily speech, such as *olman*, old man, instead of *amalaisali*, and *posi*, suppose or if, in place of *zogo*, *thogo*, or *dogo* (depending on dialect). Many words for items introduced by Europeans derived from this Papuan pidgin have an archaic flavor, such as *maskedi*, musket, for gun, and *calico* for cloth and cotton clothing.

40. British New Guinea Annual Reports (1888–1889); cf. Nelson (1976:26).

41. MacGregor (1891a:22–23), White (1893); cf. Nelson (1976:20).

42. On islander-white relations during the gold rush see Hely (1889:58) and MacGregor (1891b:68). Campbell (1898a, 1898b) records evidence of abuses by traders; see Lepowsky (1991).

43. Territory of Papua Patrol Reports (1911, 1912, 1935); see chapter 5.

44. An exception is the long-dead grandfather of a present-day big man. This ancestor, an asiara, is remembered for his aggression toward his neighbors and his taste for

human flesh, qualities described with a mixture of amusement and horror. Sorcerers still secretly take relics from his burial place for use in destructive magic.

45. Brown (1979:104–105) similarly identifies fighting leaders, peace leaders, and those who specialize in knowledge, particularly that of "medicine, sorcery and spirits"among New Guinea Highlanders. Contributors to Godelier and Strathern (1991) apply the concepts of great men and big men to a variety of Melanesian societies.

46. Cf. Lepowsky (1990b, 1991); Linnekin (1990).

3. Island Lives

1. See, for example, Lowie (1920), Linton (1940, 1942), Sahlins (1958), Fried (1967), Flanagan and Rayner (1989).

2. Fifty years ago Ralph Linton (1940, 1942) coined the term age-sex category to describe the dual nature of these positions, calling them a neglected aspect of social organization. They are still relatively neglected. Age stratification is prominent in East African pastoral societies (Eisenstadt 1956, Bernardi 1985), aboriginal Australia (Warner 1937, Elkin 1964), the Amazon (Murphy and Murphy 1974), and many societies in interior New Guinea (Herdt 1982b, Godelier 1986). Some of these have been described as gerontocracies, but if they are, they are male gerontocracies, stratified by sex as well as age.

3. Sterility among island men and women alike is probably often due to complications of gonorrhea, introduced into the region during World War II. It probably reached Vanatinai through island visitors from the northwest, with the ultimate source of infection the American naval and airbase at Milne Bay. Gonorrhea is generally treated today only through magical healing practices. Even now that there are government aidposts which (in theory) are stocked with penicillin, people are ashamed to report to them for treatment of sexually transmitted diseases (cf. Lepowsky 1990c).

4. Since teenagers are often sexually active, although irregularly, as at feasts, and only occasionally use local contraceptives, this suggests the phenomenon of "adolescent sterility"or "adolescent subfecundity"due to absent or irregular ovulation. Early menarche and early regular ovulation are related to diet and health as well as genetics. Menarche has been reported as late as age eighteen (Wood, Johnson, and Campbell 1985) in some New Guinea populations. Vanatinai diet is very low in protein and vitamin-poor, and people are debilitated by malaria and by intestinal parasites (Lepowsky 1985b), factors that undoubtedly help to inhibit conception.

5. Pregnant women are not permitted to eat any "European,"meaning store-bought, foods. Some women eat no fish or seafood in early pregnancy, but this is purely a matter of choice and may be because they are suffering from morning sickness. A pregnant woman is otherwise said to be free to eat what she likes (see Lepowsky 1985b). But during the long labor of Rara some of her woman attendants suggested that she might have eaten some of the wrong kind of fish or that she might have eaten too much fish and pig during her pregnancy, prolonging her labor and producing a very large infant.

6. Schlegel (1990) reports a pattern of female infant preference among the Hopi, who are matrilineal and largely gender egalitarian, similar to that of Vanatinai. Well-known examples of female infanticide or female child neglect come from China (Potter 1987), Taiwan (Wolf 1972), and Northern India (Miller 1981, 1987). An explicit preference

for sons has been taken for granted in European and Euro-American cultures until the new wave of feminism of recent years has made parts of these populations more self-conscious and defensive about their desires.

7. See, for example, Poole (1981), Jenkins, Orr-Ewing, and Heywood (1985), Godelier (1986).

8. Formerly a baby's ears and nose were pierced when the umbilical cord stump fell off, but, because of missionary disapproval, nose piercing has not been practiced since the late 1940s, and even ear piercing has become uncommon in the last twenty years. The custom of smearing an infant's head with charcoal made from burnt coconut husks for several months to protect it with the help of ancestor spirits and make it hard and strong has survived despite mission opposition.

9. Babies are allowed to eat no animal protein food or greens of any kind until they are walking around habitually at age two or three. Their first supplementary foods are papaya juice and the liquid from boiled root vegetables that have been cooked in coconut cream. Later they are given root vegetables or banana mashed in the cooking liquid, and finally at about age one they eat the normal soft, bland sago, yam, sweet potato, manioc, taro, banana, and coconut cream that are the staples of the adult diet (Lepowsky 1985b).

10. Sorenson (1976) concludes that Fore children of the New Guinea Highlands who are similarly permitted to play with knives and other dangerous objects thereby learn to manipulate them without ever harming themselves, but young children on Vanatinai occasionally burn themselves while playing with fire or cut themselves or those around them while playing with knives. One four-year-old girl had previously cut off the first joint of her right forefinger, an accident while playing with a fourteen-inch-long bush knife.

11. See, for example, Allen (1967), Herdt (1982b, 1984), Godelier (1986). The significance of female puberty ceremonies or initiations—much less frequent in New Guinea and less elaborate than their male counterparts—as reflection and reinforcement of egalitarian or asymmetrical gender ideologies is more open to debate (cf. Powdermaker 1933, Godelier 1986).

12. Major writings on the topics include Meggitt (1964), Langness (1967), Herdt (1982b), Meigs (1983), and Godelier (1986).

13. Gottlieb (1988, 1990) makes a similar point about the taboos of the matrilineal Beng of West Africa in which menstrual blood and the fluids produced by both males and females during sexual intercourse must be kept away from the forest, domain of supernatural creative power. Adults should also bathe each morning to "wash off sex"before they come into contact with the sacred earth in their gardens. Breaking the taboos endangers the fertility of human beings and the natural world.

14. For accounts of New Guinea Highlands beliefs about menstruation see Meggitt (1964), Langness (1967), Brown and Buchbinder (1976), and Godelier (1986). The Vanatinai case also contrasts with that of Rossel Island, twenty-five miles northeast, where women are secluded in a menstrual house during their periods and during and following childbirth, and where women were traditionally forbidden at all times to visit certain areas such as the vicinity of Loa Island (Armstrong 1928:127, 148–149, 151), a river near Jinjo (Armstrong 1928:140), the reef near a sacred stone (ibid. 145), the neighborhood of other sacred stones (ibid. 152), and the vicinity of the *ptyilöwe* dance (ibid.

91). Rossel women were also forbidden even to look at as well as to board the chiefly canoes called *nö* (ibid. 30), which are no longer built. Most of these taboos are still maintained today, including menstrual and childbirth seclusion and the proscription on women visiting certain sections of reef and other sacred locations. Armstrong (1928) observed seventy years ago that the status of women on Rossel Island is markedly lower than elsewhere in the Massim. Even though it is matrilineal, Rossel customs greatly privilege older males, who control the marriages of younger men and of women through their monopoly of the most important types of shell valuables. These are essential for bridewealth, the principal arena of exchange on the island, as opposed to the Massim, where elaborate series of mortuary feasts are the norm.

15. Malinowski (1935:301) notes that in the Trobriand Islands, "The payment given for erotic services is called buwana, and this name is, I think, derived from the word for betel nut, Buwa."He does not describe the nature, content, or direction of this payment. On the northern Massim island of Gawa, the gifts of food given to a child's spouse by his or her kin are called *buwaa* (Munn 1986). Buwa is a cognate of the reconstructed proto-Austronesian term for betel nut, *buNah* (Conklin 1958:2). The Vanatinai term for betel nut is *ghelezi* or *eledi*, depending upon dialect. Betel nut is often given to a lover and is sometimes first bespelled with love magic (Lepowsky 1982). It is possible that buwa on Vanatinai is a loan word that originally derived from the word for betel nut in many present–day Austronesian languages.

16. In these societies boys do not become men as a developmental consequence of their birth to women and the nurturance of breastmilk. Men develop through rebirth during initiation rituals secret from women, and they are nourished by semen as part of these rituals during their years–long seclusion from women prior to marriage (Herdt 1981, 1982a, 1984; Schieffelin 1976, Godelier 1986).

17. Special, named houses were formerly used by the male warriors of each clan at Misima Island but not on Vanatinai. On Vanatinai individual male warriors each formerly had a particular spot, or *yova*, on the ground whose location was known only to him, where he would go to work rituals to strengthen himself for battle. Yova is translated as "sacred place."Elders say nowadays each man may have a yova, a spot revealed to him by his father, where he goes to make magic in order to create and locate stone axe blades (tobotobo). Women are said not to have yova.

18. About 10 percent of marriages are contracted with people from elsewhere. Marriage to spouses from the East Calvados Islands, or Saisai, is most common in the western hamlets of Vanatinai, and to Rossel Islanders, in the eastern hamlets. Vanatinai people also marry Misima, Panaeati, and West Calvados Islanders, and more rarely, people from other parts of Milne Bay Province, such as the Trobriand Islands, Dobu Island, or the Milne Bay region of the mainland.

19. Fortune (1932:4–6), who found a pattern of alternate year bilocal postmarital residence for Dobu in 1928, describes more deference and avoidance behavior on the part of the affines toward the "Owners of the Village"than obtains nowadays, or is remembered from the past, for Vanatinai.

20. Author's fieldnotes for Misima; see Berde (1974) for Panaeati and Battaglia (1990) for Sabarl. Berde (1974:139) notes that in former times the young husband spent several months living with his wife's parents and doing brideservice. In these islands a widow and her children, who are normally residing and gardening on the deceased husband's

land at the time of his death, try to give enough ceremonial valuables to his matrilineage during mortuary rituals so that they may gain permanent title to it. Battaglia (1990:103–104) shows that about twice as much land is inherited in this way, generally from fathers to children, than through the matrilineage. Panaeati and Sabarl Islanders also place a much stronger emphasis on the husband's lineage's contributions or *muli* (called *mulimuli* in the Misima language), which should ideally include the gift of a sailing canoe, a *muliwagana* in the Misima language and *muliwaga* in Saisai (Berde 1974:247, Battaglia 1990, and author's fieldnotes). This greater asymmetry of affinal prestations compared to Vanatinai may also generate and reinforce a power asymmetry between husband and wife that disadvantages the woman. Panaeati and Sabarl, where people use affinal exchanges during marriage and in mortuary ritual to try to detach land from the father's matrilineage, are densely populated and short of garden land at home and on neighboring islands. Vanatinai people have plenty of land and do not need to have the same passionate concern with land inheritance. Virtually all land, held communally by the matrilineage, is inherited matrilineally. It is quite possible that more land pressure on Vanatinai would result in land becoming more contested and therefore more land would be wrested from matrilineal succession. Use rights to garden land are normally given for the asking by owners to neighbors, friends, or affines. Coresidents of a hamlet usually clear a garden together in a convenient area, with each couple having their own section. Ideally, the owners should be compensated yearly with a tribute of a greenstone axe blade and a token basket of fine seed yams. Matrilineages communally hold sago groves, and another person must ask to cut a sago palm, a favor sometimes granted and sometimes refused to neighbors or exchange partners. Tracts of forest and sections of fringing reef are also owned by matrilineages, and in precolonial days poaching on a reef sometimes triggered a war. Today residents of one dialect area do not even bother to ask permission of the owners before foraging in forest or on the reef.

21. Bazi seems to agree with John Ogbu's (1978) argument that bridewealth enhances female status by legitimizing marriage.

22. Jane Collier and Michelle Rosaldo (1981:278–279) argue that hunter-gatherer and horticulturalist societies may be divided into "brideservice"and "bridewealth"societies based upon their customary marriage arrangements, with each type exhibiting a characteristic pattern of gender roles, politics, ritual, ideology, and social organization. But Vanatinai has strong traditions of both brideservice and bridewealth. This suggests that such societies might better be conceptualized as forming a continuum, ranging from those where only brideservice is found to those where only bridewealth is customary, with Vanatinai being in the middle and sharing some attributes of each ideal type.

23. Sanday (1974, 1981) hypothesizes that where men and women contribute equally to subsistence, women's status will be higher, and suggests that the mingling of the sexes in the tasks of daily life works against the rise of male dominance. Similarly Bacdayan (1977) sees "task interchangeability"between the sexes as an important correlate of a high status of women in a particular society.

24. Female hunting is relatively rare worldwide, but it has been reported among foragers and horticulturalists in various parts of the world, such as Australian aborigines of the Kimberleys and Melville Island (Kaberry 1939, Goodale 1971), the Agta of the Philippines (Estioko-Griffin and Griffin 1981, 1985), and the Ojibwa, Montagnais-Naskapi, and Rock Cree of Canada (Landes 1938, Leacock 1978, Brightman 1993a).

25. See, for example, Simmons (1945:63–65), Meigs (1976), Poole (1981), and Brown (1982).

4. Ancestors and Other Spirits

1. As early as the 1912 edition of *Notes and Queries on Anthropology*, R. R. Marett (1912:251) notes that "the two things which theorists in various ways distinguish as magic and religion, tend to run into one another for primitive folk"and therefore should as well for the anthropological observer who "wants to reproduce . . . their point of view."He calls these "magico-religious facts."

2. Armstrong (1928:126), in the introduction to his remarkably detailed discussion of the supernatural beings that populate Rossel Island, uses the term religion "for beliefs about and ritual directly connected with the gods."By distinguishing "gods"from other place spirits inhabiting *yaba*, or sacred places, he contrasts Rossel with "the Massim culture, which contains little religion in this sense of the term"(cf. Armstrong 1923–24:10). This is a false distinction based on Armstrong's (1928:126) concept of "a hierarchy of gods on Rossel and . . . a certain system both in the way these gods are related to one another and in their treatment by the natives."Armstrong also distinguishes the entities he labeled as gods by their remembered roles in the mythological past. But he notes that the spirit beings he calls gods reside in "sacred places," which he translates in his writings as yaba (Armstrong 1928:127).

3. But Alagh has a mother named Talak. She came from Ghalagh, a flat place south of Mt. Rio where there is a big stone called Emazowara, and she named her son after this place. Alagh and Talak belong to the Goriva clan, Witamo and Eurio to the Eniela (Guau) clan, and Rodyo and Ekuneada to the Magho (Mawa) clan. Egogona's clan is unspecified. The two versions of the creation myths of Vanatinai and the later story of Alagh's departure from the island were told to me by men and women respected for their knowledge of Vanatinai myths and customs who trace their origins to Ragule, a large village that formerly existed inland below Mt. Rio. The village name Ragule is said on Vanatinai to have been transformed, because of its importance in ancient times, into the Misima and Saisai names for the entire island, Tagula or Tagule. Ragule people are regarded throughout Vanatinai as the owners of all myths about Rio and its resident spirits and most knowledgeable about customs pertaining to them.

4. The people of the Saisai-speaking islands just north and south of Vanatinai, namely Panaman and Yeina (Piron) also say their dead go to Mt. Rio, but most of the other Saisai dead go to Hanhiewa, a sandy beach just opposite Sabara on the island of Hemenehai. Hemenahai is uninhabited but used by the Sabara people to fetch water and make gardens. Saisai dead may also go to a sandy islet on the barrier reef just north of Sabara. Two boats named Yamero and Maumau are called by the magic of a living villager who knows witchcraft to carry the spirits of the recently deceased to Hanhiewa. The spirits of the Nimowa and Panatinani (Joannet Island) dead go to the easternmost point of Panatinani, which is called Bwebweso, the same name as the mountain that is the home of the dead on Duau, or Normanby Island (cf. Fortune 1932:187, Róheim 1946:223). The spirits of the dead from Kuanak and the Misima-speaking islands to the north go to the summit of the tallest mountain on Misima, Oyatau, or to a cave called Bwanagum near Hinauta at the eastern tip of Misima. I have seen dozens of old, ochre-stained

human skulls amidst fragments of clay pots in a burial cave at this spot. The term for "spirit"in the Saisai language is *balome*, cognate to the *baloma* of the Trobriand region (cf. Malinowski 1916).

5. In 1978 and 1979 a man from Siagara Village on Misima Island, the same place where Buriga, the cargo prophet of the early 1940s came from, a man who was in fact Buriga's sister's son, claimed to have received a message from the spirits of the dead that the world would end in 1980 or 1981, and all the spirits of the dead would sail back to their islands with plenty of European cargo. I was told by Misima friends that he was collecting money from some of the Misima villagers. They would then number among the elect who would receive cargo from the spirits. Many Misimans thought he was a charlatan and spoke out forcefully against him. He found a number of adherents on the island of Kimuta, south of Misima. Kimuta people have little access to cash or to European goods compared to their Misima neighbors, and some of them had recently been jailed for scavenging the wreck of an Australian yacht which had gone onto the reef near the island. The people of Vanatinai did not believe in this prophet. A small number of Misimans continued to be adherents to these new prophecies into the late 1980s in spite of the missed deadline for the end of the world (Lepowsky 1989b).

6. Totemism has fascinated ethnologists since Victorian times, and disputes over its definition and its significance for understanding cognition and religious philosophy in non-Western cultures where it is prominent have continued into the late twentieth century (e.g., Lévi-Strauss 1963). The term itself comes from an Ojibwa word (Fogelson 1991). An early edition of the ethnological bible, *Notes and Queries on Anthropology*, defines it as "the belief in a connection existing between a group of human beings and a class of animals or plants called their *totem*"(Freire-Marreco 1912:249).

7. Armstrong (1928:38–39) describes the "plant"totem (his list includes sago, taro, and coconut as well as others untranslated) as the principal totem of Rossel, and the others as bird and fish. He describes an additional snake totem, though, as a "god."He says later that each clan has "an intimate relation to a certain god . . . the name of the god is given as if it were a species of snake"(Armstrong 1928:129). He was unable to trace any continuity between Rossel clans and those of Sudest, but he cautiously notes that his evidence was insufficient (Armstrong 1928:38). I was told by a number of Vanatinai people of clans found on both islands. In two cases origins on Rossel and migrations to Vanatinai by female ancestors were remembered.

8. The term in the Misima language is *silapa*.

9. See Mead (1933), Lawrence and Meggitt (1965) on masalai. Just as Vanatinai silava in the sea may take the shape of an octopus, floating log, or stone and try to capsize a boat and drown its crew, Róheim (1948:286) describes a belief at Duau in "moving stones"called *nuakekepaki* that run after canoes and try to overturn them. They are avoided by charming small stones and throwing them or other offerings into the sea. Malinowski (1922:332–333) describes several stones in the D'Entrecasteaux Archipelago that must be propitiated by kula voyagers to prevent disease or misfortune. One of these, Gurewaya, is said to have "a big snake . . . coiled on the top . . . which looks after the observance of the taboos, and in case of breach of any of them would send down sickness on them."Armstrong (1923–24:6), who cites this Trobriand belief and notes the existence of similar ones in the southern Massim, comments that "the resemblance of

such beliefs to Rossel beliefs is a resemblance only to isolated fragments torn from their setting in a systematic cosmology."

10. It lives in a creek called Henahua. The brown head is called Ligia and is the totem snake of the Guau clan. It may be found in Jone Creek on the south side of the island above Pamela Village. The black head is called Wanobwa. It is found in Enawa Creek on the north side and is the totem snake of the Magho (Mawa) clan. (The two clans have no other special relationship to one another.) If a person visits this area it will grow dark and rain heavily, causing flooding.

11. Two caves below Mt. Rio used by people hunting for wild pig are silava. One should be slept in only by single people and the other by married people, whether or not they are with their spouses. Otherwise, the offender will develop sores on the mouth. Similarly, if you speak while paddling across a certain bay near Jiema on the north coast, you will develop sores on the mouth. A silava named Lejimolua in the shape of a snake lives at Ngyangya, a place on the smaller mountain south of Mt. Rio above Bwamumu, and anyone who sleeps in this vicinity will be eaten by the snake. There is a silava stone underwater just off the mangrove-fringed shore at Seghe (East Point Village), a stone that is markedly different from surrounding rocks and reef. If you stand on it you will develop elephantiasis. A stream on the eastern section of Yeina (Piron Island) near the barrier reef north of Vanatinai is said to be silava. If you have had intercourse the night before and you cross the stream, or if you cross it after anyone who has, even if you were celibate, you will get elephantiasis. That silava is why there are so many elephantiasis cases on Yeina. The condition is a complication of filariasis, a parasitic disease transmitted by swamp-dwelling mosquitoes that is marked by grotesque swelling of the testicles and lymph nodes of the groin. The silava beliefs mirror the associations of the disease with the genital region and with prime mosquito habitat.

12. Bambagho also brought ome, or sandalwood, to Rossel, a form of wealth used for medicinal and magical purposes abundant on Rossel and now imported though ceremonial exchange to Vanatinai, where it is rare. Rossel is also the only island in the Massim where drums are not used, a detail of cultural distribution relevant to the version of the myth that has Bambagho leaving Goodenough Island to get away from the sound of drumming. She would then by implication still be unhappy on Vanatinai, where drumming is an integral part of mortuary ritual feasts.

13. Young (1983b:83, 1987:232–236, 1989a:130–131). A young woman from Goodenough living temporarily on Vanatinai told me a variant of this myth. There was a "special snake,"male, which used to live on a pile of flat stones that was the traditional meeting place in one Goodenough village. One woman fed it going there alone each day. After her two sons had grown up she took them with her one day, cautioning them not to frighten the snake. But when they saw it, they shouted in fear, and the snake left, going to Vanatinai and Rossel Islands. It took with it all the fish and valuable shells, and that is why the waters around Goodenough are so poor while those of Vanatinai and Rossel are very rich. The Goodenough version states explicitly that the snake is the bringer of valuables and that its being carelessly frightened away resulted in impoverishment of the seas, the source of both food and of shell for making valuables. The Goodenough people still hope, she said, for the snake to return with all the valuables it once took away. When it left it created off-shore oil deposits with its belly, a source of wealth explored in the 1970s by an American company. She also said a mountain on Goode-

nough near the snake's original home is called Tuage, the same name still borne by the peak under which the snake is said to have sheltered on Vanatinai. Perhaps this myth remembers an otherwise forgotten early migration from Goodenough to Vanatinai and Rossel, or at least an early exchange voyage.

14. Róheim (1950:202), Thune (1980), cited also in Young (1987:236–237). Maddock (1978:12) notes that Australian aboriginal beliefs in the rainbow serpent vary regionally, with the serpent seen as a male being in some areas and female in others. "As there are female as well as male rainbow serpents, the way stands open for the conception of a snake-like All-Mother."Rainbow serpent myths become increasingly important in northern and northeastern Australia (Mountford 1978:94).

15. The association of wealth items with excrement is also prominent in the southern Massim society of Duau. Róheim (1932:138) describes a ritual presentation of betel nut on Duau in which the presenters boastfully describe the highly valued nuts as "my excrement."In two Duau myths kula shell-disc necklaces and armshells are found in the belly of a female pig in place of excrement (Róheim 1950:195). The kula trade, called kune on Duau, is said to have originated when the culture hero Tauhau threw handfuls of pig innards toward Murua (Woodlark Island), which became shell currency necklaces (bagi) and armshells (*mwali*) (Róheim 1932:141). On the other side of the Pacific, in another region famous for its elaborate exchanges of wealth, Dundes (1979:401) reviews the ethnographic evidence to argue for "the association of wealth, in the form of copper, with feces"in the potlatches of Pacific Northwest Coast peoples from the Tlingit of Southeast Alaska to the Salish of Washington and British Columbia.

16. I was told by Vanatinai elders that this was a myth from Ware Island. Géza Róheim (1950:192) collected a version of this myth at Duau, or Normanby Island, in which the hero, called Matakapotaiataia, is said to have intercourse with his mother. Debbora Battaglia collected several variants of this myth at Sabarl, one in which the hero is male (1990:122) and another where the hero, Katatubwai, is a girl dressed in a male pubic leaf who spears the menacing giant. She later reverts to female dress when instructed to by her mother's brother (1990:50–52).

17. The term mumuga is found in other Austronesian languages of southeastern Papua. In Duau, for example, it means myth (Róheim 1948:304).

18. Seligman (1910:646) noted eighty years ago "the essential similarity of men and animals and perhaps even trees"in Massim cultures.

19. A more elaborate set of magical customs called *tara* is unique to Vanatinai and is rare nowadays. Members of the exchange expedition prepare by fasting, purging with seawater, and eating only ginger and coconut. Their skin becomes bright and dazzles their hosts, making them dizzy with desire. But the visitors remain celibate during the journey unless male youths are instructed to seduce local women to change their luck if the party was not previously successful enough in obtaining valuables. A youth in the visiting party sits on the ground in front of the host's house with a bottle of bunama, in a basket secured to a sleeping mat, on his lap while the expedition leader delivers a ritual persuasive speech, or tara. Members of the host hamlet who have assembled to listen then give valuables to their personal exchange partners. A party of twenty men and women from Rehua visited most Vanatinai settlements in 1978 to give tara. They were especially successful in gaining valuables.

20. Mbasiri may be the same as Mbasi, the supernatural progenitor of the Rossel Islanders who was summoned to that island by its creator, Wonajö, from Sudest Island (Armstrong 1923–24:104, 1928:126–28). Armstrong (1923–24:3) relates that Mbasi, who brought the sun, moon, pig, dog, taro and sailing canoe to Rossel, was converted into a rock that lies on the reef at the east end of the island, "some little way from the shore, almost completely covered at high water."His 1928 map of Rossel Island yaba shows Mbasi's rock located between Jinjo and East Point, just as Vanatinai people say (1928:8, 144). On Vanatinai Mbasiri is remembered for having taken the present-day Rossel Island language with him when he migrated from Vanatinai to Rossel. Armstrong (1923–24:2) also remarks that "Mbasi is known on Sudest as the brother of Tamudulele, the most important figure in the mythology of at least the more easterly of the Southern Massim." I was unable to confirm this relationship although I inquired of Vanatinai people.

21. This is reminiscent of Reo Fortune's (1932) report of Dobu garden magic in which yams are convinced to walk from their home garden to that of the magician.

22. During the first month or two after the yams are planted you sometimes hear the people of Vanatinai calling to their yams in a loud ululating cry that echoes from the mountains. They are trying to "wake up the yams"and call them to come up and grow. This time of year is called *zogatine*, or "cover inside,"for the yam plants are underground. Vanatinai people say garden magic on Misima is far less elaborate, although Misima is known for its fine gardens. The Misimans stake their yams, but the Vanatinai people never do. Misimans always fence their gardens to keep out marauding wild pigs, but this is rarely done on Vanatinai, where pigs often destroy gardens. The Vanatinai people rely more on magic and the Misimans on particular gardening techniques for good harvests. The Misimans practice more intensive horticulture on that densely populated island. Vanatinai reliance on cultivation versus the gathering of wild foods has increased markedly over the last fifty years (Lepowsky 1985a:111–113, 1991b:220–222).

23. One technique of weather magic is called *vetha witawita*, meaning "small pouch with something inside," such as is used to hold a daveri, or orange shell currency piece. In this case there is a relic inside, some hair, a tooth, or a piece of skull. This small pouch is bespelled and placed in a basket on a canoe in order to blow in rain. In another kind of rain magic, *ghava*, river water is poured over round river stones and covered with leaves to the accompaniment of a spell.

24. Seligman (1910:655) records a belief at Wagawaga that a white-skinned supernatural named Tamudurere lives under the sea at the head of Milne Bay and is in charge of the ghosts of the dead. Róheim (1948:282–283) reports that on Duau Tau Mudurere, whose name means "man's pubic part tattooed," is the "husband of all the witches," who bring him human beings to eat. He is also "the chief of the underworld."Martha Macintyre (1987:215) finds similar beliefs about the powerful culture-hero called Taumudulele on the island of Tubetube. He creates, transforms, and vanquishes enemies. His name means "he-who-tattoos-female pudenda,"a female puberty rite banned by missionaries. He seduces human women, who then give him witchcraft victims in exchange for his garden magic, and he thus gains the most powerful witches as wives.

25. See, for example, Chowning (1979), Keesing (1982), Godelier (1986), Stephen (1987), Lindstrom (1990); cf. Foucault (1978, 1980).

5. Sorcerers and Witches

1. A few women on other islands as well have become known as sorcerers. For example, in the 1920s women were occasionally taught sorcery techniques on Normanby Island (Róheim 1950:207), and some Rossel Island women knew one type of sorcery (Armstrong 1928:174–175).

2. On the sorcerer as big man see Forge (1970), Marwick (1970), Zelenietz (1981), Chowning (1987), Bowden (1987). On sorcery and chiefs see Malinowski (1926), Stephen (1987b).

3. Michele Stephen (1987b) reports similar attitudes in Mekeo, where sorcerers and others know poisons, but they are considered a crude and unsophisticated mode of attack, and sorcery techniques are based on destructive magic.

4. Patrol reports are often unsigned by the writer. In some of these cases I have been able to identify the author through references by a patrol officer to an earlier patrol and the report that resulted. In most cases that I am able to document, a different officer has gone on patrol each time, testimony to the lack of continuity in administration in one of the most remote districts of Papua.

5. Heat is associated with sorcery in other parts of New Guinea, including nearby Rossel Island, where fasting produces heat, which Armstrong (1928:173) equates with *mana*. Reo Fortune (1932:161–162) describes the actions of a Dobu sorcerer at work using techniques that seem identical to some of those found fifty years later on Vanatinai: "Y drank a great quantity of salt water to parch his throat and keep himself safe from swallowing his own black spells with his saliva. He chewed great quantities of ginger and *gau* to make his body hot and heat up the spells to an effective killing temperature." *Logau*, or one who chews, refers to invisibility magic on both Dobu and Vanatinai (Fortune 1932:162). Michele Stephen (1987b:60–61) reports some similar practices among the sorcerers of Mekeo, including celibacy, seclusion, fasting, chewing ginger, and avoiding cold foods like fish, in order to induce heat and thus supernatural power. Fitz Poole (1987:152–153, 170–174) discusses ginger as a "hot sacred substance"and its uses in male initiation to induce a state of ritual heat among the Bimin Kuskusmin. Although there has been little research on this topic, it seem quite likely that ginger has psychoactive properties, especially when ingested in large quantities while chanting repetitive magical spells, fasting, and/or purging with salt water (cf. Duve 1980). Géza Róheim (1948:300) observed that on Duau (Normanby Island), which is said to be the origin of many types of Vanatinai sorcery techniques, "the witches like the cold, and the barau like the hot, things." The term *barau* means sorcerer in the Duau language and is occasionally used on Vanatinai as a loan word, where it is sometimes pronounced "balau."Martha Macintyre (1987:216–217) records the association of witchcraft with coldness on Tubetube.

6. One particular type of sorcery involving the personal leavings of the victim is called *nakinaki*. The practitioner places the leavings on top of his house where the smoke from his fire will envelope them after he has bespelled them. The victim will get thin, waste away for two or three years, and then die. Nakinaki is one of the indigenous names for tuberculosis. If the sorcerer places the leavings in the fire the victim will die right away. This form of sorcery may be reversed by putting the leavings in a cup of water and saying the appropriate magic. One man told me that only men know nakinaki because a woman would not look after the leavings properly but would allow them to

fall into the fire. His wife disagreed and said that a woman would not want to do such a thing.

7. Róheim (1948:281) writes of similar cannibalistic witches' feasts on Duau and Macintyre (1987:215–216) on Tubetube.

8. The flying witches of the Trobriand Islands (Malinowski 1922:244–248), Duau (Róheim 1948:287), and Tubetube (Macintyre 1987:216) are responsible for shipwrecks as well, hovering over the sea and magically befuddling sailors. Shipwrecks in the Louisiade Archipelago are also blamed on place spirits, or silava.

9. This is probably the incident discussed in a patrol report dated 1952–53. The officer writes, "Recently (about two weeks before this patrol) a MOTORINA canoe was lost and all lives lost. It is alleged that while search canoes were out one MOTORINA woman said to four MISIMA visitors—'Why waste their time looking for the canoe and survivors? I know that they are all dead because I made "pourri-pourri" against them.' "

10. Similarly, Róheim (1948:287, 305) reports that at Duau witches are called "our mothers,"attack their close kin, and need the permission of a victim's mothers or sisters to attack and kill. Otherwise these women will retaliate by killing and eating relatives of the offending witch. Macintyre (1987:217) writes of Tubetube women who retaliate to offenses by killing their own grandchildren with witchcraft.

11. For discussions of African witchcraft and social life see Evans-Pritchard (1937), Nadel (1952), Douglas (1963), Turner (1964), Simmons (1971). Simmons (1980) uses the rate of witchcraft accusations as an index to the social disruption caused by contact with the outside world and the resulting cultural changes in Badyaranke villages in West Africa. It is worth noting in this context that the area of Vanatinai with the worst reputation as the home of active sorcerers, a reputation that has been noted in government reports for at least several decades, is the north central coast, the place where goldmining activities and the encroachment of Europeans have in the past been the most extensive.

12. Cf. de Beauvoir (1953), Ortner (1974), Rosaldo and Atkinson (1975), and Sanday (1981:5).

6. The Living, the Dead, and Relations of Value

1. See, for example, Fortune (1932), Leach and Leach (1983), Munn (1986), and Damon (1990) on kula and Fortune (1932) and Damon and Wagner (1989) on mortuary ritual.

2. See Campbell (1983), Damon (1983a), Munn (1983), Weiner (1983), Macintyre (1983b) on the kula ring. Men from Ware Island, part of the kula ring, whom I met on exchange visits to Grass Island (Wanim), 175 miles to the southeast of their home island, told me how they had taken armshells and necklaces in a clockwise direction on expeditions by sailing canoe from Ware to Normanby (Duau) and Dobu Islands and obtained both armshells and necklaces there (Lepowsky 1983). Similarly, people from Panaeati Island told me that armshells and necklaces flow in both directions between Panaeati and Woodlark, both of which are part of the kula ring depicted by Malinowski.

3. See Berde (1983), Battaglia (1983b, 1990), and Liep (1983, 1989). Orange shell currency pieces, called daveri on Vanatinai and ndap on Rossel, circulate primarily on those two islands, according to quite different rules of ceremonial exchange (cf. Arm-

strong 1928, Liep 1983 for Rossel). They began to be used occasionally as an additional valuable in East Calvados mortuary ritual beginning about 1960 (Lepowsky 1983).
They are not found at all in the islands farther to the north and west.

4. These are also cognates to the kura of Gawa, kun of Muyuw (Woodlark), and both
the kune of Dobu and Tubetube and une of Duau briefly mentioned in chapter 4 (Malinowski 1922, Munn 1983, Fortune 1932, Macintyre 1983, Róheim 1954).

5. Malinowski notes that women from Kiriwina, Kitava, Iwa, and Gawa Islands occasionally sailed on overseas kula expeditions but did not participate in exchanges (Malinowski 1922:280; see also Munn 1986:292 for Gawa). Munn (1986:282) mentions that
"women participate directly in kula on some of the other islands south and east of
Gawa."Malinowski describes exchanges of kula valuables by the wives of a chief on Kiriwina to individuals on the same island and the custom of a man's sending his wife with
a kula valuable to an exchange partner in a neighboring village in southern Kiriwina or
on Vakuta. He also remarks that "in Dobu, the wife, or the sister of a man, is always
credited with a great influence over his Kula decisions"and must be appealed to by a visiting Trobriand man through oratory, gifts, and special magic (Malinowski 1922:
280–281). Modern researchers have documented the participation of a woman from
Kitava in the most important set of interisland kula partnerships (Damon 1980:275,
Scoditti 1983:255–256), although her father acts for her in overseas kula expeditions.

6. Big women have also been reported among the Kove and Kaulong of New Britain
and the Nagovisi of Bougainville. There have been female chiefs, or hereditary leaders,
among the Mekeo of the south Papuan coast and the Trobriand Islanders (Chowning
1979:79–81).

7. Elsewhere in the Pacific women are actively involved in exchange of wealth as
well as its production. On the Micronesian island of Belau (Palau) tortoiseshell trays are
a form of female wealth that older women give to their matrilineal heirs during mortuary exchanges (Parmentier 1985). Belauan women also ceremonially exchange
money, pigs, and foodstuffs (Margold and Bellorado 1985). Annette Weiner's experience with women's wealth in the Trobriand Islands led her to investigate female forms
of wealth in other societies, particularly objects made by women of cloth or fiber, and
their cultural consequences (see especially Weiner 1992). She reminds us of the numerous intriguing references to mats woven by women as items of exchange in the early
anthropological literature on the New Hebrides and the Solomon Islands (Weiner
1986:99), the importance of finely woven mats made by women in Samoan ceremonial exchange and politics, earlier documented by Margaret Mead (1930; Weiner
1986:104–105, 1989), and Tongan women's production of *tapa* cloth for ceremonial
exchange (Weiner 1986:99–100; see Gailey 1980 and 1987). "Fibrous wealth," in
Weiner's (1986) phrase, such as mats, cloth, or baskets, produced and often exchanged
by women, may be less obvious to an outside observer as significant objects of value in
exchange than harder and more durable goods.

In Africa Hoffer (1971:174) notes that both women and men who seek political
influence among the Mende of Sierra Leone "give gifts to supporters, the gift being a
tangible symbol of a special relationship in which the political aspirant may later ask for
a reciprocal favor." Baule women of the Ivory Coast traveled long distances to trade
cloth they had woven for gold and captives (Etienne 1980). Wiessner describes the *hxaro*
gift exchange relations of the !Kung in which women and men participate with partners

of both sexes. Items exchanged include meat, women's aprons, and "beads, arrows ostrich eggshells, clothing, blankets, bowl, pots, etc. . . . the bulk of a !Kung's material wealth"(Wiessner 1982:70). The giver expects an equivalent present in future or as needed (Wiessner 1982, 1990). In North America women as well as men are involved in accumulating and distributing valuables (sheep, goats, cash, store-bought goods, and other items) at various Navaho curing ceremonies (e.g., Reichard 1934:241, 1969:122–23). Women may take a prominent role in potlatching activities among the Gitksan (Adams 1973:57–65), Haida (Barnett 1968:70–71, Rosman and Rubel 1971: 60–62), Kwakiutl (Barnett 1968:70, Drucker and Heizer 1967:105–107), Nootka (Rosman and Rubel 1971:94–100), Tlingit (Barnett 1968:70), and Tsimshian (Rosman and Rubel 1971:24–25). Women among the Tutchone, Tagish, and other northern Athapaskan groups of the Yukon and Alaska host and participate in memorial potlatches and those following a girl's puberty seclusion (e.g., Cruikshank 1990:35–36, 91–93, 312–314). Drucker and Heizer cite a Kwakiutl who comments that "the chiefs did not like to have women [take important roles] in the potlatch"(1967:107), but according to Barnett (1968: 71), among the Haida "it is the wife who always gives one of the two most important types; namely that at the building of a house . . . the women participate on an equal footing with the men. They also have potlatches of their own among all the groups from the Tsimshian to the Salish. They follow those of the men. The host's wife is the donor and she distributes spoons, dishes and other household articles among the women."Tlingit women are and were active potlatch participants, although men of rank have the most prominent role, particularly among central and southern Tlingit (de Laguna 1972, Kan 1989:214–215, 235–236, 342). When Chilkat Tlingit men traveled to the interior of northwest British Columbia and the southern Yukon to trade with local Athapascans for furs, their host's wife would give the Tlingit visitor "moccasin boots and a caribou-skin shirt"and "she usually gave him a robe of ermine skins for his wife"(Olson 1936:213). When thirty-four Kwakiutl were arrested at Alert Bay in 1922 by the Canadian government for defying the law against potlatching, their number included six women, including a grandmother, some of whom served jail sentences (Cole and Chaikin 1990:118–123). Women's exchange activities are not limited to societies with subsistence or barter economies. Agricultural produce, handicrafts, and other commodities are primarily marketed by women in many parts of the world, particularly in West Africa, the Caribbean, Latin America, and Southeast Asia (e.g., Mintz 1971, Babb 1989).

8. Recent researchers in the northern and western Massim have described the *kitomu* (the Trobriand term; there are cognates in other languages), a kula armshell or necklace that is diverted from interisland circulation in a counterclockwise or clockwise direction and used by its temporary owner to satisfy personal ceremonial obligations in the Trobriands (Weiner 1976:129, Campbell 1983) or on Woodlark Island (Muyuw), Gawa, Normanby Island (Duau), or Tubetube (Damon 1983a, Munn 1983, Thune 1983, Macintyre 1983).

9. White (1893) describes "Native Money" during the period just before and after the British colonial conquest:

A string of red native beads about a yard long, with shell appendages called teeni, is their most valued money, one of which will purchase a canoe. The tomahawk stone is another valuable kind of money, but not so much as the beads, and different sized stones have different values, some of the small thick kind being hardly worth anything. They are also certain shells which they use as a medium of exchange, but these again are of less value than the stones.

Vanatinai elders whom I queried were unfamiliar with the word *teeni* (written as *tani* by one contemporary British colonial officer). The report that a yard-long string of shell-disc necklace "with appendages," a recognizable description of a bagi, could purchase a canoe (type unspecified) corroborates local oral histories of substantial inflation in the number of ceremonial valuables necessary to purchase canoes and satisfy obligations at mortuary feasts since the coming of Europeans (Lepowsky 1983).

10. Fortune (1932:209) and Malinowski (1935I:455–456) also wrote of exchange as peacemaking or a substitute for war on Dobu and Kiriwina, as have, more recently, Young (1971) and Macintyre (1983) for Goodenough and Tubetube.

11. The existence of the Dawin site was confirmed to me by a woman friend from Samarai who is active in exchange and who recognizes the blades' human origin. Dawin blades frequently circulate in the islands near Samarai.

12. The best daveri have the patina of extreme age and/or a deep orange-red color. Some of the ones most highly valued on Vanatinai, but not Rossel, are also long. The term daveri is sometimes used as well as a generic term for ceremonial valuables. Other kinds of valuables are either rare or no longer in circulation, including certain colors and thicknesses of shell-disc necklaces, shell-disc belts, cassowary bone lime spatulas, and the shell-decorated wooden objects called dolphin's teeth (Lepowsky 1983).

13. See Seligman (1910:607–637), Malinowski (1929:36–37, 159–160), Fortune (1932:193–200), Weiner (1976:61–120), Damon and Wagner 1989, and Battaglia 1990 for other discussions of the ethnography of mortuary ritual in Massim cultures. See Powdermaker (1933), Goodenough (1971), Iamo (1981) for coastal Melanesia, Crystal (1971) and Huntington and Metcalf (1979) for Sulawesi and Borneo, and Bloch (1971) and Huntington and Metcalf (1979) for Madagascar.

14. Peter Lawrence states that "throughout [Papua New Guinea] all ceremonies honouring the dead stress male dominance, although, as always, there is variation." He cites the Trobriand Islands and the Rai Coast of the northeastern mainland as areas where "women enjoy some degree of equality with men and have a definite, if less prominent, role in ritual life" (1973:216).

15. Even in those Massim societies where most feasting is not connected with death, such as Goodenough Island (Young 1971a: 232–233), ceremonial exchanges stress inter-lineage or affinal competition with each side striving to outgive the other (or the other's previous performance) and demonstrate its wealth, power, and generosity. Affinal exchanges with a competitive edge are a major feature of mortuary feasts in the Trobriand Islands (Weiner 1976: 61–120), Dobu (Fortune 1932:195–200), Duau (Normanby Island; Róheim 1932:124), the Bartle Bay area north of Milne Bay (Seligman 1910:636), Wagawaga on Milne Bay (Seligman 1910:620–621), Tubetube Island (Seligman 1910:624–625), and Panaeati Island in the Misima language area (Berde 1974:169–175), among other parts of the Massim. Mortuary ritual is far less elaborate on Rossel Island (Yela) than in the Massim, and bridewealth payments instead receive a much greater cultural emphasis. But certain mortuary customs on Yela are strongly reminiscent of those of Vanatinai. For example, Armstrong (1928:105) notes that a widow on Yela wears a string around her neck as a token of mourning until a feast is held at

which she is ritually fed (he does not describe how) by a member of the deceased's clan. This resembles the ritual feeding in the Vanatinai *jivia* feast. Liep (1983) describes mortuary payments on Yela made about a week after a death by the subclan of the spouse to both that of the deceased and that of the deceased's father. The latter transaction is perhaps analogous to the payments of valuables to the tau, or patrilateral cross-cousin of the deceased, on Vanatinai. The Yela mortuary payments are said by Liep to consist of greenstone axe blades, shell necklaces, ceremonial lime spatulas and ndap, the orange shell currency called daveri on Vanatinai. These same valuables figure prominently in Vanatinai mortuary ritual, particularly in the final feast, or zagaya.

16. The rigorous mourning enjoined upon a surviving spouse is linked to the belief in ritual pollution resulting from close contact with death (cf. Hertz 1907:38). But the survivor must endure stringent mourning taboos for a period lasting from one to twenty or more years to demonstrate that she or he did not cause the death by means of sorcery or witchcraft. Malinowski (1929:158) mentions similar Trobriand taboos prohibiting a widow from eating with her hands or leaving the house until a feast is made.

17. Armstrong (1928) reports a similar custom was formerly practiced on Rossel Island after the death of a "chief."

18. Polygynists may sleep with their other wives after the death of one wife, as long as she is not a kinswoman of the deceased.

19. In the three cases out of eighteen I recorded in which it was a kinsperson rather than an affine or father's child (including child of a father's brother, also a father in local kinship reckoning) who hosted a final feast, the owner of the feast was either brother or lineage brother to the (two female and one male) deceased.

20. The importance of the tau is in many ways parallel to the importance of matrilateral kin such as the mother's brother in social relations in patrilineal horticultural societies, both in New Guinea and in other parts of the world (e.g., Radcliffe-Brown and Forde 1950, Radcliffe-Brown 1952, Strathern 1972). Lowie (1919) pointed out the correspondence between the roles of paternal relatives in matrilineal societies and those of maternal relatives in many patrilineal societies more than seventy years ago.

21. A similar mechanism operates in the hagali of the Misima language area islands (Berde 1974:176 and author's fieldnotes) and in the East Calvados mortuary feasts (Battaglia 1990 and author's fieldnotes).

22. See Lepowsky (1989a). The valuables at the zagaya of a female deceased went three times to tau who were father's sister's sons, to a husband (from a clan brother), to a son, and to a husband's sister's son.

7. Fruit of the Dead

1. The spiritual essence of the mourners is captured in the glass and presented symbolically to the kin of the deceased in the way that valuables removed from a corpse remain with the spirit on its journey to the land of the dead. Similarly, one term for taking a photograph means "to take your spirit." Witches steal reflections of their victims in pools, mirrors (traditionally stone bowls filled with water), or photographs.

2. Female affinal mourners continue to wear the long mourning skirt and male affinal mourners keep their beards and wear old clothes, except in the case of the death of a child, when no further mortuary observances are made.

3. The term jivia, or "break,"referring to the sharing by the kin and the affines of the deceased of sago pudding (*moni* or *kiowak*) and roasted sago loaf or vegetables boiled in coconut cream, thus has a meaning similar both literally and symbolically to the English expression "breaking bread together,"the classic mark of friendship and trust. It is also significant that the valuable most closely associated with the ritual is the gile, or gold-lip pearl shell, a decorated version of the customary eating implement. The social death of mourning is most vividly signified by blackening the body, *ghan nyiba* (eating charcoal). Róheim (1950:204) reports that in parts of Normanby Island the corpse's belly is (or presumably was) cooked in oil with taro to make a pudding called *mona*, then eaten by distant members of the deceased's clan. This literal or symbolic endocannibalism using mona, a cognate to the moni or sago pudding of Vanatinai, is an analogous eating of the dead in mortuary ritual.

4. Kaikai and sago pudding are also essential as part of the final feast, the zagaya. Kaikai in Neo-Melanesian Pidgin is the noun "food"or the verb "to eat,"borrowed from Polynesian languages. People on Vanatinai say that the word kaikai is not derived from either Neo-Melanesian or Vanatinai Pidgin (Vanga Lumo) but is an ancient term in their language referring both to the wild legume and to the prepared food. Kaikai and sago, along with yams, were the principal staple foods on the island until the introduction of new root crop cultigens in the past century (Lepowsky 1985b, 1991). In many cultures ancient foods that are no longer commonly eaten and traditional methods of food preparation find a central place in ceremonial life (cf. Foster and Anderson 1978:269–270). This is true on Vanatinai for sago pudding, kaikai, and the custom of roasting food in a stone oven, less common in the past few generations as an increased volume of interisland trade has allowed Brooker Island clay cooking pots to become more plentiful in the households of Vanatinai.

5. For example, Taradi had gotten a certain tobotobo from a clan brother of the Grass Island woman who would "eat the feast."Custom forbids him to present it to the same lineage during the zagaya ritual, so he was appreciative when another woman offered him her own tobotobo. He exchanged it for the one he had gotten at Grass Island and later ritually presented his new one to the Grass Island woman. People often obtain a superior valuable in these cases at the expense of the host, who is supposed to agree to all reasonable exchanges. These exchanges are private and backstage, not part of public ritual in the hamlet clearing.

6. In 1978 one kina, which is Papua New Guinean paper currency, equaled about $1.30. A two-kina note is considered to be the equivalent of a daveri. Traditionalists frown on such a substitution and on other replacements of customary forms of wealth with store-bought wealth, such as a one kilo block of trade twist tobacco for a pig, or industrially made spoons for pearl shell spoons. The use of store-bought cloth and dishes is more common in East Calvados mortuary ritual than on Vanatinai, and I was told that such items had been included because the woman who ate the feast was from the East Calvados. The Vanatinai conservatism about substitutions of new forms of wealth in ritual exchanges is an interesting contrast to the potlatches of the Pacific Northwest Coast and a major difference between the way the two forms of ritual wealth distributions have been affected since contact with Europeans (Lepowsky 1991).

7. Less commonly the final feast is called either moni or kiowak, synonyms in Vanatinai dialects for the pudding of sago and green coconut that is central to the ritual, bigibi-

gi, or "things," *ngabubobo* (bobo means pig), or *mwaguvajo* ("mwagu goes over," referring to the mwagumwagu, the key ritual event). Zagaya and thagaya are cognates to the terms *sagali* in the languages of the Trobriand Islands (Malinowski 1929:223, 253, 347–348; Weiner 1976:62) and Dobu Island (Fortune 1932:199), hagali in the Misima language area islands (Berde 1974:167 and author's fieldnotes), and *sagaya* or *segaiya* in the Saisai language of the East Calvados Islands (Battaglia 1990 and author's fieldnotes). Sagali in the Trobriands refers to a ceremonial distribution of food, not necessarily a mortuary distribution. In the other islands these terms refer to major rituals held to commemorate individual deaths and thereby lift mourning restrictions from certain categories of survivors. The nature of the mortuary ritual and the customs that comprise this memorial feast vary significantly among the islands of the Massim.

8. The necessity of accumulating a surplus of food for the ritual distributions and the feeding of feast guests, often for many weeks, and the great shame of not having enough food to feed people generously and still have some left over, are another way in which zagaya resembles potlatch.

9. I never encountered Rossel Islanders at Saisai feasts. People in the communities of eastern Vanatinai, such as Rehua, Buyawe, and Seghe, told me that a generation ago it was far more common for Rossel people to sail to these hamlets to attend zagaya, because there used to be a much higher rate of intermarriage between the two islands, particularly at Seghe, or East Point Village. The number of Rossel sailing canoes declined sharply during the 1950s and as the Rossel people married at Vanatinai died their numbers were no longer replaced by young people who had met their spouses at zagaya where Rossel Islanders had sailed to Vanatinai to assist their affines.

10. Vanatinai people say that the open, though ritualized, aggression of muli presentations found at Saisai and Misima language area feasts, such as the ritual dance of *kalehe*, where affines who carry in their pigs and valuables mock throwing a spear (a mango tree branch, kalehe) at the feast house or tearing it down, is too dangerous for Vanatinai, where it would enrage a sorcerer into killing them in revenge (on kalehe see Seligman 1910 for the Milne Bay region, Battaglia 1990 for Sabarl, author's fieldnotes for Grass Island, Panatinani, and Panabari). But affinal processions at Vanatinai feasts have a challenging and almost contemptuous tone, reminiscent of descriptions of potlatch prestations. At one feast I saw four men, the host's in-laws, carry in an enormous, tusked boar on two crossed poles as two young men stood on the boar's belly, one blowing the conch shell that signals a muli. They were part of a long procession of men and women carrying yams, sago, axe blades, and several other pigs. Mortuary ritual throughout the Massim are attempts to contain conflicts generated by death by channeling and ritualizing aggression. Vanatinai feast participants may also challenge affinal or other exchange partners, present or absent, with the uraura. This is a formal, ritualized speech, often called loudly in the middle of the night, to the accompaniment of a lime spatula beating on a gourd lime pot, demanding valuables in compensation for the generosity of the speaker's past gifts. The person challenged hears about this with amazing speed, even if she or he is on another island at the time, and must either rise to the occasion or face public shame.

11. In the East Calvados and Misima areas the ritual foods, yams, and valuables presented in mortuary rituals are even more explicitly likened to the corpse, as discussed at length by Battaglia (1990) for Sabarl in the East Calvados. Berde (1974:172–179) records

that on Panaeati, in the Misima language area, a sago pudding called *moni nova* (prepared differently from the Vanatinai moni or kiowak sago pudding) is presented by female affines of the deceased to the deceased's father's sister's children. It is topped with pieces of roasted sago called *tomati piawina*, or "strips of the corpse's flesh."

12. Jane Collier and Michelle Rosaldo (1981:275–276) find, to their surprise, a lack of ritual emphasis on female fertility and maternity in hunter-gatherer and hunter-horticulturalist societies. They say women's rituals "have much less to do with the creation of life than with health and sexual pleasure."Vanatinai ritual roles exclusive to women contradict this finding.

13. See for example Berde (1974) on Panaeati and Battaglia (1990) on Sabarl. Even though mortuary ritual on Rossel Island is far less elaborate than in the Massim proper, mortuary exchanges emphasize the payment of valuables by the deceased's matrilineage to that of his father (Liep 1989). There is a neat reversal of these kinship roles on patrilineal Goodenough Island in the northern Massim. There the mother's patrilineage "eats the dead"in mortuary ritual exchanges as compensation for the loss of the deceased's mother on her marriage (Young 1989b).

14. For example, affinal presentations of yams that include women are central to mortuary ritual in Dobu (Fortune 1932:199–200), Fergusson (Chowning 1989: 114–116), and Tubetube (Macintyre 1989:143–144). In the hagali mortuary ritual of Misima (author's fieldnotes) and Panaeati (Berde 1974:170–171), affinal women present fine, perfectly arranged baskets of yams to the deceased's father's sister's children. Ritual yam exchanges are also more highly developed in the East Calvados. In the analogue to the mwagumwagu ritual there must be a pyramid of fine seed yams plus a pot of leaf-wrapped, partially steamed yams presented in addition to the pot of yams boiled in coconut cream, used on Vanatinai too, in addition to a pot of sago pudding (author's fieldnotes; cf. Battaglia 1990).

8. Gender and Power

1. See, for example, Rogers (1975) and Collier and Rosaldo (1981) on ideal versus real gender relations. Ortner (1984) summarizes approaches to practice; cf. Bourdieu (1977).

2. Meigs (1976), Kelly (1976), Poole (1981, 1985), Herdt (1981, 1982b).

3. The dualism of Vanatinai gender symbolism is significantly less even than in other matrilineal Massim cultures (cf. Berde 1974, Kahn 1986, Battaglia 1990). On two small islands relatively near to Vanatinai, Sabarl and Panaeati, men are associated with the sea and sailing canoes, constructed at Panaeati, and women with the land and gardens to a greater and more exclusive degree than on Vanatinai. Women are more strongly associated with certain kinds of valuables, such as yams and skirts, and men not only with canoes but stone axe blades and shell-disc necklaces. Battaglia (1983a, 1990) documents extensive dualistic gender symbolism in Sabarl views of the environment and of ceremonial valuables. Although Sabarl and Panaeati have strong tendencies toward gender equality, there seems to be a greater degree of gender asymmetry than on Vanatinai, as expressed in ideologies and the valuing of men's and women's productions. Also, as I noted in chapter 3, while postmarital residence on Vanatinai is bilocal, and the husband moves in with his wife and her parents at the beginning of a marriage, deferring to his

affines and giving brideservice, the ideal pattern on both Panaeati and Sabarl is virilocal residence, with the woman moving to her husband's place (Berde 1974, Battaglia 1990).

4. Another example is the young woman who complained at the feast, described in chapter 7, when the men did their ritual bathing upstream from the women. Women and men generally bathe in the same pools, either in family or same-sex groups.

5. On warfare and male superiority see Divale and Harris (1976), Friedl (1975), Harris (1974), Langness (1967), Whyte (1978), and Sanday (1981:164). On male absence and female autonomy see Schlegel (1977), Wallace (1972), and Fogelson (1990).

6. See, for example, Gailey (1987) on Tonga, Silverblatt (1987) on the Inca, Kan (1989) on Tlingit, and Linnekin (1990) on Hawaii.

7. Compare Weiner (1980), Damon (1983b), Battaglia (1985, 1990), and Strathern (1988).

8. The emphasis on feeding the father in mortuary ritual is even more pronounced on Panaeati (Berde 1974) and Sabarl (Battaglia 1985, 1990). On both islands a widow and her children, generally living virilocally, try to gain permanent rights to hamlet and garden lands of the father's matrilineage through their ritual work and gifts of valuables. Battaglia (1990:103–104) finds that most land owned by Sabarl people is actually acquired from the father's matrilineage, usually from father to children, not inherited matrilineally, in a quasi-patrilineal inheritance system.

9. The appropriateness of using the big man institution to define Melanesia versus a Polynesia characterized by chiefdoms, the relationship of big men to social equality, rank, and stratification, and the interactions of this form of leadership with colonialism and modernization are central issues in recent anthropological writings on big men (e.g., Brown 1987, Godelier 1986, Sahlins 1989, A. Strathern 1987, Thomas 1989, Lederman 1991). I discuss the implications of the Vanatinai case of the giagia at greater length in Lepowsky (1990b).

10. See, for example, Clifford (1983), Clifford and Marcus (1986), and Marcus and Fischer (1986) on representations. In this book I have followed my own cultural premises and not those of Vanatinai by publicly attributing thoughts, motives, and feelings to others and by trying to find the shapes in a mass of chaotic and sometimes contradictory statements and actions. But my Vanatinai friends say, characteristically, that my writing is "something of mine"—my business.

Glossary

Unless otherwise indicated all words are in Vanga Vanatinai—also called Vanatinai ghalingaji, the language of Vanatinai (Sudest Island)—and in the Vanga Vanazhibwa dialect, spoken in the southwestern portion of the island—literally, "the language of the place of zh,"referring to one of its most distinctive phonemes. Other words are in Vanga Lumo, literally, "the language of Europeans,"or Vanatinai Pidgin, and Papuan Pidgin, closely related to Vanga Lumo, a largely extinct pidgin formerly spoken intermittently along the south coast of New Guinea from the Gulf of Papua to the islands off the southeastern tip of the mainland that has contributed vocabulary words to various local languages. Also included in the glossary are words from Neo-Melanesian Pidgin, or Tok Pisin, one of the national languages of Papua New Guinea along with Motu and English, spoken mainly in northern Papua New Guinea and the Highlands.

Terms from many languages spoken elsewhere in the islands off eastern New Guinea are known on Vanatinai and defined here. They include words from Kilivila, the language of Kiriwina, largest of the Trobriand Islands; Duau, the language of eastern Normanby Island; Dobu, spoken on Dobu Island, adjacent small islands and nearby parts of coastal Fergusson and Normanby Islands; Ware and Tubetube, dialects of the language spoken in the Bwanabwana region or the Engineer Group and Ware Island; Pana Saisai, the language of the East Calvados Islands; Pana Misima, the language of Misima, Panaeati and the West Calvados Islands; and Yeletnye, the language of Rossel Island.

Yeletnye is in a Papuan or non-Austronesian linguistic phylum. All the other languages, including the pidgins, have an Austronesian grammar.

Glossary

Alagh	also known as Ghalagh; literally, to enlarge; male spirit driven from Mt. Rio who departed for the land of Europeans taking forms of wealth now associated with Europeans
amalaisali	old man; male elder; cognate to Vanga Lumo olman, from the English old man
amalá na	that man there; used to refer to or address a male affine
asiara	champion warrior
bagi	necklaces made from perforated discs of shell, often reddish in color; usually from the bivalves Chama pacifica or from Spondylus species; the most valuable bagi have a decorated helmet shell pendant and are many feet long; shell-disc necklaces circulating in ceremonial exchange in the Louisiade Archipelago and in kula; see soulava
bakubaku	central clearing of a hamlet
bala	Torres Strait pigeon; a totem bird
Bambagho	a female spirit being in the form of a snake who in myth brings the first ceremonial valuables and the first exchange magic
barau	sorcery; sorcerer; loan word from Duau; also balau; see ribiroi, susudi, puripuri
bigibigi	things; used to refer to material possessions, including as brought by returning spirit beings; see kago; ceremonial valuables other than those of shell or stone exchanged at mortuary feasts; synonym for zagaya, or final mortuary feast
bobo	pig
bobo bwejám	wild pig; literally, pig of the forest
boda	person; people, as to refer to a crowd; kinsperson; exchange partner
bubu	reciprocal affectionate diminutive term of address used between grandparents and grandchildren; from rubugu
buda	what; as in, Budai? What is it?
budai idai	literally, What is the name of this? as in, What does X mean?
bukumutula	bachelors' house; Kilivila
bunama	magically enhanced scented coconut oil
buwa	lover's gift to a woman's matrilineal kin
bwa	water
bwabwali	visitors
bwam	type of smaller greenstone axe blade; synonym of tawai; see tobotobo

bwanbwanleo	fairylike spirit being(s); Pana Misima; see lokulokubaji
bwarabwarama	type of spirit; may bring messages to humans; synonym of ghiyoghiyo and ngyau
bwarogi	fish; generic term for larger marine animals, a category of totem; also used to refer generically to animal foods both marine and terrestrial
bwauyezovo	war magic; other forms of malicious or destructive magic
bwawi	fishing magic
bwebwe	father; daddy
calico	cotton cloth; cotton garment; European style skirt, blouse, or dress; from Vanga Lumo; from the English calico
daveri	shell currency piece(s), usually orange in color, made from various species of Spondylus; ceremonial valuables used in exchange on Vanatinai, Rossel Island, and recently in the East Calvados Islands; generic term for shell and stone ceremonial valuables; see ndap
dia	Piper betel; betel pepper chewed with Areca nut (betel nut) and powdered coral lime
doga	boar's tusk necklace; type of kula valuable; Kilivila
dogo	to sort; as in the ritual sorting of roasted vegetables at feasts
Duau	Normanby Island; eastern Normanby Island; people from Normanby and Dobu Islands; language of Normanby Island
Ediriwo	female supernatural patron of illness; lives on Mt. Rio
Egogore	female supernatural patron of health; lives on Mt. Rio
Emuga	female supernatural who first knew the secret of fire and cooking food; literally, of custom
enima	ceremonial wooden axe handle, usually with a carved bird's head at the apex and curvilinear designs along its length; used for the ritual presentation of greenstone axe blades, or tobotobo
euria	givers of good things; respectful generic term for spirit beings
Eurubi	female spirit being who with her sister Jinrubi is a supernatural patron of garden food
gama	child; plural, gamagai; used for children of both sexes from birth to puberty
gamaina	young girl; literally, child female; girl or woman between puberty and young adulthood, usually until a lasting marriage
gamau	firstborn child
Gamayawa	Pleiades; appearance in eastern sky in June and July signals the yam harvest

gana	fence; antisorcery magic
garegare	wisdom; knowledge
gatu	assistants; as of a sorcerer
gau	chew
gaugau	generic term for ceremonial valuables; see ghune
gavagu	my sister (woman speaking); my brother (man speaking); my same-sex sibling; my co-wife (woman speaking)
gavamani	Vanga Lumu; Papuan Pidgin; now a loan word in Vanga Vanatinai
ghabubu	taboo; sacred; closed; forbidden
ghalaghe	sago-making magic; literally, to enlarge
ghalingaji	language; literally, their speech; as in Vanatinai ghalingaji, the language of Vanatinai; ghalingada: our (inclusive we) speech or language
ghan	eat; ighan: he, she or it eats
ghan nyiba	literally, to eat charcoal; to blacken the body with burnt coconut husk as a sign of mourning
ghanika	food; yams
ghanika moli	literally, true food; yams, other tubers, and bananas boiled in coconut cream
ghanmaghamaghada	feast honoring champion warriors
ghanrakerake	literally, food goes out; mortuary feast releasing taboos on preparing or eating food in a house inhabited by the deceased
ghava	type of rain magic
gheba	literally, place; hamlet, village
ghelezi	betel nut; nut of the Areca palm, wild and cultivated, picked unripe and green or ripe and yellow; a stimulant; valuable item in interisland trade and ceremonial exchange; eledi in central and eastern dialects
ghenagá	large decorated wooden lime spatula; a ceremonial valuable
ghiva	travel in search of ceremonial valuables
ghiyoghiyo	see bwarabwarama
ghomoli	man; male; husband, as in leghomoli, her husband
ghu	matrilineal clan
Ghubughububala	female supernatural in the form of a Torres Strait pigeon (bala) who lives in the forest; a patron of the forest and wild foods
ghubwa	tree; wood; a particular hardwood tree, a clan totem

ghuma	garden
ghuma tanuwagai	owner of the garden
ghumu	stone
ghumughumu	stone oven
ghune	ceremonial valuables; ceremonial exchange; une or kune in central and eastern dialects; occasionally pronounced kune in western dialects; ceremonial exchange; Duau; cognate to Kilivila kula
ghunoi	fruit; also used as in Vanatinai ghunoi, literally, fruit of the motherland, the people of Vanatinai; gheba ghunoi, people of the village; or enima ghunoi, fruit of the ceremonial axe handle, a greenstone axe blade; also essence
gia	give; giver; big man or big woman; plural giagia
giarova	greenstone axe blades from Rossel Island; literally, give Rossel
giazagu	long greenstone axe blades
gida	illness caused by magical attack
gile	polished gold-lip pearl shell spoons; a ceremonial valuable
goreye	yes
hagali	mortuary feast; Pana Misima; see zagaya
ibotewa	he/she doesn't want to; synonym of ma nuagu
ighan zagaya	literally, she/he eats the feast; the person who receives valuables at a mortuary feast, especially the final feast
ighan ghunoi	literally, he/she eats its fruit; the person who receives valuables at the final mortuary feast
ijupokiki	she/he takes care of him/her/it; he/she/it holds on
ikebenuanua	he/she commits suicide
ikwan	she/he is lying
ilukautinga	he/she takes care of it; from the English look out; Vanga Lumo; now a synonym of ijupokiki
inde	type of war magic
irada	she/he is crying
iragi	literally, he/she goes out; feast after the birth of a firstborn at which mother's matrilineage gives valuables to father's; ends seclusion of mother and child
ivaiye	cousin; child of the mother's brother or father's sister; cross-cousin
ivwe	spear; prick; cut
jamjám	forest

Jinrubi	female spirit being who with her sister Eurubi is a supernatural patron of garden food
jivia	first mortuary feast after a burial; literally, to break, referring to the ritual breaking and feeding of baked sago loaf
kago	from the English cargo; things; material possessions; Vanga Lumo; Papuan Pidgin; Neo-Melanesian Pidgin; may refer to valuables brought by returning spirit beings, as in cargo cult beliefs; see bigibigi
kaikai	large wild legume, poisonous until leached and roasted; a staple food in ancient times and still a feast food; Vanga Vanatinai; food; Neo-Melanesian Pidgin; Papuan Pidgin
kaiwa	work
kaka	spirit
kalehe	mango; mango tree branch; Pana Saisai; Pana Misima; danced ritual challenge of affinal visitors to a feast who have brought five or more pigs
kelumo	metal or European axe
kiowak	boiled pudding of sago and green coconut water ritually presented at the final mortuary feast; synonym of moni
kitomu	ceremonial valuable circulating in kula used in satisfaction of a personal debt or ritual obligation; Kilivila
Kiriwina	largest of the Trobriand Islands; Kilivila; used on Vanatinai to refer to the people and language of the Trobriand Islands
kukura	magic; magical spell; also kukula
kula	ceremonial exchange system in which shell disc necklaces circulate clockwise and armshells counterclockwise among many of the islands off the east end of New Guinea accompanied by other valuables; Kilivila; cognates include Vanga Vanatinai ghune, kune, une; Muyuw kun; Gawa kura; Dobu and Tubetube kune; and Duau une; in Vanga Vanatinai kula refers to magic for finding copal gum
kulakula	call out
kunai	type of long coarse grass; Neo-Melanesian Pidgin
kune	ceremonial valuables; exchange magic; also une or ghune; ceremonial exchange; Duau; cognate to Kilivila kula
labe	help
laisali	old woman; female elder; synonym of mankwés
latamata	ancestor spirits; synonym of kaka; probably a loan word from Pana Misima in which it literally means our dead ones
lema ma	our (exclusive we) bird, referring to totem bird

Glossary

Len ma budá?	What is your bird? inquiry about one's totem bird and thus one's matrilineal clan
loboda	my kinsperson; my exchange partner; literally, my person
logau	see rogau
logu	my brother (woman speaking); my sister (man speaking); my cross-sex sibling
lokulokubaji	fairylike spirit beings who live in or near forests, lakes, or streams
loleh	person; someone; euphemism referring to a sorcerer
lumo	European (singular)
lumolumo	European (singular and plural)
ma	bird; not (western dialects)
machisi	matches; from English; originally Vanga Lumo
maje	type of tree bearing edible nuts
Malek	Misima Island; now rarely used
man	bird; Pana Saisai; Pana Misima
mana	wind; Pana Misima; sacred power in Polynesian languages
manighighi	type of bird with a high trilling cry; said to deliver warning messages from ancestor spirits
mankwés	old woman; female elder; also mankwesi
manuwijiwiji	bat
maruo	no; synonym of nandele (central dialects) and ningia (eastern dialects)
masalai	place spirit; Neo-Melanesian Pidgin
maskedi	gun; from Vanga Lumo; from the English musket
mbasiri	convincing magic
Mbasiri	male supernatural; patron of convincing magic and a patron of exchange; now lives on Rossel Island
memeyoa	male loin covering of pandanus palm leaf, often with incised designs unique to each clan, held up by cord wound around the hips, now rarely worn; garment worn by both male and female sorcerers
monamona	type of hunting magic
moni	boiled pudding of sago and green coconut water ritually presented at the final mortuary feast; sometimes used to refer to the zagaya or final mortuary feast; synonym of kiowak
muli	affinal presentation of valuables, especially at a final mortuary feast
mumuga	custom; also Papuan Pidgin

muramura	relic of the dead such as a bone or tooth used in magic, sorcery, or ritual; from mura, or to blow
Murua	Muyuw or Woodlark Island; people and language of Woodlark and adjacent small islands
mwadai	its price
mwagumwagu	central ritual of the final mortuary feast in which mourners draped with ceremonial valuables are publicly presented to the heirs of the deceased; synonym for zagaya; see zagaya
mwaguvajo	final mortuary feast; synonym for zagaya; literally, mwagu goes over, referring to the transfer of valuables in the mwagumwagu; see zagaya
mwaje	type of tree bearing edible nuts
Mwajemwaje	male supernatural dwelling in the forest; a patron of wild foods
mwali	decorated Conus armshell; a ceremonial valuable circulating counterclockwise among islands along with other valuables in kula; Kilivila
mwaoli	type of forest plant; tea made from a type of forest plant used as a tonic for the sick, for nursing mothers, and as a refreshing drink while on a work break in the garden
mwaoni	ceremonial valuables; generic term; also mwaon
Mwaoni	male supernatural living on Mt. Rubi; a patron of ceremonial valuables
mwata	snake; a category of totem
mwata re	snake's excrement; in myth, the first shell valuables, or daveri
nago	request or ask; as in inago, he/she requests
nakinaki	personal leavings sorcery; tuberculosis
narugu	my child
ndap	shell currency piece, usually orange in color, made from species of Spondylus; ceremonial valuable used in exchange on Yela, or Rossel Island; Yeletnye; known as daveri on Vanatinai where they also circulate in exchange
negenege	dizzy with desire; a state usually induced by magic
ngabubobo	final mortuary feast; suffix bobo means pig; rarely used synonym of zagaya
ngangaya	garden magic; literally, talk to
ngyau	see bwarabwarama
noi	mother; mommy
nuaroru	type of mourning song

olman	old man; from English; Vanga Lumo; synonym of amalaisali, which it has by now largely replaced
ome	sandalwood bark; used in magic and sorcery
Panaeati	Panaeati Island; used to refer to the people of Panaeati and Panapompom Islands, who build outrigger sailing canoes
Panatinani	Joannet Island; people of Joannet Island; in Pana Saisai, literally, motherland; mainland or large island
posi	if; Vanga Lumo; from the English suppose; now a synonym of zogo (western dialects), thogo (central dialects), or dogo (eastern dialects)
ptyilöwe	type of male ritual dance; Yeletyne
puripuri	sorcery; sorcerer; Papuan Pidgin; see ribiroi, barau, susudi
raibok	leprosy
rama	father; infrequently used synonym of bwebwe
ramagu	my father; formal mode of address also used ocasionally to refer to a father's sister's child or a member of the father's matrilineage, whether male or female
rausi	drumming by men using long hardwood drums with monitor lizard skin heads; all-night ceremonial drumming and singing at a final mortuary feast
rawa	island; often refers to smaller coral islands as opposed to a nearby larger island known as the mainland, or vanatinai; analogous to saisai in Pana Saisai
renuanga	thought; thoughts
ribiroi	sorcery; sorcerer; literally, poison; synonyms include the euphemistic loleh; Vanga Lumo susudi; barau, a loan word from Duau; and the Papuan Pidgin puripuri
Rodyo	male creator spirit who lives on Mt. Rio; supernatural patron of the spirits of the dead who dwell with him; a patron of sorcery and war magic; sometimes in snake form
rogana	magic used to make food abundant at feasts; literally, fenced one
rogau	literally, one who chews; used for chewing betel nut; may refer to a person practicing magic or sorcery; invisibility magic; also logau
Rova	Rossel Island; called Yela in Yeletnye
rubugu	reciprocal term of address used by grandparents and grandchildren
saisai	island; often refers to smaller coral islands as opposed to a nearby larger island known as the mainland; Pana Saisai; analogous to Vanatinai rawa

Glossary

Saisai	people and language of the East Calvados Islands; Vanga Vanatinai and Pana Saisai
samakupo	shell-disc necklace that reaches to the collarbone worn daily by many people of both sexes
sibawa	widower
silava	place spirit; place inhabited by such a spirit; also sirava; cognate to Pana Misima silapa; Yeletnye yaba
sisiga	naughty
sobu	women's dance that moves counterclockwise around a group of men drumming and singing, or performing rausi; women may sing as they dance; women's dance often performed at the final mortuary feast
soi	mortuary feast; Ware; Tubetube; Duau; Dobu
soulava	decorated shell-disc necklaces circulating in a clockwise direction among islands along with other valuables in kula; Kilivila; term recorded by Malinowski in 1915–1918 but unusual by 1970s; synonym of vaiguwa (Malinowski: vaygu'a), bagi
sowasowa	pyramid of yams ritually presented at a mortuary feast; Pana Saisai
stoa	store; from English; from Vanga Lumo
susudi	sorcery; sorcerer; from the English sorcery; Vanga Lumo; see ribiroi; puripuri; barau
tagarugu	wild shrub (Gnetum gnemon) whose young leaves are eaten boiled in coconut cream
Tagula	Vanatinai or Sudest Island; Pana Misima and the Sabarl dialect of Pana Saisai; frequently used in goverment publications and on maps and nautical charts as the "indigenous" name of the island
Tagule	Vanatinai or Sudest Island; Pana Saisai dialects from Panawina and eastward
tamja	literally, squeezed one; yams and other tubers or bananas boiled in coconut cream, made by squeezing grated coconut meat with a small amount of water; sometimes called ghanika moli, or true food
Tamudurere	male supernatural who lives in the deep sea outside the barrier reef; a supernatural patron of sorcery, witchcraft, and war; also Taumudulele
tanokau	man who officiates at a hamlet's yam planting ritual; see yola
tanuwagai	owner; supernatural patron; plural tanuwagaji
tara	type of ritual for requesting valuables; type of exchange magic

tau	designated member of the father's matrilineage, often a father's sister's child, who nurtures one in life and who must be compensated with valuables after one's death; reciprocal term, as in zimantau, they are tau to one another; also people; ancestors
taubwaragha	the way of the ancestors; custom; tradition
tawai	type of smaller greenstone axe blade; synonym of bwam; see tobotobo
tina	mother; synonym of noi
tinagu	my mother; formal mode of address; sometimes used to address spirit beings
tinai	his/her/its mother
tobotobo	long, thin axe blades of finely polished greenstone, or hornfels, that circulate in ceremonial exchange throughout the Louisiade Archipelago and in kula; analogous to the Kilivila beku; may also refer to the axe blades and their carved ceremonial handles or enima; generic term for ceremonial valuables
topwake	tobacco; from English; tabak in Vanga Lumo
Tova	male supernatural; patron of wild pigs and dogs
udi	love magic
une	see ghune
unga	you say
uvaghona	you write that down; you count that
vana	place, land
Vanatinai	Sudest Island; literally, land of the mother; also mainland or large island as opposed to small island, rawa; Vanatina in central and eastern dialects
vanga	language; speech
vaghan	adopt or foster; literally, take and feed
vazavó	bridewealth; literally, toward the wife
vo	woman; wife; as in levo, his wife
vearada	literally, for crying; mortuary feast honoring those who cried at a burial
velaloga	literally, for walking; mortuary feast releasing widow or widower from taboos against leaving the hamlet
vetha witawita	type of weather magic; literally, a small pouch with something inside
via	large aroid similar to taro

vivirelavare	category of supernatural beings often in animal form who are patrons of particular domains of human affairs
volevole	type of grass used for a medicinal tea
vowo	claim by a matrilineal kinsperson to be the rightful heir of valuables at a mortuary feast
vwatai	summit; peak; shoulder
wabwi	widow
wadala	type of medicinal tea
wadawada	witchcraft; witch; cognate to Pana Saisai wadewade; analogous to Pana Misima olal
waga	sailing canoe; paddling canoe; boat; motor vessel
waghena	moon
wakinie	behind or in back of; menstruation; probably related to waghena
Wanim	Grass Island
wevo	woman; female
Witamo	male supernatural who left Mt. Rio for Rossel Island or parts unknown
wivwara	type of food magic
wonamo	turtle
wonamo jilevia	tortoiseshell lime spatula; a ceremonial valuable
wughulumo	rain forest plant with white aromatic root used in magic and sorcery
yaba	place spirit; Yeletnye; cognate to silava
Yamba	Vanatinai or Sudest Island; Yeletnye; probably from mountain, visible to the west from Yela
yagoau	parents of a firstborn; reciprocal term of address between parents
yam	knee-length skirt of shredded coconut leaf tied around the hips; usually worn in layers of two or three
yogeyoge	mourning skirt of coconut palm leaf cut in wide strips; worn ankle length by widows and mothers of a firstborn and calf length by other female affinal mourners and daughters mourning a father
yola	woman; respected woman; woman who performs ritual at her hamlet's yam planting; see tanokau
yola na	literally, that woman there; used to refer to or address female affines

yova	sacred place; male warrior's secret location for performing magical rituals
zagaya	final mortuary feast; thagaya in central dialects; synonyms include mwagumwagu, mwaguvajo, ngabubobo, bigibigi; cognate to Pana Misima hagali and Kilivila sagali
zawazawara	healing magic; thawathawara in central and eastern dialects
zegezege	year
zegezege posuye	literally, nose of the year; new year; October
zeva	male youth from puberty to young adulthood, usually until a lasting marriage
zeyala	ginger root
zhuwe	type of tree bearing edible nuts
ziazio	vine; a category of totem; cord made from shredded and woven vine fibers used to lash houses or canoes together
zilidá	literally, they lay the mat; referring to the laying out and public counting of ceremonial valuables after the mwagumwagu ritual during a final mortuary feast; synonym of zagaya
zogatine	November, December; literally, to cover inside, referring to newly planted yams
zogazoga	ritual covering of a woman's body after childbirth and during mourning
zogo	if; thogo in central dialects; dogo in eastern dialects; now often replaced by the Vanga Lumo posi

Bibliography

Abu-Lughod. 1991. "Writing Against Culture." In Richard Fox, ed., *Recapturing Anthropology: Working in the Present*. Santa Fe: School of American Research Press.

Adams, John W. 1973. *The Gitksan Potlatch: Population Flux, Resource Ownership and Reciprocity*. Toronto: Holt, Rinehart and Winston.

Affleck, Donald. 1983. "Manuscript 18: Information on Customs and Practices of the People of Woodlark Island, by Carlo Salerio." *Journal of Pacific History* 18(1):57–72.

Allen, Jim. 1977. "Sea Traffic, Trade, and Expanding Horizons." In J. Allen, J. Golson, and R. Jones, eds., *Sunda and Sahul: Prehistoric Studies in Southeast Asia, Melanesia, and Australia*. London: Academic Press.

Allen, J., T. Flannery, C. Gosden, R. Jones, and J. P. White. 1988. "Pleistocene Dates for the Human Occupation of New Ireland, Northern Melanesia." *Nature* 331:707–709.

Allen, M. R. 1967. *Male Cults and Secret Initiations in Melanesia*. Melbourne: Melbourne University Press.

—— 1984. "Elders, Chiefs, and Big Men: Authority Legitimization and Political Evolution in Melanesia." *American Ethnologist* 11:20–41.

Appadurai, Arjun. 1990. "Disjuncture and Difference in the Global Cultural Economy." *Public Culture* 2(2):1–24.

—— 1991. "Global Ethnoscapes." In Richard Fox, ed., *Recapturing Anthropology: Working in the Present*. Santa Fe: School of American Research Press.

Ardener, Edwin. 1975. "Belief and the Problem of Women." In Shirley Ardener, ed., *Perceiving Women*. London: Malaby.

Armstrong, W. E. 1923–24. "Rossel Island Religion." *Anthropos* 18–19:1–11.

—— 1928. *Rossel Island: An Ethnological Study*. Cambridge: Cambridge University Press.

Atkinson, Jane. 1982. "Anthropology." *Signs* 8:236–258.

Babb, Florence. 1989. *Between Field and Cooking Pot: The Political Economy of Marketwomen in Peru*. Austin: University of Texas Press.

345

Bibliography

Bacdayan, Albert. 1977. "Mechanistic Cooperation and Sexual Equality Among the Western Bontoc." In Alice Schlegel, ed., *Sexual Stratification: A Cross-Cultural View*. New York: Columbia University Press.

Bachofen, Johann. 1967 [1861]. *Myth, Religion, and Mother Right: Selected Writings of J. J. Bachofen*. Tr. Ralph Manheim. Princeton: Princeton University Press.

Bamberger, Joan. 1974. "The Myth of Matriarchy: Why Men Rule in Primitive Society." In Michelle Rosaldo and Louise Lamphere, eds., *Woman, Culture, and Society*. Stanford: Stanford University Press.

Barnett, Homer. 1968 [1938]. "The Nature and Function of the Potlatch." Ph.D. diss., Department of Anthropology, University of Oregon. Mimeograph.

Barth, Fredrik. 1987. *Cosmologies in the Making: A Generative Approach to Cultural Variation in Inner New Guinea*. Cambridge: Cambridge University Press.

Battaglia, Debbora. 1983a. "Projecting Personhood in Melanesia: The Dialectics of Artefact Symbolism on Sabarl Island." *Man* (n.s.) 18(2):289–304.

—— 1983b. "Syndromes of Ceremonial Exchange in the Eastern Calvados: The View from Sabarl Island." In Jerry Leach and Edmund Leach, eds., *The Kula: New Perspectives on Massim Exchange*. Cambridge: Cambridge University Press.

—— 1985. " 'We Feed Our Fathers': Paternal Nurture Among the Sabarl of Papua New Guinea." *American Ethnologist* 12(3):427–441.

—— 1990. *On the Bones of the Serpent: Person, Memory, and Mortality in Sabarl Island Society*. Chicago: University of Chicago Press.

—— 1991. "Punishing the Yams: Leadership and Gender Ambivalence on Sabarl Island." In Maurice Godelier and Marilyn Strathern, eds., *Big Men and Great Men: Personifications of Power in Melanesia*. Cambridge: Cambridge University Press.

Beauvoir, de, Simone. 1953. *The Second Sex*. New York: Knopf.

Bellwood, Peter. 1979. *Man's Conquest of the Pacific: The Prehistory of Southeast Asia and Oceania*. New York: Oxford University Press.

Bendann, Effie. 1930. *Death Customs: An Analytical Study of Burial Rites*. London: Kegan Paul, Trench, Trubner.

Berde, Stuart. 1974. "Melanesians as Methodists: Economy and Marriage on a Papua and New Guinea Island." Ph.D. diss., Department of Anthropology, University of Pennsylvania.

Bernardi, Bernardo. 1985. *Age Class Systems: Social Institutions and Polities Based on Age*. Cambridge: Cambridge University Press.

Berndt, R. M. 1965. "The Kamano, Usurufa, Jate, and Fore of the Eastern Highlands." In P. Lawrence and M. J. Meggitt, eds., *Gods, Ghosts and Men in Melanesia*. Melbourne: Oxford University Press.

Bevan, Theodore. 1890. *Toil, Travel, and Discovery in British New Guinea*. London: Kegan Paul, Trench, Trubner.

Birdsell, Joseph B. 1977. "The Recalibration of a Paradigm for the First Peopling of Greater Australia." In J. Allen, J. Golson, P. Jones, eds., *Sunda and Sahul: Prehistoric Studies in Southeast Asia, Melanesia, and Australia*. London: Academic Press.

Bloch, Maurice 1971. *Placing the Dead: Tombs, Ancestral Villages, and Kinship Organization in Madagascar*. London and New York: Seminar Press.

Bowden, Ross. 1987. "Sorcery, Illness, and Social Control in Kwoma Society." In Michelle Stephen, ed., *Sorcerer and Witch in Melanesia*. New Brunswick: Rutgers University Press.

Bibliography

Bourdieu, Pierre. 1977. *Outline of a Theory of Practice*. Tr. R. Nice. Cambridge: Cambridge University Press.

Briffault, Robert. 1931. *The Mothers: The Matriarchal Theory of Social Origins*. New York: Macmillan.

Brightman, Robert. 1993a. "Biology, Taboo, and Gender Politics in the Sexual Division of Foraging Labor." Department of Anthropology, Reed College. Manuscript.

—— 1993b. *Grateful Prey: Rock Cree Human-Animal Relationships*. Berkeley: University of California Press.

British New Guinea Annual Reports. 1888–1898.

Brown, Judith. 1970a. "A Note on the Division of Labor by Sex." *American Anthropologist* 72:1073–1078.

—— 1970b. "Economic Organization and the Position of Women Among the Iroquois." *Ethnohistory* 17(3–4):151–167.

—— 1975. "Iroquois Women: An Ethnohistorical Note." In Rayna Reiter, ed., *Toward an Anthropology of Women*. New York: Monthly Review.

—— 1982. "Cross-Cultural Perspectives on Middle-Aged Women." *Current Anthropology* 23(2):143–156.

Brown, Paula. 1979. "Chimbu Leadership Before Provincial Government." *Journal of Pacific History* 14:100–116.

—— 1987. "New Men and Big Men: Emerging Social Stratification in the Third World, A Case Study from the New Guinea Highlands." *Ethnology* 26:87–106.

Brown, Paula, and Georgeda Buchbinder, eds. 1976. *Man and Woman in the New Guinea Highlands*. Washington, D.C.: American Anthropological Association.

Buckley, Thomas, and Alma Gottlieb. 1988. "A Critical Appraisal of Theories of Menstrual Symbolism." In Thomas Buckley and Alma Gottlieb, eds., *Blood Magic: The Anthropology of Menstruation*. Berkeley: University of California Press.

Campbell, Alexander. 1898a. "Report of the Resident Magistrate for the South-Eastern Division." Colonial Reports-Annual. British New Guinea. Appendix O.

—— 1898b. Letter from A. M. Campbell, Resident Magistrate, with appended typed copies of statements, dated 7th July 1898, Samarai, British New Guinea, to the Government Secretary, Port Moresby. Port Moresby: National Archives of Papua New Guinea.

—— 1899. "Report of the Resident Magistrate for the South-Eastern Division." Colonial Report-Annual. British New Guinea.

Campbell, Shirley. 1983. "Kula in Vakuta: The Mechanics of Keda." In Jerry Leach and Edmund Leach, eds., *The Kula: New Perspectives on Massim Exchange*. Cambridge: Cambridge University Press.

Capell, A. 1943. *The Linguistic Position of Southeastern Papua*. Sydney: Australasian Medical.

Chowning, Ann. 1973a. *An Introduction to the Peoples and Cultures of Melanesia*. Addison-Wesley Module in Anthropology, no. 38. Reading, Mass.: Addison-Wesley.

—— 1973b. "Child Rearing and Socialization." In Ian Hogbin, ed., *Anthropology in Papua New Guinea: Readings from the Encyclopaedia of Papua and New Guinea*. Melbourne: Melbourne University Press.

—— 1979. "Leadership in Melanesia." *Journal of Pacific History* 14:66–84.

—— 1987. "Sorcery and the Social Order in Kove." In Michelle Stephen, ed., *Sorcerer and Witch in Melanesia*. New Brunswick: Rutgers University Press.

347

——— 1989. "Death and Kinship in Molima." In Frederick Damon and Roy Wagner, eds., *Death Rituals and Life in the Societies of the Kula Ring*. De Kalb: Northern Illinois University Press.

Clifford, James. 1983. "On Ethnographic Authority." *Representations* 1:118–146.

——— 1986. "On Ethnographic Allegory." In James Clifford and George Marcus, eds., *Writing Culture: The Poetics and Politics of Ethnography*. Berkeley: University of California Press.

Clifford, James, and George Marcus, eds. 1986. *Writing Culture: The Poetics and Politics of Ethnography*. Berkeley: University of California Press.

Cole, Douglas and Ira Chaiken. 1990. *An Iron Hand Against the People: The Law Against the Potlatch on the Northwest Coast*. Seattle: University of Washington Press.

Collier, Jane and Michelle Rosaldo. 1981. "Politics and Gender in Simple Societies." In Sherry Ortner and Harriet Whitehead, eds., *Sexual Meanings: The Cultural Construction of Gender and Sexuality*. Cambridge: Cambridge University Press.

Colson, Elizabeth. 1958. *Marriage and the Family Among the Plateau Tonga*. Manchester: Manchester University Press.

Conklin, Harold. 1958. *Betel Chewing Among the Hanunóo*. Special Reprint Paper, no. 56. Proceedings of the Fourth Far-Eastern Prehistory Conference. National Research Council of the Philippines.

Corris, Peter. 1968. " 'Blackbirding' in New Guinea Waters, 1883–84: An Episode in the Queensland Labour Trade." *Journal of Pacific History* 3:85–105.

Crystal, Eric. 1971. "Toradja Town." Ph.D. diss., Department of Anthropology, University of California, Berkeley.

Cruikshank, Julie. 1990. *Life Lived Like a Story: Life Stories of Three Yukon Native Elders*. Lincoln: University of Nebraska Press.

Damon, Frederick. 1980. "The Kula and Generalised Exchange: Considering Some Unconsidered Aspects of the Elementary Structures of Kinship. *Man* (n.s.) 15:267–294.

——— 1983a. "What Moves the Kula: Opening and Closing Gifts on Woodlark Island." In Jerry Leach and Edmund Leach, eds., *The Kula: New Perspectives on Massim Exchange*. Cambridge: Cambridge University Press.

——— 1983b. "Muyuw Kinship and the Metamorphosis of Gender Labour." *Man* 18:305–325.

——— 1990. *From Muyuw to the Trobriands: Transformations along the Northern Side of the Kula Ring*. Tucson: University of Arizona Press.

Damon, Frederick, and Roy Wagner, eds. 1989. *Death Rituals and Life in the Societies of the Kula Ring*. De Kalb: Northern Illinois University Press.

De Laguna, Frederica. 1972. *Under Mount St. Elias: The History and Culture of the Yakutat Tlingit*. Smithsonian Contributions to Anthropology, no. 7 (three parts). Washington, D.C.: Smithsonian Institution Press.

Divale, William, and Marvin Harris. 1976. "Population, Warfare, and the Male Supremacist Complex." *American Anthropologist* 78(3):521–538.

Douglas, John. 1887. "The Special Commissioner to the Governor of Queensland Reporting Return of Louisiade Islanders." Appendix C. Papers Relating to Her Majesty's Colonial Possessions. British New Guinea: British Parliamentary Papers.

————— 1888–89. "Sudest Island and the Louisiade Archipelago." Royal Geographical Society of Australasia—Proceedings of the Queensland Branch. Fourth session. 2-16.

Drucker, Philip and Robert Heizer. 1967. *To Make My Name Good: A Reexamination of the Southern Kwakiutl Potlatch*. Berkeley: University of California Press.

Drummond, Lee. 1981. "The Serpent's Children: Semiotics of Cultural Genesis in Arawak and Trobriand Myth." *American Ethnologist* 8(3):633–660.

Dundes, Alan. 1979. "Heads or Tails: A Psychoanalytic Study of Potlatch." *Journal of Psychological Anthropology* 2(4):395–424.

Duve, R.N. 1980. "Highlights of the Chemistry and Pharmacology of Wild Ginger (*Zingiber zerumbet* Smith)." *Fiji Agricultural Journal* 42(1):41–43.

Egloff, Brian. 1978. The Kula Before Malinowski: A Changing Configuration. *Mankind* 11(3):429–435.

Eisenstadt, S. N. 1956. *From Generation to Generation: Age Groups and Social Structure*. New York: Free Press.

Elkin, A. P. 1964. *The Australian Aborigines*. New York: Anchor.

Ember, Melvin, and Carol Ember. 1971. "The Conditions Favoring Matrilocal Versus Patrilocal Residence." *American Anthropologist* 73(3):571–594.

Engels, Frederick. 1972 [1891]. *The Origin of the Family, Private Property, and the State*. New York: International Publishers.

Errington, Frederick, and Deborah Gewertz. 1988. "Myths of Matriarchy Re-examined: Indigenous Images of Alternative Gender Relations." In Deborah Gewertz, ed., *Myths of Matriarchy Reconsidered*. Oceania Monograph, no. 33. Sydney: University of Sydney Press.

Estioko-Griffin, Agnes, and P. Bion Griffin. 1981. "Woman the Hunter." In Frances Dahlberg, ed., *Woman the Gatherer*. New Haven: Yale University Press.

————— 1985. "Woman Hunters: The Implications for Pleistocene Prehistory and Contemporary Ethnography." In Madeleine Goodman, ed., *Women in Asia and the Pacific: Towards an East-West Dialogue*. Honolulu: Women's Studies Program, University of Hawaii.

Etienne, Mona. 1980. "Women and Men, Cloth and Colonization: The Transformation of Production-Distribution Relations Among the Baule (Ivory Coast)." In Mona Etienne and Eleanor Leacock, eds., *Women and Colonization: Anthropological Perspectives*. New York: Praeger.

Etienne, Mona, and Eleanor Leacock, eds. 1980. *Women and Colonization: Anthropological Perspectives*. New York: Praeger.

Evans-Pritchard, E. E. 1937. *Witchcraft, Oracles and Magic Among the Azande*. Oxford: Oxford University Press.

————— 1965. *The Position of Woman in Primitive Societies and Other Essays*. London: Faber.

Favret-Saada, Jeanne. 1980. *Deadly Words: Witchcraft in the Bocage*. Cambridge: Cambridge University Press.

Feil, D. K. 1978. "Women and Men in the Enga Tee." *American Ethnologist* 5(2):263–279.

Flanagan, James. 1989. "Hierarchy in Simple 'Egalitarian' Societies." *Annual Review of Anthropology* 18:245–266.

Flanagan, James, and Steve Rayner. 1988. "Introduction." In James Flanagan and Steve

Rayner, eds., *Rules, Decisions, and Inequality in Egalitarian Societies.* Aldershot: Avebury.

Fogelson, Raymond. 1990. "On the 'Petticoat Government' of the Eighteenth-Century Cherokee." In David Jordan and Marc Swartz, eds., *Personality and the Cultural Construction of Society.* Tuscaloosa: University of Alabama Press.

———— 1991. "The Origins of Totemism." Department of Anthropology, University of Chicago. Manuscript.

Forbes, Henry. 1886. Letter to John Douglas, Her Majesty's Special Commissioner for British New Guinea, Regarding the Craig Massacre, Joannet Island. 2 November, Samarai, Dinner Island. Port Moresby: National Archives of Papua New Guinea.

Forge, Anthony. 1970. "Prestige, Influence, and Sorcery: A New Guinea Example." In M. Douglas, ed., *Witchcraft Confessions and Accusations.* London: Tavistock.

Fortes, Meyer, and E. E. Evans-Pritchard, eds. 1940. *African Political Systems.* London: Oxford University Press.

Fortune, Reo. 1963 [1932]. *Sorcerers of Dobu: The Social Anthropology of the Dobu Islanders of the Western Pacific.* New York: Dutton.

Foster, George, and Barbara Anderson. 1978. *Medical Anthropology.* New York: Wiley.

Foucault, Michel. 1978. *The History of Sexuality.* Volume 1, *An Introduction.* New York: Random House.

———— 1979. *Discipline and Punish: Birth of the Prison.* Tr. Andrew Sheridan. New York: Vintage.

———— 1980. *Power/Knowledge: Selected Interviews and Other Writings, 1972–1977.* New York: Pantheon.

Frankel, Stephen. 1984. "Peripheral Health Workers are Central to Primary Health Care: Lessons from Papua New Guinea Aid Posts." *Social Science and Medicine* 19(3):279–290.

———— 1986. *The Huli Response to Illness.* Cambridge: Cambridge University Press.

Frazer, James. 1913. *The Golden Bough: A Study in Magic and Religion.* London: Macmillan.

Freire-Marreco, Barbara. 1912. "Religion. A Note on Some Recent Observations and Theories." In Editorial Committee of the British Association, *Notes and Queries on Anthropology.* 4th ed. London: Harrison and Sons.

Fried, Morton. 1967. *The Evolution of Political Society.* New York: Random House.

Friedl, Ernestine. 1975. *Women and Men: An Anthropologist's View.* New York: Holt, Rinehart and Winston.

Gailey, Christine. 1980. "Putting Down Sisters and Wives: Tongan Women and Colonization." In Mona Etienne and Eleanor Leacock, eds., *Women and Colonization.* New York: Bergin/Praeger.

———— 1987. *Kinship to Kingship: Gender Hierarchy and State Formation in the Tongan Islands.* Austin: University of Texas Press.

Gewertz, Deborah. 1981. "An Historical Reconsideration of Female Dominance Among the Chambri of Papua New Guinea." *American Ethnologist* 8:94–106.

———— 1983. *Sepik River Societies: A Historical Ethnography of the Chambri and their Neighbors.* New Haven: Yale University Press.

Gladwin, Thomas, and Seymour Sarason. 1953. *Truk: Man in Paradise.* Viking Fund Publications in Anthropology, no. 20. New York: Wenner-Gren Foundation for Anthropological Research.

Glasse, R. M. 1965. "The Huli of the Southern Highlands." In P. Lawrence and M. J. Meggitt, eds., *Gods, Ghosts and Men in Melanesia*. Melbourne: Oxford University Press.

Glick, Leonard. 1973. "Sorcery and Witchcraft." In Ian Hogbin, ed., *Anthropology in Papua New Guinea: Readings from the Encyclopaedia of Papua and New Guinea*. Melbourne: Melbourne University Press.

Godelier, Maurice. 1986. *The Making of Great Men: Male Domination and Power Among the New Guinea Baruya*. Cambridge: Cambridge University Press.

Godelier, Maurice, and Marilyn Strathern, eds. 1991. *Big Men and Great Men: Personifications of Power in Melanesia*. Cambridge: Cambridge University Press.

Goodale, Jane. 1971. *Tiwi Wives*. Seattle: University of Washington Press.

Goodenough, Ward. 1971. "The Pageant of Death in Nakanai." In Lewis Langness and John Wechsler, eds., *Melanesia: Readings on a Culture Area*. Scranton, Pa.: Chandler.

Goody, Jack, and S. J. Tambiah, eds. 1973. *Bridewealth and Dowry*. Cambridge: Cambridge University Press.

Gottlieb, Alma. 1988. "Menstrual Cosmology Among the Beng of the Ivory Coast." In Thomas Buckley and Alma Gottlieb, eds., *Blood Magic: The Anthropology of Menstruation*. Berkeley: University of California Press.

———— 1990. "Rethinking Female Pollution: The Beng Case (Côte d'Ivoire)." In Peggy Sanday and Ruth Goodenough, eds., *Beyond the Second Sex: New Directions in the Anthropology of Gender*. Philadelphia: University of Pennsylvania Press.

Grimshaw, Beatrice. 1908. The Truth about Papua. *Sydney Morning Herald*, May 9, p. 7; May 16, pp. 6–7; May 23, p. 13.

———— 1911. *The New New Guinea*. London: Hutchinson.

Guiart, Jean. 1951. "Forerunners of Melanesian Nationalism." *Oceania* 22:81–90.

———— 1952. "John Frum Movement in Tanna." *Oceania* 22:165–175.

Haddon, A. C. 1894. *The Decorative Art of British New Guinea*. Dublin: University Press.

———— 1947. "Smoking and Tobacco Pipes in New Guinea." Royal Society of London Philosopical Transactions, series B, *Biological Sciences* 232(586):1–278.

Hammond, Dorothy, and Alta Jablow. 1973. *Women: Their Economic Role in Traditional Societies*. Reading, Mass.: Addison-Wesley.

Hamy, E. T. 1888. "Etude sur les Papouas de la Mer D'Entrecasteaux." *Revue D'Ethnographie* 7:503–519.

Harris, Marvin. 1974. *Cows, Pigs, Wars, and Witches*. New York: Vintage.

Hely, B. A. 1889. "Administrative Visits of Inspection. Mining. Sudest." Papers Relating to Her Majesty's Colonial Possessions. British New Guinea. British Parliamentary Papers.

Henderson, Jim, and Anne Henderson. n.d. "Languages of the Louisiade Archipelago and Environs." In *Three Studies in Languages of Eastern Papua*. Ukarumpa, Papua New Guinea: Summer Institute of Linguistics.

Herdt, Gilbert. 1981. *Guardians of the Flute: Idioms of Masculinity*. New York: McGraw-Hill.

———— 1982a. "Fetish and Fantasy in Sambia." In Gilbert Herdt, ed., *Rituals of Manhood: Male Initiation in Papua New Guinea*. Berkeley: University of California Press.

———— 1984. *Ritualized Homosexuality in Melanesia*. Berkeley: University of California Press.

Bibliography

———— 1990. "Social Change, Western Schooling, and New Gender Roles in Rural Highland Papua New Guinea." Committee on Human Development, University of Chicago. Manuscript.

Herdt, Gilbert, ed. 1982b. *Rituals of Manhood: Male Initiation in Papua New Guinea.* Berkeley: University of California Press.

Herdt, Gilbert, and Fitz Poole. 1982. " 'Sexual Antagonism': The Intellectual History of a Concept in New Guinea Anthropology." In Gilbert Herdt and Fitz Poole, eds., *Sexual Antagonism, Gender, and Social Change in Papua New Guinea. Social Analysis.* Special issue, no. 12.

Herdt, Gilbert, and Fitz Poole, eds. 1982. *Sexual Antagonism, Gender, and Social Change in Papua New Guinea. Social Analysis* (special issue), no. 12.

Hertz, Robert. 1960 [1907]. *Death and the Right Hand.* Tr. R. Needham. Glencoe, Ill.: The Free Press.

Hill, Jonathan. 1988. "Introduction: Myth and History." In Jonanthan Hill, ed., *Rethinking History and Myth: Indigenous Perspectives on the Past.* Urbana: University of Illinois Press.

Hochschild, Arlie. 1983. *The Managed Heart: Commercialization of Human Feeling.* Berkeley: University of California Press.

Hoffer, Carol. 1974. "Madam Yoko: Ruler of the Kpa Menda Confederacy." In Michelle Rosaldo and Louise Lamphere, eds., *Woman, Culture, and Society.* Stanford: Stanford University Press.

Hunter, R. L. 1839. "Gower's Harbour, New Ireland." *Nautical Magazine* 8:37–39.

———— 1840. "Pacific Ocean—New Islands. Woodlark Island." *Nautical Magazine* 9:300–302.

Huntington, Richard, and Peter Metcalf. 1979. *Celebrations of Death: The Anthropology of Mortuary Ritual.* Cambridge: Cambridge University Press.

Huxley, Julian, ed. 1935. *T. H. Huxley's Diary of the Voyage of H.M.S. Rattlesnake.* London: Chatto and Windus.

Iamo, Warilea. 1981. "Death of a Kinsman in a Keakalo Village." Paper presented at the Second Conference on the Kula and Massim Exchange. Charlottesville, Virginia.

Irwin, Geoffrey. 1981. "Archaeology in the Kula Area." Paper presented at the Second Conference on the Kula and Massim Exchange. Charlottesville, Virginia.

———— 1989. Letter to author.

Jacobs, Thomas Jefferson. 1844. *Scenes, Incidents, and Adventures in the Pacific Ocean, or The Islands of the Australasian Seas, During the Cruise of the Clipper Margaret Oakley under Capt. Benjamin Morrell.* New York: Harper and Brothers.

Jenkins, Carol, Alison Orr-Ewing, and Peter Heywood. 1985. "Cultural Aspects of Early Childhood Growth and Nutrition Among the Amele of Lowland Papua New Guinea." In Leslie Marshall, ed., *Infant Care and Feeding in the South Pacific.* New York: Gordon and Breach.

Kaberry, Phyllis. 1939. *Aboriginal Woman: Sacred and Profane.* London: Routledge.

Kahn, Miriam. 1986. *Always Hungry, Never Greedy: Food and the Expression of Gender in a Melanesian Society.* Cambridge: Cambridge University Press.

Kan, Sergei. 1989. *Symbolic Immortality: The Tlingit Potlatch of the Nineteenth Century.* Washington, D.C.: Smithsonian Institution Press.

352

Bibliography

Keesing, Roger. 1978. "Politico-Religious Movements and Anticolonialism on Malaita: Maasina Rule in Historical Perspective." Part 1. *Oceania* 48:241–261.
——— 1982. *Kwaio Religion*. New York: Columbia University Press.
Kelly, Raymond. 1976. "Witchcraft and Sexual Relations: An Exploration in the Social and Semantic Implications of the Structure of Belief." In Paula Brown and Georgeda Buchbinder, eds., *Man and Woman in the New Guinea Highlands*. Washington, D.C.: American Anthropological Association.
Kirch, Patrick. 1987. "Lapita and Oceanic Cultural Origins: Excavations in the Mussau Islands, Papua New Guinea." *Journal of Field Archaeology* 14:163–180.
——— 1988. "Long-Distance Exchange and Island Colonization: The Lapita Case." *Norwegian Archaeological Review* 21:103–117.
——— 1990. "Specialization and Exchange in the Lapita Complex of Oceania (1600–500 B.C.)." *Asian Perspectives* 29(2):117–133.
Kirkpatrick, John. 1983. *The Marquesan Notion of the Person*. Studies in Cultural Anthropology, no. 3. Ann Arbor: UMI Press.
Lamphere, Louise. 1977. "Anthropology." *Signs* 2(3):612–627.
Landes, Ruth. 1938. *The Ojibwa Woman*. New York: Columbia University Press.
Langness, L. L. 1967. "Sexual Antagonism in the New Guinea Highlands." *Oceania* 37:161–177.
——— 1976. "Discussion." In Paula Brown and Georgeda Buchbinder, eds., *Man and Woman in the New Guinea Highlands*. Special Publication of the American Anthropological Association, no. 8. Washington, D.C.: American Anthropological Association.
Lawrence, Peter. 1973. "Religion and Magic." In Ian Hogbin, ed., *Anthropology in Papua New Guinea: Readings from the Encyclopaedia of Papua and New Guinea*. Melbourne: Melbourne University Press.
——— 1987. "De Rerum Natura: the Garia View of Sorcery." In Michelle Stephen, ed., *Sorcerer and Witch in Melanesia*. New Brunswick: Rutgers University Press.
Lawrence, Peter, and M. J. Meggitt, eds. 1965. *Gods, Ghosts and Men in Melanesia: Some Religions of Australian New Guinea and the New Hebrides*. Melbourne: Oxford University Press.
Leacock, Eleanor. 1978. "Women's Status in Egalitarian Society: Implications for Social Evolution." *Current Anthropology* 19:247–276.
Lederman, Rena. 1986. *What Gifts Engender: Social Relations and Politics in Mendi, Highland Papua New Guinea*. Cambridge: Cambridge University Press.
——— 1990. "Contested Order: Gender and Society in the Southern New Guinea Highlands." In Peggy Sanday and Ruth Goodenough, eds., *Beyond the Second Sex: New Directions in the Anthropology of Gender*. Philadelphia: University of Pennsylvania Press.
——— 1991. " 'Interests' in Exchange: Increment, Equivalence, and the Limits of Bigmanship." In Maurice Godelier and Marilyn Strathern, eds., *Big Men and Great Men: Personifications of Power in Melanesia*. Cambridge: Cambridge University Press.
Lepowsky, Maria. 1982. "A Comparison of Alcohol and Betelnut Use on Vanatinai (Sudest Island)." In Mac Marshall, ed. *Through a Glass Darkly: Beer and Modernization in Papua New Guinea*. Monograph 18, Boroko, Papua New Guinea: Institute of Applied Social and Economic Research.

———— 1983. "Sudest Island and the Louisiade Archipelago in Massim Exchange." In Jerry Leach and Edmund Leach, eds., *The Kula: New Perspectives on Massim Exchange.* Cambridge: Cambridge University Press.

———— 1985a. "Gender, Aging, and Dying in an Egalitarian Society." In Dorothy and David Counts, eds., *Aging and Its Transformations.* Association for Social Anthropology in Oceania Monograph, no. 10. Washington, D.C.: University Press of America.

———— 1985b. "Infant Feeding and Cultural Adaptation on Vanatinai (Sudest Island), Papua New Guinea." *Ecology of Food and Nutrition* 16(2):105–126. Reprinted in Leslie Marshall, ed., *Infant Care and Feeding in the South Pacific.* New York: Gordon and Breach, 1985.

———— 1989a. "Death and Exchange: Mortuary Ritual on Vanatinai (Sudest Island)." In Frederick Damon and Roy Wagner, eds., *Death Rituals and Life in the Societies of the Kula Ring.* De Kalb: Northern Illinois University Press.

———— 1989b. "Soldiers and Spirits: The Impact of World War II on a Coral Sea Island." In Geoffrey White and Lamont Lindstrom, eds., *The Pacific Theater: Island Representations of World War II.* Pacific Monograph Series, vol. 8. Honolulu: University of Hawaii Press.

———— 1990a. "Gender in an Egalitarian Society: A Case Study from the Coral Sea." In Peggy Sanday and Ruth Goodenough, eds., *Beyond the Second Sex: New Directions in the Anthropology of Gender.* Philadelphia: University of Pennsylvania Press.

———— 1990b. "Big Men, Big Women, and Cultural Autonomy." *Ethnology* 29(10):35–50.

———— 1990c. "Sorcery and Penicillin: Treating Illness on a Papua New Guinea Island." *Social Science and Medicine* 30(10):1049–1063.

———— 1991. "The Way of the Ancestors: Custom, Innovation, and Resistance." *Ethnology* 30(3):217–235.

———— n.d.1. "Gold Dust and Kula Shells." Manuscript.

———— n.d.2. "Islanders, Ancestors, and Europeans on the Coral Sea Frontier." Manuscript.

Lévi-Strauss, Claude. 1963. *Totemism.* Boston: Beacon Press.

———— 1969a. *The Elementary Structures of Kinship.* Ed. Rodney Needham. Tr. J. Bell and J. von Sturmer. Boston: Beacon Press.

———— 1969b. *The Raw and the Cooked.* Tr. J. and D. Weightman. New York: Harper and Row.

Levy, Robert. 1988 [1973]. *Tahitians: Mind and Experience in the Society Islands.* Chicago: University of Chicago Press.

Liep, John. 1983. "Ranked Exchange on Rossel Island." In Jerry Leach and Edmund Leach, eds., *The Kula: New Perspectives on Massim Exchange.* Cambridge: Cambridge University Press.

———— 1989. "The Day of Reckoning on Rossel Island." In Frederick Damon and Roy Wagner, eds., *Death Rituals and Life in the Societies of the Kula Ring.* De Kalb: Northern Illinois University Press.

Lindstrom, Lamont. 1990. *Knowledge and Power in a South Pacific Society.* Washington, D.C.: Smithsonian Institution Press.

Linnekin, Jocelyn. 1990. *Sacred Queens and Women of Consequence: Rank, Gender, and Colonialism in the Hawaiian Islands.* Ann Arbor: University of Michigan Press.

Bibliography

Linton, Ralph. 1940. "A Neglected Aspect of Social Organization." *American Journal of Sociology* 45:870–886.

———— 1942. "Age and Sex Categories." *American Sociological Review* 7(5):589–603.

Lowie, Robert. 1919. "The Matrilineal Complex." *University of California Publications in American Archaeology and Ethnology* 16(2):29–45.

———— 1920. *Primitive Society*. London: George Routledge.

MacCormack, Carol, and Marilyn Strathern, eds. 1980. *Nature, Culture, and Gender.* Cambridge: Cambridge University Press.

Macgillivray, John. 1852. *Narrative of the Voyage of H.M.S. Rattlesnake. Commanded by the late Owen Stanley, R.N., F.R.S. and During the Years 1846–1850. Including Discoveries and Surveys in New Guinea, the Louisiade Archipelago, etc.* 2 volumes. London: T. and W. Boone.

MacGregor, William. 1891a. British New Guinea Annual Reports.

———— 1891b. British New Guinea Annual Reports. Appendix R.

Macintyre, Martha. 1983. "Kune on Tubetube and in the Bwanabwana Region of the Southern Massim." In Jerry Leach and Edmund Leach, eds., *The Kula: New Perspectives on Massim Exchange*. Cambridge: Cambridge University Press.

———— 1987. "Flying Witches and Leaping Warriors: Supernatural Origins of Power and Matrilineal Authority in Tubetube Society." In Marilyn Strathern, ed., *Dealing with Inequality: Analysing Gender Relations in Melanesia and Beyond*. Cambridge: Cambridge University Press.

———— 1988. "The Unhappy Wife and the Dispensable Husband—Myths of Matrilineal Order." In Deborah Gewertz, ed., *Myths of Matriarchy Reconsidered*. Oceania Monograph, no. 33. Sydney: University of Sydney Press.

———— 1989. "The Triumph of the *Susu*: Mortuary Exchanges on Tubetube." In Frederick Damon and Roy Wagner, eds., *Death Rituals and Life in the Societies of the Kula Ring*. De Kalb: Northern Illinois University Press.

Maddock, Kenneth. 1978. "Introduction." In Ira Buchler and Kenneth Maddock, eds., *The Rainbow Serpent: A Chromatic Piece*. The Hague: Mouton.

Malinowski, Bronislaw. 1954 [1916]. "Baloma: The Spirits of the Dead in the Trobriand Islands." In Bronislaw Malinowski, *Magic, Science, and Religion, and Other Essays*. New York: Doubleday.

———— 1922. *Argonauts of the Western Pacific*. New York: Dutton.

———— 1926. *Crime and Custom in Savage Society*. Totowa, N.J.: Littlefield, Adams.

———— 1929. *The Sexual Life of Savages in North-Western Melanesia*. New York: Harcourt, Brace and World.

———— 1934. "Stone Implements in Eastern New Guinea." In E. E. Evans-Pritchard et al., eds., *Essays Presented to C. G. Seligman*. London: Kegan, Paul, Trench, Trubner.

———— 1935. *Coral Gardens and Their Magic: A Study of the Methods of Tilling the Soil and of Agricultural Rites in the Trobriand Islands*. 2 vols. New York: American Book. Reprint 1978 in one volume. New York: Dover.

———— 1954. *Magic, Science, and Religion, and Other Essays*. New York: Doubleday.

———— 1962. *Sex, Culture, and Myth*. New York: Harcourt, Brace and World.

Marcus, George, and Michael Fischer, eds. 1986. *Anthropology as Cultural Critique: An Experimental Moment in the Human Sciences*. Chicago: University of Chicago Press.

Marett, R. R. 1912. "The Study of Magico-Religious Facts." In Editorial Committee of the British Association, *Notes and Queries on Anthropology*. 4th ed. London: Harrison and Sons.

Margold, Jane, and Donna Bellorado. 1985. "Matrilineal Heritage: A Look at the Power of Contemporary Micronesian Women." In Madeleine Goodman, ed., *Women in Asia and the Pacific: Towards an East-West Dialogue*. Honolulu: Women's Studies Program, University of Hawaii.

Marwick, Max. 1970. "Witchcraft as a Social Strain-Gauge." In Max Marwick, ed., *Witchcraft and Sorcery: Selected Readings*. Harmondsworth: Penguin.

Mason, Otis. 1895. *Woman's Share in Primitive Culture*. New York: Macmillan.

Mauss, Marcel. 1954 [1925]. *The Gift*. Tr. I. Cunnison. London: Cohen and West.

Mead, Margaret. 1928. *Coming of Age in Samoa*. New York: William Morrow.

—— 1930. *Social Organization of Manu'a*. Honolulu: Bishop Museum Publications.

—— 1933. "The Marsalai Cult Among the Arapesh, with Special Reference to the Rainbow Serpent Beliefs of the Australian Aboriginals." *Oceania* 4(1):37–53.

—— 1935. *Sex and Temperament in Three Primitive Societies*. New York: William Morrow.

Meggitt, M. J. 1964. "Male-Female Relationships in the Highlands of Australian New Guinea." In James B. Watson, ed., *New Guinea: The Central Highlands*. Special Publication, no. 66 (vol. 4, part 2). Washington, D.C.: American Anthropological Association.

—— 1965. "The Mae Enga of the Western Highlands." In P. Lawrence and M. J. Meggitt, eds., *Gods, Ghosts and Men in Melanesia*. Melbourne: Oxford University Press.

Meigs, Anna. 1976. "Male Pregnancy and Reduction of Sexual Opposition in a New Guinea Highlands Society." *Ethnology* 15:393–408.

—— 1983. Discussion with author.

—— 1984. *Food, Sex, and Pollution: A New Guinea Religion*. New Brunswick: Rutgers University Press.

—— 1990. "Multiple Gender Ideologies and Statuses." In Peggy Sanday and Ruth Goodenough, eds., *Beyond the Second Sex: New Directions in the Anthropology of Gender*. Philadelphia: University of Pennsylvania Press.

Miller, Barbara. 1981. *The Endangered Sex: Neglect of Female Children in Rural North India*. Ithaca: Cornell University Press.

—— 1987. "Female Infanticide in India." In Nancy Scheper-Hughes, ed., *Child Survival: Anthropological Perspectives on the Treatment and Maltreatment of Children*. Dordrecht: D. Reidel.

Mintz, Sidney. 1971. "Men, Women, and Trade." *Comparative Studies in Society and History* 13:247–269.

Morauta, Louise. 1981. "Social Stratification in Lowland Papua New Guinea: Issues and Questions." Paper presented at a seminar on Social Stratification in Papua New Guinea, May 1981, Department of Political and Social Change, Research School of Pacific Studies, Australian National University, Canberra.

Morgan, Lewis Henry. 1877. *Ancient Society*. New York: Holt and Company.

Mountford, Charles. 1978. "The Rainbow-Serpent Myths of Australia." In Ira Buchler and Kenneth Maddock, eds., *The Rainbow Serpent: A Chromatic Piece*. The Hague: Mouton.

Mukhopadhyay, Carol, and Patricia Higgins. 1988. "Anthropological Studies of Women's Status Revisited: 1977–1987." *Annual Review of Anthropology* 17:461–495.

Munn, Nancy. 1983. "Gawan Kula: Spatiotemporal Control and the Symbolism of Influence." In Jerry Leach and Edmund Leach, eds., *The Kula: New Perspectives on Massim Exchange*. Cambridge: Cambridge University Press.

——— 1986. *The Fame of Gawa: A Symbolic Study of Value Transformation in a Massim (Papua New Guinea) Society*. Cambridge: Cambridge University Press.

Murphy, Yolanda, and Robert Murphy. 1974. *Women of the Forest*. New York: Columbia University Press.

Nadel, S. F. 1967 [1952]. "Witchcraft in Four African Societies: An Essay in Comparison." In Clellan S. Ford, ed., *Cross Cultural Approaches: Readings in Comparative Research*. New Haven: HRAF Press.

Nash, Jill. 1987. "Gender Attributes and Equality: Men's Strength and Women's Talk Among the Nagovisi." In Marilyn Strathern, ed., *Dealing with Inequality: Analysing Gender Relations in Melanesia and Beyond*. Cambridge: Cambridge University Press.

Nelson, Hank. 1976. *Black, White and Gold: Goldmining in Papua New Guinea, 1978–1930*. Canberra: Australian National University Press.

Ogbu, John. 1978. "African Bridewealth and Women's Status." *American Ethnologist* 5:241–262.

Olson, Ronald. 1936. "Some Trading Customs of the Chilkat Tlingit." In *Essays in Anthropology Presented to A. L. Kroeber in Celebration of His Sixtieth Birthday*. Berkeley: University of California Press.

Ortner, Sherry. 1974. "Is Female to Male as Nature Is to Culture?" In Michelle Rosaldo and Louise Lamphere, eds., *Woman, Culture, and Society*. Stanford: Stanford University Press.

——— 1984. "Theory in Anthropology Since the Sixties." *Comparative Studies in Society and History* 26(1):126–166.

——— 1990. "Gender Hegemonies." *Cultural Critique* 15:35–80.

Ortner, Sherry, and Harriet Whitehead. 1981. "Introduction: Accounting for Sexual Meanings." In Sherry Ortner and Harriet Whitehead, eds., *Sexual Meanings: The Cultural Construction of Gender and Sexuality*. Cambridge: Cambridge University Press.

Ortner, Sherry, and Harriet Whitehead, eds. 1981. *Sexual Meanings: The Cultural Construction of Gender and Sexuality*. Cambridge: Cambridge University Press.

Osborne, D. H. 1942. "Old Days in the Louisiades. Memories of the First Recruiter." *Pacific Islands Monthly* 13(3):34.

Parmentier, Richard. 1985. "Gendered Wealth: Male and Female Valuables in Belau Mortuary Exchange." Paper presented at the American Anthropological Association Annual Meeting, Denver, Colorado.

Pawley, A., and R. C. Green. 1976. "Dating the Dispersal of the Oceanic Languages." *Oceanic Linguistics* 12:1–67.

Peletz, Michael. 1988. *A Share of the Harvest: Kinship, Property, and Social History Among the Malays of Rembau*. Berkeley: University of California Press.

Bibliography

Petersen, Glenn. 1982. "Ponapean Matriliny: Production, Exchange, and the Ties That Bind." *American Ethnologist* 9:129–144.

Poole, Fitz. 1981. "Transforming 'Natural' Woman: Female Ritual Leaders and Gender Ideology Among Bimin Kuskusmin." In Sherry Ortner and Harriet Whitehead, eds., *Sexual Meanings: The Cultural Construction of Gender and Sexuality*. Cambridge: Cambridge University Press.

———— 1985. "Coming Into Social Being: Cultural Images of Infants in Bimin-Kuskusmin Folk Psychology." In Geoffrey White and John Kirkpatrick, eds., *Person, Self and Experience: Exploring Pacific Ethnopsychologies*. Berkeley: University of California Press.

———— 1987. "Ritual Rank, the Self, and Ancestral Power: Liturgy and Substance in a Papua New Guinea Society." In Lamont Lindstrom, ed., *Drugs in Western Pacific Societies: Relations of Substance*. Association for Social Anthropology in Melanesia Monograph, no. 11. Lanham: University Press of America.

Potter, Sulamith. 1987. "Birth Planning in Rural China: A Cultural Account." In Nancy Scheper-Hughes, ed., *Child Survival: Anthropological Perspectives on the Treatment and Maltreatment of Children*. Dordrecht: D. Reidel.

Powdermaker, Hortense. 1931. "Mortuary Rites in New Ireland." *Oceania* 2(1):26–43.

———— 1933. *Life in Lesu: The Study of a Melanesian Society in New Ireland*. New York: Norton.

Pratt, Mary Louise. 1986. "Fieldwork in Common Places." In James Clifford and George Marcus, eds., *Writing Culture: The Poetics and Politics of Ethnography*. Berkeley: University of California Press.

Price, Charles, and Elizabeth Baker. 1976. "Origins of Pacific Island Labourers in Queensland, 1863–1904: A Research Note." *Journal of Pacific History* 11(1–2):106–121.

Radcliffe-Brown, A. R. 1952. *Structure and Function in Primitive Society*. Glencoe: Free Press.

Radcliffe-Brown, A. R., and Darryll Forde, eds. 1950. *African Systems of Kinship and Marriage*. London: Oxford University Press.

Read, Kenneth. 1954. "Cultures of the Central Highlands, New Guinea." *Southwestern Journal of Anthropology* 10:1–43.

Reichard, Gladys. 1934. *Spider Woman: A Story of Navajo Weavers and Chanters*. New York: Macmillan.

———— 1969 [1928]. *Social Life of the Navajo Indians*. New York: AMS Press.

Richards, Audrey. 1950. "Some Types of Family Structure Amongst the Central Bantu." In A. R. Radcliffe-Brown and Darryl Forde, eds., *African Systems of Kinship and Marriage*. London: Oxford University Press.

———— 1956. *Chisungu: A Girls' Initiation Rite Among the Bemba of Northern Rhodesia*. London: Faber and Faber.

Rivers, W. H. R. 1914. *Kinship and Social Organisation*. London: Constable.

Rogers, Susan Carol. 1975. "Female Forms of Power and the Myth of Male Dominance: A Model of Female/Male Interaction in Peasant Society." *American Ethnologist* 2:727–756.

Róheim, Géza. 1932. "Tauhau and the Mwadare." *The International Journal of Psychoanalysis* 13:121–174.

———— 1937. "Death and Mourning Ceremonies at Normanby Island." *Man* 37(56-7):49–50.

———— 1946. "Ceremonial Prostitution in Duau (Normanby Island)." *Journal of Clinical Psychopathology and Psychotherapy* 7:753–764.

———— 1948. "Witches of Normanby Island." *Oceania* 13(4):279–308.

———— 1950. *Psychoanalysis and Anthropology: Culture, Personality and the Unconscious.* New York: International Universities Press.

———— 1954. "Cannibalism in Duau, Normanby Island, D'Entrecasteaux Group, Territory of Papua." *Mankind* 4(12):488–492.

Rosaldo, Michelle. 1974. "Woman, Culture, and Society: A Theoretical Overview." In Michelle Rosaldo and Louise Lamphere, eds., *Woman, Culture, and Society.* Stanford: Stanford University Press.

———— 1980. "The Use and Abuse of Anthropology: Reflections on Feminism and Cross-Cultural Understanding." *Signs* 5(3):389–417.

Rosaldo, Michelle, and Jane Atkinson. 1975. "Man the Hunter and Woman: Metaphors for the Sexes in Ilongot Magical Spells." In Roy Willis, ed., *The Interpretation of Symbolism.* New York: John Wiley.

Rosaldo, Michelle, and Louise Lamphere, eds. 1974. *Woman, Culture and Society.* Stanford: Stanford University Press.

Rosaldo, Renato. 1980. *Ilongot Headhunting 1883–1974: A Study in Society and History.* Stanford: Stanford University Press.

———— 1984. "Grief and a Headhunter's Rage: On the Cultural Force of Emotions." In Edward Bruner, ed., *Text, Play, and Story.* Seattle: American Ethnological Society.

———— 1989. *Culture and Truth: The Remaking of Social Analysis.* Boston: Beacon.

Rosman, Abraham, and Paula Rubel. 1971. *Feasting with Mine Enemy: Rank and Exchange Among Northwest Coast Societies.* New York: Columbia University Press.

———— 1978. *Your Own Pigs You May Not Eat: A Comparative Study of New Guinea Societies.* Chicago: University of Chicago Press.

Sacks, Karen. 1974. "Engels Revisited: Women, the Organization of Production, and Private Property." In Michelle Rosaldo and Louise Lamphere, eds., *Woman, Culture, and Society.* Stanford: Stanford University Press.

Sahlins, Marshall. 1958. *Social Stratification in Polynesia.* Seattle: University of Washington Press.

———— 1963. "Poor Man, Rich Man, Big Man, Chief: Political Types in Melanesia and Polynesia." *Comparative Studies in Society and History* 5:285–303.

———— 1989. "Comment: The Force of Ethnology: Origins and Significance of the Melanesia/Polynesia Division." *Current Anthropology* 30:36–37.

Sanday, Peggy. 1973. "Toward a Theory of the Status of Women." *American Anthropologist* 75:1682–1700.

———— 1974. "Female Status in the Public Domain." In Michelle Rosaldo and Louise Lamphere, eds., *Woman, Culture, and Society.* Stanford: Stanford University Press.

———— 1981. *Female Power and Male Dominance: On the Origins of Sexual Inequality.* Cambridge: Cambridge University Press.

———— 1990a. "Androcentric and Matrifocal Gender Representations in Minangkabau Ideology." In Peggy Sanday and Ruth Goodenough, eds., *Beyond the Second Sex: New Directions in the Anthropology of Gender.* Philadelphia: University of Pennsylvania Press.

Bibliography

———— 1990b. "Introduction." In Peggy Sanday and Ruth Goodenough, eds., *Beyond the Second Sex: New Directions in the Anthropology of Gender*. Philadelphia: University of Pennsylvania Press.

Sanday, Peggy, and Ruth Goodenough, eds. 1990. *Beyond the Second Sex: New Directions in the Anthropology of Gender*. Philadelphia: University of Pennsylvania Press.

Schieffelin, Bambi. 1990. *The Give and Take of Everyday Life: Language Socialization of Kaluli Children*. Cambridge: Cambridge University Press.

Schieffelin, Edward. 1976. *The Sorrow of the Lonely and the Burning of the Dancers*. New York: St. Martin's.

Schlegel, Alice. 1972. *Male Dominance and Female Autonomy: Domestic Authority in Matrilineal Societies*. New Haven: HRAF Press.

———— 1977. Towards a Theory of Sexual Stratification. In Alice Schlegel, ed., *Sexual Stratification: A Cross-Cultural View*. New York: Columbia University Press.

———— 1990. "Gender Meanings: General and Specific." In Peggy Sanday and Ruth Goodenough, eds., *Beyond the Second Sex: New Directions in the Anthropology of Gender*. Philadelphia: University of Pennsylvania Press.

Schneider, David. 1953. "Abortion and Depopulation on a Pacific Island." In B. D. Paul, ed., *Health, Culture, and Community*. New York: Russell Sage.

———— 1961. "Introduction: The Distinctive Features of Matrilineal Descent Groups." In David Schneider and Kathleen Gough, eds., *Matrilineal Kinship*. Berkeley: University of California Press.

Schneider, David, and Kathleen Gough, eds. 1961. *Matrilineal Kinship*. Berkeley: University of California Press.

Schwartz, Theodore. 1979. "Cult and Context: The Paranoid Ethos in Melanesia." *Ethos* 1:153–174.

Scoditti, Giancarlo, with Jerry Leach. 1983. "Kula on Kitava." In Jerry Leach and Edmund Leach, eds., *The Kula: New Perspectives on Massim Exchange*. Cambridge: Cambridge University Press.

Seligman, C. G. 1909. "A Classification of the Natives of British New Guinea." *Journal of the Royal Anthropological Institute* 39:246–275.

———— 1910. *The Melanesians of British New Guinea*. Cambridge: Cambridge University Press.

Silverblatt, Irene. 1987. *Moon, Sun, and Witches: Gender Ideologies and Class in Inca and Colonial Peru*. Princeton: Princeton University Press.

Simmons, Leo. 1945. *The Role of the Aged in Primitive Society*. New Haven: Yale University Press.

Simmons, William. 1971. *Eyes of the Night*. Boston: Little, Brown.

———— 1980. "Powerlessness, Exploitation, and the Souleating Witch: An Analysis of Badyaranke Witchcraft." *American Ethnologist* 7(3):447–465.

Sorenson, E. Richard. 1976. *The Edge of the Forest: Land, Childhood and Change in a New Guinea Protoagricultural Society*. Washington: Smithsonian Institution Press.

Spriggs, Matthew. 1984. "The Lapita Cultural Complex: Origins, Distribution, Contemporaries, and Successors." *Journal of Pacific History* 19:202–223.

Stanley, Owen. 1849. Unpublished journal. Photocopy in New Guinea Collection, Library of the University of Papua New Guinea.

Stephen, Michelle. 1987a. "Contrasting Images of Power." In Michelle Stephen, ed., *Sorcerer and Witch in Melanesia*. New Brunswick: Rutgers University Press.

———— 1987b. "Master of Souls: The Mekeo Sorcerer." In Michelle Stephen, ed., *Sorcerer and Witch in Melanesia*. New Brunswick: Rutgers University Press.

Stephens, William. 1967. "A Cross-Cultural Study of Menstrual Taboos." In Clellan S. Ford, ed., *Cross-Cultural Approaches: Readings in Comparative Research*. New Haven: Human Relations Area Files Press.

Strathern, Andrew. 1971. *The Rope of Moka: Big Men and Ceremonial Exchange in Mount Hagen, New Guinea*. Cambridge: Cambridge University Press.

———— 1972. *One Father, One Blood*. Canberra: Australian National University Press.

———— 1987. "Social Classes in Mount Hagen? The Early Evidence." *Ethnology* 26:245–260.

Strathern, Marilyn. 1972. *Women In Between: Female Roles in a Male World*. London: Seminar (Academic) Press.

———— 1980. "No Nature, No Culture: The Hagen Case." In Carol MacCormick and Marilyn Strathern, eds., *Nature, Culture, and Gender*. Cambridge: Cambridge University Press.

———— 1981. "Self-Interest and the Social Good: Some Implications of Hagen Gender Ideology." In Sherry Ortner and Harriet Whitehead, eds., *Sexual Meanings: The Cultural Construction of Gender and Sexuality*. Cambridge: Cambridge University Press.

———— 1987. "Introduction." In Marilyn Strathern, ed., *Dealing with Inequality: Analysing Gender Relations in Melanesia and Beyond*. Cambridge: Cambridge University Press.

———— 1988. *The Gender of the Gift: Problems with Women and Problems with Society in Melanesia*. Berkeley: University of California Press.

———— 1990. *Partial Connections*. Association for Social Anthropology Special Publication, no. 3. Lanham, Maryland: University Press of America.

Territory of Papua 1911, 1912, 1934, 1935, 1943, 1948, 1951, 1951–52, 1952–53, 1953, 1954, 1959, 1960–61, 1962, 1971, 1972. Patrol Reports on Sudest Island, Misima Sub-District, Milne Bay District.

Thomas, Nicholas. 1989. "The Force of Ethnology: Origins and Significance of the Melanesia/Polynesia Division." *Current Anthropology* 30:27–34.

Thune, Carl. 1980. "The Rhetoric of Remembrance: Collective Life and Personal Tragedy in Loboda Village." Ph.D. diss., Department of Anthropology, Princeton University.

———— 1983. "Kula Traders and Lineage Members: The Structure of Village and Kula Exchange on Normanby Island." In Jerry Leach and Edmund Leach, eds., *The Kula: New Perspectives on Massim Exchange*. Cambridge: Cambridge University Press.

Turner, Victor. 1964. "Witchcraft and Sorcery: Taxonomy Versus Dynamics." *Africa* 34:314–325.

Tuzin, Donald. 1980. *The Voice of the Tambaran: Truth and Illusion in Ilahita Arapesh Religion*. Berkeley: University of California Press.

Vansina, Jan. 1990. *Paths in the Rainforests: Toward a History of Political Tradition in Equatorial Africa*. Madison: University of Wisconsin Press.

Wagner, Roy. 1972. *Habu: The Innovation of Meaning in Daribi Religion*. Chicago: University of Chicago Press.

———— 1975. *The Invention of Culture*. Englewood Cliffs, N.J.: Prentice-Hall.

———— 1991. "The Fractal Person." In Maurice Godelier and Marilyn Strathern, eds.,

Bibliography

Big Men and Great Men: Personifications of Power in Melanesia. Cambridge: Cambridge University Press.

Wallace, Anthony. 1972. *The Death and Rebirth of the Seneca.* New York: Vintage.

Warner, W. L. 1937. *A Black Civilization.* New York: Harper and Row.

Wawn, William T. 1893. *The South Sea Islanders and the Queensland Labour Trade.* London: S. Sonnenschein.

Weiner, Annette. 1976. *Women of Value, Men of Renown: New Perspectives in Trobriand Exchange.* Austin: University of Texas Press.

——— 1980. "Reproduction: A Replacement for Reciprocity." *American Ethnologist* 7(1):71–85.

——— 1982. "Sexuality Among the Anthropologists: Reproduction Among the Informants." In Fitz Poole and Gilbert Herdt, eds., *Sexual Antagonism, Gender, and Social Change in Papua New Guinea. Social Analysis* (special issue) 12:52–65.

——— 1986. "Forgotten Wealth: Cloth and Women's Production in the Pacific." In Eleanor Leacock and Helen Safa, eds., *Women's Work: Development and the Division of Labor by Gender.* South Hadley, Mass.: Bergin and Garvey Publishers.

——— 1989. "Why Cloth? Wealth, Gender, and Power in Oceania." In Annette Weiner and Jane Schneider, eds., *Cloth and Human Experience.* Washington, D.C.: Smithsonian Institution Press.

——— 1992. *Inalienable Possessions: The Paradox of Keeping-While-Giving.* Berkeley: University of California Press.

Weist, Katherine. 1973. "Giving Away: The Ceremonial Distribution of Goods Among the Northern Cheyenne of Southeastern Montana." *Plains Anthropologist* 18(60): 97–103.

Welsch, Robert. 1983. "Traditional Medicine and Western Medical Options Among the Ningerum of Papua New Guinea." In Lola Romanucci-Ross, Daniel Moerman, and Lawrence Tancredi, eds., *The Anthropology of Medicine: From Culture to Method.* New York: Praeger.

White, David. 1893. "Descriptive Account, by David L. White, Esquire, of the Customs, etc. of the Natives of Sudest Island." British New Guinea Annual Reports, Appendix U, 73–76.

Whyte, Martin. 1978. *The Status of Women in Pre-Industrial Society.* Princeton: Princeton University Press.

Wiessner, Polly. 1982. "Risk, Reciprocity, and Social Influences on !Kung San Economics." In Eleanor Leacock, ed., *Politics and History in Band Societies.* Cambridge: Cambridge University Press.

——— 1990. "The Participation of Men and Women in Exchange Networks Among the !Kung San." Paper presented at the Fifth International Hunter-Gatherer Conference. Fairbanks, Alaska.

Wolf, Eric. 1982. *Europe and the People Without History.* Berkeley: University of California Press.

Wolf, Margery. 1972. *Women and the Family in Rural Taiwan.* Stanford: Stanford University Press.

Wood, J., P. Johnson, and K. Campbell. 1985. "Demographic and Endocrinological Aspects of Low Natural Fertility in Highland New Guinea." *Journal of Biosocial Science* 17:57–79.

Bibliography

Worsley, Peter. 1968. *The Trumpet Shall Sound: A Study of "Cargo" Cults in Melanesia.* 2d augmented ed. New York: Schocken.

Young, Michael W. 1971a. *Fighting with Food: Leadership, Values and Social Control in a Massim Society.* Cambridge: Cambridge University Press.

———— 1971b. "Goodenough Island Cargo Cults." *Oceania* 42:42–57.

———— 1983a. "The Theme of the Resentful Hero: Stasis and Mobility in Goodenough Mythology." In Jerry Leach and Edmund Leach, eds., *The Kula: New Perspectives on Massim Exchange.* Cambridge: Cambridge University Press.

———— 1983b. *Magicians of Manumanua: Living Myth in Kalauna.* Berkeley: University of California Press.

———— 1987. "The Tusk, the Flute and the Serpent: Disguise and Revelation in Goodenough Mythology." In Marilyn Strathern, ed., *Dealing with Inequality: Analysing Gender Relations in Melanesia and Beyond.* Cambridge: Cambridge University Press.

———— 1989a. "Illness and Ideology: Aspects of Health Care on Goodenough Island." In Stephen Frankel and Gilbert Lewis, eds., *A Continuing Trial of Treatment: Medical Pluralism in Papua New Guinea.* Dordrecht: Kluwer Academic Publishers.

———— 1989b. " 'Eating the Dead': Mortuary Transactions in Bwaidoka, Goodenough Island." In Frederick Damon and Roy Wagner, eds., *Death Rituals and Life in the Societies of the Kula Ring.* De Kalb: Northern Illinois University Press.

Zelenietz, Martin. 1981. "Sorcery and Social Change: An Introduction." *Social Analysis* 8:3–14.

Index

Abortion, 85, 163

Abu-Lughod, Lila, 308*n*10

Adolescence, 97–98; adolescent subfecundity, 312*n*4; *see also* Youth

Adoption, 85–90; and warfare, 61

Adultery, 110; as a crime, 71; and divorce, 111

Adulthood, 107–19

Affinal relations, 46–47, 109–10; affinal exchange, 108–10, 112, 143, 219, 252, 263, 269–74, 325*n*15; avoidances, 112, 245; and childbirth, 271–72; competition in, 269–70; and mortuary ritual, 220–21, 233–34, 238–40, 244–47, 250, 253, 262, 267, 269–76, 298–99, 326*nn*15, 16, 19, 20, 21, 22, 328*n*10

Age: grading, 38, 83; roles, 83–84; stratification, 312*n*2

Age-sex categories, 312*n*2

Aggression: and gender relations, 32, 307*nn*6, 7; male, as personal quality, 58, 292, 307*n*7; and socialization, 58; and warfare, 73–74, 292–93, 307*n*6; against women, 73

Agta (Philippines), 315*n*26

Aid posts, 70, 196, 312*n*3

Alagh: and magic, 161; in myth, 129, 133–35, 144, 316*n*3

Alotau, 1, 2, 3, 70, 77, 105, 197

Amazonia: age stratification in, 312*n*2; myths, 145, 149, 154

America: and ancestors, 24–25, 135; wartime relations with Americans, 26, 27, 68

American Museum of Natural History, 24

Ancestors: honoring, 278, 280; way of the ancestors, 30, 48, 151–52, 219, 291, 293–94

Ancestor spirits, ix, xiii, 77–78, 134–37, 152; Europeans as, 23–28, 171; and knowledge, 165–66, 228, 280; and magic, 157–58, 166, 220, 228; and mortuary ritual, 220, 251, 260, 267–68; relations with, 220, 226–28, 267–68; and warfare, 75

Animals: and humans, 137; in myth, 147–50; as totems, 136–37

Annie Brooks, 59

Araida (Village), 104, 184, 213

Archeology, and Vanatinai history, 49–51

Argonauts of the Western Pacific, xi

Armlets, fern-fiber, 206–7; and mortuary ritual, 247, 255, 258, 260, 277

Armshells: Conus, in exchange, 36, 59, 209–10, 322*n*2, 324*n*8; Conus, prehistoric trade in, 50–51; Trochus, as ornament, 156

Armstrong, W. E., 13, 139–40, 146, 217, 310n31, 314n14, 316n2, 317nn7, 8, 9, 320n20, 325n15, 326n17

Arrival, xiv; as trope, xiv

Ashanti (Africa), 296

Asiara, *see* Warrior

Asymmetry, gender or sexual, 32, 123–24, 129, 131, 166, 205, 283–84, 287–88, 290, 292, 329n3

Athapaskans, Northern (North America), 324n7

Atkinson, Jane, 32

Australia: Australian New Guinea Administrative Unit (ANGAU), 67–68; Australians, 63, 66, 76; and labor trade, 63; *see also* Government, colonial

Australian aborigines, 145, 311n34, 312n2, 315n24, 319n14

Australasian Methodist Missionary Society, 3, 68

Austronesian(s), 49–50, 220

Authority, 78, 279, 285–86; of big men and big women, ix, 40–42, 175–76; female, 47–48, 307n7; male, vii, viii, 47–48, 281; in matrilineal societies, 298; political, 40, 76–77, 208, 292–94, 296–97, 301–2, 306; of sorcerers, 176, 194

Autonomy, viii, xii, 39–40, 118, 123–24; cultural, 78–79, 219; female, xii, xv, 32–33, 78–80, 118, 291, 293, 296–97, 330n5; personal, 286, 291, 293, 304–6

Axe blades, greenstone, 329n3; as bridewealth, 108–9; as compensation to allies, 61–62; in courtship, 104; in exchange, xiii, 36, 41, 59, 61, 77, 87–88, 209–10, 213, 215–16, 218; individual names of 256, 258; magic of, 156–57; in mortuary ritual, 13–14, 221–22, 244–46, 249–50, 254–58, 261, 263, 266, 269, 275–77, 279, 326n15; as tribute to landowners, 301; types, 156, 216–18

Axe handles, ceremonial, 217; male carving of, 115, 217, 249, 255, 277

Axes, metal, in trade with Europeans, 54–59, 65

Azande (Africa), 171

Bagi, *see* Necklaces, shell-disc

Bagodi (pseudonym), 252–60

Bambagho, xiii, 125–27, 130, 134, 143–44, 146–51, 156, 217, 311n31, 318n12

Banana (plantain), 10, 44; in mortuary ritual, 241, 253–54; in myth, 147–49; in precolonial era, 52; in trade with Europeans, 56

Barnett, Homer, 324n7

Barracuda, 42; as totem, 42, 136–37

Bartle Bay, 325n15

Baruya (New Guinea), 74–79, 152–54

Baskets: in exchange, 215; as female wealth 323n7; and food magic, 258–59, 302–3; manufacture, 115, 221; in mortuary ritual, 221–22, 241–43, 250, 252, 255, 257, 265, 276; in mourning, 12–13, 229, 241; pandanus leaf, 20; and paraphernalia, 163

Bats: and sorcery, 142, 191; and witchcraft, 142

Battaglia, Debbora, 314–15n20, 319n16, 328n11, 329n13, 329–30n3, 330n8

Baule (Africa), 323n7

Bêche-de-mer, 311n34; trade with Europeans, 54, 58–60, 62–64, 75

Belau (Micronesia), 323n7

Bemba (Africa), 296

Beng (Africa), 313n13

Berde, Stuart, 214, 314–15n20, 328–29n11, 329n13

Berkeley, University of California at, x–xi

Betel nut (Areca nut), 11, 12, 16, 114, 248–49, 252, 254, 290, 303; and courtship, 314n15; in exchange, 44, 61, 207, 215, 266, 269; in magic, 169; in myth, 147; in mortuary ritual, 232, 235, 256; in sorcery, 189, 191–92

Betel pepper, 44
Biak (New Guinea), 135
Big men, ix, 40–42, 74–75, 211–12, 288, 297, 301, 312*n*45, 330*n*9; *see also* Giagia; Great men
Big women, ix, 40–42, 74–75, 211–12, 265–66, 297, 301, 323*n*6; *see also* Giagia
Bimin Kuskusmin (New Guinea), 132, 321*n*5
Birds: and humans, 137; as messengers, 142, 227; as place spirits, 138; as totems, 45–46, 136–37, 309*n*19, 317*n*7
Bishop of Norwich, 55
Boboghagha (Village), 70, 213, 309*n*24, 310–11*n*31
Bontoc, Western (Philippines), 290
Borneo, 325*n*13
Bosavi, Mt. (New Guinea), 173
Bougainville (Island), 40
Bougainville, Louis de, 54
Bourdieu, Pierre, 37
Bramble, 55, 56
Breadfruit, 10, 44
Brideservice, 88, 107, 109, 314–15*n*20, 315*n*22, 329–30*n*3
Bridewealth, 103, 108–9, 111, 215, 217, 272, 274, 315*nn*21, 22, 325*n*15
Brierly, Oswald, 55
Briggs, Jean, 307*n*7
Brisbane *Courier*, 59
British: early voyages, 54–58; opinion on labor trade, 63
British New Guinea, 2, 53, 64–66, 170; *see also* Government, colonial
Bronchitis, 178
Brooker (Island), 12, 52; cooking pots, 52, 215–16, 269, 276, 327*n*4; exchange, 214–16, 276
Bundles, banana-leaf, 277
Burfitt, George, 67–68
Burial, 188, 222–26, 228, 241, 243–44, 250–51, 274, 316–17*n*4
Buriga (Bulega), 67–68, 317*n*5
Buwa, 102–4

Buyawe (Village), 67
Bwanagum (cave), 316–17*n*4
Bwebweso, Mt., 316*n*4
Bwetha (clan), 51

Calvados Chain (Islands), 5, 42–43, 71, 134; and cargo cults, 67–68, 135; exchange, 44, 167, 169–70, 209–11, 214–16, 218–19, 269, 322–23*n*3; languages, 50, 309*n*18, 310*n*26; mortuary ritual, 221, 251–52, 255, 260, 265–66, 275, 326*n*21, 327*n*6; 328*nn*7, 9, 10, 11, 329*n*14; peoples of, 40, 50, 69–70, 104, 115, 201, 253; and sorcery, 202; and warfare, 51–52, 59–61; and witchcraft, 168, 172, 173, 201, 204; women in, 210–11, 214, 218–19, 221
Cancer, 197, 198
Cannibalism, 61, 73, 74, 230, 244, 268, 285–86, 327*n*3
Canoes, paddling or poling, 9, 215
Canoes, sailing, 2–3, 73; construction, 115, 137, 215, 289; and early contacts with Europeans, 54–57; in exchange, 44, 59, 210, 212–16, 218–19, 269, 278, 324–25*n*9; men and, 329*n*3; in myth, 51, 151; purchase, 215; Rossel Island, 314*n*14; sailing to feasts, 251–52, 261, 266, 275; in warfare, 60
Cape Deliverance (Rossel Island), 55
Cape York (Australia), 56
Cargo, 25; beliefs, 131, 133–35, 145; cults, 67–68, 135, 181, 315*n*5; and myth, 133–35
Cash: economy, 45, 48, 71, 77; in mortuary ritual, 256–58, 327*n*6
Census, 66, 69
Challenge, ritual, 263–64, 328*n*10
Cherokee (North America), 292, 296
Chiefs, 38, 281–82, 321*n*2; and big men/big women, 40, 301–2; female, 323*n*6; and Polynesia, viii, 330*n*9
Childbirth, 81–86, 116, 203, 313–14*n*14
Children, 17, 40; abduction in warfare, 61; attitudes toward, 82, 89–90, 123; child-

care, 17, 92–93, 116, 124, 290, 306; child rearing, 89–93, 123, 313*n*10; gender socialization, 91–93, 96
Child spacing, 84–85
Childwealth, 87–88, 215, 272
China: Chinese laborers, 59; Chinese trade goods, 12; female infants in, 312*n*6; trade with, 54, 311*n*34
Chowning, Ann, 74
Christianity, xiii, 128, 129, 135, 226; *see also* Mission(s)
Clam, Tridacna, 43, 71, 88, 115; in myth, 288; and place spirits, 140–41; smoked, in exchange, 215, 269
Clans, 45–46; origins, 51; and totems, 135–57, 151–52
Class, 40; and gender, 38
Cloth, 65, 70; as female wealth, 323*n*7
Coconut, 10, 114; in diet, 10–11, 43, 63; in European trade, 55, 56; in magic, 41, 156, 162, 319*n*19; and mortuary ritual, 226, 232, 235, 241, 244, 247, 252–58, 261, 265, 327*nn*4, 7, 329*n*14; in myth, 125–26; plantations, 65; in settlements, 44
Collier, Jane, 329*n*12
Colonialism, 293; *see also* Government, colonial
Combs, in mortuary ritual, 244, 255, 258, 277
Conception, 84–85, 120
Conch shell, and mortuary ritual, 252, 275, 328*n*10
Conservatism, cultural, xiii, 71–72
Contested gender roles and ideologies, 35, 282, 290, 330*n*4
Contraception, 84–85, 163, 312*n*4
Cook, Captain James, 138
Cooktown (Australia), 64
Copal gum: as commodity, 45, 65, 70; in early contacts, 53; magic and, 161
Copra, 3, 5, 45, 53, 65, 70
Coral Sea, 42; Battle of, 24, 26, 29, 67; early European voyages in, 53–55; frontier, 59–64
Corn, 63

Corpse, symbolism of, 238–40, 270, 278–79, 285, 287–88, 303–4, 328*n*11; *see also* Burial
Cosmology, xv, 127–128
Courtship, 102–4, 215, 259, 262, 273, 314*n*15
Cowley, C. F., 182
Cousins, cross-cousins, 46; *see also* Heir of deceased
Crabs, 43, 89
Crime, 71
Crocodiles, 4, 42, 206; commercial hunting, 45, 70; subsistence hunting, 45, 114; as totems, 42, 45, 136–37; and witchcraft, 195
Croton, 224
Crow (North America), 46, 296
Cultural change, 71–72; and gender, 48, 78–80; on Vanatinai, 48–80
Cultural innovation, 48–49, 71–72
Custom, xii, 4, 143, 148, 151–52; and gender, 283
Cyclones, 10, 51, 168–70, 195; and exchange, 269

Dancing: at feasts, 11–12, 14–15, 259, 261; taboos, 11, 232
Daveri, *see* Shell currency pieces
Dawin (New Guinea), 51, 216–17, 325*n*11
Deaf, communication with, 21
Death, 87, 116, 120, 203, 207, 244–46, 251; of a child, 326*n*2; emotions and, 267; and exchange, 219–24, 238–40, 261; and sorcery, 170, 174–76, 200–1, 220, 224, 233, 326*n*16; and taboo violation, 138–40, 170; and witchcraft, 170, 195–201, 233, 326*n*16; *see also* Burial; Mortuary ritual
Dedehai (Island), 134, 214
D'Entrecasteaux, Bruny, 54
Derris root, 43, 114
Diaz, May, xi
Diet, 63, 148, 312*n*4, 313*n*9, 327*n*4
Divorce, 98, 107, 111, 118–19, 300

Dobu (Island), 2, 135, 176; affinal relations on, 314*n*19; kula and exchange, 211, 322*n*2, 323*nn*4, 5, 325*n*10; magic, 320*n*21; mortuary ritual, 13, 325*n*15, 328*n*7, 329*n*5; residence, 309*n*21, 314*n*19; sorcery, 178, 321*n*5; witchcraft, 173

Doldrums, 43

Douglas, John, 59

Drought, 62, 63; and exchange, 269

Drums: drumming at feasts, 11, 259; taboos, 232

Drunkenness, 200

Dugong: hunting, 45, 114; as totem, 42, 45

Dulubia, 61

Dundes, Alan, 319*n*15

Dysentery, 64, 178

Ebora (Village), 195

Economy: and gender, 46; Vanatinai subsistence, 42–45; women's participation in, ix

Edaikorighea (hamlet), 213

Ediriwo, 162, 203

Eel, 43, 89, 249–50

Egalitarian societies, vii, x, 32–33, 35, 38, 46–47, 286, 298; and big men, ix, 330*n*9; and gender, 295, 305–6; Vanatinai as egalitarian, xii, 31–32, 35, 36, 38–42, 46–47, 290, 293, 298, 305–6

Egogona, 129, 133, 316*n*3

Egoregore, 162, 203

Ekuneada, 129, 133–34, 156, 316*n*3

Elderly: activities of, 120–22; attitudes toward, 199–22, 198; and magical knowledge, 120, 123; in small-scale societies, 40; as sorcerers or witches, 120–21

Elephantiasis, 140–41, 318*n*11

Embambalia (Village), 6

Emuga, 147–51

Enga (New Guinea), 214

Engineer Group (Islands), 51–52, 66, 309*n*25

England, in myth, 135

English (language), 4, 15, 76, 80, 96, 138, 253, 293

English, Father Kevin, 139

Estuaries, as resource, 43

Etadiwewa (hamlet), 17–18, 222

Ethnographic authority, xiii

Ethnographic representation, 305, 330*n*10

Ethnoscapes, 291

Etienne, Mona, 33

Eurio, 51, 129, 316*n*3

Europeans: and crop introductions, 52, 63; and cultural change, 48; early contacts with, 54–64; early voyages, 53–64; male advantage with, 75–76; in myth, 133–35, 144; relations with, 6–7, 16–17, 26–30, 42, 45, 53, 65–71, 134, 293–94; technology, 48; and women in colonial era, 65, 75

Eurubi, 158

Evans-Pritchard, E. E., 171–72

Exchange, viii, xi, xii, 35–39, 72–75, 115, 259; and compensation, 215; and cultural change, 48, 219, 291, 293–94; decisions, 43, 47; and gender, xv, 35–38, 208–14, 277–80, 286–87; goods, 215–16; journeys, 206–8, 212, 263, 278; and kinship, 219; and life cycle, 116–19, 212, 261, 267, 275; of like for like, 254, 268–69, 327*n*5; and mortuary ritual, 207–9, 215, 217–22, 254, 267–80; myths, 125–27, 143–46, 166; partners, viii, 39, 40, 166, 206–12, 215–19, 263–6, 275, 278, 280, 291, 300; prehistoric, 50–51; and residence, 47; and surplus production, 268; women in, viii, 41–42, 146, 206–14, 218–19, 290–91, 300–1, 306, 323–24*n*7

Fallow, 22, 44–45

Father: death of, 46, 229, 232–34; father's matrilineage, 46; and mortuary ritual, 274; relations with children, 46; *see also* Nurture, paternal

Favret-Saada, Jeanne, 171

Feasts, 6, 10–15, 23–24, 48, 167–70; for child, 87–88; cooking at, 115; and decisions of women, 47; food sharing at, 192, 245–46, 302–3; food sorting at, 258–59, 302–3; and government, 76–77, 265; precolonial, 52; *see also* Mortuary ritual

Feeding, ritual, 242–46, 256, 258, 270, 272

Feil, Darryl, 214

Feminist scholarship, xii, 32–35, 219, 282–83, 285

Fergusson Island, 35, 329*n*14

Fern fronds, in diet, 43

Fertility, 100

Fire: in myth, 147–50; significance of 121, 148; and witches 149

Firefly: as messenger, 142, 227; and sorcery or witchcraft, 142

Fish: and magic, 190; as place spirits, 138; smoked, in exchange, 269; taboos and, 140; as totems, 45–46, 136–37, 317*n*7

Fishing, 15, 42–43, 63, 114, 289, 304; metal fishhooks, 65, 70, rights, 39

Flying fox, 45, 114

Foraging, 45, 114–15, 247, 290, 320*n*22; inheritance and use rights, 46; societies and gender relations, 38, 295–96

Fore (New Guinea), 313*n*10

Forest, 1, 15, 22, 44, 45, 53; meanings of, 150–51; and spirits, 160–61; and sorcery, 172–73

Forman, Captain, 59

Fortune, Reo, 2, 13, 176, 178, 211, 314*n*19, 320*n*21, 321*n*5

France, 285

Frazer, Sir James, 128

Freudian theories, and myth, 145–46

Fried, Morton, 39

Frigate bird, as totem, 136–37

Frogs, as place spirits, 140–41

Fruit bat, 45, 114

Gaiba (pseudonym), 248

Garia (New Guinea), 172, 178

Garden(s), 16, 46–47, 250; clearing new, 22–23, 289; and exchange, 41, 269; magic, 23, 44, 113; and mortuary ritual, 235, 250; new cultigens, 63; planting, 44, 113; and prestige, 74–75, 304; produce in mortuary ritual, 241–43, 245, 251–59, 261–66, 268, 271, 273, 276, 278, 302–3; rights to, 39, 46–47; ritual experts, 47–48; and sexual division of labor, 113–14, 329*n*3; women as owners of, 47, 63, 113, 262–63, 276, 286, 290–91

Gawa (Island), 314*n*15; kula and exchange, 209, 323*n*5, 324*n*8; and witchcraft, 286

Gender, x, xv; complementarity, 281; equality, vii, vii, ix, xv, 32–33, 35, 40, 154, 219, 221–22, 238, 281–82, 289–94, 305–6, 307*n*7; equivalence, 279, 281; hegemonies, 34–35; hierarchies, viii; in historical context, xiii, 48, 72–80, 282, 291–94; ideologies and philosophies, 32, 34–35, 40, 142–55, 271–74, 281–85, 287–89, 307*n*5, 308*n*10; inequality, vii, xv, 38, 282, 292, 294, 298, 302; and the life cycle, 83–84; materialist approaches to, 31–32, 37–38, 281–82, 294–96, 329*n*3; symbolism, xv, 32, 142–55, 203–5, 209, 284, 286, 302–4; theories of, vii, 31–35, 289–90, 302–4, 307*n*7

Generosity, ix, 37–38, 274, 287; as moral quality, 279–82, 300, 303, 304; and mortuary ritual, 251, 269, 271, 278, 301

Germans, in New Guinea, 70

Gerontocracies, male, 297, 312*n*2

Gerret, Frank, 59

Gesila (Village), 140

Ghanrakerake, 169, 222, 248, 251

Ghayawa (pseudonym), 212–13, 275–76

Ghejegheje, 161–62

Ghubughububala, 141, 161

Giagia, ix, 39, 41, 117–18, 304, 330*n*9; and gender symbolism, 279; and government, 76–79; and mortuary ritual, 234, 252, 267, 270–71, 279–80; qualities of 78; and sorcery/countersorcery, 175–76; wealth and, 279; women as, 73–74, 79, 211, 275
Giazagu (pseudonym), 186–87
Ginger: and magic, 82–83, 156, 159–60, 162–64, 190, 228, 319*n*19; and sorcery, 189–90, 228, 321*n*5
Ginuba (psuedonym), 206–8
Gitksan (North America), 324*n*7
Giving: as moral, 143; paradox of, 271; as parental nurture, viii; and power, 208–9, 305
Gladwin, Thomas, 97
Godelier, Maurice, 74–75, 79, 152–54
Gold: and labor, 53; mining, 45, 64–66, 68, 294; in myth, xiii, 133; rush, and illness, 178; rush, and relations with Europeans, 64–66, 311*n*42
Gonorrhea, 163, 312*n*3
Goodenough Island, 35; cargo beliefs, 145; exchange, 325*nn*10, 15; mortuary ritual, 329*n*13; myths, 125, 131, 132, 144–45, 311*n*31, 318–19*n*13
Goriva (clan), 316*n*3
Gottlieb, Alma, 313*n*13
Government: colonial, 48–49, 64–70, 72; and exchange, 168–69; and gender, 75–80, 293–94; national, 48–49, 70–72; and sorcery, 168, 170, 176–85, 219; *see also* British New Guinea; Papua New Guinea; Papua, Territory of
Grandparents, 121
Grass Island (Wanim), 52; alliance with, 52, 61; exchange, 214, 322*n*2, 327*n*5; mortuary ritual, 251–52, 255–56, 260–61, 265–66
Grasslands, 9, 18
Great men, 74–75, 312*n*45
Griffin Point, 69
Groomwealth, 274

Guau (clan, also Eniela), 126–27, 136–37, 300, 316*n*3, 318*n*10
Guns, *see* Warfare; Weapons

Hagen, Mt. (New Guinea), 150, 153
Haida (North America), 296, 324*n*7
Hamlets, 9–10, 44
Hanhiewa, 316*n*4
Hawaii, 330*n*6
Healing, 140, 162–65; as countersorcery, 75, 162, 287; as counterwitchcraft, 162; and prestige, 75, 118, 304
Heir of deceased (tau), 46, 213, 234–39, 250, 255–56, 260, 273, 275–76, 279–80, 286, 326*nn*15, 20, 21, 22; women as, 278, 286
Hina (Martin), 9, 16, 21
Hoffer, Carol, 323*n*7
Homosexuality, 104–5
Hopi (North America), 296–97, 307*n*7, 312*n*6
Horticultural societies, and gender, xi, 33, 38, 63, 296–97, 329*n*12
Horticulture, changing patterns of, 63
Host, of mortuary feast, 211, 213, 233–34, 245, 249–51, 253–54, 260, 264, 275–76, 280, 301, 326*n*19
House: construction, 10, 115, 137, 289; payments, 215
Household tasks, 115–16; gender and prestige, 123–24, 289–90
How to Learn an Unwritten Language (Sarah Gudschinsky), 20
Hua (New Guinea), 285, 307*n*6
Huli (New Guinea), 174
Hunting, 15, 304, 318*n*11; female, 45, 114, 204, 286, 289, 315*n*24; male, 45, 114, 123, 204, 289–90; rights, 39
Huxley, Thomas H., 6–7, 54–56, 216

Ijau (pseudonym), 265–66, 275
Ilahita Arapesh (New Guinea), 285
Illness: and Europeans, 178; and healing, 162–65, 196–201; and place spirits, 138–42; and sorcery, 157, 170, 178–79, 190, 196; and taboo viola-

tion, 138–41, 170; and witchcraft, 170, 196–201
Iloga (pseudonym), 137
Ilongot (Philippines), 290
Inca (South America), 330n6
India, 54, 312n6
Individual, respect for, 290, 300, 306; see also Autonomy
Inequality, social, 38, 308n16; see also Gender inequality
Infanticide, 85, 312n6
Infants, 86–89, 222, 249; care of, 313n8, 313n9; sex preferences, 82, 86–87, 312–13n6
Influenza, 178
Ingham, W. B., 59–60
Inheritance, 35, 39, 46–47, 163, 315n20; and gender, 46–47, 295–96, 306; and magic, 155, 188; and mortuary ritual, 234, 238
Initiation, 74–75, 284; female, 38, 98, 313n11; male, 38–39, 98, 153, 314n16, 321n5
Inuit (North America), 307n7
Iron, in trade, 56
Iroquois (North America), 292, 296
Iwa (Island), 323n5
Iyen (Island), 8–9, 185

Jacobs, Thomas Jefferson, 54
Japanese, and World War II, 26, 66–67
Jealousy, 187, 194, 197
Jelewaga (Village), 5–15, 69, 140, 183, 206, 207, 212, 213, 224
Jinjo (Village), 139, 156
Jinrubi, 158
Jivia, 222, 225, 229, 241–46, 248–49, 256, 270; and gender, 244–45; symbolism of, 326n1, 327n3
Jolanden (hamlet), 213

Kaikai, 52, 159, 247, 327n4
Kalinga, 61
Katatubwai, 319n16
Kaulong (New Guinea), 40, 323n6
Keminana (pseudonym), 257–58

Kimuta (Island), 317n5
Kinship, 45–46, 72; see also Matrilineality
Kiriwina, 3–4, 153, 215, 297; see also Trobriand Islands
Knowledge: and influence, 304; inheritance of, 155, 166, 299, 305; and magic, 155–66, 306; and myth, 143; ownership of, 155, 166, 299, 305; as power, 75, 155, 165–66, 171, 201–5, 297, 299, 301; as private, 305; and sorcery, 187–88, 201–5
Koita, 126–27, 260
Kove (New Guinea), 40, 323n6
Kuanak (Island), 50
Kula, 115, 125, 155, 297, 322n1; and gender, 210–11; magic, 317n9; in prehistory, 50–51; ring, 209–10, 322n2; valuables, 36, 41, 144, 209–10, 215, 322n2, 324n8; women in, 211, 323n5; see also Armshells; Exchange; Necklaces; Valuables
Kunai grass, 44, 164
!Kung (Africa), 323–24n7
Kwakiutl (North America), 324n7
Kwaraiwa (Island), 52, 61

Labor, wage, 45, 53, 78–80, 105–6, 179; as crew of European vessels, 59–60; and government office, 76; indentured, on sugar plantations, 62–64
Lagoon, 8–10; as resource, 42–43
Lamphere, Louise, 33, 307n7
Land: ownership, 47, 72, 73, 282, 295, 301–2, 315n20; purchase, 215, 270; use rights, 270, 282, 298, 315n20
Langness, Lewis, 150
Language, Vanatinai, 49; dialects, 49, 300, 309n24; learning, 15–20; taboos, 138, 140
Lapita, 49, 50–51
Lawes, Mrs., 66
Lawrence, Peter, 178, 325n14
Leacock, Eleanor, 32–33, 293
Leadership, 74–75, 301, 330n9; see also Big men; Big women; Chiefs; Great men

Lederman, Rena, 35, 214
Leglets, as ornaments, 247
Leprosy, in myth, 126
Lesu (New Guinea), 297
Lévi-Strauss, Claude, 142, 149
Life cycle, and gender, xi–xii, xv, 83–84,
    96, 106, 122–24, 281–82, 284,
    288–89, 291
Lime, powdered coral, in exchange, 44,
    214–15
Lime pots, 191, 328n10
Lime spatulas, ceremonial: carving by
    men, 115; in exchange, viii, 41, 55,
    208, 210, 213, 215; in mortuary ritu-
    al, 13, 249, 255–58, 263, 276, 326n5,
    328n10
Linguistics, and Vanatinai history, 48–50
Linton, Ralph, 312n2
Loa (Island), 138–40
Local Government Councils, 75–80; and
    gender relations, 75–80; Louisiade, 5,
    69–70, 76–77; Yeleyamba, 70, 77,
    169
London Missionary Society, 59
Louisiade Archipelago, xiv, 3, 42, 76;
    early contacts with Europeans, 53–64,
    311n34; exchange in, 209–11,
    214–15, 264, 274; settlement, 50;
    totems, 136; witchcraft, 172; and
    World War II, 66–68
Lowaida (pseudonym), 255–56
Lowie, Robert, 326n20
Ludi, 85

McFarlane, Reverend, 59
McOrt, John, 59–61
Macgillivray, John, 54, 56–58, 216
MacGregor, Sir William, 53, 65
Macintyre, Martha, 149, 211, 320n24,
    321n5, 322nn7, 10
Mackerel, 71; canned, 14–15
Madagascar, 220, 325n13
Madawa (Village), 69
Maddock, Kenneth, 319n14
Mader, Lt., 67–68
Magho (clan), 316n3, 318n10

Magic, xv, 23–24, 74–75, 137, 304–5;
    antisorcery, 165; childbirth, 82–83,
    86; contraception, 84; convincing,
    157, 169, 190; and Europeans, 170;
    exchange, 41, 74–75, 106, 125–27,
    143, 146, 155–57, 162, 206–7,
    216–18, 220, 228, 247, 314n17,
    319n19; finding wild foods, 161;
    food, 106–61, 242, 252–54, 258–59,
    261, 264, 276, 302–3; fishing, 161,
    220; garden, 155, 157–60, 220,
    320n21, 321n22; and gender, 155–66,
    283, 286; healing, 140, 155, 162–65;
    hunting, 161, 188; invisibility, 165,
    191, 321n5; as knowledge, 165–66,
    279, 305; love, 102–3, 106, 162, 218,
    247, 260, 314n15; and mortuary ritu-
    al, 160; and myth, 125–27; and place
    spirits, 140–41, 162; and pigs, 165;
    and religion, 127–28, 316n1; sago
    making, 161; war, 62, 146–47,
    164–65, 188, 286; weather, 161–62,
    168, 182–83, 193, 320n23; women
    and, 41, 62, 146–47, 158, 161,
    164–65, 276
Mahony, Elizabeth, 25, 30, 65–66
Malaria, 64, 116, 312n4; and healing,
    163; and magic, 140
Malays, 59, 311n34
Male cults, 38–39, 297, 299
Male dominance, xv; and big men, 40;
    definitions, 32, 100, 307nn5, 7; ide-
    ologies of male superiority, vii–viii,
    xii, 32, 37–38, 76, 142–43, 152–54,
    278–79, 281, 283–85, 292, 295, 297,
    307n6, 330n5; myth of, 285; and
    prestige, 37; and sexual division of
    labor, 289; universality of, vii, xii, 32,
    33, 282, 306, 307n4
Male gender roles, studies of, 31–32
Malinowski, Bronislaw, xi, xiii, 3–4, 26;
    on adolescence, 97–98; on courtship,
    314n15; on kula, 36, 209–11, 215–16,
    322n2, 323n5; on magic, 317n9; on
    myth, 130–31, 146; on religion, 128;
    on status of women, 35–36, 308n13

Mango, 10, 44, 63
Mangroves, 9, 252; mangrove swamps, 10, 42, 43
Manioc, 10, 44; introduction of, 52, 63; magic, 159; and mortuary ritual, 241, 254
Mankaputaitai, 137, 146–47
Marai (pseudonym), 175, 185, 187, 193, 253
Margaret Oakley, 54
Marquesas (Islands; Polynesia), 97
Marriage, 102, 104, 106–9, 118–19, 192, 245, 274, 288, 300; and the life cycle, 98, 117, 284; and mortuary ritual, 220, 222, 262, 273, 269, 299; patterns, 107, 314*n*18; precolonial, 49, 52; proscriptions, 46, 105, 122; *see also* Affinal relations
Marett, R. R., 316*n*1
Martin (Peter), 5–6, 15, 19, 53
Massim, xi, 35–36, 38, 73, 308*n*12; adolescence in, 97–98, 106; exchange in, 209–11, 214, 216–17, 269, 301, 325*n*15; gender symbolism, 329*n*3; and high status of women, xi, 211, 214, 221; magic and religion, 128; matrilineal societies in, 297–99; mortuary ritual in, 220–21, 233, 277, 325*n*13, 325–26*n*15, 328*n*7; myths, 130–32, 137, 144–45, 319*n*15; and natural world, 319*n*18; religion in, 316*n*2; sorcery, 171, 173; totems, 136, 309*n*19; witchcraft, 149, 171–72
Matriarchy, myths of, 154; theories of, 308*n*9
Matrilineages, 45–46, 47, 300; and child-wealth, 87–88; and exchange, 219; and inheritance, 46; and land tenure, 47; and mortuary ritual, 239–40, 244–45, 250, 267, 271–75, 279, 299, 303
Matrilineality, ix, xi, 35, 308*n*9; father in, 298–99; and gender relations, 33–34, 46, 296–300; and male authority, 33–34, 296–98; "matrilineal puzzle"

and, 298–99; and stratification, 296–97; and totems, 135–36, 151
Mats, 10, 252; in exchange, viii, 41, 47, 215, 323*n*7; manufacture, 115, 221, 276; in mortuary ritual, 221, 224–25, 229, 276
Matthews, R., 182–83
Mbasiri, 156–57, 310–11*n*31, 320*n*20
Mead, Margaret, viii, 304, 323*n*7
Medicines, herbal, 81, 84–85, 89, 162–65; in exchange, 215
Meigs, Anna, 285
Mekeo (New Guinea), 177; female chiefs, 323*n*6; sorcery, 172, 174, 177, 321*nn*3, 5
Melanesia, vii–viii, 38, 303; and big men/big women, ix, 40, 74–75, 301, 330*n*9; and egalitarian societies, vii; knowledge in, 166; and male dominance, viii, 245; male initiation in, 307*n*3; matrilineal societies in, 296–97; Melanesian paradox, 305; myths in, 145; prehistory, 50–51; ritual in, 245; sorcery and witchcraft in, 171; worldview in, 176, 284
Melbourne (Australia), 71
Men, as life-takers, ix, 32, 124, 133, 178, 203–5
Mende (Africa), 323*n*7
Mendi (New Guinea), 35, 214
Menopause, 119, 284
Men's house, x, 32, 38–39
Menstruation, 99–101, 153, 288–89, 313*nn*13, 14
Mental illness, 165, 180–81; and witchcraft, 198–200
Micronesia, adolescence in, 97, 106
Migration, 39, 44, 96, 105, 282; and sorcery, 8–9, 185–86
Milne Bay, 2, 24, 26; Battle of, 29; Province, 49, 70, 77, 170; wartime labor at, 67–68; witchcraft, 173
Milne Bay Provincial Government, 5, 77
Minangkabau (Indonesia), 296–97
Minister, Nicholas, 60, 62–63

Misima (Island), xi, 2–6, 105, 125,
308*n*12; and cargo cults, 67–68,
317*n*5; exchange, 44, 195, 210, 215,
266; gardening, 44, 158, 320*n*22; and
government, 69–70; goldmining at,
64, 71; healing, 200, 204; language,
50, 253, 309*nn*18, 25, 310*n*26; mortuary ritual, 221, 260, 277, 326*n*21,
328*nn*7, 10, 11, 329*n*14; and missions, 68–69, 94; in myth, 125, 134,
147; postmarital residence on, 108;
sorcery and, 201, 202; spirits, 142;
totems, 45–46; witchcraft, 168, 172,
173, 195–201, 204; women on, 210,
221
Mission of the Sacred Heart (Roman
Catholic), 12, 29, 30, 69–70, 77,
93–95, 105–6, 139; and sorcery, 170,
177, 202
Mission(s), 3, 4–5, 45, 48, 68–69, 71,
77–78, 219, 308*n*12; and gender, 78,
293–94; and schools, 69, 70, 77; and
syncretism, 129–30; and wage labor,
53
Mobility, female, viii, 17, 150–51, 271,
293, 300; increased after pacification,
66, 77, 79, 179, 293; residential, 17,
108, 300
Monitor lizard, 45, 289
Monsoon, northwest, 18, 43
Montagnais-Naskapi (North America),
315*n*24
Morrell, Captain Benjamin, 54
Mortar and pestle, stone, 247
Mortuary ritual, viii–ix, xi, xii, xiii, xiv,
11–15, 40–42, 71, 115, 325*n*13,
325–26*n*15, 326*nn*19, 20, 21, 22; and
aggression, 221; female roles in,
121–22, 152, 221–22, 233–34,
244–45, 247, 251, 264–67, 275–76,
286–87, 291; gender and, 248,
271–80, 286–87; and inheritance, 46,
233, 244, 250; male roles in, 245–46,
264–65, 267; and personal and gender
identity, 278; precolonial, 61–62, 74,
230, 302–3; and sacrifice, 230;

sequence, 219–22, 244–48, 250–51,
261–62; *see also* Burial; Feasts; Ghanrakerake; Jivia; Mourning; Vearada;
Velaloga; Zagaya
Mother, as ancestor, 166; ritual roles of,
271–72; *see also* Nurture, maternal
Motor vessels, 1–2, 42, 266
Motorina (Island), 59; and cargo cult,
67–68; and witchcraft, 195–96
Motu (language, New Guinea), 76
Mourning, 6, 224–25; affinal mourners,
224–25, 228, 233, 241–50, 267,
272–73, 272, 275, 280, 287, 303,
326*nn*1, 2, 327*n*3; and compensation,
267; crying, 224–25, 251, 257, 267;
and exchange, 217; principal female
mourner, 225, 229, 238, 244, 246,
271–76, 303
Mulia, 17–20
Mundurucú (South America), 308*n*1
Munn, Nancy, 286, 323*n*5
Murphy, Yolanda and Robert, 154,
308*n*11
Mwagumwagu, 13, 229, 255–59, 270,
273, 275–77
Mwajemwaje, 160, 161
Mwaniku (pseudonym), 259–61
Mwaoni, 156–58, 160
Myth(s), xii, 72; animals in, 42, 125–27,
143; of European wealth, xiii, 131,
133–34, 144; of female dominance,
154; of first exchange, ix, xiii,
125–27, 143–46, 166, 217, 295,
318–19*n*13; of first fire, ix, 147–50; of
first menstruation, 288; and gender,
xv, 129–33, 143–55, 282–83; of
migration, 310–11*n*31; motifs in,
144–47, 319*n*16; origin, ix, 128–33,
166, 301–2, 316*n*3; and witchcraft,
195

Nagovisi (New Guinea), 40, 297, 323*n*6
Nainhil (hamlet), 185
Naming, 88
Nasikwabu (Island), 195, 309*n*25
National Science Foundation, xi, xv

Nature-culture opposition, 142–43,
146–55
Navaho (North America), 324n7
Nayar (India), 296
Ndembu (Africa), 296
Necklaces, shell-disc (bagi), 36, 41,
325n12; in bridewealth, 108–9; as
compensation to allies, 61–62, 216; in
courtship, 103–4; and European
trade, 66; in exchange, 61, 88,
169–70, 209, 213, 215–16, 218–19,
266, 279, 322n2, 324n8, 324–25n9;
and gender, 278–79, 329n3; and land
purchase, 65; magic and, 156–57;
manufacture, 32, 115, 209–10, 216,
218–19; in mortuary ritual, 13–15,
221–22, 226, 248, 254–58, 260, 263,
265, 275–77, 326n15; and prehistoric
exchange, 50–51
New Britain, 40
New Guinea, vii, 43, 54, 135, 139, 284;
age stratification in, 312n2; early
European contact with, 54, 57; and
female pollution, viii, 99–101; and
gender role diversity, viii; and male
dominance, viii, 154; place spirits,
140; settlement of, 49–50; Trust Territory of, 70
New Guinea Highlands, 35; and cultural
change, 53–54; and gender studies,
31–32, 150, 152–54; leadership in,
74–75, 312n45; and male dominance,
101, 132, 152–53, 214, 307n6; sorcery in, 174; women and exchange
in, 214
New Hebrides, 62, 323n7; *see also* Vanuatu
New Ireland, 50
Nigaho (Island), 181, 218–19
Nimowa (Island), 12, 66, 68, 69, 214
Ningerum (New Guinea), 174
Non-Austronesian languages, 49–50
Nootka (North America), 324n7
Nora (Moses), 7, 9, 11–12, 15–16, 21,
23–24
Normanby Island (Duau), 259; kula and

exchange, 209, 215, 264, 322nn2, 4,
324n8, 325n15; and magic, 158,
317n9; mortuary ritual, 327n3; and
myths, 129, 145, 319nn15, 16; sorcery, 178, 321nn1, 5; supernaturals,
320n24; wealth on, 319n15; witchcraft, 149, 173, 320n24, 322nn7, 8, 10
Notes and Queries on Anthropology, 316n1,
317n6
Nurture, 281, 305; of corpse, 278,
303–4; female and maternal, 124,
204, 285–87, 303–4, 306; male and
paternal, 124, 232, 238–39, 274,
286–87, 292, 298–99, 303–4
Nutrition, 63, 312n4
Nuts, wild: magic for finding, 161; in
myth, 126

Octopus, 42; as place spirit, 138–40; as
totem, 42
Oil palm, 45
Ojibwa (North America), 315n24, 317n6
Opossum, 45, 89, 289
Oral traditions, 48, 49, 51; and precolo-
nial diet, 52; and precolonial
exchange, 52, 310n31; and precolo-
nial settlement patterns, 51–52; and
warfare, 51–52, 60–62, 72–74
Ortner, Sherry, 32, 34–35, 37, 38,
142–43, 150, 152, 283–84, 308n10
Osborne, D. H., 62
Oven, stone, 11, 115, 302, 327n4; magic
and, 161, 302–3; and mortuary ritual,
241, 247, 249, 253–54, 258, 265
Owen Stanley Range, 43
Owl: and sorcery or witchcraft, 142; as
totem, 136
Oyatau, Mt., 316n4
Oysters, 43

Pacification, colonial, 66, 79, 293
Paddles, sago-stirring, 254, 277
Pamela (Village), 104, 147, 184, 213
Panabari (Panawina Island), 68, 265
Panaeati (Island), 2–3; affinal relations,
314–15n20; exchange, 210, 214–16,

251–52, 266, 269, 275, 322*n*2; feasts, 214; land inheritance, 314–15*n*20, 330*n*8; language, 50; and missions, 68–69; mortuary ritual, 221, 277, 325*n*15, 328–29*n*11, 329*nn*13, 14, 330*n*8; postmarital residence, 108, 314–15*n*20; and sorcery, 202; women on, 210, 214, 221, 329–30*n*3; and World War II, 67–68; *see also* Canoes, sailing

Panaman (Island), 134, 214
Panapompom (Island), 59
Panasesa (Island), 2
Panatinani (Joannet Island), 57, 64, 67, 69, 121, 214
Pantava (Village), 180, 184
Papaya, 44
Papua, Territory of, 5, 66, 70
Papuan coast, south, 43, 50, 51
Papua New Guinea, xi, xv, 1, 45, 70, 76, 77
Paranoid ethos, 176, 203
Parrot, green, 136, 248
Patrilineal societies, 296–97, 326*n*20
Patrol officers, 66, 69, 179–85, 321*n*4
Paulisbo, Patrick, 70
Person, concepts of, 170–71, 208–9, 218, 238–40, 286–88, 304; in mortuary ritual, 270, 277–79, 303
Personality: in children, 91–93; variation in, 40, 118–19, 304
Philosophy, 278–79, 282, 287; and gender, 283
Pidgin: Papuan, xiii, 173–74; Neo-Melanesian, 76, 140, 311*n*39, 327*n*4; Vanga Lumo, 63, 139–40, 174, 311*n*39, 327*n*4
Pigs, 9, 46, 77, 150; care of, 115; in diet, 87; distribution, 46–47; in exchange, 36, 41, 59, 61, 109, 268; inheritance of, 39, 46; magic and, 160; and mortuary ritual, 12, 45, 115, 222, 230, 232–35, 237, 241, 243, 245, 251–52, 254, 259, 262–75, 277–78, 327*n*6, 328*nn*7, 10; in myth, 147–48; ownership of, 45, 76, 114, 290–91; value of,

148; and warfare, 60, 61; wild, 45, 114, 148, 150, 207, 299
Pindewe, 147
Pineapples, 44, 63
Plantations: coconut, 65–66; sugar, 62–64
Plants: and humans, 137, 320*n*24; and magic, 158–65; and sorcery, 189–90; as totems, 136–37
Platters, wooden: in exchange, viii, 41, 215; in mortuary ritual, 252, 303
Pleiades, 159
Pneumonia, 116, 178, 186–87
Polio, 247
Pollution, female, viii, 98–101, 105, 119–20, 132, 281, 288–89, 297
Polygyny, 111–12, 288, 326*n*18
Polynesian(s): adolescence, 97, 106; ancestors of, 50; as missionaries, 68–69; and taboo, 138
Poole, Fitz, 321*n*5
Population: 71, 72–73, 84, 108; density, 39, 44; growth and warfare, 60; and political authority, 301–2
Porpoise, 42; as totem, 42
Port Moresby, 1, 2, 66, 70
Positioned subject, xiii
Potlatch, 37, 319*n*15, 327*n*6, 328*nn*8, 20; women in, 324*n*7
Pottery, and Lapita peoples, 50
Pots, clay: in cooking, 43, 247, 327*n*4; in exchange, viii, 12, 41, 61, 215–16, 266, 269, 276; in mortuary ritual, 222, 241, 248–49, 253, 255–58, 276, 328–29*n*11, 329*n*14
Power: and cultural change, 291–94; and exchange, 278–79; gender and, viii, 38–39, 72, 127, 165–66, 170, 219, 221, 279, 281–84, 300, 306, 307*n*7, 308*n*10; ideologies of, xii, 80, 208–9, 281–83, 294–95; and mortuary ritual, 221; supernatural, ix, xv, 127–28
Practice, 283, 295, 308*n*10, 329*n*1
Prawns, 249–50
Pregnancy, 81, 84–85, 109, 312*n*5

Prestige: and exchange, 270–71, 301; and gender, ix, 36, 37–39, 72–74, 123–24, 219, 281, 283–84, 287, 290–91, 295, 306, 307n5; and giagia, 78; and mortuary ritual, 118, 221, 234, 269, 272–73; and warfare, 72–74, 292–93
Ptyilöwe (dance), 313–14n14
Public and domestic, 36–37, 40, 123, 219, 306
Pueraria, 45, 70
Pumpkin, 63, 203

Queensland, 59; and gold rush, 64; labor trade, 62–63, 311n39

Ragule (hamlet), 309n24, 316n3
Rambuso (Village), 69
Rank: and big men, 330n9; and gender, 38, 296–97, 302, 330n6
Rape, 32, 292
Rara (pseudonym), 81–83
Raré, 161
Rattlesnake, HMS, 6, 54–58, 64, 216
Raw and the Cooked, The, 149
Read, Kenneth, 31–32
Reefs: as obstacle to shipping, 8–9, 42, 54, 55, 57–58, 71, 294; ownership of, 73; and place spirits, 138–41; as resource, 42–43
Rehua (Village), 65, 69, 183, 218–19, 311nn37, 39, 319n19
Relics, 25; and magic, 156–58, 162, 188–89, 228, 320n23; and sorcery, 188–89, 228, 312n44
Religion, xv; definitions of, 316n2; and gender, 127–28; in Melanesia, 128; relations with supernaturals, 128, 188
Renown, 270–71, 280, 287, 304, 306
Research methods, 15–23
Residence, postmarital: bilocal, 47, 108, 250, 309n21, 329n3; and gender, 46, 47, 108, 110, 296–97, 309n21, 329–30n3; and matrilineality, 108; virilocal 108, 330n3; of widow(er), 270

Resistance, xiii, 49, 53–54, 71–72, 79, 219, 291, 294
Rice, 65; in mortuary ritual, 253, 261
Richards, Audrey, 298
Rio, Mt., 316n3; and place spirits, 134–35, 142, 156, 162, 203, 318n11; and spirits of the dead, 24–25, 27, 42, 51, 129–30, 132–33, 150–52, 226–27, 316n4
Ritual, 39; and change, xiii; expertise, 74–75; and gender relations, ix, xv; roles of women in, 271–74; *see also* Mortuary ritual
Rock Cree (North America), 315n24
Rodyo: and cargo myth, 133–34, 144; clan of, 316n3; as creator spirit, 42, 51, 129–33, 151–52; and destructive magic, 165; and exchange magic, 156–57; and sorcery, 162, 164, 180, 187; and spirits of the dead, 129, 132–33, 227; and warfare, 164
Rogers, Susan Carol, 285
Róheim, Géza, 149, 211, 317n9, 319nn15, 16, 321nn5, 7, 322n10, 327n3
Role overlap, viii, 289–90, 306, 315n23
Rosaldo, Michelle, xi, 32, 290, 329n12
Rosaldo, Renato, xiii
Rossel Island (Yela), 5, 71; axe blades, 156, 216–17; bridewealth, 314n14; clans, 317n7; contacts with Europeans, 53, 54, 55, 62; exchange with Vanatinai, 167, 215, 216, 328n9; female taboos, 313–14n14; language, 49, 310n26; magic and, 156, 157, 168, 180; male dominance on, 297; mortuary ritual, 325–26n15, 326n17, 329n13; and myths, 126, 134, 144–46, 310–11n31, 318nn12, 13, 320n20; place spirits, 137–40, 156, 316n2, 317–18n9; rank on, 140; relations with government, 70; religion, 316n2; settlement, 50; shell currency (ndap), 13, 144, 145–46, 217; shell disc necklace manufacture, 66, 209, 216; sorcery, 170, 173, 321nn1, 5;

totems, 136, 317*n*7; women on, 138, 211, 314*n*15

Rubi, Mt., 156, 158

Sabarl (Island; Sabara), 50, 52, 69; affinal relations on, 314–15*n*20, 330*n*3; exchange, 214; gender on, 329–30*n*3; inheritance of land, 314–15*n*20, 330*n*8; language, 309*n*18; mortuary ritual, 328–29*n*11, 329*n*13, 330*n*8; myths, 132, 319*n*16; warfare, 66, 214

Sacrifice, and mortuary ritual, 268

Sago (palm), 15; in construction, 10; in diet, 10–11, 44, 63; in exchange, 41, 44, 52, 61, 215, 266, 269–70, 299; fed to pigs, 44, 77; and men, 82, 114; in mortuary ritual, 232, 234–35, 241–47, 249–58, 261, 264, 266, 268, 271, 275–78, 327*nn*3, 7, 328*n*10, 328–29*n*11, 329*n*14; in myth, 125–26, 143, 146; rights to, 39; Solomon variety, 59; swamps, 18, 42, 44; as totem, 317*n*7; in warfare, 60; women and, 114

Sahlins, Marshall, 40, 211, 301

Sahul, 50

Saisai, *see* Calvados Chain

Sale, 53

Salish (North America), 319*n*15, 324*n*7

Samarai (Island), 2, 3, 170, 325*n*11

Samoa (Polynesia), 97, 323*n*7

Sanaroa (Island), 125

Sandalwood: in magic, 180–81; in myth, 126

Sanday, Peggy, 32, 110, 129, 131–32, 307*n*7, 315*n*23

Sarason, Seymour, 97

Scarlet lories, 9; in myth, 149; as totem birds, 136, 149

Schlegel, Alice, 34, 108, 110, 307*n*7

Schneider, David, 97, 298

Schools, 69–70, 76, 80, 93–96, 115; *see also* Mission(s)

Schwartz, Theodore, 176

Seclusion, ritual, 87–88, 229, 271, 313–14*n*14

Seghe (Village), 51

Seligman, Charles, 128, 136, 309*n*19, 319*n*18, 320*n*24

Semen, 100, 143, 146, 153

Settlement patterns, 44; precolonial, 51–52; and World War II, 68

Sex roles, x, 31–32, 83–84; *see also* Gender

Sexual antagonism, 154; in New Guinea Highlands, 31–32

Sexual division of labor, 33, 63, 123; in adulthood, 113–16; and gender, 282–83, 289–91, 298; role overlap in, 289–90; supernatural, 204; in youth, 98–99

Sexual equality, xii; definitions, 32–33; *see also* Gender

Sexuality: and exchange, 106, 212, 319*n*19; and jealousy, 110; and magic, 159; and taboo, 247, 288–89; and youth, 101–3, 106

Shame, 86, 170, 305, 328*nn*8, 10

Sharks, 71; in myth, 126, 137; as totem, 42, 136–37; and witchcraft, 195

Shell: black lip and gold lip pearl, Trochus, as commodity, 45, 53, 70; Conus, in exchange, 209; and European trade, 54, 58–60, 63, 64, 66, 75; gold lip pearl, in household use, 207, 327*n*3; gold lip pearl, in magic and ritual, 61, 158, 242–44, 327*nn*3, 6; for making valuables, 115, 228; Trochus, 115

Shell currency pieces (daveri), 145–46, 207–8, 213, 217; and burial, 224–25; in exchange, 36, 41, 322–23*n*3, 325*n*12; in mortuary ritual, 13–14, 217, 244, 246, 249, 255–58, 261, 326*n*15; in myth, 125–26, 145, 217

Shellfish: in diet, 43; and place spirits, 140–41

Shifting cultivation, 44

Shipping: Australian, 138–39; in Milne Bay Province, 1–3

Shipwreck, 71, 317*n*5; and place spirits, 137–40; and witchcraft, 157, 195–96

Shrimp, 43, 250
Silava, *see* Spirits, place
Simmons, William, 322*n*11
Singapore, 54
Singing, at feasts, 11, 14, 259–61
Skirts, xii, 329*n*3; cloth, 6; coconut leaf, 6; in exchange, viii, 41, 210, 213–15; manufacture, 115; in mortuary ritual, 13–15, 221–22, 253, 255–56, 260, 265, 272–73, 276–77; as signal in warfare, 62, 286
Skulls, as valuables, 61–62, 74, 216
Smith, Lt. Sidney, 68, 181
Snakes: beliefs about, 131; and humans, 137, 151; in myth, 125–27, 129–31, 217, 318–19*n*13; as place spirits, 137–40, 317*n*9, 318*n*10; and sorcery, 179–80; as totems, 45, 136, 309*n*19, 317*n*7, 318*n*10
Social stratification, 302; and big men, 330*n*9; and egalitarian societies, 33, 38
Sociality, 281; and gender, 299–300, 302–3, 308*n*10
Societies, small-scale, 300, 305
Solomon Islands, 51, 62, 70, 98, 135, 139, 323*n*7; men at Brooker Island, 59
Solomon Sea, 42; early European voyages in, 54, 55
Sorcerers of Dobu, 2
Sorcery, ix, xii, xiii, 2, 4, 73, 75, 84, 142, 271, 279, 282, 300–1, 304; accusations, 39, 167–70, 171, 174, 186, 192–93, 203; and aggression, 202; assistants in, 182, 192; and big men/big women, 175–76, 192, 198, 321*n*2; and chiefs, 321*n*2; as a crime, 2, 71, 167–68, 175, 177, 179–80, 182, 184–85, 245; definitions of, 171–72; and disputes, 9, 14, 181; and divination, 193; and the elderly, 198; and exchange, 212; and extortion, 174–75, 179–80, 181, 184–85, 192, 215; and government, 176–85; and heat, 189, 321*n*5; in illness and death, 170, 186–87, 249; learning, 188;

magic and, 165, 174; as male, 124, 133, 161, 172, 193–94, 203–5, 289, 302; in Milne Bay Province, 170; and mortuary ritual, 189, 191, 237–38, 242, 246–47, 253–54, 270, 286–87, 303; and poison, 173, 179, 192, 246, 303, 321*n*3; and power, 201–5, 286; research on, 171; revenge, 193; and secrecy, 188; and social conflict, 203, 322*n*11; and social control, 202, 305; and spirits, 129, 151, 164–65, 179–80; terms for, 173–74; threats, 183; valuables and, 174–75, 184, 186–87, 192, 196, 253; warfare and, 164, 177–78, 194, 201–2; women and, 172, 175–77, 188, 193, 204–5, 285, 321*n*1, 321–22*n*6
Sorenson, E. Richard, 313*n*10
Southeast Asia, 220
South Korea, 71, 138
Spears, 55–57, 62, 99; as male monopoly, 93, 114, 286, 289; in myth, 147
Spirit(s), ix; creator, 129–33, 166; of the dead, 24–25, 68, 129, 220, 226, 228, 316–17*n*4; and humans, 137, 141–42, 151; place, 43, 137–42, 141–52, 162, 165, 187, 317*nn*8, 9, 318*nn*10, 11, 320*n*20; and power, 127–28, 165; *vivirelavare,* 139, 141–42; *see also* Ancestors
Squid, giant, 42; as place spirit, 42
Stephen, Michele, 321*nn*3, 5
Stanford University, xi
Stanley, Captain Owen, xii, 49, 54–58
Stonefish, 163
Stones, as place spirits, 140, 151
Strathern, Marilyn, 150, 153, 302, 308*n*10
Strength, as personal quality, ix, 279–80, 283
Suau (New Guinea), 51, 69, 216–17
Sulawesi (Island; Indonesia), 325*n*13
Sudest Island, x, xi, 1; name, 54; stereotypes of, 2, 4; *see also* Vanatinai
Sugarcane, 44, 63
Suicide, 165

Suloga (stone quarry, Woodlark Island), 216–17
Summer Institute of Linguistics, 45
Surplus, control of, 46–47
Sweeping, as female role, 115–16, 261, 290–91
Sweet potato, 10, 44, 46; introduction of, 52, 63; and magic, 159; and mortuary ritual, 241, 249, 253–55
Swordfish, in myth, 126
Sydney, 54, 55, 135
Symbolic capital, 37–38, 118, 123, 219, 270–71, 281

Taboo (s), 138, 283; affinal, 112; food, 87–89, 244, 246, 249–50, 268, 284, 312*n*5, 313*n*9; language, 140; menstrual, 99–101, 288–89, 313–14*n*14; mourning, 11, 219–20, 222, 228–33, 239, 244, 246–51, 256, 259–60, 262, 267–68, 270, 272–73, 279, 326*n*16; and place spirits, 138, 140–41, 162; postpartum, 85–89; prepartum, 86; sibling, 112–13; totem and, 137
Tagarugu (Gnetom gnemon), in diet, 43
Tagula, 309*n*18; see also Sudest Island; Vanatinai
Tagula Station, 5, 7, 45, 69–70, 105–6
Tahiti (Polynesia), 97
Taineghubwa, 25, 51
Taiwanese, poaching, 71
Talak, 316*n*3
Tamudurere, 320*nn*20, 24; and magic, 165; and mortuary ritual, 268; and sorcery, 133, 141, 164, 180, 187; and warfare, 141, 164
Taradi (pseudonym), 252–58, 327*n*5
Taro, 10, 44, 46, 63; in mortuary ritual, 253, 255; in precolonial era, 52; as totem, 317*n*7
Tauhau, 129, 319*n*15
Tax, 66, 69–71, 77, 79
Thomas (Robutu), 25
Tierra del Fuego, myth, 154
Tiwi (Australia), 296–97

Tlingit (North America), 296, 319*n*15, 324*n*7, 330*n*6
Tobacco, 11, 16, 18, 53, 65, 68, 70; and early trade with Europeans, 53, 59; and mortuary ritual, 327*n*6; and sorcery, 189
Tobotobo, see Axe blades, greenstone
Tonga (Africa), 296
Tonga (Polynesia): female wealth in, 323*n*7; islanders as missionaries, 69; women and rank in, 330*n*6
Tools, steel, 53, 70
Torres, Luiz de, 54
Torres Strait, 54; islanders in Louisiade, 59
Torres Strait pigeon: and spirits, 141, 161; as totem, 136, 161
Tortoise (turtle), 42; shell in early trade with Europeans, 54, 55, 58; as totem, 42, 45, 136–37; see also Lime spatulas, ceremonial
Totems, 45–46, 135–36, 151–52, 309*n*19, 317*nn*6, 7
Tourism, 3–4
Tova, 161
Trade, with Europeans: 28–29, 54, 58–66, 68, 219; goods, 56, 59, 60, 62–66; and Vanatinai gender relations, 64; and weapons, 52; see also Exchange
Tradestore(s), 12, 65–66, 70; goods, 70; goods in mortuary ritual, 242–43, 255–57, 260–61, 303, 327*n*6
Tradewinds, southeast, 43, 158
Trading, commercial, 3, 5, 45
Tradition, x, xii, xii; see also Custom; Ancestors
Trees: and place spirits, 151; as totem, 136–37
Trobriand Islands, 3–4, 16, 38; adolescence in, 97–98, 106; chiefs, 297–98, 301–2, 323*nn*5, 6; father in, 299; kula and exchange, 35–36, 115, 144, 145, 209–11, 213–16, 299, 323*n*5, 324*n*8, 325*nn*10, 14, 15, 328*n*7; magic, sorcery, and witchcraft, 128, 158,

308*n*13, 322*n*8; myths, 130–32; prehistory, 50–51; spirits, 128; women in, 308*n*13, 323*nn*5, 7, 326*n*16; *see also* Kiriwina
Truk (Micronesia), 97
Tsimshian (North America), 296, 324*n*7
Tuage, Mt., 125–26, 217, 318–19*n*13
Tuberculosis, 116, 178, 185, 187, 224, 321–22*n*6
Tubetube (Island), 52; female puberty rite, 320*n*24; kula and exchange, 209, 211, 323n4, 323*n*8, 325*n*10; mortuary ritual, 325*n*15, 329*n*14; supernaturals, 320*n*24; witchcraft, 149, 320*n*24, 321*n*5, 322*nn*8, 10; women on, 211
Tuna, yellowfin, 42, 71
Tuzin, Donald, 285

United Church Mission, 3, 69, 94–95; *see also* Mission(s)
University of Papua New Guinea, 2

Valuables, ceremonial, viii, 36, 39, 40, 42, 76, 325*n*12; and exchange, 209–19; and food magician, 160; inflation of, 61–62, 73; inheritance of, 46, 250; and land, 315*n*20; and mortuary ritual, 221–22, 224–26, 234–36, 245–47, 249–51, 254–58, 260–80, 303–4, 326*n*15; in myth, 125–26; and paternal nurture, 298–99, 303–4; and spirits, 129; and warfare, 61, 74, 216
Vanatinai: language and dialects, 309*n*24, 310*n*26; name, x, xii, 19
Vanuatu, 98, 135, 297; *see also* New Hebrides
Vearada, 222, 251; *see also* Mortuary ritual
Velaloga, 222, 231–32, 244, 246–48; *see also* Mortuary ritual
Veora River, 56, 68, 140, 206; dialect, 309*n*24
Vines: in making cord, 45; as totems, 45, 137
Violence, viii; against men, 110; against women, 110, 292; and power, 289;

and sorcery, 110, 181, 292–93; and valuables, 181
Vuo (hamlet), 206
Vuti (pseudonym), 257

Wagawaga (Village), 320*n*24, 325*n*15
Waghena (pseudonym), 257
Ware (Island): exchange, 44, 77, 209, 215–16, 264, 266, 269, 322*n*2; missions on, 59; myth, 319*n*16
Warfare, xiii, 49, 57, 59–62, 64, 72–74, 78, 291–92; and exchange, 60–62, 216, 294, 325*n*10; and gender relations, 32, 58, 64, 72–74, 205, 307*n*6, 330*n*5; magic and, 164–65, 188, 314*n*17; and settlement patterns, 60–61; women and, 57, 58, 60, 62, 75, 204
Warrior: male role of, 58, 61, 62, 64, 73–75, 79, 114, 205, 287, 292–93, 302, 307*n*6, 311–12*n*44; men's houses and, 314*n*17; in myth, 146–47; societies, 154
Wawn, William, 309*n*18, 311*n*37
Wealth, 269; and cultural change, 291–92; European, in myth, 133–34; and exchange, 270–71; female, 323–24*n*7; and gender, 72, 146, 219, 251, 281
Weapons: and Europeans, 52, 55–56, 57, 59–60, 62; and exchange, 55; and warfare, 52, 57, 72, 74; *see also* Spears
Weiner, Annette, xi, 35–36, 98, 210–11, 277, 323*n*7
Wiessner, Polly, 323–24*n*7
Western Point, 1, 156
Whalers, 54
White, David, 19, 64, 130, 164, 179, 192, 302, 324–25*n*9
Whitehead, Harriet, 37, 38
White heron: in myth, 137; as totem, 136–37
Whooping cough, 178
Widowers, 120, 221; as feast hosts, 233; and mourning, 221, 222, 229–31, 246–48, 270, 279

Widows, 120, 121, 221, 330*n*8; and exchange, 212, 265–66, 275; as feast hosts, 233; and mortuary ritual, 253, 255–61; and mourning, 15, 120, 221, 222, 229–31, 246–49, 270, 279

Wisdom, ix, 165, 278–80, 283; wise woman motif, 143–47, 166; women and, 143, 283; *see also* Knowledge

Witamo, 134, 311*n*31, 316*n*3

Witchcraft, ix, xii, 75, 124, 247, 282, 285–86, 300, 301, 322*n*11; and cannibalism, 172, 194, 204, 285–86; and coldness, 190, 199, 322*n*10; definitions of, 171–72; and the elderly, 198; and familiars, 195; and fire, 149; in illness and death, 162–63, 196–201, 27; inheritance of, 172; and kinship, 175, 195–96, 322*n*10; in myth, 147, 195; and power, 201–2; and shipwreck, 157, 195–96, 322*nn*8, 9; and social control, 202, 305; and social disruption, 322*n*11; and spirits, 151, 164; techniques, 172, 194–200; and women, 194, 197, 204–5, 285–86, 289, 304

Woman, Culture, and Society, xi

Women: and control of means of production, 295–96, 298, 306; and exchange cross-culturally, 323–24*n*7; as exchange leaders, 210, 212–13; as life-givers, ix, 32, 124, 133, 203–5, 271, 278, 285–89; qualities of, 283; and relations with Europeans, 56–58, 65, 293–94; in small-scale societies, 40; status of, x, xii, 83–84, 282, 308*nn*10, 13, 315*n*23; *see also* Gender

Wona (pseudonym), 212–13

Wonajö, 310*n*31, 320*n*20

Woodlark Island (Muyuw): axe blades, 216–17; kula and exchange, 209,

216–17, 322*nn*2, 4, 324*n*8; in myths, 132, 144

World War II, 24, 66–68, 70, 182; and conscription, 67; and relations with Europeans, 24–26, 67–68, 312*n*3

Wozhoga (clan), 51, 161

Writing: ethnographic, xiii, xiv, 305, 330*n*10; travel, xiv

Yam(s), 46, 63; in diet, 63, 207, 327*n*4; distribution, 46–47; in exchange, 41, 61, 210, 214, 274; gardening, 44, 113–14, 115, 158–59, 288–89, 300; harvest, 16, 57, 159; magic and ritual, 44, 47–48, 157–60, 320*n*22; and mortuary ritual, 10, 221–22, 234, 241, 249, 252–55, 265, 268–69, 270, 275–77, 328*n*10, 329*n*14; in precolonial era, 52; taboos, 100–1; trade with Europeans, 55–57; and warfare, 60, 61; women as distributors of, 46–47, 57, 276, 287, 302–3, 329*n*3

Yap (Micronesia), 97

Yeina (Piron Island): in myth, 126; place spirits, 318*n*11

Young, Michael, 131, 144

Youth: activities of, 98–99; female, 97–106; as life stage, 97–106; male, 97–99, 101–6; Pacific Island patterns of, 98, 106; and sexuality, 101–3, 106

Zagaya, 222, 231, 250–78, 327–28*n*7; preparations for, 262–65, 328*n*8; timing of, 265; *see also* Feasts; Mortuary ritual

Zeyala (pseudonym), 157, 162, 167–70, 182, 186, 193–94

Zhuwa (pseudonym), 249